ROBERT LYMAN was for twenty years an officer in the British Army. Educated at Scotch College, Melbourne and the Royal Military Academy, Sandhurst, he has degrees from the Universities of York, Wales, London and Cranfield.

**Praise for *Slim Master of War***

'A tour-de-force.' *Major Gordon Graham MC and Bar*

'This is a first-rate book, and without doubt the best account of Bill Slim's conduct of the Burma Campaign. It was said that Slim had 'the head of a general and the heart of a private soldier.' Reading Robert Lyman's beautifully written and carefully researched account, we can see why.'
*Dr Richard Holmes*

'Robert Lyman makes a powerful case that Bill Slim was the greatest British general of the Second World War. I think he is right.'
*Dr Gary Sheffield*

'Lyman is good on strategy ... A former army officer, he is also astute on what it took to fight the war on the ground, with stretched supply lines and the need for long-range air drops.' *The Sunday Times*

'The first full length biography of Slim for 30 years – an excellent book.'
*Royal British Legion*

# SLIM, MASTER OF WAR

## BURMA AND THE BIRTH OF MODERN WARFARE

## ROBERT LYMAN

ROBINSON
LONDON

Constable & Robinson Ltd
3 The Lanchesters
162 Fulham Palace Road
London W6 9ER
www.constablerobinson.com

First published in the UK by Constable,
an imprint of Constable & Robinson Ltd 2004

This paperback edition published by Robinson,
an imprint of Constable & Robinson Ltd 2005

A copy of the British Library Cataloguing in
Publication Data is available from the British Library

ISBN 978-1-84529-223-3

Printed and bound in the EU

1 3 5 7 9 10 8 6 4 2

To Milos Stankovic, who persuaded me that this was possible.
Like Slim, 'a true manoeuvrist'.

And in memory of Yolande Beale, who
supported me throughout.

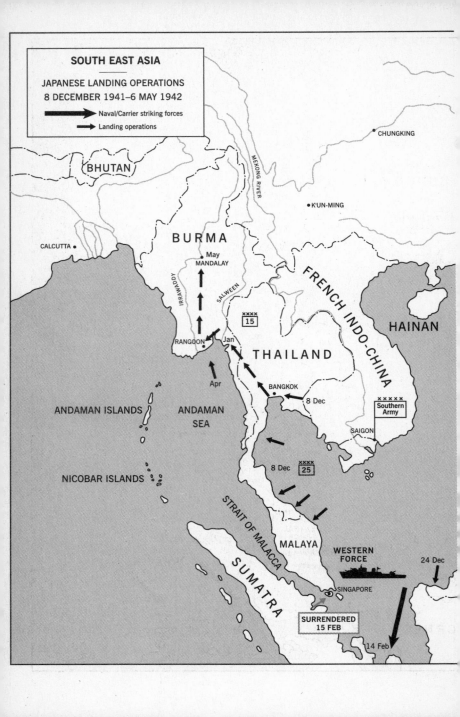

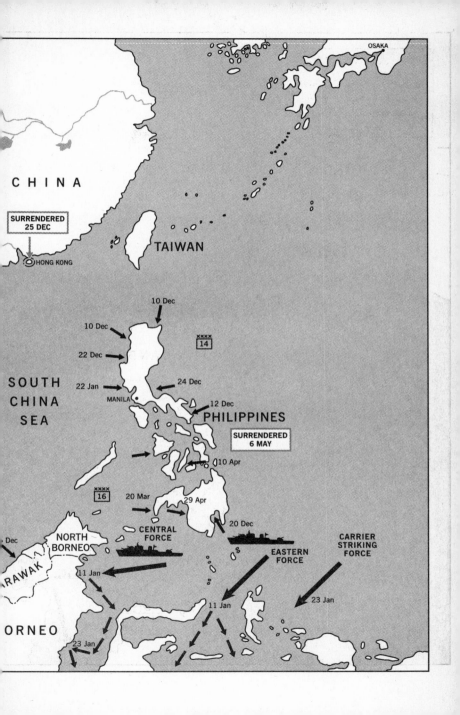

'The reconquest of Burma by the 14th Army under Slim remains a classic in the art of generalship. Only a man of the highest judgement, nerve and skill could have achieved this *tour de force*. History may well decide that there are more important lessons to be learned from Slim's handling of this campaign than from some of the larger and more spectacular battles on other fronts . . .' – Earl Mountbatten of Burma, 15 December 1970

# Contents

# Contents

# Acknowledgements

An undertaking of this kind cannot take place without the support and guidance of a great number of people. Many contributed significantly to the writing of this book. My family in particular laboured with me for five years in the study of 'Uncle Bill' Slim, and journeyed with me through the arguments, histories, battles and reminiscences that make up this story. Thank you for staying the course.

I would like to acknowledge a number of the academic staff at the Royal Military Academy Sandhurst, the Joint Services Command and Staff College and the War Studies Department of King's College, London, who assisted me generously. Professor Geoffrey Till, Dr Gary Sheffield, Dr Christina Goulter and Dr Duncan Anderson, himself a Slim scholar, provided much early encouragement. The librarians and custodians of various libraries and manuscript repositories in the United Kingdom – the Public Record Office at Kew; the British Library; the Liddell Hart Centre at King's College, London; the John Ryland Library at the University of Manchester; the Churchill Archives at Churchill College Cambridge; the Imperial War Museum; and the Hartley Library, home of Mountbatten's 'Broadlands Archives' at the University of Southampton – were unfailing in their patience. I am very grateful for the respective permission of each of these libraries and their trustees to quote from the documents and manuscripts in their charge, as without their material this book would never have been possible. Particular thanks are due to the Master, and Fellows and Scholars of Churchill College, Cambridge University and to the Controller of Her Majesty's Stationery Office.

I am also grateful to a wide variety of other people for their support in this project, too many to list here. I would, however, like to mention in particular Major Milos Stankovic MBE, Major Frank Golding, Mr John Harding and Mr James Moorehead of the Ministry of Defence's Whitehall Library, and Mrs Valerie Laycock MBE, all of whom, in their own way contributed to the writing of this story. Brigadier Tim Tyler and Colonel Ben Barry, at the time respectively the British Army's Director of Army Staff Duties and Colonel, General Staff, kindly allowed me considerable time for research. Major-General Ian Lyall Grant MC and Mr Tamayama (joint authors of the remarkable *Burma 1942: The Japanese Invasion*); Brigadier A.D.R.G. Wilson CBE; Lieutenant Colonel J.N. Cormack MBE MC; Colonel S.M.W. Hickey (author of *The Unforgettable Army: Slim's 14th Army in Burma*); George MacDonald Fraser (author of *Quartered Safe Out Here*); General Sir Charles Harington and Major General Cliff Kinvig all gave generously of their time, viewpoints and memories. The redoubtable Eric Morris and his assistant Greg Grylls shared some of their own research into the life of Slim during the early part of my research. I am also thankful to those copyright holders who allowed me to quote from their books.

It was a delight to correspond with an enthusiastic but dwindling band of Burma war veterans from around the world, most of whom are members of the remarkable 'Burma Star Association'. I trust that they will see their own perspective of Slim as a 'humble man-among-men' reflected in my own telling of the Burma story. To you all, I am immensely grateful: Mr Manny Curtis, Mr Michael Milton, Major Michael Brown TD, Mr Ron Gibbins, Mr Gerald Fitzpatrick, Mr C Fairweather, Mrs Daphne Grant, Mrs Irene Craig, Mr John Peacock, Major G.W. Robertson MC, Professor Robin Higham, Sergeant G. Kelly, Lieutenant-Colonel James Tysoe, Mr Clive. L. Brammer, Mr George E, Penfold, Mr John A.L. Hamilton, Mr Peter Toole and the Revd P.P.S. Brownless.

I am extremely grateful for the support of Viscount Slim in this project and for his kind agreement to allow me to quote from his father's magisterial account of the Burma war, *Defeat into Victory* (London, Cassell, 1956). To present as uncomplicated a text as possible, quotations from *Defeat into Victory* are not referenced directly.

As an aid to comprehension, references in the text to Japanese commanders, units and formations have been placed in *italics*.

The maps were originally prepared by the now defunct Institute of Army Education in January 1966 and were bound in *A Map Book for Students of Military History*. I am grateful to Brigadier Mark St John Filler, the current Director of Educational and Training Services (Army), for permission to use the maps here.

Last but by no means least I would like to thank the fantastically professional staff at Constable & Robinson. From the outset of this venture they have been unfailing in their support and patience. To Carol O'Brien, Alexander Stilwell, Josephine McGurk, Max Burnell, Dan Hind and Anna Williamson: thank you.

# Illustrations

Maps

# Maps

# Introduction

Slim was one of the pre-eminent soldiers of his generation. Tough, wise, accessible to all, he was the epitome of the great commander. Physically imposing, Slim had a prominent square chin that gave him a look of purposefulness and determination. His physical appearance was not deceptive. Slim, against the most formidable of obstacles, helped to transform Allied fortunes in Burma such that profound defeat in 1942 was turned into overwhelming and comprehensive victory in 1945. Lord Louis Mountbatten, who commanded the Allied war effort in the south-east Asian theatre of war from November 1943, concluded that Slim was 'the finest general the Second World War produced.'[1] To a large extent, however, his flame has been extinguished in the popular memory of great British military commanders. While many today have heard of Field-Marshal Montgomery of Alamein, few have heard of Slim. Far from home and far down the priority list, his soldiers in 14th Army were by early 1944 calling themselves the 'Forgotten Army'. Slim, their commander for close on two years, can aptly be described as the 'Forgotten Commander' of this army. Despite the fact that he commanded the only Allied army comprehensively to defeat a Japanese Army on land in the Second World War, rose to the highest rank and position in the British Army – Chief of the Imperial General Staff – and retained the affection and loyalty of his soldiers in a manner equalled only by commanders of the stature of Admiral Nelson and the Duke of Wellington, his contribution to the art of war has largely been forgotten.

Slim's contribution to eventual Allied victory in the Second World War was not that he achieved outstanding battlefield success, significant though that was. Slim's real contribution to the art of war was to provide a practical bridge between the original theory of the 'indirect approach' expounded by Major-General J.F.C. Fuller, Sir Basil Liddell Hart and other members of the 'English' school of military strategy during the inter-war era, and the modern doctrine of 'manoeuvre warfare'. Indeed, Slim was the foremost British exponent in the Second World War of the 'indirect' approach to war and in his conduct of operations in 1944 and 1945 he provided a clear foreshadowing of 'manoeuvre' warfare. The common wellspring of both doctrines is the notion that the art of strategy is to undermine an enemy's mental strengths and his will to win, through the concentration of force to achieve surprise, psychological shock, physical momentum and moral dominance. It is an approach to war that sits in stark contrast to the idea of matching strength with strength, and force with force, and where the goal of strategy is not simply to slog it out with an enemy in an attritional confrontation. A 'manoeuvrist' commander, to use the rather jangling modern parlance, prizes above all the virtues of cunning and guile, seeks shamelessly to trick and deceive the enemy and bases his operational plan firmly upon the ruthless exploitation of the enemy's weaknesses.

Slim's espousal of these principles and his successful application of them to the prosecution of the war in India and Burma in 1944 and 1945 – and thus his contribution to the development of modern warfare as a whole – has never been properly recognized. This was largely because he developed and practised his ideas on the battlefield – and a relatively obscure battlefield at that – rather than in the classroom or the textbook. Slim has, accordingly, left behind no extensive body of knowledge for successive generations to remember his contribution to modern strategy and his legacy has largely been lost. Liddell Hart himself failed to recognize Slim's contribution to the practice of war in his *History of the Second World War* published posthumously in 1970.* This present book is intended to make a start in redressing this balance and to present

* B.H.Liddell Hart, *History of the Second World War* (London: Cassell & Co Ltd, 1970).

the unknown Slim, the full-orbed military commander in whom both strategy and humanity were artfully combined. Who was he?

Born into straightened financial circumstances in 1891 – the son of an iron merchant – he had spent his youth in Birmingham dreaming of a military career. Under normal circumstances a boy of his background would have been denied the chance to go to Sandhurst or Woolwich to gain a commission in the Army, as his family had not the funds to support him in what was an expensive endeavour. The First World War gave him this opportunity. He proved to be a good soldier and a natural leader. Service in Gallipoli and Mesopotamia, two wounds, the award of a Military Cross and a transfer, *via* the West India Regiment, to the Indian Army in 1919 – an opportunity granted to very few – and thence to the 6th Gurkha Rifles in 1920, saw Slim embarking on the career of which he had always dreamed. He loved the Gurkhas, whom he had first met as a subaltern in the Royal Warwickshire Regiment at Gallipoli in 1915, and with whom he would spend the remainder of his regimental life. He was made adjutant of the battalion in 1922.

Despite the slowness of peacetime advancement he had marked himself out as a man of immense ability. There is no doubt that Slim was one of the outstanding talents of the day. He came top in the entrance exam for the Indian Army Staff College at Quetta in 1926, and two years later graduated as the top student. He was universally acknowledged to have 'gained the respect and friendship of his contemporaries and was without doubt the outstanding student of his time.'[2] In 1934 he was selected to be the Indian Army's representative at Camberley, following his colleague, Lieutenant-Colonel Sir John Smyth VC, and was given the brevet rank of Lieutenant-Colonel in 1935. It was here that he made his first impact on his British peer group. None failed to be impressed. 'Both his fellow instructors and his students testify to his qualities of stability, keen intellect, down-to-earth manner, keen sense of humour and affability at all times' affirmed one of his biographers.[3]

A fellow instructor at Camberley, Lieutenant-Colonel Archibald Nye,* was later to remark that

> he was a class by himself and I rated him as probably the best all round officer of his rank in the Imperial Army. One could not fail

---

* Later to become Vice Chief of the Imperial General Staff (VCIGS).

to respect him since he had two qualities at a very high degree – quality of character which included complete integrity and at the same time the quality of a very good intellect. One does not often come across a man with both these qualities so developed.[4]

The commandant at the time, Lord Gort, sought Slim's immediate promotion to Colonel because he was 'so clearly a commander (and) . . . well above the average of his rank.'[5]

Slim's time at Camberley was followed, not by battalion command, but with selection to attend the Imperial Defence College in London, a course designed to equip selected senior officers for higher command. Thus, his period of battalion command arrived somewhat late in life, and was relatively short. Some have assumed that the lateness by which Slim received his appointment to command a battalion (he was forty-six) was indicative of a mediocre peacetime career. This, however, is incorrect.[6] The reason for Slim's appointment to command a battalion coming at such a late age was precisely because his star had taken him to a variety of other high powered appointments in the meantime, appointments which were denied to all but the best in the Indian Army. When it came for his return to India and selection for regimental command the only doubt was whether he needed, at his age and given the high profile of his previous jobs, even to command a battalion. But rules were rules and it was decided that even Slim had to jump through this particular hoop. Not, that is, that he minded doing so. Command of a battalion is what all good infantry officers aspire to, and Slim was no exception, despite the many years he had spent away from regimental soldiering. He was duly given the command of the 2nd Battalion, 7th Gurkha Rifles in 1938, if only for a year before promotion to Brigadier in 1939 to command the Indian Army Senior Officer's School at Belgaum.

The outbreak of war saw a hurried trip to New Delhi to badger GHQ into giving him a field command. He was rewarded for his persistence with 10 Indian Infantry Brigade, which was forming up in Jhansi at the time in preparation for despatch the following year to the Middle East.

Active service in Eritrea and the Middle East followed, first with 10 Indian Infantry Brigade and then as commander of 10 Indian Infantry Division on promotion to Major-General in May 1941. It might appear that Slim was fortunate to be given divisional command. Commanding his brigade in Eritrea in 1940, he had failed to capture the border town of Gallabat from the Italians, and a battalion of the Essex Regiment in his brigade broke and ran in the face of Italian air attack. Such failure could easily have ended his career. But General Sir Claude Auchinleck, the Commander-in-Chief (C-in-C) India at the time, was convinced of Slim's potential for high command. He had already appointed Slim as the Brigadier General Staff (BGS) to General E.P. Quinan, commander of the Indian Army force sent to Iraq – Force Sabine. 'I think his recent war experience ought to be of great value to you' Auchinleck wrote to Quinan on 10 March 1941.[7] Two days later Auchinleck wrote to Wavell, then Commander-in-Chief Middle East: 'I have nominated Quinan as Commander of the Force and have sent his name home to the War Office. I propose to give him Slim as his BGS and I think the combination should be a good one.'[8] Quinan and Slim left India for Iraq together on 4 May 1941.[9]

Auchinleck had his eye on Slim for even better things. The opportunity came far sooner than anybody expected. On 11 May 1941, Auchinleck wrote to the Viceroy, Lord Linlithgow:

> I heard today from General Quinan that Major-General W.A.K. Fraser, the Commander of the 10th Division, who went with the first contingent of troops to Basra, had asked to be relieved of his command on the grounds that he had no longer the confidence of his subordinate commanders. General Quinan recommended the immediate acceptance of his request and added that the strain of the past few weeks had undoubtedly adversely affected General Fraser's power of command. I have cabled General Wavell asking his concurrence to the replacement of General Fraser in command of the 10th Division by Brigadier Slim, who is Brigadier, General Staff, to General Quinan. I have every reason to expect that Slim's energy, determination and force of character generally will prove equal to the task.[10]

Slim accordingly took up the appointment on 15 May 1941 in the temporary rank of Major-General.

Interestingly, the 'Auk's' recommendation to Wavell that Slim be given divisional command brought Slim to Wavell's attention for the first time. Wavell, of course, was a British Service officer who did not have the detailed knowledge of Indian Army officers possessed by Auchinleck.

What Wavell heard of Slim made him seek to bring Slim back from Iraq to be his own Chief of Staff when he swapped places with Auchinleck in June 1941, and became C-in-C India. Auchinleck, however, would have none of this, and argued that neither Slim nor the other officer on Wavell's short list of candidates had 'the reputation, personality and experience which would give the Indian Army full confidence in their ability.'[11] This must have surprised Wavell somewhat, given Auchinleck's strong support for Slim the previous month. But Auchinleck had an ulterior motive in making this judgement: he did not want to lose Slim from the Middle East, where his division was to do sterling work both in Iraq and Persia during the following year. Nine months later Auchinleck relented, however, and agreed to Wavell's proposal to move Slim to the command of Burma Corps in Burma in March 1942.[12] It was here that this story begins.

# 1

# Poisoned Chalice

It was dusk on 8 March 1942. The Lysander Army Co-operation aircraft of the Indian Air Force drifted over the vastness of the shimmering Irrawaddy River to land at the old civil airfield at Magwe in central Burma. It was high summer. Daytime temperatures reached into 100 degrees Fahrenheit and the scarce shade in this part of the 'dry belt' of Burma did little to alleviate the heat. Nights, too, offered little respite and despite the obvious largesse of the Irrawaddy, water was scarce away from the deep-sunk village wells. The monsoon, which struck each year in May, changed all this, of course, but this was still two months away. When it did arrive, the rain fell from the heavens in ferocious torrents to drown the countryside, up to 200 inches in places. Chaungs – rivers beds that lay dry and dormant in high summer – now coursed with both life and destructive power, as roads and tracks were washed away and transport on dry-weather roads was brought to a standstill.

The Lysander had flown that day from Akyab, on the Arakan coast, where the plane's occupants had been briefed on the fate that had befallen Burma since the Japanese *15 Army* had invaded the country from Thailand six weeks before. After a short stay the passengers reboarded the cramped shell of the aircraft and it crawled into the air again, this time changing course to head due east towards Magwe.

The two principal passengers in the aircraft that day were Lieutenant-General Sir Edwin (Ted) Morris, Chief of the General Staff (CGS) of the

Indian Army* and his guest, Major-General William Joseph Slim. Morris had a much better idea of the situation in Burma at the time than Slim. This was hardly surprising. Slim had no idea why he was in the aircraft in the first place. About four days before he had been snatched from Iraq where he had been the commander of 10 Indian Infantry Division, and instructed to return immediately to India to prepare for a reconnaissance of Burma. Without asking too many questions he did as he was ordered.†

What little Slim knew about the situation in Burma when he arrived at Magwe he had picked up from Morris in the Lysander as it had made its slow and dangerous journey from Calcutta into the heart of Burma. This was sufficient to inform him of two things. First, Burma was an awful place in which to fight a war. The sheer enormity and diversity of Burma's physical geography made an immediate impact on Slim as he saw the country for the first time. The distance between its capital, Rangoon, and Imphal, the capital of Manipur state in north eastern India, represents a comparable distance between London and Marseilles: Burma's 240,000 square miles could easily fill both France and Belgium. The country is surrounded on its northern and eastern sides by rugged mountains and on the western side by sea. The Himalayas guard the northern extremities of Burma and then flow deep into the heart of the country, petering out into a thick belt of high, precipitous and tangled hills. Of these the Naga Hills in the north and the Chin Hills in the centre boast heights of 8,000–12,000 feet while the Arakan Yomas in the south forms a natural barrier between central Burma and the coastal strip to the north and south of Akyab.

Wide prairie-like plains in the centre of the country offer sharp contrast to the tropical jungle in the south and east. A long, thin jungle-entwined finger stretches down from the body of the country into the Bay of Bengal with its southernmost extremity at Victoria Point.‡ This 400-mile stretch of coastline – Tenasserim – which for the most part lies no more than forty miles wide, provided the point of access for the Japanese *blitzkrieg* into Burma in late January 1942.

Vast rivers – the Irrawaddy, Chindwin, Sittang and Salween – split the country like giant wedges. The Irrawaddy flows more than 1,300 miles from the northernmost reaches of the country and the Salween even

* Morris, late Royal Engineers, was a British Service officer.
† See Appendix 1 for the story of Slim's appointment.
‡ Now called Kawthaung.

further, but while the former was bridged, at Mandalay, the latter was not. The huge distances of this country were made even more formidable by the paucity of strategic routes of communication. In 1941 there were few roads or railways with inland trade and communications largely conducted on the great rivers. The few roads and railways in Burma that did exist tended to run north–south with the grain of the country, following the line of the rivers. Although some effort had been made to build a road from India to Burma from December 1941 (from Imphal *via* Tamu to Kalewa on the Chindwin) this was not complete when it was required in May 1942. Only one road of significance ran into China (the 1,500-mile-long 'Burma Road'), and only one road ran into northern Thailand. The few tracks that existed were not suitable for all weather use, particularly by vehicles, and were liable to interruption by floods and landslides during the monsoon.

The lack of a land link between Burma and India meant that the possession of Rangoon, with its port, was key to the defence of the country. Without the port the Burma Army could not be supplied as its line of communication would have to run for more than a thousand miles overland back to either India or China. The prospect of either was daunting.

The second reality pressed upon Slim during his visit was that the defence of the country was unravelling at great speed. The once mighty British Empire in the Far East was collapsing under the onslaught of a Japanese advance that, in terms of its audacity, speed and surprise, matched in every way the Wehrmacht's *blitzkrieg* attack on France two years before.

War had come as a considerable shock to Burma. In virtually every sense the country was completely unprepared for invasion. Burma was a colonial backwater, and its very insignificance seemed to guarantee its security. Its forces, both British and Burmese, were weak and poorly equipped. The main part of the peacetime garrison, 1 Burma Division,* was based at Toungoo in the Shan States and consisted of 1 and 2 Burma Brigades together with 13 Indian Brigade. In its ethos, dispositions and training the Burma Army was far from ready for war.[1] Prior to the

---

* Major-General Bruce Scott. The Burma Army contained two regular British battalions, 1st Battalion Gloucestershire Regiment (1 Gloucesters) and the 2nd Battalion King's Own Yorkshire Light Infantry (2 KOYLI).

Japanese invasion there had been little effective planning or training for war, troop levels were low and equipment of all kinds was in desperately short supply. When, in December 1941, war with Japan suddenly became a reality, General Sir Archibald Wavell, whose India Command suddenly became responsible for Burma, appointed one of his senior staff from New Delhi to oversee the defences of the country. Lieutenant General Sir Thomas Hutton, CGS of the Indian Army, whom Wavell considered to be a first-rate administrator and just the sort of person Burma required at this juncture, duly arrived in Rangoon on 27 December 1941. Burma's peace was not considered by most observers to be under immediate threat while Malaya lay threatened, and both Wavell and Hutton expected to have several months to plan the defence of the country, despite the aerial bombing of Rangoon in the days before Christmas. The attack from Thailand into Tenasserim by the 14,000 men of *Lieutenant-General Takeuchi*'s *55 Division*, part of *General Iida*'s *15 Army** on 20 January 1942 therefore came as a considerable shock. The capable and well-trained Gurkha brigades (16 and 48) of 17 Indian Division† which had arrived in Rangoon by ship in early January to assist in the defence of the country, were immediately engaged, with 2 Burma Brigade, in Tenasserim. Unable to stem the Japanese advance towards Rangoon, however, these makeshift defences crumbled gradually during February. On 23 February 17 Indian Division suffered a devastating blow when the vital bridge over the Sittang River was demolished prematurely, leaving over half of the division on the enemy side of the river. Rangoon, together with the rest of Burma, lay open to the exultant Japanese.

In the weeks that followed confusion and disaster pursued the retreating British. Wavell, directing from afar, became increasingly critical of Hutton's management of the crisis, and disagreed with him about the ability of the Burma Army to hold Rangoon. Despite the evidence of the previous month, Wavell consistently underrated the abilities of the Japanese and insisted that Rangoon be held, considering any talk of otherwise to be rank defeatism. Disappointed with what he considered to be Hutton's uninspired performance he asked London for an experienced operational commander to take over the Burma

* *33 Division* (16,000 men) under *Lieutenant-General Sakurai*, crossed the border in early February 1942 to secure *55 Division*'s northern flank.
† Major-General Sir John Smyth VC

Army. Churchill responded to Wavell's request by sending out General Sir Harold Alexander, who had commanded 1 Division of the British Expeditionary Force in France in 1940.

It appeared to many British troops in early 1942 that a new type of warfare and a new type of enemy had engulfed them. Tough, frugal and determined, the Japanese were far better prepared and equipped for a savage jungle-based war than the British, Indian and Burmese soldiers who opposed them in 1941 and 1942. Japanese tactics were designed above all to achieve shock and paralysis in their enemy. In this they proved to be resoundingly successful. The seemingly inaccessible jungle, a place of fear for many British and Imperial troops, was used extensively for movement. Commanders sought routinely to disrupt and confuse their enemy. Roads and headquarters were attacked in order to paralyse British command and control arrangements, overload commanders and cause confusion among the troops. The Japanese had a particular penchant for emerging from the jungle far to the rear of a main position and setting up roadblocks on the all-important lines of communication upon which the British relied for movement and supplies. By infiltrating behind and through British defensive positions, they would make the defenders believe that they were cut off with no hope of escape, and by moving quickly through thick jungle to appear far behind the 'front line' they would induce panic in rear echelon troops. They moved quickly and lightly, unencumbered with the scales of transport and materiel of war that characterized the Anglo-Indian forces. At the outset of their campaign the Japanese were amazed at the ease with which they could psychologically dominate their opponents, sometimes achieving their objectives without having to do much fighting.[2]

During their relentless advance through Burma in the first five months of 1942 the Japanese forced the British to play to their tune. The Japanese method of war, their single minded determination to win, together with their savagery and wanton disregard for life, either their own or their enemy's, came as a brutal shock to the European military tradition and its deeply rooted codes of military conduct and chivalry that still held sway in the Indian and Burma Armies. To the ordinary fighting man – but particularly the British soldier – the Japanese soldier quickly gained fame as a fearsome fighting beast for which none of their training had prepared them. James Lunt, who was a subaltern in 2 Burma Brigade during the retreat, remembered the 'speed with which they seized the fleeting chance; the exploitation of every weakness; the ruthlessness with which they drove forward across terrain considered impassable; the skilful handling of their mortars; their stamina and, let it be said, their courage.'[3] The ferocity of the onslaught *Iida* launched against them gave the Japanese an immediate psychological advantage over the troops of the Burma Army, and allowed them to dominate the battlefield, creating an aura of invincibility about the Japanese 'superman' that was to take two years for the British to erase.

It was not just the Japanese or the British who had an interest in Burma at this time. Both the Chinese and the United States had much at stake in the country. American supplies to the Chinese nationalist forces of Chiang Kai-shek found their way from Rangoon to Yunnan *via* the 'Burma Road'. Chiang Kai-shek's armies were at the time tying down twenty Japanese divisions in China, which amounted to about half of the fighting formations of the Japanese Imperial Army. This was sufficient justification for Roosevelt to lavish many thousands of tons of 'lend lease' supplies on the Chinese during 1940 and 1941.[4]

Roosevelt and Churchill had appointed Chiang Kai-shek to be the Supreme Commander of the China War Theatre, a move designed formally to bind the Chinese into the higher command structure of the anti-Axis alliance. In return Chiang Kai-shek agreed to the appointment of the American General Joseph 'Vinegar Joe' Stilwell in March 1942 as his deputy and head of the Chinese Expeditionary Force to Burma. A day after his first visit to Rangoon, on 21 December 1941, Wavell flew to Chungking, Chiang Kai-shek's mountain stronghold 1,000 miles from Rangoon, to confer with the 'Generalissimo'. Wavell's primary objective was to secure the services of the American Volunteer Group (AVG)* for the defence of Rangoon. Chiang Kai-shek offered him the major part of 6th Chinese Army, already on the Yunnan-Burma border, for the defence of Burma, as well as 5th Chinese Army. Concerned not to overburden the Burma Army's already fragile supply arrangements, Wavell accepted

* Two squadrons of the AVG, flying P40 Tomahawks, commanded by Colonel Chennault of the United States Army Air Force (USAAF) but under the control of Chiang Kai-shek, protected the Burma road.

at the time only 6th Chinese Army, although he was later also to accept 5th Chinese Army as well.

However, command and control arrangements between the British and Chinese in Burma proved to be anything but clear. In late March Chiang Kai-shek asked Alexander to assume overall command of the Chinese as well as the British and Empire forces in Burma. 'Nominally I commanded all the Allied Forces', wrote Alexander in his Despatch.

> General Stilwell commanded the Chinese V and VI Armies but he had to issue all his orders through a Chinese Commander, General Lou. There was, moreover, a system of liaison officers working under the Generalissimo and it appeared that no orders of a major nature issued by myself, by General Stilwell or by General Lou could be carried out unless they had the sanction of the Generalissimo, which had to be obtained through the latter's Liaison Mission, whose head was General Lin Wei in Lashio, and who in turn had a forward liaison officer in General Hou at Maymno. Such an arrangement was obviously quite unsuitable for modern war since quick decisions for the employment of the Chinese forces were impossible to obtain and this, together with the almost total lack of knowledge of staff duties which existed in the Chinese forces, caused considerable delay in the execution of vital movements.[5]

The Chinese were a mixed blessing. When they fought at all they fought well. The difficulty lay in persuading their commanders to fight in the first place. Chinese commanders regarded their armies to be their own private fiefdoms: their continued power and prosperity involved retaining these forces, not in frittering them away in battle. The protracted war against the Japanese over the previous decade had forced them to conserve forces and avoid pitched battles. Large scale actions and offensives were fought only when the Chinese, not possessing artillery or air support, otherwise enjoyed overwhelming odds over the Japanese.

To a large extent this explained their notorious unreliability, from which Slim was to suffer on more than one occasion. Although the bravery of their soldiers, once battle had been joined, was for the most part faultless, their campaign style was largely reprehensible. Like the Japanese they had a deep disregard for human life and treated the Burmese with considerable brutality. Supplies that could not be garnered from the British were taken from the local population by force or stripped from the countryside. They were deficient in transport, heavy weapons, trained staff and communications. The latter was a particular problem for Stilwell, as keeping contact with both Alexander and Slim proved extremely difficult throughout the campaign.

In the weeks following the Sittang disaster 17 Indian Division was reinforced with the newly arrived 63 Indian Brigade.* 7 Armoured Brigade† also arrived to join Burma Army just before Rangoon fell. With just under 7,000 troops, 17 Indian Division had less than half its normal establishment. Many units had been completely shattered and were patched up as best they could for the next stage of the campaign. Wavell blamed Smyth for the disaster and replaced him with Major General 'Punch' Cowan, who was to command the division until the end of the war.

Alexander flew into Magwe airfield on 4 March 1942, the newly appointed C-in-C Burma, in the midst of what one of his biographers has described as 'the military poverty and disillusionment of Burma.'[6] A day later he arrived in Rangoon in the last plane to land before it fell. He had been travelling for more than a week. As soon as his aircraft touched down he hurried forward to 17 Indian Division's HQ at Hlegu where he met both Cowan and Hutton, taking command of British forces in Burma at 3 p.m. Hutton remained, rather reluctantly, as Alexander's chief of staff.

During a brief stop over in Calcutta on 3 March Wavell had impressed on Alexander the need to hold on to Rangoon. The retention of the whole of Burma was equally important, Wavell stressed, to maintain the connection with China, to protect north eastern India with its war industries, and as an essential air base for prosecution of attacks on the Japanese.[7] Without the port, Alexander was told, Burma Army could not be reinforced or re-supplied until a land route could be pushed through from India, something that was in hand but which would not be complete for many more months.

---

* Brigadier J. Wickham

† Brigadier J.H. Anstice (7 Queens Own Hussars [QOH] and 2 Royal Tank Regiment [2RTR]). Both regiments were equipped with Stuart 'Honey' light tanks and had distinguished themselves in North Africa.

These orders remained imprinted on Alexander's mind, and dictated his conduct of the campaign thereafter. Critically, however, Wavell failed to provide Alexander with an overall mission for the defence of Burma as a whole. Nor did he give him any advice as to what he should do if the unimaginable happened and Rangoon fell.

In the first hours of his arrival outside Rangoon Alexander was confronted with a stark choice. He could accept Hutton's assessment that the defence of Rangoon was now untenable and immediately withdraw 17 Indian Division from Pegu, evacuate Rangoon and draw back the Burma Army onto the Irrawaddy. Alternatively, he could obey Wavell's instructions and launch attacks to close the gap that had developed between 1 Burma and 17 Indian Divisions with the intention of defending Rangoon to the last. Mindful of Wavell's orders and as yet not fully conversant with the realities of the battle situation west of the Sittang, Alexander chose the latter. Against the frantically proffered advice of Hutton, Brigadier 'Taffy' Davies, Hutton's Chief of Staff, and Cowan, he countermanded Hutton's order for a withdrawal and ordered attacks to be launched by both divisions into the area between Pegu and Waw.

Predictably, the attacks proved abortive. Neither of Burma Army's two divisions was in any way able to carry out Alexander's instructions. One Burma Division did not even move. Brigadier Wickham, of the newly arrived 63 Indian Brigade, was severely wounded and all three of his battalion commanding officers were killed in an ambush, rendering the newly arrived and untried brigade virtually helpless.*

This setback convinced Alexander that he had no choice but to risk Wavell's disapproval and evacuate Rangoon. The alternative, as Alexander now recognised, was catastrophe. As Alexander himself was later ruefully to admit, his decision to disregard Hutton's advice on 5 March was made on the basis of instructions that differed markedly from the reality of the situation. To his credit, it took him only twenty-four hours to recognise that Wavell's ambitions for the retention of Rangoon, even to turn it into a 'second Tobruk', were wholly unrealistic and, if implemented, would have meant the complete loss of the Burma Army. At midnight on 6 March, therefore, he ordered Rangoon to be evacuated and the remaining

---

* Wickham was replaced two weeks later by Brigadier A.E. Barlow.

demolitions to be blown. The garrison began its withdrawal north towards Prome in the early hours of 7 March.

The narrowness of Alexander's escape became apparent on 7 and 8 March when, during the withdrawal north, the remnants of the Rangoon Garrison, which included Alexander's Army HQ and 1 Gloucesters, were halted by a roadblock twelve miles north of the burning city. *Lieutenant-General Sakurai* had been ordered to attack Rangoon with his *33 Division* from the north, advancing on the city to the west of the main road that led to Prome. In order to allow himself an unimpeded advance around the north of Rangoon he placed a block on the road to Prome at the village of Taukkyan. Despite repeated but piecemeal attacks by the withdrawing elements of Rangoon garrison trying to effect their escape northwards throughout 7 March the block proved impossible to break. Thousands of troops, including the new Army commander, and hundreds of vehicles in a nose-to-tail convoy stretching for 40 miles, were trapped.

By luck alone, they managed to escape. It had never occurred to the Japanese that the British would abandon Rangoon without a fight and the regimental commander responsible for establishing the block had been instructed not to get too embroiled in a battle while the bulk of *33 Division* crossed the road to the north. In strict observance of his orders, the battalion commander at the block lifted the roadblock at first light on 8 March when *33 Division*'s crossing was safely complete. The way was thus clear to allow Alexander and the remnants of the Rangoon garrison to make good their escape.

When Wavell received the message that Alexander had evacuated Rangoon he was incensed that his clear instructions to defend the city had been ignored. He immediately sent a terse telegram demanding to know whether battle had taken place. When he received this cable, on 10 March, Alexander, even more tersely, replied that he and the remnants of Burma Army had escaped only by the narrowest of margins.

The directive I was given was to hold Rangoon as long as possible but not to allow my force to be shut up there and destroyed. This has been accomplished but by a very narrow margin. With part of my force isolated in Pegu and most of it cut off from north there was for some time grave danger of the whole Army being surrounded . . . Most of troops have fought extremely well especially

armoured brigade who although their scope was limited by nature of
ground have done work beyond all praise . . . You are of course aware
of state of force when I assumed command and partially trained 63
Infantry Brigade could not turn the scale.[8]

Wavell, taken aback by the unexpected vehemence of Alexander's reply,
responded merely by congratulating Alexander on his escape. Wavell
never acknowledged how close he had brought the Burma Army to
disaster, commenting merely in his Despatch that 'On balance, I am
satisfied that we gained by the delay.'[9]

On Slim's return to Calcutta on 11 March following his reconnaissance of
Burma he was still unsure of Morris' purpose for him. His greatest fear was
that he was to be made Chief of Staff to Alexander, a prospect that filled
him with trepidation. Staff work and administration, even in the field,
were not, he believed, his forte. Whatever he was as a field commander,
he told himself, he 'was certainly worse as a staff officer.' Slim was called
to Government House to be interviewed by Wavell. Only at this stage
did Wavell tell him that he wanted Slim to command the corps that he
intended to form in Burma, thus better to co-ordinate the fight against
the Japanese. 1 Burma Division and 17 Indian Division, together with 7
Armoured Brigade, were to form 1 Burma Corps.

It is clear that in giving him command of Burma Corps Wavell
continued to believe that the Japanese offensive could be halted. Despite
the severe setbacks during the previous six weeks, including the loss of
Rangoon, Wavell was convinced that, if its commanders showed more
fortitude in battle than they had shown hitherto, Burma Army could
yet redeem the situation. Even at this stage Wavell harboured some
considerable delusions about the scale of the threat posed by the Japanese
and about the ability of his disparate and poorly prepared troops to halt
the invaders. But he did recognise, nevertheless, the complexity of the
task. Calmly, he told Slim: 'I want you to go back to Burma to take
command of the corps that is to be formed there. Alexander has a most
difficult task. You won't find yours easy. The sooner you get there the
better.'

Slim, under no illusions that 'a command in Burma was more likely to
be a test, and a tough one, than a triumph', but obviously relieved that he

was not destined to become a staff *wallah* in Alexander's headquarters, responded promptly that he would start off the next morning. As the blistering sun fell finally over the wide and murky waters of the Irrawaddy on the evening of 12 March 1942, the newly promoted Lieutenant-General found himself once again strapped into a Lysander flying into the now familiar Magwe airfield.

Slim formally took command of Burma Corps on 19 March 1942, setting up his HQ in the now derelict Law Courts in Prome, a dusty, straggling river port on the east bank of the Irrawaddy. Of all the strange situations in which he had found himself this, he admitted, beat them all. 'This was not the first, nor was it to be the last, time that I had taken over a situation that was not going too well. I knew the feeling of unease that comes first at such times, a sinking of the heart as the gloomy facts crowd in . . .'. As he was soon to discover, he could not have been handed a more poisonous chalice.

The one bright spot on arrival was the unexpected discovery that several of his key subordinates were old friends. By some 'trick of fate', he recalls, his two divisional commanders were fellow officers from the 1st Battalion, 6 Gurkha Rifles, and his Chief of Staff (the 'Brigadier, General Staff', or BGS) Brigadier 'Taffy' Davies, had commanded a battalion in Slim's old brigade. Bruce Scott commanded 1 Burma Division and 'Punch' Cowan commanded 17 Indian Division. Furthermore, Brigadier 'Welcher' Welchman, a gunner with whom he shared the shrapnel from an Italian mortar bomb in Eritrea, was on the staff of HQ 17 Indian Division. Slim records of Scott and Cowan that 'We had served and lived together for twenty-odd years . . . I could not have found two men in whom I had more confidence or with whom I would rather have worked. The fact that we were on those terms was more than a help in the tough times ahead.' He was equally delighted to find Davies by his side. 'A tall, thin, emaciated Welshman,' commented James Lunt, 'he combined driving energy with a first class tactical brain.'[10] 'I had known him for a long time . . .' writes Slim. 'If I had been lucky in my divisional commanders I was equally fortunate in my BGS.' As for Welchman, Slim immediately poached him from Cowan and made him commander of what little corps artillery he possessed.

The loss of Rangoon removed at a stroke Alexander's ability to sustain his forces for a protracted campaign in central Burma. Hutton had fortuitously stockpiled stores in central Burma during January and February, but these were sufficient to support Alexander for only another two months. Likewise the Japanese capture of the airfields in southern Burma rendered Burma useless in Britain's wider prosecution of the war in the Far East. Alexander nevertheless realised that his immediate imperative was to prepare defences to the north of Rangoon to prevent *Iida's* inevitable exploitation towards Mandalay, given that the Japanese were likely immediately to pour reinforcements into Rangoon from the sea.

Hutton's original plans to fall back on the Irrawaddy offered a ready-made solution for Alexander. When he had first considered how best to continue fighting if Rangoon had to be evacuated, Hutton had suggested leaving the Chinese to cover the Sittang Valley, assisted by 1 Burma Division, while 17 Indian Division retired on Prome, as a forward defence for the vital oilfields at Yenangyaung. Prome was important for another reason. Much of the large stocks of stores shipped out of Rangoon before the fall of the city, and necessary for the continued sustenance of Burma Army, littered the docks and required back loading up river to Mandalay.

Building on Hutton's plans, Alexander decided to create a general defence line running from Tharrawaddy in the west through to Nyaunglebin on the Sittang in the east. Successful holding of this line would allow contact to be maintained with the Chinese and provide time for India to build up her defences. There was no thought as yet of a withdrawal to India, although the task now facing the Burma Army was daunting.

The geography of central Burma played a considerable part in determining first Hutton's, and then Alexander's, plans. The city of Mandalay dominated, then as now, the centre of the country, and sits astride the mighty Irrawaddy as it traverses due south from the roof of Burma, before turning south west to Yenangyaung and then falling south again towards its mouth at Rangoon. The Sittang, which falls due south to the Gulf of Martaban from its source in the Karen Hills just south of Pyinmana, flows parallel to the Irrawaddy but closer to the Thai frontier. These two rivers are separated by an eighty-mile-wide range of roadless and thickly forested hills called the Pegu Yomas.

The two principal routes to Mandalay from Rangoon in 1942 were by road and rail through the Sittang Valley and by road along the Irrawaddy, to the west and east of the Pegu Yomas respectively. Alexander's defence of both the Irrawaddy and Sittang valleys was based on the not unreasonable assumption that the Japanese would use both these routes to make their way to Mandalay. Alexander did not know, however, where *Iida's* main effort would fall. Consequently he felt constrained to guard against the eventuality of a Japanese advance northwards on both routes. By doing this, however, he accepted that he was dividing rather than concentrating his forces, an issue which was later to strain his relationship with Slim. The plan was simple. Alexander decided to block any Japanese advance by placing the Burma Army in the Irrawaddy Valley and the 5th Chinese Army roughly parallel in the Sittang.

Concerned not to repeat the mistakes which he had seen at first hand in France in 1940, when the German breakthrough had bypassed and marginalised the static French defences, Alexander intended to use defensive tactics similar to those articulated by Wavell in a letter to Hartley, his new Chief of the General Staff, on 23 February. Wavell had proposed an approach based not on a static line defended proportionally by both divisions, 'but by widely separated mobile brigade groups or even smaller columns operating from railway as base and converging rapidly on any body of enemy between railway and river. By such methods' he suggested, a 'wide area can be covered offensively and enemy infiltration tactics defeated by immediate attack often from several directions. Use can be made of natural obstacles to protect flanks and to drive enemy against. We have advantages' he concluded, 'of railways, base and better communications.'[11]

To the newly arrived Army Commander these notions made perfect sense.[12] Accordingly, Alexander planned to place Brigade Groups in Prome and Allanmyo, which were to be made defended localities and stocked with supplies and ammunition for twenty-one days. If the Japanese got round these, the garrisons were to remain and fight on. The remainder of Burma Corps were to form mobile groups ready to counter-attack Japanese incursions into the defence zone when required.

Hutton, however, opposed these plans, not because of any criticism of the theory behind Alexander's approach, but because he was convinced that these ideas simply did not take into account the ragged state of the Burma Army. Alexander would be hard pressed to provide the counter-attack forces with sufficient mobility and striking power, and without the benefits of air supply it would be impossible to supply the defended localities when they were inevitably cut off by Japanese encirclement. Hutton's concern was that the Japanese would bypass these 'strong points' with ease, and then starve them into submission or attack and defeat them in detail once the 'mobile forces' had been pushed back.

The viability of Alexander's initial plans were also dealt a sharp blow by a decision by Chiang Kai-shek not to allow 5th Chinese Army to deploy any further south than the town of Toungoo. The town provided the key bridge over the Sittang river taking the Burma Road through the Shan States and up to Lashio and from thence to China. If the town were lost it would close the Burma Road and turn the whole of the Allied left flank. Not being able to defend forward of the town thus placed a severe restriction on Alexander's freedom of action, as it forced him to balance his forces on the Irrawaddy with those on the Sittang.

Chiang Kai-shek's ruling meant that, in order to keep the defending armies on a line roughly level with each other Alexander had no choice but to withdraw 1 Burma Division from the lower Sittang Valley. On 13 March, only minutes after Slim's first arrival at Alexander's HQ, he gave orders to 1 Burma and 17 Indian Divisions to withdraw north. 1 Burma Division was to move back through the Chinese and thence withdraw to Prome, some elements crossing the Pegu Yomas to the Irrawaddy Valley while the remainder entrained for Taungdwingyi. 17 Indian Division was ordered to move to Okpo, a village some sixty miles south east of Prome, by 15 March.

Following their fortuitous escape from Rangoon, the garrison and HQ Burma Army had met up with 17 Indian Division north of Taukkyan, withdrawing to the area of Tharrawaddy by 10 March, many troops marching on foot. Thereafter 17 Indian Division attempted to reorganize itself as best it could after the disastrous Sittang River battles. During this time Scott's division, which was covering the Sittang Valley south of Nyaunglebin, had mounted an offensive south on both sides of the Sittang on 11 March but had achieved indifferent results. The withdrawal to Tharrawaddy was accomplished without a fight, but in the process some eighty miles were sacrificed, and huge quantities of rice stockpiled for the two Chinese armies were lost.

Alexander's decision to defend both the Irrawaddy and the Sittang Valleys bore out to the full Hutton's fears that it would encourage the Japanese to use infiltration against the widely dispersed Allied forces, a tactic which they had by now developed to perfection and which, after the battles in Tenasserim, had become such a bogey to the Burma Army. In such circumstances it was simply not possible to be everywhere at once, and the inevitable consequence of Alexander's decision was that wide gaps were created across the Allied line, easily identifiable to the Japanese from both aerial reconnaissance and local Burmese fifth columnists. In particular, the opportunity existed for the Japanese to attempt to turn either of the flanks by driving a wedge deep through the eighty-mile gap in the Pegu Yomas.

Some have argued that an alternative approach to the defence of the Prome–Toungoo line would have been to place light forces on the floors of both the Irrawaddy and Sittang valleys. These could have blocked any Japanese advance, while mobile strike forces hidden in the tangled mass of the Pegu Yomas itself could have launched attacks upon the advancing Japanese columns. As Alexander's official biographer, William Jackson, asserts, this 'would have been the classic manoeuvre'.[13] However, for such a plan to succeed Alexander would have had to have been able to prevent the Japanese at the same time from conducting a wide envelopment up either the Irrawaddy to the west or through the Shan States to seize Mandalay from the east, either of which would have served to cut off Burma Army from the possibility of escape. Alexander simply did not have a means of blocking the Irrawaddy and his troops were not trained, equipped or confident enough to operate in this way. Nor, of course, did they have the air support that would have been essential to the success of this strategy. Such an approach was, according to Major-General Ian Lyall Grant, author of a detailed analysis of the retreat, 'pie in the sky' in 1942, insisting that the cruel realities of the situation gave Alexander no choice but to attempt to cover both routes northwards as best he could.[14]

The only other option would have been to give up that part of Burma which lay to the south of Mandalay entirely and adopt instead a defensive posture on the north bank of the Irrawaddy. At the certain risk of losing the Burma Road altogether, this would at least have given the Allies time to recover from the effects of the Sittang disaster. Crucially, it would also have reduced the extreme vulnerability of the RAF and aircraft of the American Volunteer Group (AVG) in the airfields in the Irrawaddy valley and would have drastically shortened the long and rickety line of communication to India. It would also have acted to remove what Slim derided as the 'rather nebulous idea of retaining territory', a policy which inevitably led to the dispersion of forces over wide areas and created 'a defensive attitude of mind'. Such an approach, however, was undoubtedly too radical at the time for Churchill, Alexander, Wavell and Chiang Kai-shek, for whom any further loss of territory to the encroaching Japanese was anathema.

Whatever the merits or demerits of Alexander's strategic plan, however, Slim was convinced, with Wavell, that offensive action was the only way to wrench the initiative from the Japanese. Slim remained hopeful that *Iida* might become too confident and over extend himself, and make his divisions vulnerable to sharp and timely counter-attack. If Burma Corps did not attack, Slim reasoned, it would relinquish the initiative, however momentarily and locally, and would therefore always be at the mercy of the Japanese. This was something that he was determined to avoid. He instinctively understood that, in order to defend, he must attack, and his desire for offensive action repeats itself strongly in the pages of *Defeat into Victory*, Slim's best selling account of the war in Burma. In order to wrest the initiative from the Japanese it was necessary, he wrote of his first assessment of the problem, to 'hit him, and hit him hard enough to throw him off balance. Could we do so? I thought so.' He knew that an army that failed to attack would quickly lose its fighting spirit and as rapidly thereafter succumb to despair and defeat. Fully expecting his left flank in the Prome–Allanmyo area to be turned by Japanese exploitation of the largely unguarded Pegu Yomas, Slim intended to form a powerful reserve to strike and defeat this attack, using his trump card, 7 Armoured Brigade, whenever and wherever the Japanese attack emerged.

Slim gave orders on 22 March for 1 Burma Division to concentrate in the Allanmyo area while 17 Indian Division held the open country lying to the south of Prome. He needed time to gather the scattered elements of 1 Burma Division together after their withdrawal through Toungoo and had hoped to have at least ten days at Prome–Allanmyo to recover, re-equip and re-position his corps. 'The last thing I wanted' he wrote, 'was to commit any portion of it to action before the whole was ready.'

In the event, Alexander's defensive plans came to nothing. This was in part because of the virtual elimination of the Allied air forces in Burma in late March 1942 after devastating raids on the remaining British air base at Magwe. It was also due to the successful Japanese offensive against

200 Chinese Division at Toungoo, which removed any hope Slim had of fighting his Corps as a single entity because he was forced into a premature commitment of his already weakened forces.

During the first two weeks of March *Sakurai* rested and replenished *33 Division* in Rangoon while *55 Division* continued to probe northwards along the Sittang Valley against 1 Burma Division. Possession of Rangoon allowed the Japanese to be substantially reinforced. The *56* and *18 Divisions*, along with two tank Regiments, artillery and supporting troops, made available by the fall of Singapore on 15 February, arrived during March and April. The Japanese plan was for *55 Division* to advance on the right flank up the Sittang Valley, seize the airfield at Toungoo and then advance on Meiktila. *33 Division* was to advance in parallel up the Irrawaddy Valley to Prome with the aim of occupying the Yenangyaung oilfields by mid-April. Thereafter *56 Division* was to move through *55 Division* to seize Taunggyi by way of Toungoo and Meiktila. *Iida* was confident that the decisive battle for Mandalay would be over by the middle of May, when the British would be forced to fight with their backs to the Irrawaddy, and that the opening of this door would be followed by the rapid collapse of northern Burma.

The Japanese began to probe forward in strength in both the Irrawaddy and Sittang Valleys on 16 March. Attacks against Toungoo began on 19 March, just as 1 Burma Division was handing responsibility for the town to the 5th Chinese Army. Scott managed to extricate himself safely and make his way to Allanmyo. Although 200 Chinese Division, one of the best equipped and trained divisions in the Chinese Army, fought hard to retain Toungoo, the town was cut off on 24 March by *55 Division* and an assault with considerable air support was launched on 26 March. With the situation looking increasingly desperate, Stilwell ordered 22, 55, and 96 Chinese Divisions to counter-attack in support of 200 Chinese Division, but the order was not obeyed. Stilwell, in desperation, asked Alexander to take the offensive in the Irrawaddy Valley to relieve the pressure on Toungoo.

On 28 March Alexander met Chiang Kai-shek at Chungking, and repeated Stilwell's plea for him to do something to relieve the hard-pressed 200 Chinese Division at Toungoo. The request placed Alexander in an awkward predicament. He knew that Burma Corps was not yet ready to take offensive action, following its withdrawal to Allanmyo–Prome, but he also recognized the strategic necessity to hold Toungoo. At the same time Alexander knew that failing to help the Chinese in their hour of need would allow Chiang Kai-shek an excuse for withholding assistance from Alexander at a time when the British might require it in the future. But how exactly could Burma Corps assist the Chinese Division?

There seemed to be two options. The first was to launch an attack through the Pegu Yomas against the Japanese at Toungoo. But given the state of Slim's forces and their inherent immobility this option was dismissed as quickly as it was raised. The newly trained Indian formations had only recently been mechanized in preparation for deployment to the Middle East and were still excessively tied to what Slim expressively described as 'the ribbon of the road'. However hard they tried throughout the withdrawal, he complained, Burma Corps was unable to 'shake loose from the tin-can of mechanical transport tied to our tail'. This constraint made the British vulnerable not just to constant air attack but also to outflanking actions by the enemy and constant punishment at the hands of the roadblock.

The only other option was to mount an offensive sweep south from Prome in the hope of engaging the forward elements of 33 Division and thereby frustrate their plans to advance deep into Burma, perhaps even of forcing them to relax their grip on Toungoo. This in the circumstances was all that Alexander felt he could do and accordingly he ordered Slim to mount an immediate offensive.

These orders provided Slim with an option of difficulties. From even a superficial evaluation Slim recognized that there was nothing the offensive could conceivably do to assist the Chinese in Toungoo, and there was virtually no information on Japanese movements in the Irrawaddy Valley with which to form a detailed plan. In obedience to Alexander's orders, Slim decided to launch a thrust southward by 17 Indian Division with the strongest mobile force Cowan could cobble together, with the simple aim of causing maximum havoc to any Japanese advance. The instructions to Cowan were unavoidably vague. Cowan dutifully created a 'strike force' based on the 7 Hussars and a total of one-and-a-half battalions of infantry were hastily brought together from the remnants of four depleted battalions. Commanded by Brigadier Anstice of 7 Armoured Brigade, the force set off on 29 March towards Okpo through the villages of Shwedaung and Paungde.

Unbeknown to either Slim or Cowan, who did not now have the benefit of air reconnaissance, the move towards Paungde on 29 March coincided with a Japanese advance up the Irrawaddy to seize the straggling river-side village of Shwedaung. At a stroke this move cut Anstice off from Prome. Rather than becoming a threat to *33 Division*, Cowan's force had been outflanked long before it had the opportunity even to engage the enemy. By evening, after sharp skirmishes around Paungde, news of the Japanese block behind the force reached Anstice. Cowan, recognizing immediately that there was now a very real chance that he would be cut off, promptly ordered Anstice to withdraw to Prome.

In Prome, Cowan was now aware that he was faced by an advancing column up the railway from the south-west and a strong force at Shwedaung which threatened to cut-off his force completely. Accordingly, he placed a block on the railway which led to Paungde and ordered a counter-attack on Shwedaung from the north to assist Anstice's now retreating troops.

The block at Shwedaung proved to be impossible to break, however. Anstice's troops threw themselves boldly against it throughout the evening of 29 March in the knowledge that if they could not break through they would otherwise not make good their escape to Prome. That night the Japanese in Shwedaung were further reinforced from the Irrawaddy. The entrapped British column stretched back down the road to Paungde and was attacked throughout the following day. In desperation Anstice launched attacks on the Shwedaung block on 30 March, but these were only partially successful. When it became apparent that bludgeoning their way through was unlikely to succeed in rescuing the whole of the trapped force, and that the cost was ever increasing casualties, units were forced to break off the engagement and escape as best they could across country to Prome.

The Prome offensive was a disaster for Slim's weak Corps. It suffered just over 400 killed and missing and many more wounded and lost two 25-pounder field guns and ten tanks, all for no real purpose.[17] Indian Division was now severely weakened. The First battalion Gloucestershire Regiment and a company of 1 West Yorkshire Regiment were down to 100 all ranks; 1 Cameronians were down to 100 and 2 Duke of Wellington's Regiment were down to 150. The 'wasting disease' affecting Burma Corps was all the more desperate for the fact that there was no cure. As Ronald Lewin comments, the mathematics was inescapable: 'Next time there would be less armour available, and next time less still. It was a one-way process.'[15] Worse still, morale plummeted. Hutton had firmly opposed the idea of an offensive at this time, considering it premature and foolhardy and partly as a consequence asked to be relieved as Alexander's CGS. In retrospect he was right. There is no doubt that insisting on an offensive with such an ill-defined objective before Burma Corps was in a position to carry it out was a considerable error of judgement. A thousand miles away in Chungking Alexander was simply too far distant to make a valid assessment of the situation, although the pressure applied by Chiang Kai-shek 'to do something' to assist the Chinese at this critical juncture of the battle for Burma was undoubtedly considerable.

The whole episode was galling to Slim. Like Alexander, he was convinced that he had to attack if he was ever to gain the initiative but this was not the time or the place for an offensive. Slim blamed Alexander at least in part for the debacle for insisting on an offensive for political rather than military reasons. Although 200 Chinese Division fought doggedly and courageously in the defence of Toungoo, it was the only one of the six available Chinese Divisions to be engaged at the time, and its two sister divisions in 5th Army had flatly refused Stilwell's orders to go to its assistance. As it was, the Chinese were only two days away from abandoning Toungoo when 17 Indian Division launched its ill-fated thrust south. 'To maintain solidarity with Chiang, such sops were unavoidable', comments Lewin, 'though it is difficult to see how the investment of Toungoo could have been substantially affected by operations at Prome.'[16] If action were to be taken at all, it should have been in direct support of the Chinese at Toungoo, which Burma Corps, on the wrong side of the Pegu Yomas, was incapable of offering. Burma Corps was to pay handsomely for this mistake.

As Anstice's battered force crept back to Prome on 30 March, 200 Chinese Division's grip on Toungoo on the other side of the Pegu Yomas was itself finally loosened. The newly arrived *56 Division* attacked the town of Toungoo from the east after crossing the key bridge over the Sittang on the road north to Lashio, which the Chinese had failed to destroy, following a wide outflanking movement through the Shan States. The Chinese, although having fought well, suffered heavy casualties, lost all of their heavy equipment and were forced to withdraw. Because it served to uncover Alexander's eastern flank and unbalanced the defence line, Slim came to regard the loss of Toungoo to be 'a major disaster second only to our defeat at the Sittang bridge.'

The way was now open for the Japanese to exploit deep into the Shan States, which in turn served to force the British on the Irrawaddy to withdraw in tandem to avoid being encircled and trapped from the north-east. *Iida* needed no encouragement to exploit his success at Toungoo. He immediately trucked *56 Division* across the Sittang and headed for Lashio, intending to cut the Burma Road and destroy the 6th Chinese Army, which was supposed to be covering Alexander's left flank in the Southern Shan States.

Prome was not easy to defend and the abortive offensive of 29 and 30 March made it even less so. The town had been bombed on 28 March and large areas of it gutted by fire. 17 Indian Division was now very weak, but the state of 1 Burma Division shocked Slim when he first met its units straggling towards the Allanmyo area at the end of March. It had little heavy equipment and artillery and its units were largely Burmese, many of whom deserted as they found themselves further and further from their villages and families. By 3 April Wavell was reporting to the War Office: 'British troops fighting very well but are weak in numbers. Some Indian units shaken and not very reliable. Remaining Burmese units of little fighting value.'[17]

Slim's plan for the defence of Prome involved the weak 63 Indian Brigade holding the town and its straggling southern outskirts, 48 Indian Brigade guarding the road that ran south-east along the railway to Paungde, while 16 Indian Brigade guarded the open left flank of the division at Tamagauk, just to the north of the town, facing onto the Pegu Yomas.

Slim admits that in retrospect he made a mistake in planning his preliminary corps dispositions for the defence of Prome–Allanmyo. 17 Indian Division was initially deployed in the open country forward of the town but Slim, fearful of the threat to his flanks from the direction of both the Irrawaddy on the right and the Pegu Yomas on the left, withdrew the division on to Prome itself. 'I was anxious at this stage to gain time for the corps concentration,' he wrote. 'I should have done better to leave the 17th Division forward and to concentrate the 1st Burma Division about Prome. Apart from all else it was a mistake to begin my command by a withdrawal if it could have been avoided.'

The loss of Toungoo on 30 March made the retention of Prome impossible, as Burma Corps found itself too far down the Irrawaddy and now threatened by the possibility of the Japanese outflanking it by a wide movement up the Sittang Valley. Accordingly it was agreed on 1 April, during a fleeting visit to Burma by Wavell, who met with Alexander and Slim at the latter's HQ in Allanmyo, that 17 Indian Division should be withdrawn from Prome immediately and Burma Corps concentrated further north to defend the Yenangyaung oilfields.

Before this could be carried out, however, *33 Division* launched a sudden assault on Prome's defences on the night of 1–2 April and overwhelmed a battalion of 63 Indian Brigade. Throughout the crisis of that night, neither Slim nor Davies slept. Early the next morning, with 63 Indian Brigade in some disarray and falling back through the town, Cowan feared, correctly as it transpired, that the Japanese were about to establish roadblocks to his rear, and sought Slim's permission to withdraw to Allanmyo. Slim agreed and the withdrawal of 17 Indian Division began at midday on 2 April. This withdrawal prevented Cowan's division from being completely encircled.

17 Indian Division now faced a prolonged trial of discipline and endurance as it withdrew northwards into the notorious 'dry belt' of central Burma to Allanmyo. The countryside presented a stark contrast to the jungles of Tenasserim. It was dry and ferociously hot. Lunt recalled the horror of this two-day march. 'The heat was intense, the road dusty and the march a severe trial to the troops. Water was scarce and it was difficult to prevent the men crowding around the infrequent water holes.'[18] Constant Japanese air attacks added to the difficulties of the withdrawal although fortunately the exhausted Japanese did not press the pursuit.

The lack of air support compounded Slim's difficulties and became a daily nightmare to the retreating troops of Burma Corps. The problem was only slightly exaggerated by Burma's retreating colonial governor, Reginald Dorman-Smith, in a telegram he sent from Maymyo to the Secretary of State for Burma in London on 30 March, when he declared that 'at this moment our total air strength is one aged [Tiger] Moth.'[19] Not only did a lack of aircraft severely restrain Slim's ability to observe forward of his positions and so gain intelligence about Japanese movements, but the

Japanese air force roamed at will across Burma's skies, entirely dominating the few roads during the hours of daylight. Allied casualties were high and morale suffered as a result. 'Enemy air activity continued throughout 3 and 4 April,' Alexander reported to Delhi and London on 6 April, 'dive bombing and machine gunning our troops and transport. Casualties estimated as 100 killed and wounded sustained by 63 Brigade, by bombing attack 3 April south of Dayindabo.'[20]

The day before, Alexander despatched a short telegram to Wavell pleading for more air support. 'Complete lack of air support' he wrote, 'is adversely affecting morale of troops under my command. Request as matter of urgency that aircraft, particularly fighter aircraft, be made available. The three or four transport aircraft serving this theatre are totally inadequate.'[21] Wavell replied that wished he could do more but he simply had no more aircraft to give. He explained in a signal to the War Office on 13 April that with only forty Hurricanes and Mohawks available for the defence of Calcutta and North-East India, he did not want to fritter the few precious aircraft he had in pursuance of what he increasingly regarded as a forlorn hope in Burma.[22] Command of the air was undoubtedly one of the critical factors in the Japanese victory in 1942. In addition to being able to attack Slim's forces at will the Japanese were able to conduct widespread and indiscriminate attacks against towns and villages throughout Burma. The largely wooden towns were methodically destroyed in attacks that exacerbated the panic in the civil population and removed the last vestiges of civil government and public morale.[23] The lesson of Japanese air supremacy was not lost on the British–Indian Army. In fairness, however, it was a lesson that did not need to be learned. Imperial air forces had been weak for several decades and the Burma Army was now being punished not for defective doctrine but for the failure of successive pre-war political administrations in London to meet the full air-power requirements of the Far-Eastern garrisons.

On 6 April Alexander wrote to Wavell admitting that the state of the troops under his command was causing him anxiety. 'The 17th Division was tired and dispirited', he said, 'and consequently did not fight well at Prome. Unit commanders were complaining that they had been fighting for over three months without relief, that as no reinforcements were arriving their units were getting weaker and weaker, and that they had had to suffer constant bombing and machine-gunning from low altitudes without any support from British aircraft.[24] Major-General Ian Lyall Grant regards Alexander's assessment of 17 Indian Division here to be somewhat harsh. The real problem, he avers, was exhaustion in both 48 and 63 Indian Brigades, although he admits that some British infantry units were certainly demoralized after Shwedaung.[25]

Morale, however, was a constant concern for Slim. To many of his troops the sullen hostility of some Burmese, the lack of any certain role or destination, the knowledge that there would no further reinforcements, the almost complete loss of air support, the intense heat and lack of water, the condition of the thousands of desperate refugees who were clogging the roads, the prevalence of malaria and cholera and their complete isolation from news or mail from home, offered the potential for widespread hopelessness. There was an acute lack of essential stores, from ammunition to vehicle spares and maps, and a lack of information led to floods of rumours which themselves exacerbated the decline in morale. A paucity of proper medical attention for the wounded, together with the bitter knowledge that the Japanese invariably bayoneted wounded prisoners rather than go to the trouble of looking after them, was also a constant worry. Seemingly pointless offensives, such as the one launched out of Prome at the end of March, did nothing to help. For these reasons James Lunt described March 1942 'as possibly the most depressing month in my life.'[26]

Following the collapse of the Prome–Toungoo line, Alexander tried desperately to create a new defence line further north. Wavell had given him three imperatives during his fleeting visit at the beginning of the month. These were to concentrate Burma Corps to the north of Prome, to continue to take every opportunity for offensive action and to make preparations to withdraw to the area south of Magwe–Taungdwingyi. Wavell commented to the War Office at the time: 'This is our only force in Burma. We cannot reinforce for some time and we must keep it in being even at expense of loss of ground. I think Slim will probably have severe fighting north of Prome in immediate future.'[27]

Alexander decided to place his forces along a new east–west line running from the Irrawaddy through to Loikaw in the Southern Shan States. This would serve to defend the extensive oilfields at Yenangyaung as well as preserve the Army's base at Mandalay. The line ran through the towns of Taungdwingyi and Pyinmana, with Taungdwingyi approximately mid-way. Alexander intended that the Chinese would garrison the left flank of the Taungdwingyi Line and Burma Corps the right.

The problem was that Burma Corps' frontage amounted to nearly sixty miles, which was considerably more, in Slim's judgement, than his limited forces could hope to defend properly. A further problem then emerged. Alexander directed that Slim place forces in Taungdwingyi itself to protect Mandalay to the north and to maintain a firm link with the 5th Chinese Army on the left flank. He saw only too clearly, as did Slim, that the loss of Taungdwingyi would serve to drive a wedge between the British right flank and the Chinese left. This instruction, however, limited the depth Slim was able to provide to the whole of his frontage. It also meant that he now had insufficient forces to create the reserve he needed to counter the inevitable Japanese infiltration between his widely dispersed brigade locations. Keeping a firm hold of Taungdwingyi, regardless of where the Japanese point of main effort emerged was, Slim considered, a mistake. Slim feared that if he was forced to fight two separate divisional battles, one based on Taungdwingyi and the other on Magwe, his two weak and geographically diverse divisions would be no match for the concentrated might of *33 Division*. He was convinced that if he were able to fight the forthcoming battle with his two divisions working closely together he would have a much better chance of challenging *Iida* and even, as he hoped, of counter-attacking him decisively. But to do this he needed the entire 17 Indian Division to be freed from its responsibilities for Taungdwingyi and given over entirely to the task of counter-attacking the main Japanese thrust against the oilfields. Alexander was aware of Slim's difficulty but felt constrained by the need to keep on good terms with Chiang Kai-shek, believing that if the British abandoned Taungdwingyi it would enable the Chinese to claim that the British were not serious about defending Burma.

Unable to concentrate his corps, and with Alexander insistent on the need to defend Taungdwingyi, Slim did the only two things open to him. First, he shortened his line. This required a further withdrawal from Allanmyo to the area just south of Magwe, which was completed by 6 April. The Japanese occupied the town on the day the troops of 1 Burma Division departed. 'I did not like the idea of another withdrawal,' Slim wrote: 'We were fast approaching the dangerous state when our solutions to all problems threatened to be retreat, but I hoped this would be the last.' But at least this withdrawal reduced the extent of his responsibilities to about forty miles. Burma Corps was complete on the Taungdwingyi Line by 8 April.

Second, Slim asked Alexander to give responsibility for Taungdwingyi to the 5th Chinese Army. Alexander accordingly on 6 April asked Stilwell for help in defending the town. Stilwell agreed to help, and a Chinese regiment was promised for the task. But, as in so much of his dealings with the Chinese, Slim was to be disappointed. 'We waited expectantly for them to arrive,' he wrote. 'We waited in vain.' Despite the promise of logistical help and attempts by Burma Corps to tempt the Chinese by dumps of rice, which Slim likened to 'enticing a shy sparrow to perch on your windowsill', no Chinese arrived. Unbeknown to Slim, Chiang Kai-shek had countermanded Stilwell's order and instructed him not to provide the regiment after all. It seemed that 'neither Chiang Kai-shek nor Stilwell had any faith in Slim's ability to hold up the Japanese', comments James Lunt, 'and despite offers of help were not prepared to risk their own troops in this venture.'[28] Slim now had no choice but to hold the whole of the Allied right flank himself, including Taungdwingyi and the vital oilfields at Yenangyaung.

Not aware of any sign that might indicate that the Chinese would not do what they had promised, Slim went ahead and issued orders for the defence of the line on 6 April. Water was so scarce that he was forced to base unit dispositions on the location of village wells. 2 Burma Brigade was tasked with holding Minhla on the west bank of the Irrawaddy and 1 Burma Brigade was given the area of Migyaungyi on the east bank. 63 and 16 Indian Brigades held the left flank at Taungdwingyi itself. From the remainder, including 13 and 48 Indian Brigades and 7 Armoured Brigade, Slim intended to form a powerful 'strike force' under the command of Bruce Scott, which would counter-attack against the flanks of the enemy whenever and wherever the Japanese thrusts developed.

John Hedley, a young British officer in the Indian Army, recalled Slim explaining his plan to the assembled officers of 63 Indian Brigade during this realignment of the defence line. Slim told them,

You've probably been wondering why we have had these everlasting withdrawals and I sympathise with you. I've loathed them too. The reason, however, is that I must have good open country where the tanks can operate with good effect against the Japs, and this is it. And this is my plan: You, 63 Brigade, are to hold Taungdwingyi, 1 Burma Division is in Magwe, 48 Brigade and the Tanks are in the middle. Now, wherever the Japs attack, the other two will close in, and we'll really knock him this time.[29]

The problems of attempting to hold too much ground with too few troops now became apparent. Scott's brigades were in no way self-supporting, with wide gaps between the four principal defensive positions. 48 Indian and 7 Armoured Brigades found themselves at the town of Kokkogwa ten miles to the west of Taungdwingyi while 13 Indian Brigade was placed a further eight miles to the west. Partly in order to make up some of his deficiencies in battlefield intelligence, Slim placed an observation screen, made up of troops from the Burma Frontier Force, some sixteen miles to the front of the position, in order to provide information about the direction of the Japanese advance.

To complicate matters even further, the main road between Taungdwingyi, Magwe and Yenangyaung, the only line of communication between Slim's dispersed units, ran just behind the front line. Blocking this road would cut Slim's units off from each other. This vulnerability exacerbated an already serious communications weakness in Burma Corps. 'Battalions had only one telephone and this was connected to Brigade HQ,' recalled Ian Lyall Grant. 'Using runners was the only other means of passing messages. Of any one area there was only one map (black and white) per battalion.'[30]

Slim's HQ was no better off. Micheal Calvert, a young Royal Engineers officer who fought throughout the war in Burma and who, amongst other things, wrote a short biography of Slim in 1973, recalls that when Slim arrived he was presented with a signal detachment that had been

scraped together from Burma Army HQ and only four wireless sets whose batteries had to be recharged by operating a pedal driven generator. Transport was scarce and trained staff officers were few. This was, however, a blessing in disguise, as it meant that his headquarters was small and therefore very mobile.[31]

'We were, of course' recalled Slim, 'a tactical battle headquarters only – the whole of our 'G' branch, for instance, moved on two jeeps, one truck and a couple of motor cycles – and orders were more often than not verbal.'

Despite these deficiencies 'Taffy' Davies managed to run an efficient and effective HQ. 'We were never out of touch with our formations', affirms Slim; 'we quickly knew their dispositions and movements; we never failed to feed and ammunition them to the extent possible, and we never failed to get our orders to them in time.'

The lack of adequate radio communications between Slim and his divisional commanders was a constant headache. As a result, Slim was forced to rely on his divisional commanders understanding his overall intentions without the benefit of detailed orders and instructions. Fortuitously, this did not prove to be a problem for either Cowan or Scott. There was no substitute for adequate radio communications, however. The Japanese, by contrast, were immeasurably better equipped. Following their capture of British tanks and their radios at Shwedaung, the Japanese quickly exploited the British habit of transmitting signal messages in clear speech, rather than in code, on the assumption that the Japanese could not understand English. However, the Japanese had some extremely good English-speaking soldiers in their ranks and made widespread use of them to keep their commanders informed of British battlefield activity and intentions.[32] In time Burma Corps learned the importance of radio security. During the battle for Yenangyaung, when Slim was in contact with Scott's HQ inside the pocket through the radios of 7 Armoured Brigade, both used an extensive, home made code in Gurkhali to confuse the Japanese they knew to be listening.

*Iida*'s plan was to seize the oilfields at Yenangyaung before the British could destroy them, as they would be vital for subsequent operations in northern Burma. This, and not Mandalay, was to be his main effort. *33 Division* was to advance up both banks of the Irrawaddy, exploiting to the full the opportunities the vast river provided for the transport of troops and supplies. *Sakurai* intended to hold British attention to the area between Magwe and Kokkogwa while inserting a strong river-borne force up the Irrawaddy to seize the oilfields. This would also serve to cut off Slim from the rear. It was a classic Japanese manoeuvre and it very nearly succeeded.

Japanese patrol actions developed against positions held by 1 Burma, 13 and 48 Indian Brigades on 10 April. The following day attacks were launched in strength against 1 Burma and 48 Indian Brigades at Kokkogwa. Success in either of these attacks would have driven a wedge between 17 Indian and 1 Burma Divisions. But Slim's left flank held firm. 48 Indian Brigade succeeded brilliantly in halting the attack against Kokkogwa throughout the period 11–14 April, a battle which Slim described as 'one of the bitterest fought actions of the whole campaign' and which *33 Division* regarded as their one defeat of the 1942 campaign.[33]

However, the situation was far less secure on Slim's right flank where 1 Burma Brigade was fighting a confused battle on the banks of the Irrawaddy to the south of the vulnerable Magwe–Taungdwingyi road. Considerable infiltration had taken place through the Burma Corps position in the period from 10 April onwards, much of it by Japanese disguised either as refugees, Chinese soldiers or members of the Burma Frontier Force. British and Indian troops were caught out regularly by such ruses, which were difficult to counter. During 12 April the threat of a strong Japanese advance towards the oilfields forced Scott to withdraw 1 Burma Brigade westward in order to reinforce the village of Migyaungye. The enemy, however, seized the village before 1 Burma Brigade could secure it, and the village could not be retaken in a counter-attack launched by Scott on 13 April. 'The Striking Force, moving down to counter-attack,' recalled Slim, 'became involved in a series of fights with enemy groups, and exhausted itself by marching and counter-marching to deal with them.'

The truth was that Alexander's positioning of the Taungdwingyi Line was able to do very little to prevent the Japanese threatening Yenangyaung. Indeed, Alexander's plan served to sacrifice Yenangyaung in favour of securing the link with the Chinese right flank. A key village dominating the east bank of the Irrawaddy was now in *Iida*'s hands, and British counter action was feeble and confused. Grant levels the blame for this confusion squarely on Scott and Slim. 'There was still a belief at the higher levels of command that aggressive action would neutralise the apparent Japanese superiority,' he argues; '1 Burma Division was therefore directed to strike at this Japanese force advancing from the south. This was distinctly unrealistic. 1 Burma Division was only partially trained, was numerically weaker and was far less experienced than its opponent.'[34] This is undoubtedly true. Scott's division was probably incapable at this stage of mounting more than aggressive patrols against the highly professional *33 Division*. The problem for both Scott and Slim at this time was that the alternatives were appallingly stark, and they sought every opportunity to regain the initiative.

Slim consistently held out hope that something could be done to recover the situation by the use of offensive action. By 14 April, nevertheless, the whole of Slim's right flank had begun to crumble. By midday on 13 April it was already clear to both Slim and Scott, when they met at Magwe to discuss the deteriorating situation, that Japanese gains threatened to outflank 1 Burma Division entirely. A powerful divisional sized counter-attack against the flank and rear of *33 Division* might succeed in removing the threat to Yenangyaung but Slim could only launch this if Alexander allowed him to relinquish his grip on Taungdwingyi. This Alexander, constrained as he was by the political necessity of retaining a firm link with the Chinese on the left flank of Burcorps, would not permit.

Seventeen years later, when writing *Defeat into Victory*, Slim could hardly restrain his frustration at this lost chance to inflict a grievous blow on *Sakurai's* over-stretched regiments. During the days preceding the first Japanese attacks on 10 April, it was obvious to Slim that *Iida* would make a concerted effort to seize the Yenangyaung oilfields along the course of the Irrawaddy. He remarks candidly that when he could not persuade Alexander to agree to reduce the Taungdwingyi garrison, he ought to have done it himself, with or without the sanction of the Army Commander. Foregoing the link with the Chinese for a time might, he believed, have enabled him to achieve a decisive strike against *Sakurai*. The strategic realities of the situation in which Burma Corps found itself, however, meant that both divisions now had no choice but to fight separate battles.

With 1 Burma Division on the Yin Chaung Shin recognized that he now had no hope of holding the oilfields and on 15 April ordered their destruction. The following day he moved his HQ north to Gwegyo. In disaster now stalked 1 Burma Division. The troops were in a state close to exhaustion and the awful heat, lack of water, contact harassment from the air and relentless demoralization of retreat conspired to force Scott to consider resting his troops before continuing the withdrawal to the Yin Chaung. Not realizing how close the Japanese were to cutting his

# 2

# Through the Shadows of Darkness

On 13 April Slim duly ordered 1 Burma and 13 Indian Brigades to disengage and withdraw to temporary positions on the line of the Yin Chaung. This almost dry water course, lying ten miles to the south of Magwe, followed a meandering south-easterly course from the Irrawaddy, some thirty miles south of the Yenangyaung oilfields, to Taungdwingyi. The only source of water north of the Yin Chaung was at the Pin Chaung, which lay just to the north of Yenangyaung. Slim also transferred two battalions from 17 Indian Division to Scott. Slim's units were now becoming dangerously depleted as casualties and sickness reduced his force every day, a factor that had an inevitably negative effect on the morale of those remaining. Even after it had been reinforced following the battle for Shwedaung, 1 Cameronians, for example, was again reduced to only 215.[1] On the same day 48 Indian Brigade and 7 Hussars withdrew from Kokkogwa to Taungdwingyi.

With 1 Burma Division on the Yin Chaung, Slim recognized that he now had no hope of holding the oilfields and on 15 April ordered their destruction. The following day he moved his HQ north to Gwegyo. Disaster now stalked 1 Burma Division. The troops were in a state close to exhaustion and the awful heat, lack of water, constant harassment from the air and relentless demoralization of retreat conspired to force Scott to consider resting his troops before continuing the withdrawal to the Pin Chaung. Not realizing how close the Japanese were to cutting him off from his escape route over the Pin Chaung, Scott decided to take this risk and rest his exhausted division for twenty-four hours.

But it was a near-fatal error. In the early hours of 16 April *Sakurai* used the opportunity to outflank Scott's division to the east, infiltrating a whole regiment in small groups through Scott's thinly held defences in a race to slam shut the Pin Chaung gate. At the same time attacks were made on 1 Burma and 13 Indian Brigades' hastily prepared positions on the Yin Chaung. The Yin Chaung proved to be nothing like the obstacle Scott had hoped for and the retreating 1 Burma Division was too exhausted and had too few resources to cover every part of it. Both brigades were unable to hold the Japanese attack and were pushed back, withdrawing during the remainder of the night to the Kadaung Chaung, which followed the southern outskirts of Yenangyaung. While this attack was going in *Sakurai's* outflanking force managed to get a force across the Pin Chaung and cut the road running north out of Yenangyaung to Kyaukpadaung. Another block was quickly placed at the village of Twingon, south of the ford, and a strong force put on the ford itself. Scott's only escape route to the north was now blocked.

Worse was to come. During the oppressively hot day that followed (17 April) *Sakurai* managed to insert troops into Yenangyaung itself by boats from the Irrawaddy. Not only was Scott cut off from the north, at the Pin Chaung, and pursued from the rear, but the Japanese were also now in Yenangyaung itself.

The withdrawal of 1 Burma Division into the Yenangyaung pocket over the period 17 and 19 April, and into the trap *Sakurai* had set for it, proved in every respect to be the severest trial yet faced by Slim's troops. It turned out to be not a battle for the oilfields, as these had already been destroyed, but rather a battle for the survival of 1 Burma Division. A taste of the agonies to come had been provided by the withdrawal from Prome to Allanmyo over a week earlier, but this was far worse. The most pressing physical trial was caused by the intense heat and the lack of water. For much of the route to Yenangyaung 'the scrub and occasional palm trees ceased and the country was bare and shadeless', recalled Grant. 'Moreover, it was very broken, with small hills and deep nullahs, and marching off the road became impracticable.'[2] There was virtually no fresh water as the east bank of the Irrawaddy, the only source of water, was now in Japanese hands.

Although having denied *Iida* the opportunity to exploit the wealth of the oilfields, it was now clear to Slim that, with 1 Burma Division on the verge of extinction, *Iida* was likely to take advantage of Slim's weakening right flank to make a powerful thrust up the Irrawaddy to threaten Mandalay. It was crucial therefore that Scott held on for as long as he could. Despite his earlier experience with the promise of Chinese assistance for the defence of Taungdwingyi, Slim realized that with no reserve of his own, Scott's only hope of relief lay in assistance from the Chinese. If he could engineer a Chinese attack into the pocket, across the Pin Chaung, combined with a breakout attack by 1 Burma Division, Scott might have a chance of escape. Nothing else looked likely to succeed. Fortunately, Stilwell was able to comply with Slim's request for urgent assistance, and gave him 38 Chinese Division. This was commanded by one of Chiang Kai-shek's ablest commanders, Lieutenant-General Sun Li Jen. Slim rated Sun highly, considering him 'a good tactician, cool in action, very aggressively minded, and, in my dealings with him, completely straightforward.' But the Chinese once again proved themselves to be something of a mixed blessing. Taking a considerable risk, Slim, partly as he admits to gain Sun's confidence, placed all his available tanks and artillery under Sun's direct command. This served to enhance considerably Sun's personal standing before his men. It was a masterly piece of diplomacy and, despite the initial anguish of Brigadier Anstice, the arrangement worked remarkably well. But it was not simply good politics: unity of command for all forces involved in the battle required a single commander and a clear, unambiguous chain of command. Slim could conceivably have taken command himself but this may, perversely, have served to prevent Sun's troops from fighting at their best.

Slim's plan was for 38 Chinese Division to attack from the north on the morning of 18 April while 1 Burma Division, within the pocket, fought its way out. The attack was a failure, however, and the Japanese retained their grip on both the ford and the village of Twingon. The day was one of torment for Scott's beleaguered troops. With no means of escape the situation for 1 Burma Division could not have been more desperate. Slim recalled it as 'a brutal battle ... The temperature that day was 114 degrees; the battlefield was the arid, hideous, blackened shale of the oilfield, littered with wrecked derricks, flames roaring from the tanks, and shattered machinery and burning buildings everywhere. Over it all hung that huge pall of smoke. And there was no water.' The wounded lay untreated, and men were beginning to die from the heat. To make matters worse Japanese machine gun and artillery fire played constantly over the exposed positions to which Scott's beleaguered and depleted units now clung desperately, although there was a welcome respite from air attack during the day.

Scott sought Slim's permission in the late afternoon of 18 April to break out of the pocket that night across the Pin Chaung. It would be fraught with risk and would result in Scott's abandonment of all his remaining vehicles and heavy weapons. But Slim held out one last hope that he could break the Japanese stranglehold, and relieve Scott's division. Using 2RTR's radio truck, now his only means of communication with the troops in the pocket, Slim asked Scott to hold on until the following morning, when a further attack over the Pin Chaung towards Twingon by 38 Chinese Division was planned. If this went well, as Slim hoped it would, it would prove decisive in securing the relief of Scott's division. 'I was afraid, too', wrote Slim, 'that if our men came out in driblets as they would in the dark, mixed up with Japanese, the Chinese and indeed our own soldiers, would fail to recognize them and their losses would be heavy.'

Scott and Slim were old and close friends, and a sentimental response would have been for Slim to agree with Scott's desperate request to withdraw. Major Brian Montgomery, the Intelligence Staff Officer in Slim's tiny headquarters, watched and listened to Slim talking into the microphone in the back of the radio truck, telling Scott to hold on. He recorded 'how gently and courteously he talked to Scott, never relaxing the iron grip of authority but never domineering or dictating.'[3] Trusting therefore to the promise of relief the next morning, Scott agreed to hold on and 1 Burma Division dug in to its tenuous positions on the eastern outskirts of Yenangyaung. The Japanese kept up constant pressure on the perimeter throughout the remainder of the day and during the night that followed.

The next day began badly, however. The Chinese attack was scheduled to begin at 7 a.m. on the morning of 19 April. Late the previous night Alexander had ordered Slim to meet with himself and Stilwell at Pyawbwe on the 19th, to discuss the future conduct of the campaign. But the first news of the morning was that the Chinese attack would not be ready on time. This came as a considerable blow, given the assurances he had given Scott the previous afternoon, and Slim immediately took steps to get the attack going before handing over the reins to 'Taffy' Davies and departing for Pyawbwe. Despite the failure to attack when planned, Slim was sufficiently content that General Sun would do his utmost to attack at the earliest opportunity. It is clear that, although Slim did not consider the battlefield situation on the morning of 19 April to be stable, he nevertheless felt that he had little choice but to obey Alexander's instructions to meet with him at Pyawbwe. To complicate matters an attack by British infantry and armour also failed to materialize during the day, as erroneous reports of Japanese troops outflanking the position to the north caused someone in Slim's HQ to cancel the attack and divert the troops elsewhere to meet this new 'threat'.

If Slim had remained at his tactical HQ during the day, could he have ensured that Sun delivered his attack over the Pin Chaung when it was promised? In all likelihood, probably not. Although the situation was maddening, there was little that Slim could have done to assist Sun's preparations for the attack. He records that with the Chinese 'lack of signalling equipment, of means of evacuating wounded and of replenishing ammunition, and their paucity of trained junior leaders it was not surprising that to sort themselves out, reform, and start a fresh attack took time.' Slim was invariably impressed with what he saw of the Chinese soldier in action, but their support and command functions were shockingly poor and a source of constant frustration to all who had occasion to operate with them.

Inside the pocket on 19 April, as the hours dragged by with no sign of relief, Scott determined that he now had no choice but to break out that day. His only other alternative was the unthinkable recourse of surrendering his exhausted division to the Japanese. Scott therefore ordered his troops to break out along a track that led to the Pin Chaung. They managed to do so, with great difficulty, by nightfall. It had been a costly engagement. Scott had lost at least one fifth of his force of about 4,000, including most of the division's vehicles and guns, none of which could be replaced, and had escaped only by the skin of his teeth. The promised Chinese attack had been delayed repeatedly throughout the day. When it finally went in at 3 p.m., it successfully captured the ford and penetrated into Yenangyaung, but it was launched too late to help 1 Burma Division and failed to wrest Twingon from the Japanese.

While 33 Division had failed to seize the oilfields intact, they had still inflicted a severe defeat on 1 Burma Division. Slim returned from

Pyawbwe in the evening in time to watch the survivors of Scott's division come out of the pocket. It was a moving experience. 'The haggard, red-eyed British, Indian and Burmese soldiers who staggered up the bank were a terrible sight' he recalled, 'but every man I saw was still carrying his rifle. The two brigades of the division had reached Yenangyaung at a strength of not more than one'.

At the Pyawbwe conference Alexander had sought to reinforce the need to hold a defensive line running through Chauk, Kyaukpadaung, Meiktila and Thazi. Slim, however, was convinced that the effort required to ensure the creation and maintenance of a viable defence line would be wasted without a serious attempt to counter-attack the advancing Japanese. With *33 Division* deeply investing Yenangyaung, Slim reiterated forcefully the need for a powerful counter-attack against *Sakurai* in the Irrawaddy Valley, and argued that 17 Indian Division should be allowed, with Stilwell's help, to attack westwards. Only a single, concerted offensive against *33 Division*, he argued, promised to do anything to halt the Japanese advance up the Irrawaddy. If successful, as Slim believed it had every chance of being, it would allow the British to transfer support to the Chinese in the Sittang Valley. The only alternative to offensive activity of this type was to continue to fight separate actions across the whole of the front. In setting this case forward Slim was simply repeating his arguments of the previous week, arguments which Alexander had at that time rejected. However, it is unlikely that Slim realized at the time the extent to which *Sakurai* was being supplied by boat up the Irrawaddy and was thus less vulnerable to counter-attack than Slim expected because he did not have an extensive logistical 'tail'.[4] Slim acknowledged openly that his hopes for a counter-offensive were ambitious, and often little more than 'a house of cards', but believed, as did 'Taffy' Davies, his 'mainstay in these difficult times', in the essential correctness of his ideas.

This time, in the face of these arguments Alexander gave way. He directed that Burma Corps, with Stilwell's help, launch an offensive on 22 April against the exposed Japanese flank running south along the Irrawaddy from Yenangyaung. This was what Slim had long wanted. There was a sting in the tail, however. Alexander continued to refuse to release 17 Indian Division from Taungdwingyi. This left only Scott's battered division, which now amounted to not much more than a brigade, and which was largely unfit for further action, supplemented by any units Stilwell could provide. Without the support of 17 Indian Division the impact of any attack was never going to be substantial. Stilwell was nevertheless eager to contribute. He agreed that Sun's 38 Chinese Division be placed under Slim's command and he also allocated 200 Chinese Division and one regiment of 22 Chinese Division to the offensive. Stilwell planned, at the same time, to counter-attack with the 5th Chinese Army south of Pyinmana.

However, between 18 and 20 April disaster struck again. The Japanese proceeded to break through in the east at Loikaw and Pyinmana on Alexander's left flank, effectively negating all of Slim's plans. The 6th Chinese Army fell apart with such alarming speed that Stilwell had to reinforce it with the 5th Chinese Army's 200 Division, the same troops who only three weeks before had been forced out of Toungoo and who were now earmarked for Slim's counter-offensive against *33 Division*.

With the threat of a wide envelopment deep into the Shan States Slim's hoped-for offensive against *33 Division* now had to be abandoned and his forces rapidly rearranged to meet the requirements of the deteriorating situation. As had been clear from the outset of the withdrawal from Rangoon, the ability of the Japanese to turn either the Sittang or the Irrawaddy fronts would make the other untenable. The security of central and northern Burma depended on both fronts being held together. Now, with the left flank apparently shattered, Slim's position on the right flank was now impossible to sustain. It looked increasingly inevitable that continued fighting was useless and the only choice confronting Alexander was to withdraw his troops from Burma entirely.

Alexander had received instructions on 18 April from Wavell, the day before the Pywabwe conference. This was the first written directive Alexander had received since 4 March, and gave him direction as to what he was to do if the situation necessitated a wholesale evacuation of Burma. Wavell still expected much of the Burma Army. Alexander was instructed to keep in close touch with Stilwell's 5th and 6th Chinese Armies, to which were to be attached one of Slim's brigades, to cover the route that led from Kalewa through to Tamu in Assam and to retain as many 'cards of re-entry' as possible so as to facilitate future offensive operations into Burma. He was also instructed to maintain the integrity of his fighting troops so that a 'force in being' could eventually be withdrawn for the defence of Assam.

There were two possible routes back to India. The first, and least practicable, was *via* Mogaung or Myitkyina through the Hukawng Valley to Ledo. While there was a good road and railway link with Myitkyina, the route into Ledo thereafter was by foot only, through the Hukawng Valley. The area was remote and mountainous and interspersed by rivers passable only with considerable difficulty. This was the route chosen by many escaping civilians, and many thousands of those unable to escape by air from Myitkyina died in its wooded vastness.

The second was the cross-country route that led north-west from Shwebo to Kalewa on the Chindwin, through the notoriously malarial Kabaw Valley to Tamu in Assam, and thence to Imphal. Alexander decided that the only viable option for the evacuation of Burma Army was by the latter route, even though this would itself be fraught with difficulty. Almost a month earlier Wavell had agreed to a plan formulated by Alexander to effect an evacuation of Burma using this route. 1 Burma Division was to cover the approaches to India by Kalewa. 17 Indian Division (less one brigade) was to withdraw to India on the axis Mandalay–Shwebo–Katha so as to cover the projected route from Ledo through the Hukawng Valley. 7 Armoured Brigade, together with an Infantry Brigade or four infantry battalions from 17 Indian Division, was to accompany the 5th Chinese Army to China *via* Lashio, and the 6th Chinese Army was to withdraw to China by way of Lashio and Kentung.

But the prospect of having to divide his carefully husbanded corps and to despatch even a small element to China to an uncertain fate was anathema to Slim and something he opposed strongly from the moment he heard of it. He knew that above all 'the men, both British and Indian, would be horribly depressed at the prospect.' The Chinese province to where they would withdraw, Yunnan, was in the grip of a severe famine and it would have been impossible to sustain the troops by airlift from India. Given the tenuous nature of Chinese supply and administration it was inevitable that British forces would have either to starve or turn into the same kind of scavengers as their hosts. Either way they would lose any residual military value they took with them into exile.

The issues of morale, supply and future usefulness had not been exposed in the consideration of the problem by Wavell and Alexander, who, prompted by Churchill, had been primarily concerned with issues of high politics and diplomacy. Lunt caustically remarks that these issues never occurred to Alexander because he 'never pretended to be a logistician.'[5] The CIGS, Alan Brooke, fortunately for Slim, was also far from enamoured with the idea.[6]

On 23 April Alexander gave Slim and Stilwell orders for the further defence of Burma. Even at this stage it was not certain that a withdrawal would take place. Alexander was still hopeful that Mandalay could be held. Burma Corps was to hold the area west of the Mu River, with 1 Burma Division on both sides of the Chindwin River, a strong element covering the exposed Myittha Valley which ran northwards up to Kalewa. Brigadier Anstice's 7 Armoured Brigade, together with Sun's 38 Chinese Division, were to hold the area between the Irrawaddy and the Mu River, while 22, 28 and 96 Chinese Divisions were to hold the area south of Mandalay, including the crossings over the Myitnge River. So that there would be no repeat of the Sittang experience, Alexander ordered that in the event of its defences becoming untenable his forces were to withdraw across the Irrawaddy in the Mandalay area and the Ava Bridge, the only one to span the river, was to be destroyed.

Despite Alexander's optimism, however, the situation on his left flank now deteriorated rapidly. Two days after these instructions had been promulgated Alexander recognized that he was now faced with the evacuation of Burma and he called another meeting of his senior commanders. Alexander, Slim and Stilwell met again at the small town of Kyaukse, thirty miles south of Mandalay, on 25 April. All were agreed that the events of the past week meant that it was now not possible for either the British or the Chinese to retain any significant forces in northern Burma, and the only choice left to them was a complete withdrawal to Assam and China. It was at this meeting that Slim forcefully rejected Alexander's plan for any elements of Burma Corps to fall back on Yunnan. 'I was more than ever convinced', Slim writes, 'that to send any of our British units in their present state to China would be a grave military and political error.' Major Brian Montgomery, who accompanied Slim to the meeting, later commented: 'I so well remember that . . . Slim clearly dominated the scene, and made certain once and for all that no British or Indian troops would retreat into China. Alexander gave me, at any rate, the impression of being rattled.'[7]

Alexander bowed to Slim's objections, and announced the following day that the British forces would withdraw to India and the Chinese to China. It was a momentous decision. For the first time during the campaign the final objective had been made clear. Once this decision had been made there was no time to be lost. The withdrawal north of the Irrawaddy began that night, and was to be complete within a week, after which a general withdrawal to India and China was to take place. The decisive issue during the first stage was speed in getting all elements of the British and Chinese armies safely across the Irrawaddy before *Iida* had the chance to catch Alexander with his back to the river.

Upon returning to his HQ at Taungtha Slim issued his orders for the first phase of the withdrawal, which was to recover Burma Corps to the north side of the Irrawaddy while providing rearguard security for the withdrawal of the scattered and collapsing 5th Chinese Army. Slim's plan was for 38 Chinese Division to cover Kyaukpadaung while 1 Burma Division completed reorganizing itself following the escape from Yenangyaung prior to moving on Taungtha. 17 Indian Division was to move immediately from Taungdwingyi to Meiktila to allow 22 and 96 Chinese Divisions to complete their withdrawal northwards from Meiktila.

The 5th Chinese Army was already reeling from the Japanese offensive and needed protection as it attempted to move northward and cross safely over the Irrawaddy. The use of Burma Corps as a secure rearguard for the Chinese paid an immediate dividend over the following days as the Japanese applied pressure across the front in an attempt to unbalance Alexander's defence of the Irrawaddy. Slim pays tribute in *Defeat into Victory* to Cowan's division and Anstice's armoured brigade for ensuring the brilliant success of this difficult rearguard action. Both formations had recovered much of their previous confidence, in large part due to skilful handling by their respective commanders. Following the successful clearance of the Meiktila area, Slim ordered Cowan to withdraw north to the Irrawaddy through the towns of Wundin and then Kyaukse, which was to be held by 48 Indian Brigade.

48 Indian Brigade and 7 Hussars had only just reached Kyaukse during the night of 26 April, and were busy preparing a strong defensive position as the remainder of Cowan's division passed through the town on their way north. In the event this gave them only a day's respite before *18 Division*, as yet unbloodied in Burma, attacked the town on the evening of 28 April. The attack was launched in the midst of a ferocious thunderstorm, but the defenders were well prepared and it was bloodily repulsed. The brigade positions emerged largely unscathed and a counter-attack on the

morning of 29 April was successful in ejecting parties of Japanese from positions to the front of the town. However, the incurable wasting disease afflicting Burma Corps – an inexorable rise in casualties as the withdrawal continued with no hope of reinforcements to compensate for these losses – meant that even the most determined stand was not guaranteed to last for long, and, their task completed, the brigade, now only about 1,700 strong, withdrew from their positions at 6 p.m. that evening.

It had been a truly creditable achievement for 48 Indian Brigade. The same troops who had delivered the bloody repulse against *Iida* at Kokkogwa had now halted the advance of *18 Division* long enough for Slim to effect a successful withdrawal across the Irrawaddy. 'The action' concluded Slim, 'was a really brilliant example of rearguard work. It not only enabled the last of the Chinese to cross the Ava bridge without molestation and gave us all a breathing space, but it inflicted heavy casualties on the enemy at extremely small cost to ourselves.'

On the day that *18 Division* was repulsed at Kyaukse, Slim received final instructions from Alexander for the evacuation to India. Alexander ordered Slim to place a 'strong detachment' to cover the Myittha Valley on the vulnerable western flank, and the remainder of Burma Corps, including 38 Chinese Division, was to withdraw on Kalewa *via* the rough and incomplete track that traversed the 120 dry and dusty miles from Ye-U on the eastern side of the river.

From his new HQ at Sagaing on the northern side of the Irrawaddy as the great river turns west from Mandalay, Slim immediately issued his own instructions to Burma Corps. The troops of 1 Burma Division were to cross over a number of hastily prepared ferries at Sameikkon, while the remainder of Burma Corps, together with all vehicles, tanks and guns, were to cross *via* the Ava Bridge at Mandalay. Once over the Irrawaddy, 2 Burma Brigade was to withdraw up the Myittha Valley to protect Slim's vulnerable left flank, while 1 Burma and 13 Indian Brigades withdrew to Kalewa, following the course of the Chindwin River, the former by boat and the latter securing the river port of Monywa. This town lay some fifty miles north of the confluence of the Irrawaddy with the Chindwin and commanded all movement along the latter. The remainder of the Corps was to hold the northern bank of the Irrawaddy and the road to Monywa against Japanese infiltration across the river for as long as was necessary. Thereafter Burma Corps would converge from its various approach marches on Kalewa, before

rejoining for the final move up the malarial Kabaw Valley to Tamu for
the relative safety of India.

On the surface the plan sounded simple, but the task facing Alexander
and Slim was vast. The Burma Army was exhausted, and was noticeably
diminishing in size and strength by the day. Lunt comments that, despite
the desperate necessity for such plans, the implications of a general
withdrawal to India were perhaps not readily apparent to Alexander,
Slim or Stilwell at the time. The extent of the challenge posed to a
successful withdrawal to India by the physical geography of the region
was daunting.

> All three had arrived in Burma by air. Most of the fighting since then
> had been taking place in the relatively open country of central Burma
> where the road system, however indifferent, was incomparably better
> than anything to be found in the vast tract of country lying between
> the west bank of the Irrawaddy and the border with India. Nor
> had they experienced Burma in the monsoon, when the whole
> countryside is completely transformed.[8]

The harsh reality, however, was that without sufficient aircraft to evacuate
the Army together with the thousands of pitiful refugees who continued to
clog the few dusty tracks that led to safety over the mountains, Alexander
and Slim had no choice. Walking to India by the most direct route was
now the only way to save what remained of the Burma Army. No other
possibility for redemption offered itself. It was march or die, and it had
all to be completed before the monsoon broke in all its destructive ferocity
in mid-May.

Slim's skilful handling of the Irrawaddy crossings and the rearguard
actions that protected the crossings from interference by the Japanese
averted a repeat of the disastrous Sittang experience. Despite some nervous
moments, such as the discovery that the maximum capacity of the two
cantilevered roads on the Ava Bridge was a mere six tons, while the
Stuart tanks of 7 Armoured Brigade weighed some thirteen tons each,
the crossings were successfully completed and the central spans of the Ava
Bridge were blown into the fast flowing waters of the river at midnight
on 30 April. 1 Burma Division, including 500 oxen and 250 bullock carts
crossed the Irrawaddy by ferries at Sameikkon on 28 April.[9] It was a
masterpiece of organization and control, all carefully orchestrated by Slim.

As this evacuation was taking place the Japanese seized Lashio on 29 April, cutting the Burma Road and opening the way to Bhamo and Myitkyina, making it doubly necessary now for all of the Burma Army to make its way to India with the greatest of speed.

Despite the successful crossing of the Irrawaddy, disaster continued to stalk Burma Corps. After crossing the river, Scott despatched 2 Burma Brigade from Pakokku on the evening of 28 April on the first part of its journey to the Myittha Valley, which ran due north to Kalewa some sixty miles west of the Chindwin. The security of the extreme left flank of the Burma Army's withdrawal route was vital, as without this protection Slim was concerned that *Iida* might slip a quick left hook up the Myittha Valley to seize Kalemyo before Slim could withdraw his troops to the town from the east bank of the Chindwin.

However, consideration of the security of his left flank created another potentially catastrophic problem in the area between Pakokku on the Irrawaddy, and Monywa on the Chindwin. Slim had planned to protect Monywa from a Japanese incursion up the west bank of the Chindwin. But instead of making for Monywa with best speed after successfully crossing the Irrawaddy on 28 April, Scott allowed the remainder of his exhausted division (1 Burma and 13 Indian Brigades) to rest on the north bank of the Irrawaddy on 29 and 30 April. The division did not continue its withdrawal to Monywa until late on 30 April. Alexander was content to allow this delay because it gave an opportunity for the stream of wounded and the thousands of refugees cluttering the withdrawal routes to get a head start before the main body of the Army withdrew.[10]

But despite the exhaustion of Scott's troops this delay was a very grave error, the second mistake of this kind by Scott. The departure of 2 Burma Brigade for Pauk on 28 April allowed the road leading from Pakokku to Monywa to remain entirely unprotected throughout the period 28 to 30 April. The route to Monywa along the west bank of the Chindwin was thus wide open for exploitation by the Japanese.

The Japanese seized the opportunity offered to them. Following his failure to destroy 1 Burma Division at Yenangyaung, and his subsequent failure to trap Alexander on the south side of the Irrawaddy, *Iida* had ordered his four divisions on 26 April 'to strike wide and deep in [the] rear of the Allied forces, so as to cut their lines of retreat and thus destroy them in one blow.'[11] *33 Division* was to form the left flank of the Japanese advance with the object of preventing Alexander from withdrawing his

troops successfully to India and was instructed to seize Monywa and
Ye-U. *55 Division* was to form the right flank with the objective of
advancing on Myitkyina. In compliance with these orders, *Sakurai* drove
*33 Division* so hard that he occupied Pakokku on the evening of 28 April,
the same day that Bourke had left the town. Surprised to see that the
town lay undefended, and suspecting that the door to Monywa might be
wide open, the regimental commander trucked an advance guard up the
road to the point where, forty-five miles later, the road came to a halt in
the jungle opposite the unsuspecting town of Monywa. It was dusk on
Thursday 30 April.

The regimental commander's enthusiasm now got the better of him and
that night he attacked Monywa with artillery, mortar and machine-gun
fire from the west bank of the Chindwin, revealing his presence many
hours before he made an attempt to cross the river to Monywa itself.
At his HQ some miles to the north of the town on the Monywa–Ye-U
road, Slim first feared that the outbreak of firing indicated that Monywa
had already been lost. Alive to the serious threat this would now pose to
Shwegyin–Kalewa and the prospect yet again of looming disaster, Slim
ordered 1 Burma Division immediately to recapture the town. He also
ordered Cowan to divert a battalion of 48 Indian Brigade, as well as all
of 63 Indian Brigade, together with a squadron of tanks, to gather at
Chaungu, fifteen miles south of Monywa, in order to assist Scott. The
remainder of 17 Indian Division were instructed to make best speed to
Ye-U to prepare for what would now be a rapid evacuation to Shwegyin
and Kalewa. Slim then gathered up some 300 stragglers in the vicinity
and sent them on to Monywa. Scott now had three brigades assembling,
albeit all very weak, with which to attack and recover Monywa the next
morning.

Additionally, in order to expedite the withdrawal of the Corps to
Kalewa once the situation in Monywa had stabilized, Slim advised
Winterton, Alexander's Chief of Staff, to commandeer all vehicles, dump
their loads and personnel and send them on to Shwegyin, the river port
on the Chindwin a few miles to the south of Kalewa. Winterton was later
to recall 'that it was this action that, above all else, saved the bulk of the
Burma Army from being captured. As it was, the Japanese were beaten to
Shwegyin, where transhipment across the Chindwin had to take place, by
the very shortest of short heads.'[12]

Early on the morning of 1 May the Japanese crossed the river and attacked Monywa, dispersing Scott's HQ and occupying the town. The situation was complicated by the fact that the town was considerably swollen by refugees and two thousand rear echelon staff awaiting evacuation up river to Kalewa. 63 Indian Brigade counter-attacked from the south in the morning but was unable to penetrate into the town. Alexander and Stilwell met at Ye-U on 1 May and, in view of the situation at Monywa, agreed that the withdrawal from the Irrawaddy line should begin without further delay. Stilwell also agreed that 7 Armoured Brigade, which had been assisting in the withdrawal of the 5th Chinese Army through the Shwebo area, should be allowed to rejoin Burma Corps for the withdrawal to India. Following his failure to eject the Japanese from the town on 1 May, Scott planned to attack Monywa on 2 May with all the forces at his disposal. 63 Indian Brigade and a squadron of 7 Hussars were to attack astride the railway from the south with 13 Indian Brigade attacking from the east. 1 Burma Brigade was to be the divisional reserve.

The attack, although vigorously pressed, failed a second time to eject the Japanese from the town. As the battle continued during the afternoon, an order to withdraw, purporting to come from Alexander himself, led Scott to break off the engagement and move 1 Burma and 63 Indian Brigades north to Alon. But no such order had been issued by Alexander or his HQ. It is possible that the message emanated from the Japanese who were now very experienced in monitoring and interfering with Burma Corps signals from British tanks captured at Shwedaung. If the order had been genuine, it would have been given to Scott by Slim in the first instance. Slim, however, knew nothing of it. That night 16 Indian Brigade was sent to secure the crossing at Shwegyin, as the capture of Monywa now gave the Japanese control of the direct route up the Chindwin to this vital crossing.

Lunt describes the delay which led to Sakurai's exploitation of the unguarded gap at Pakokku as 'Slim's costly miscalculation'.[13] Likewise, Lewin asserts that Slim had discounted the possibility of the Japanese seizing Monywa.[14] Neither is true. The gap was entirely unintentional. Slim knew from the outset just how vital the security of Monywa was to his plan for the withdrawal of Burma Corps. The retention of the town was important to allow Slim to move considerable quantities of stores, heavy equipment and troops up river to Kalewa without the necessity of carting them laboriously over the jungle track from Shewbo to Ye-U and

thence to Shwegyin–Kalewa. For the same reason it was important that
the Japanese were denied control of the town as otherwise they could
use the Chindwin to insert troops to outflank the Burma Army toiling
slowly overland to Kalewa. Alexander and Slim both recognized this,
as Alexander's original orders on 25 April to place a brigade on both
sides of the Chindwin at Monywa indicate. Slim's instructions on 27
April could not have been clearer in this regard. Scott was directed to
place a strong brigade group (13 Indian Brigade) on the west bank of
the Chindwin at Monywa, and for the remainder of the division, less 2
Burma Brigade, together with a brigade group from 17 Indian Division,
to hold the Chindwin – on both banks – as far south as possible.[15]

Likewise, there was no miscalculation in Slim's decision to send more
than a 'strong detachment' to guard the Myittha Valley, as Alexander had
first wished. The risk that *Iida* would exploit Slim's left flank to seize
Kalemyo by *coup de main* before the Allies could withdraw through the
town and up the Kabaw Valley to Tamu demanded that it be guarded well.
The fact that this potential risk demanded some form of insurance by Slim,
even though in the event *Iida's* main effort did not fall in this area, was
not a miscalculation but rather the outworkings of prudent generalship.

Similarly, in sending Bourke to guard the Myittha Valley, Slim in no
wise assumed any lessening of the importance of Pakokku as guardian
of the approach to Monywa. The problem stemmed solely from Scott's
failure to hold Pakokku at the same time as he inserted the required
protection into Monywa itself. The door left open at Pakokku after
Bourke's departure for Pauk, and before Monywa and the west bank
of the Chindwin could be properly secured, created the difficulties that
now confronted Burma Corps.

Characteristically Slim blamed himself for this failure to keep this door
closed, in particular for not delaying the march of 2 Burma Brigade until
Monywa had been secured. 'Threats were growing in many directions
with competing claims on our slender resources', he wrote. 'Forgetting
the speed with which the Japanese might come up the river by boat,
I chose to meet the wrong one, and we paid heavily for my mistake.'
While commendable, Slim's admission of guilt hides the fact that Scott,
as the divisional commander, should have taken adequate steps to ensure
the security of the vital road that ran alongside the west bank of the
Chindwin to Monywa.

To do this Scott could have done one of two things. First, he could have held back 2 Burma Brigade until either of his remaining two brigades had secured Monywa. Alternatively, he could have forgone the period of rest he granted his division following the crossing of the Irrawaddy. Neither would have been easy. Slim's requirement for a presence in the Myittha Valley was urgent, and any undue delay in Pakokku may well have jeopardized the security of Kalemyo itself if the Japanese had managed to get a force on the route before Slim. Equally, the period Scott gave the rest of his division to rest on 29 and 30 April was given not out of charity but of utter necessity. Most units were now at no more than company strength, and few soldiers were free from the effects of prolonged exhaustion and illness. His command had only just survived the agonies of Yenangyaung and in its exhausted state a major river crossing had taxed the division to its limit.

On 3 May 1 Burma Division and 7 Armoured Brigade began the withdrawal to Ye-U, the start of the track to the Chindwin. Most of Burma Corps reached Ye-U by 4 May, following a 100-mile forced march from Monywa, in desperate conditions, harassed for much of the time from the air. The Army was now in a pitiful state, with battalions reduced to scores rather than hundreds of men. 'We were by this time accustomed to serious situations,' writes Slim. 'We were faced with one now.'

There were three immediate threats to the survival of Burma Corps in what was now a race for Kalewa and the safety of India. The first was that *Sakurai* would manage to cut off Slim's forces on the Ye-U track from Shwegyin and Kalewa, by inserting troops up the Chindwin. This would have cut off the British escape route to India and brought the retreat to an ignominious end. But the second threat was equally pressing. The monsoon was due to break in mid-May, and would make the track to Tamu impassable to vehicles and the task of evacuation and resupply of the Army immeasurably more difficult. The third problem was that of supply. As soon as the decision to withdraw to India had been taken, great efforts were made to stock the route to Kalewa with the provisions required for the retreating Army, and similar action was taken from the Imphal end of the track. This was not easy, and as a precaution the troops were placed on half rations. The task was immensely hampered, Lunt records, 'by the thousands of refugees tramping along this route, dying in their scores beside the track from hunger, thirst or disease.'[16]

Slim wasted no time in Ye-U. The withdrawal to Shwegyin and Kalewa
got underway even before the evacuation of Monywa had been completed.
The urgent imperative now was to get all his units, including vehicles and
heavy equipment, to Shwegyin and then ferried across the Chindwin to
Kalewa with the greatest possible speed. With *Iida* on his heels any delay
would prove finally to be fatal. But the track was atrocious. 'Anyone
seeing this track for the first time', wrote Alexander, 'would find it
difficult to imagine how a fully mechanised force could possibly move
over it.'[17] For the most part it was unmade and difficult for wheeled
vehicles and was made passable to vehicles only through strenuous efforts
by engineers. Many sections of the route had no water.

Ever mindful of the Japanese penchant for inserting devastating blocks
on to withdrawal routes, Slim ordered 17 Indian Division to picket the
route to Pyingaing. Likewise a plea by Alexander to GHQ India brought
a series of successful British air attacks on the Chindwin over the period 3
to 5 May which considerably delayed the Japanese advance up the river. To
reduce pressure on the Shwegyin–Kalewa crossing, Slim ordered 1 Burma
Brigade to branch north off the track at Pyingaing and make for Pantha,
from whence they successfully crossed the Chindwin on 13 May. The
remainder of Burma Corps, with the ubiquitous 7 Armoured Brigade
providing the rearguard, made direct for Shwegyin, which it reached
between 8 and 9 May.

Shwegyin provided a small ferry service up the river to Kalewa, but
the weight of thousands of pitiful refugees, together with the assembled
units of Burma Corps, was too much for the limited capacity of the ferries
and the embarkation point at Shwegyin, known as the 'basin', became
hopelessly clogged with the detritus of a defeated army. Some accounts
recall that refugees lay dying amidst scores of abandoned civilian vehicles
and military equipment. Shwegyin became the graveyard for the Burma
Army: it was literally the end of the road for virtually all of Burma Corps'
remaining vehicles, tanks, guns and other heavy equipment. What could
not be carried to Kalewa had to be destroyed where it stopped.

Just as Slim had feared, and despite a security screen in the jungle to the
south, *Sakurai* managed by luck to insert a battalion rapidly by boat up the
Chindwin. This arrived unnoticed on the hills to the south and east of the
'basin' at Shwegyin, early on 10 May. Slim, having inspected the ferrying
arrangements upriver at Kalewa, landed at Shwegyin himself on the early
morning of 10 May just as the Japanese assault on the basin began. Battle

was immediately engaged, but despite this display of Japanese initiative they were unable to penetrate the perimeter of 17 Indian Division's defence during the day, and the last desperate evacuation of stores and personnel continued amidst constant fire.

Their presence, nevertheless, severely disrupted the pace and equanimity of the evacuation process. Cowan was forced to divert 48 Indian Brigade to support the defence of Shwegyin but, despite the attempts by the Japanese to break in, the ferries managed to continue shipping out personnel during the day. By 4 p.m., however, Cowan was told that only one more ferry journey would be made to Shwegyin. With no more reason to hold the position, he ordered the destruction of all remaining vehicles and equipment. As darkness fell and remaining troops prepared to march through the jungle along the east bank of the Chindwin to Kalewa, all remaining tanks and guns fired off their ammunition. By late on 11 May what remained of Burma Corps was safely on the west bank of the Chindwin. 2 Burma Brigade, after an agonizingly slow march for 200 miles through the Myittha Valley, during which movement was only possible at night, reached Kalemyo on 10 May.

Burma Corps now limped slowly into India through Tamu along the recently completed dry weather road to Imphal, having beaten the full force of the monsoon by only a few days. The last unit of Burma Corps passed through Tamu on its way to Imphal on 19 May. Although mercifully now not pressed by the Japanese, Slim recalled this final part of Burma Corps' march into India as 'sheer misery'. The Japanese reached Kalewa on 14 May but were too exhausted themselves to follow across the Chindwin.

Virtually all men of Burma Army were sick with malaria but, while everyone was exhausted, Slim noted proudly that the fighting elements marched into the Imphal Plain as soldiers.

On the last day of that nine-hundred-mile retreat I stood on a bank beside the road and watched the rearguard march into India. All of them, British, Indian and Gurkha, were gaunt and ragged as scarecrows. Yet, as they trudged behind their surviving officers in groups, pitifully small, they still carried their arms and kept their ranks, they were still recognizable as fighting units. They might look like scarecrows, but they looked like soldiers too.

They had been defeated, he admitted, but not disgraced. 'Taffy' Davies watched Slim take the salute from the ragged remnants of Burma Corps as they marched into India, remarking afterward that 'I thought his eyes had misted a bit.'[18]


The withdrawal had been an incredible feat. Despite the humiliation and bitterness of defeat, Burma Corps had not collapsed or surrendered, and for the most part had held together under the most trying circumstances imaginable. As the Official British Historian asserts, 'the Army in Burma, without once losing its cohesion, had retreated nearly one thousand miles in some three and a half months – the longest retreat ever carried out by a British Army – and for the last seven hundred miles had virtually carried its base with it.'[19] That this was the case was largely due to the skill and exertions of one man: 'Bill' Slim.

Slim had ample opportunity after he had relinquished his command of Burma Corps to consider why the imperial army had been so humiliated in Burma. In *Defeat into Victory* he rehearsed the issues of lack of preparation, the lack of any viable land communications between India and Burma, the smallness and unsuitability of the forces in Burma at the time of the Japanese invasion, the inadequacy of the air forces available to him, the hostility of some of the local population, the 'extreme inefficiency of the whole intelligence system' and the lack of training of the Burma Army. Two factors in particular, however, he considered to have been critical determinants in the defeat. The first was the quality of Japanese generalship relative to the Allies, and the second was the overwhelming effectiveness of Japanese tactics. Slim was in no doubt that the British had been outgeneralled to the point of embarrassment. 'The outstanding and incontrovertible fact' he concluded, 'was that we had taken a thorough beating. We, the Allies, had been outmanoeuvred, outfought and outgeneralled.' Stilwell, equally expressively, commented 'I claim we got a hell of a beating. We got run out of Burma and it is humiliating as hell.'[20] *Iida* and his divisional commanders were, Slim wrote, 'confident, bold to the point of foolhardiness, and so aggressive that never for one day did they lose the initiative.' By contrast Allied generals were slow to grasp the potential for decisive and aggressive action and consistently underestimated the ability of the Japanese to achieve what the British would consider impossible in the jungle. Commanders as a whole lacked vision, single-mindedness and the moral and mental robustness necessary to withstand the succession of shocks delivered by the Japanese. The Allies appeared constantly to be wrong-footed. The reasons for this were obvious to Slim in retrospect. The Japanese object was 'clear and definite', Slim argued, and 'was the destruction of our forces; ours, a rather nebulous idea of retaining territory. This led to the initial dispersion of our forces over wide areas, an error which we continued to commit, and worse still it led to a defensive attitude of mind.'

Slim's comments regarding generalship were intended to have wide applicability. They included, of course, his own performance. 'For myself,' he comments, 'I had little to be proud of: I could not rate my generalship high. The only test of generalship is success, and I had succeeded in nothing I had attempted.' Although Slim was remarkably – perhaps excessively – self-critical, his criticisms were directed at the broadest spectrum of senior leadership concerned with the campaign, from Wavell downwards. Implied criticism was levelled at both Wavell and Alexander for their combined failure to explain the purpose and scope of Allied strategy in Burma following the fall of Rangoon.

> It was then, that we needed from the highest national authority a clear directive of what was to be our purpose in Burma. Were we to risk all in a desperate attempt to destroy the Japanese Army and recover all that had been lost? Ought we to fight to the end on some line to retain at least part of Burma? Or was our task to withdraw slowly, keeping our forces intact, while the defence of India was prepared? Had we been given any one of these as our great overall object it would have had an effect, not only on the major tactics of the campaign, but on the morale of the troops. No such directive was ever received.

Indeed between 3 March and 18 April Alexander received no instructions from India at all. Wavell had offered no guidance either way and consequently the overall objective of the campaign and thus the answers to these questions were never clear. This remained the case until the final stages of the campaign, noted Slim, 'and I think we suffered increasingly in all our actions from this.' Slim was kept in the dark until 25 April, when Alexander announced a general withdrawal to Assam.[21]

Wavell's lack of a clear vision for the Burma Army delayed Alexander's recognition that he now had little choice but to prepare the Army for the inevitable withdrawal to India. Wavell saw no requirement to evacuate Burma. On 7 March, the very day Alexander abandoned Rangoon, Wavell cabled the Chiefs of Staff in London: 'I will do everything possible to maintain a hold on Burma.' But Alexander's faith in Wavell's optimism, communicated to him so forcefully on 4 March, dissipated quickly. As March slipped into April, and defeat followed defeat, Alexander belatedly realized that the Burma Army was not strong enough in terms of trained troops, supplies and equipment, particularly aircraft, to do more than slow down the enemy advance. Eventually, to save the remnants of Burma Army, he would have to get it back to India.[22] As Nigel Nicholson, one of his biographers asserts, 'Alexander was never ordered to evacuate the country: he did so because the Japanese and his supply-situation forced him to.'[23]

But while it was to take some time for Alexander to realize that he needed to choose between retreat to India or prolonged resistance in Burma, to both Hutton and Davies the need to retire on Assam was self-evident. As early as 27 February Davies had reported to Hartley that, because 17 Indian Division had been destroyed as a fighting formation, a 'retirement on Assam road may be only course possible' left to the Burma Army. He asked Hartley to investigate the 'possibility of deploying forces from India at end of Assam road.'[24] Wavell had in fact initiated work on the road from Imphal to Tamu and beyond in December 1941. This farsightedness contributed significantly to the eventual survival of Burma Army. Twenty years later, in 1962, Alexander admitted that 'I ought to have ordered an earlier evacuation of Burma. But at the time I was not prepared to admit defeat before I had done everything possible.'[25] One of the reasons for Alexander's delay to order what many of his subordinates saw to be inevitable was the Army Commander's natural optimism and his refusal to be burdened by pessimistic reports. 'He was therefore sometimes critical of [Slim's] down-to-earth comments', records Lunt, 'preferring himself to give the impression that victory was just around the corner.'[26] Alexander's optimism occasionally pressed absurd limits, however. Dorman-Smith reported on 30 March, the day that Toungoo fell and Slim's southward offensive from Prome ended in ignominy, that Alexander had spoken to the Burmese Chamber of Commerce representatives, 'and painted a heartening picture.'[27] It is little wonder that many had difficulty reconciling these public statements with the reality of defeat and destruction they could see around them, and thus lost any confidence they had in the Colonial Government's ability to defend them from the Japanese. A false confidence in these circumstances, particularly when there are otherwise few grounds for optimism, is every bit as dangerous as rampant defeatism. Burma was to see both in 1942.

Slim was undoubtedly frustrated by Alexander's generalship.[28] 'Taffy' Davies avers that, while Slim trusted Alexander and found him personally charming, he was frustrated by his apparent inability to make quick decisions. In a devastatingly frank assessment years later Slim confessed, 'I don't believe he had the faintest clue what was going on.'[29] By contrast Slim, recalled Davies, 'could think terribly simply, get through any problem and find the right answer. And having found the answer he was equally capable of handing it on to his subordinates with the greatest of clarity and simplicity.'[30] Alexander's inability to take risks grated with Slim, who recognized that risks needed to be taken in concentrating his forces if Burma Corps was to have any chance of mustering sufficient strength to counter-attack quickly and effectively. One of Alexander's biographers acknowledges with regard to Alexander's generalship in Burma that there are grounds 'for feeling that a more inspired operational concept might have been possible'.[31]

Slim remained convinced that the tables could have been turned on *Iida*, even as late as April 1942, and the situation stabilized in central Burma, if some risks had been taken. 'Time and again I had tried to pass to the offensive and to regain the initiative', Slim complained, 'and every time I had seen my house of cards fall down as I tried to add its crowning storey.' He blamed, first, his unpreparedness for the extent of the risks the Japanese took on the battlefield. With Yenangyaung and Monywa in mind, he wrote: 'I had not realized how the Japanese, formidable as long as they are allowed to follow undisturbed their daring projects, are thrown into confusion by the unexpected. I should have subordinated all else to the vital need to strike at them and thus to disrupt their plans.' He chided himself for not, 'in spite of everything and at all costs', collecting the whole strength of his corps before attempting any counter-offensive. In a clear dig at Alexander Slim asserted: 'Thus I might have risked disaster, but I was more likely to have achieved success. When in doubt as to two courses of action, a general should choose the bolder. I reproached myself that I had not.'

The second significant British failing in 1942, Slim believed, lay in the dramatic inferiority of British tactics. Relative to the innovation and imagination apparent in the Japanese approach to war, the Allies had been completely outclassed. 'The Japanese could – and did – do many things that we could not', Slim wrote. 'The chief of these and the tactical method on which all their success were based was the "hook" . . . Time and again the Japanese used these tactics, more often than not successfully, until our troops and commanders began to acquire a road-block mentality which often developed into an inferiority complex.' The 'hook' was merely a classic 'turning' movement: that many units in Burma Corps were unable to counter this relatively simple tactical device testified to their profound lack of confidence in dealing with an aggressive and inventive enemy. The power of the 'hook' lay in the psychological dislocation brought about by the awful sensation of being trapped, which to inexperienced troops could be devastating. The inability to counter these tactics allowed the Japanese to retain the initiative on the battlefield. The 'liveliest memories of the retreat' recalled James Lunt, were 'of confusion, disorder and near escapes from disaster, all of which were brought about by the relentless pressure of the enemy.'[32]

A variety of solutions were possible, including the use of air supply to counter the debilitating dependence of the British on the road. Grant suggests that the idea of using aerial resupply to relieve besieged localities was first mooted during the retreat. A solitary Blenheim bomber, flying from India, dropped stores to the troops at Ye-U on 4 May, and serious discussion about the possibilities of air supply ensued.[33] These concepts were not new to Slim. Several years before he had advocated the use of aerial resupply for garrisons along the North-West Frontier. In the context of Burma, however, aerial resupply did offer one solution, but one that was dependent entirely on the availability of large numbers of aircraft and, of course, on command of the air over the operational area. But overall the real problem in 1942 was that the Japanese consistently moved faster and more decisively than the British. Until they could reverse this trend, Slim knew that the British were unlikely ever to defeat the Japanese.

Slim emerged from the campaign a defeated general by his own standards but a victor by those of his troops. He had rescued them from the clutches of defeat and brought them back, ragged, ill and starving nevertheless, through what Calvert expressively described as 'the shadows of darkness', to safety in India.[34] Slim's success between March and May 1942 lay in ensuring that even though Burma Corps had been defeated, it had not been routed. More importantly, the threat of the Army's surrender on the pattern of Singapore was averted. Undoubtedly Slim had succeeded remarkably in snatching a measure of success from the jaws of defeat: he had prevented Burma Corps from falling into the hands of the Japanese and thus denied them the full enjoyment of their undoubted victory in Burma.* Indeed, it was remarkable that Burma Corps managed to escape at all. Given the indifferent manner in which Burma was prepared for war and the disastrous outcome of the first two months of fighting, failure seemed almost inevitable. Slim was pitched into command of a retreating Corps consisting of one badly mauled division and another that had yet to be committed to battle but which had already been milked of units and afflicted by desertion and sickness. In any case neither division had been trained, equipped or mentally prepared to take on an enemy like the Japanese.

The retreat was a valuable learning experience for Slim, the best possible preparation for the long and ugly war that loomed ahead. The unknown divisional commander from the military backwaters of Iraq had proven his considerable abilities under the most trying of circumstances. Indeed, it could be argued that the retreat to India was the greatest test of his leadership, even more so than the long, hard battles against the Japanese in 1944 and 1945. Throughout the severest trial he exhibited a constant, calm and unruffled professionalism.

He had proven two things. First, that he was able to plan, organize and command in circumstances of overwhelming crisis. The campaign had marked him out as a commander of considerable mental stamina, a man who was tough and tenacious in the face of almost overwhelming adversity, and who refused to give up when all the facts seemed to indicate that there was no hope for his bedraggled and defeated forces. Second, he had proved that he could keep his head and display quite remarkable resilience and imperturbability when the military situation appeared irretrievable. 'He was not afraid of anything', recorded Stilwell, 'and he looked it.'[35] Frank Messervy, who served under Slim in 1944 and 1945, commented that 'I never saw him cross – never. I never saw him edgy.'[36] Even after the lost battles for Prome and Yenangyaung, Calvert recalled that Slim

---

* The remnants of Burma Army totalled some 30,000 troops, having suffered around 13,000 killed, wounded and missing during the campaign.

'presented an indomitable and unshaken front in the face of these disasters, and his rather ponderous jokes cheered his staff and commanders when they were at their lowest ebb.' He 'was stubborn' Calvert wrote; 'he had an indomitable spirit and, like the British troops, he never knew when he was beaten.'[37] By retaining his composure he was able to retain the confidence of his men. Such was the impact of his generalship during the retreat that, on the basis of this campaign alone, James Lunt was led to equate him in greatness to Oliver Cromwell, Lunt listing his honesty, humour, 'unstuffiness' and humanity as Slim's crowning characteristics.[38]

But perhaps the most striking characteristic of Slim as a commander was the way in which, utterly naturally and without any form of affectation, he associated himself with the troops under his command. The first task Slim set himself on taking over Burma Corps in March 1942 was to gain the measure of these men. By nature friendly and approachable, he was an inveterate visitor and his appointment to command Burma Corps reinforced his conviction that commanders must see and be seen. Following his arrival, Slim visited widely and talked to as many men, officers and soldiers of all ranks, as he could. *Defeat into Victory* is populated with constant though unselfconscious references to visits he made to his troops.

The confidence these visits provided formed an important backdrop to his command of Burma Corps and is a point emphasized repeatedly by those who served under him. One infantry battalion commanding officer in 1942 asserted: 'I cannot say what General Slim meant to his subordinate commanders during that arduous retreat. He habitually visited the formations, scattered all over the front, by jeep or car. He was always accessible and when he was in the offing and I was able to talk to him, I invariably returned full of confidence and pep.'[39] Bruce Scott agreed. 'He immediately imposed his personality to the extent that we felt that someone behind had taken charge of us', he recalled after the war. 'Up to then we had been left to our own devices.'[40] For this reason, despite the agonies of the loss of the Sittang Bridge and the subsequent fall of Rangoon, Slim's appointment acted on the troops of the newly formed Burma Corps, as the historian Duncan Anderson affirms, 'like a tonic'.[41]

Establishing leadership and authority in an Army conditioned to defeat was not easy. 'The most important thing about a commander is his effect on morale', Slim was later to write. It was the leader's job to stamp his personality on his men. Slim was able to do this in an entirely natural and uncontrived fashion. Never engaging in histrionics or tricks of oratory, Slim had charisma but not flamboyance. He was the first to admit nevertheless that it required a degree of showmanship and repeated public appearances to make himself known to the officers and men whom he commanded. When, nineteen months later, he became the commander of 14 Army, he made a point of speaking to every combatant unit, or at least to its officers and NCOs, whenever he had the opportunity to get away from his HQ. 'My platform was usually the bonnet of my jeep with the men collected anyhow around it', he wrote. 'I often did three or four of these stump speeches in a day.'

It is not an overstatement to say that Slim's approach was unusual for the time. It was vastly different, for example, to the aloofness and reserve of the Army commander. Major-General Ian Lyall Grant's balanced and engaging account of the 1941 and 1942 campaign provides an interesting commentary on the contrasting command styles of the two men. In the second week of April Alexander and Slim visited the Taungdwingyi garrison together. The retreat had only six weeks left to run. Grant writes:

> General Alexander, cool as ever, arrived in a shiny black saloon car with a flag on the front. As the road was regularly patrolled by Japanese aircraft, and likely at any moment to be the target for Japanese patrols, this display of courage by the Army Commander was much admired. But otherwise his visit made little impact. In contrast, General Slim went round the garrison talking to all the officers in small groups. It was the first time most had seen him. He gathered the officers round him informally and spoke easily and well. He said the usual things about the importance of holding Taungdwingyi firmly and of his confidence in 'Punch' Cowan. Then he added "General Cowan and I were at Staff College together – but I'm bound to say that some of the things that we learnt there don't seem to work too well out here!" This was encouraging. Many felt that they now had a leader who realised that new methods were required to counter Japanese tactics and was prepared to think them out.[42]

Slim's success in maintaining the fighting spirit of his men was thus even the more remarkable given the increasing fragility of their morale as the months passed by.

The secret to Slim's relationship with his men lay in the way in which he identified with them as co-workers in the same great enterprise and as members of the same family. As Calvert asserts, 'This identification of himself with his men, added to his innate kindness and compassion, was his greatest achievement.'[43] His official biographer makes the point that he 'inspired such affection among the men of the 14th Army . . . that they always spoke of fighting *with*, not *under*, him'.[44] This was no mere attempt at spurious adulation. So unusual is this trait amongst the senior military commanders of history that the psychologist Norman Dixon, in his study of military leadership, described Slim as the antithesis of the norm. He concluded that the affection shown to him by British, Indian, Nepalese, African, Chinese and American troops led to him being loved by his polyglot army 'perhaps more than any other commander has been loved by his men since Nelson.'[45] 'He was a great leader – true,' wrote an officer who served on his staff later in 1942; 'he was a great commander – true; but to us he was, above all, the well-loved friend of the family.'[46]

Despite the wave of propagandized adulation for Alexander in the British press that followed the successful withdrawal to India, it was Slim, rather than the Army commander, who had been principally responsible for the 'success' of the British Army's longest retreat. Grant writes that during the long march to Imphal from Tamu in the last stages of the retreat.

> General Slim, riding in a jeep, had been much in evidence. He watched his troops intently, asking the name of each unit as it passed and making some encouraging remark. General Alexander did not appear. On the 20th he [Alexander] handed over command of the Burma Army to General Irwin of 4 Corps in Imphal and then left to report to Wavell and return to England.'[47]

Stilwell, upon hearing a broadcast at the end of the retreat which extolled Alexander as 'a bold and resourceful commander of the war, [who] has fought one of the great defensive battles of the war,' expressively and characteristically retorted 'crap!' to his diary.[48]

His men, too, had no doubt who was responsible for bringing them out of Burma. As Slim said farewell to his troops in the days before his departure from Imphal on 20 May he received an accolade reserved only for the likes of a Napoleon or a Wellington: his troops cheered him. 'To be cheered by troops whom you have led to victory is grand and exhilarating,' he commented. 'To be cheered by the gaunt remnants of those whom you have led only in defeat, withdrawal and disaster, is infinitely moving – and humbling.' In the depths of defeat, Slim was the victor.

# 3

# In the Wilderness at Ranchi

Morale in both Indian and British forces had been dealt a devastating blow by the retreat from Burma. Depression and gloom was all pervasive and Slim was as affected as anybody. Michael Calvert met Slim at Ranchi soon after completing his own remarkable escape from Burma. 'He looked tired and thinner than when I had last seen him in Burma', recalled Calvert. 'For a commander the fruits of victory are sweeter than for those serving under him, but the converse of that is also true. Although Slim had taken over a hopeless situation when he came to Burma Corps it was obvious that the bitter taste of defeat was still with him.'[1] But with a new corps to train and much to do Slim could not afford the indulgence of self-pity. For one thing there was no time for recriminations. Nor was there, in the general confusion following the retreat, any enthusiasm for a witch-hunt to apportion blame. Equally, as he acknowledged, a good general has to learn to live with defeat as well as victory. His failure at Gallabat against the Italians in November 1940 had taught him that no benefit was ever gained by worrying about mistakes or errors of judgement that were, in time, remediable. In any case the retreat was a victory of sorts: that Burma Corps had managed to extricate itself at all from Burma was itself nothing short of a miracle and Slim, perhaps more than anybody else, had been instrumental in bringing that miracle about. Slim therefore allowed himself only the briefest moment for introspection before thrusting out his chin and getting on with the business in hand. At a time like this, he averred, the defeated general had to stamp on the failures of the past 'and remember only the lessons to be learnt from defeat – they are more than victory.'

The business of the moment was to prepare a new corps, 15 Corps, for war. He was to find, however, that there were no quick solutions to rebuilding a beaten army. The first, and unexpected, hurdle was to overcome the perception amongst some in India that Burma Corps was little more than a defeated rabble. Indeed, the commander of 4 Corps, Lieutenant-General Noel Irwin, responsible for the forward defence of eastern India and charged with the reception arrangements for the returning troops, regarded Burma Corps with undisguised hostility. However, even though Irwin seemed to view the troops (and their officers) with disdain for having failed to hold Burma against what he regarded to be a clearly inferior enemy, he had virtually no resources to spare to bring comfort to Slim's ragged survivors. No preparations had been made to receive Burma Corps when it arrived in Imphal and the rickety line of communication another thousand miles back to Calcutta prevented the rapid alleviation of Burma Corps' miseries. As it was, Irwin had no boots, bedding or tentage. Weapons, rations and medical facilities were not even sufficient to cope with the needs of his own troops, let alone the half-starved and sick remnants of Burma Corps.[2]

The same debilitating lack of resources confronted Slim when, after a short sojourn in Ranchi, he flew to Barrackpore, near Calcutta, to take command of 15 Corps on 2 June 1942.[*] Of the two formations in his new command, the best equipped was Major-General Wilfred Lloyd's 14 Indian Division, at Comilla.[†] Until March 1942 the division had been at Quetta preparing for service in the Middle East. Yet it was raw, under-manned and under-equipped. In this state it was none the less responsible for the defence of the whole of India's south-eastern frontier with Burma, including Arakan. It had been issued with its equipment and transport, but its training for jungle fighting was far from complete. Slim's other formation, 26 Indian Division, based in Calcutta and commanded by Major-General Clive Lomax, was in a

---

[*] *Vice* Lieutenant-General Sir Noel de la P. Beresford Pierse.

[†] At this time 14 Indian Division contained 47, 55, 88 and 123 Indian Infantry Brigades.

far worse state. It was responsible for the internal security and coastal defence of the states of Bengal and Orissa. But it was not, wrote Slim 'a mobile or battle-worthy division at all, being woefully short of all forms of transport; nor could it, by any stretch of the imagination, be regarded as a trained formation.' 15 Corps was, with 4 Corps in Assam, part of Eastern Army, which was commanded by Irwin following his promotion in July.* His headquarters was at Ranchi in Bihar State. In addition Irwin had, under command, the experienced 70 British Division† and 50 Tank Brigade as the Army Reserve.

The 1942 monsoon brought a halt to offensive activity in Burma and eastern India and provided welcome respite to the troops of Eastern Army. The Japanese were as exhausted as the British, having suffered upwards of 30 per cent casualties during the campaign. Unknown to the British at the time they had no intention of pursuing their defeated foe into India. The relief bought by the monsoon was desperately needed as India struggled to prepare itself for war. The expansion of the Indian Army continued apace. Units were formed, joined the Army's order of battle and began training, and essential resources were garnered from across India and carefully husbanded for the time when offensive action would be resumed. But the rapid expansion of the Indian Army continued to bring with it the problems that had bedevilled the Burma Army late in 1941 and was complicated by widespread civil disturbances in August in support of the Congress Party's anti-British 'Quit India' campaign. It was still far too early for India to provide anything like the required numbers of well-trained and experienced formations able to fight the enemy on equal terms.

Despite these difficulties the need to plan offensive operations asserted itself from the outset. Even before Slim had got his troops over the Irrawaddy Churchill had sent a memorandum to the Chiefs of Staff stating that he wanted plans framed for 'a counter-offensive on the Eastern front in the summer or autumn.'³ During the spring and early summer he continued to pressure Wavell for decisive action to recover

* Lieutenant-General Geoffrey A.P. Scoones replaced Irwin as commander of 4 Corps.

† Major-General George Symes.

some of Britain's lost fortunes in the region, although Churchill's initial dream of recovering Rangoon by the end of 1942 quickly faded as the lack of amphibious shipping, troops and resources required to mount this scale of operation became apparent. Prompted by Churchill's instructions, Wavell minuted Morris on 16 April 1942, instructing him 'to begin as soon as possible consideration of an offensive to reoccupy Burma.'[4] The pressure on Wavell to do *something* was irresistible. Doing nothing, with Churchill's continual pressure for warlike activities on all fronts, was never an option.

In 1942 the only place where the British could take effective action against the Japanese was Arakan. The long Burmese coastline against which lapped the Bay of Bengal was weakly defended and far easier to get to than Central or Northern Burma. Akyab Island itself was the jewel in Arakan's crown, as it contained at least one strategic airfield. Its possession offered the prospect of air attacks being mounted against Rangoon – only 330 miles away – and the Japanese line of communication into central Burma. Equally, it would prevent the Japanese from launching aerial attacks on the valuable industrial areas around Calcutta. It also offered the possibility of a sideways door into Burma proper when the time came to attempt the reconquest of the country.

However, although distances were not great, Arakan contained in microcosm some of the worst features of Burma's topography. The Mayu Peninsula stretched like a bony finger down the Arakan coast ninety miles from the coastal port of Maungdaw to Foul Point, which was separated from Akyab Island by the estuary of the Mayu River. Along the centre of the Peninsula ran the Mayu Range, a ridge of densely forested and precipitous hills which rose to some 2,000 feet above sea level. On the eastern side of the Peninsula the Mayu River, which in its higher reaches above Buthidaung was called the Kalapanzin, flowed down the centre of the Mayu Valley. At Buthidaung the Mayu Valley stretched some ten miles wide: it was wider still at its mouth as it entered the Bay of Bengal opposite Akyab. The river was itself a formidable obstacle to movement, as for most of its length it was tidal, which meant that even the smallest *chaungs* were difficult to cross at high tide. Through a parallel valley further inland flowed the Kaladan river, which also found its exit at Akyab.

The Mayu Range was crossed by an all-weather road in only one place, between the coastal port of Maungdaw and the river port of Buthidaung, the route between which passed through two tunnels. Possession of this road and the 'Tunnels' secured the whole of north Arakan. Apart from this road the Arakanese infrastructure was, in 1942, virtually non-existent. The situation was made doubly worse in the monsoon when fair weather roads became impassable to vehicles, the standard means of transport became water borne, and even foot patrols had difficulty moving away from tracks and paths. The single greatest debilitating factor from the British perspective, still heavily dependent on wheeled transport, was the almost complete lack of motorable roads. That the country was highly malarious added to the nightmare. Arakan was to be universally loathed by the troops of the British–Indian Army.

Not unreasonably, Slim, whose geographical responsibilities included the frontier region with Arakan, assumed that should an offensive be mounted to seize Akyab, 15 Corps would be given the task. On taking command he accordingly ordered Lloyd to deploy patrols well forward of the main divisional positions, regardless of the monsoon. He wanted Lloyd's troops to gain a feel for Japanese dispositions and to find out their intentions: he also wanted to ensure that 14 Indian Division did not forget that their ultimate intent was offensive. Slim then began planning for an advance in Arakan. He assumed from the outset that he would have insufficient shipping and landing craft to mount an all-out amphibious assault on Akyab, which seemed to him to offer far and away the best chance of success. After studying the problem with Lloyd, Slim decided that the least attractive option would be a straightforward advance down the peninsula. It lacked any sparkle of imagination, would fail to surprise the Japanese and, given the nature of the terrain, would guarantee only to be slow.[5] This left only two realistic alternatives. The first was a series of 'hop, skip and jump' minor amphibious operations working down the coast in hooks behind the successive Japanese positions, using a flotilla of small coastal vessels – the 'Sunderbans Flotilla' – which Slim had been instrumental in gathering together for the coastal defence of Bengal and Orissa. The second was a long-range penetration expedition to the rear of the Japanese positions, possibly against their line of communication into Arakan. Wavell had recently appointed Brigadier Orde Wingate to train a brigade for long range 'hit and run' type operations behind enemy lines, and Slim believed that this type of formation would be ideal for an attack on Akyab from a direction the Japanese would least expect.

Slim's final plan involved a combination of all three ideas. 14 Indian Division would exercise frontal pressure against the Japanese in north Arakan while a series of short amphibious hooks were made to outflank the Japanese positions down to Akyab Island, with Wingate's long-range penetration brigade assisting by hooking in from the east.

However, in July 1942 Irwin told Slim that he wanted to take personal control of the Arakan offensive himself, and would swap locations with Slim to facilitate this. 'He would take direct command of the 14th and 26th Divisions', Slim recalled, 'and I should form and train a new 15 Corps at Ranchi.' Despite his matter-of-factness when writing *Defeat into Victory* in 1956, Slim could not hide his surprise at Irwin's decision. It was, he thought, militarily inexplicable. 'Whether it was wise to eliminate a corps headquarters in the chain of command to the Arakan I doubt,' he wrote. Not only did this decision remove at a stroke an essential layer in the hierarchy of military command but it prevented Slim, the only senior commander still in India with a detailed knowledge of the Japanese, and with experience of fighting them, from contributing directly to the planning and conduct of operations. It also meant that the Army Commander himself would personally control a campaign in addition to looking after the plethora of military duties for which he remained responsible throughout the length and breadth of eastern India. Wavell's acceptance of Irwin's convoluted command arrangements is likewise not easy to understand.

The truth may have resided in Irwin's ill-concealed antipathy to Slim. Irwin had already formed a severe dislike for Slim, in the main because he regarded Slim to have been responsible for the loss of Burma. His perception was undoubtedly coloured by the fact that the retreating Burma Corps was preceded to Imphal by gangs of ill-disciplined and unit-less troops intent only on saving their own skins. Irwin concluded that this riffraff must be representative of the whole of Slim's corps. Brigadier 'Taffy' Davies attended Slim's first meeting with Irwin. 'Irwin adopted a hectoring and sarcastic attitude towards the Burma Corps generally,' Davies recalled. 'Slim said how much he hoped the troops of the Burma Corps would be given a rest, maybe some leave and a reasonable degree of comfort now they were not right in the forefront of the battle. Irwin's reaction was that they certainly would not get any rest, they could not be afforded any leave and as for comfort they could not expect anything except what they'd got with them, which was practically nothing ... To me listening in,' Davies continued, 'he seemed to be rather pleased that the useless, cowardly Burma Corps units would continue to live and fight, in extreme discomfort and without any sort of sympathy or help. Slim quite bluntly lost his temper and was very short with Irwin, expressing the view that the latter seemed to be quite out of the picture ... I don't think he ever forgave Irwin. (Irwin's) bloody minded attitude towards this badly hammered formation which was deficient of everything ... was lamentable.' When Slim complained that Irwin was being rude, Irwin snapped, 'I can't be rude; I'm senior.' The relationship between the two remained strained throughout the course of the following year.[8]

Irwin was also, by nature, a meddler. He trusted no one but himself, and involved himself constantly in detail which should have been no concern of an Army Commander. He gave little or no latitude to his subordinates to use their own initiative and ensured that in every point of detail his orders were carried out without discussion or deviation. This made him dangerously inflexible, finding it difficult to change his mind and approach when the situation demanded it.

There was another reason for Irwin's high handed approach to Slim. Irwin had been commissioned into the Essex Regiment, the 1st Battalion of which had served under Slim in 10 Indian Brigade. At Gallabat in November 1940 elements of 1 Essex had broken and fled under Italian air attack, destroying Slim's chances of capturing the Italian-held fort. Slim sacked the Commanding Officer, who was a friend of Irwin. Irwin never forgave Slim for what he regarded as a slight on his old regiment.[7]

To rub salt into the wound, Irwin somewhat peremptorily dismissed Slim's provisional planning for the Arakan offensive. Slim's imaginative approach using his flotilla of small boats was rejected in favour of the very option which Slim had discarded, namely an orthodox, direct advance overland. At the same time Wavell decided to use Wingate's brigade elsewhere and so the option of deep penetration from a wide flank was unavailable to Irwin had he wanted to employ it.

Despite Irwin's decision, Slim dutifully did as he was ordered. He was not a man given to histrionics or public debates with his superiors, and indeed eschewed any show of public dissension with senior commanders, although in private, if he felt the situation merited it, he would press issues forcefully. Slim had far more subtle means of achieving his objectives than through public disagreement or debate. He would often take the risk of taking what he knew to be the right course of action, even if this was in contravention of orders. But he would do so quietly and methodically so that the favourable effect was achieved and his superior brought around gradually and almost imperceptibly, to his own point of view. 'The curious thing', commented Davis 'was that while accepting an order without any sign of disgruntlement he would invariably succeed in carrying on in accordance with his own plans and achieving a way of doing things which he considered to be sound. Even so far as his own views and plans were concerned he was always prepared for things to go wrong and had worked out an alternative plan to which he could change without undue difficulty.'[8] 'In spite of his humility about his own exploits', recalled Brigadier Michael Roberts, 'he knew when and how to be insubordinate. During the invasion of Burma [in 1945] he used the Nelson blind eye technique over anything that didn't fit in with his conduct of the campaign.'[9]

Fifteen Corps accordingly exchanged locations with HQ Eastern Army in the last days of August 1942: Slim went to Ranchi and Irwin moved into Barrackpore. In so doing Slim took on responsibility for 70 British Division, 50 Tank Brigade, Corps Troops and, for a time, 36 British Division.* Slim's consolation prize was to train the remainder of Eastern Army for war. Putting the disappointment of his exclusion from the Arakan operation behind him, Slim threw himself into this task. If one imperative was abundantly clear to Slim from his experience of the retreat it was the necessity for realistic, imaginative and demanding training. Individual training was the bedrock on which all training was built, after which followed collective training at unit, brigade and then divisional levels. It was the widely acknowledged failure of the Burma Army to prepare sufficiently and adequately for the rigours of fighting a 'new' type of war – where the enemy fought by a different set of rules – that had led so quickly to the collapse of British arms in Burma earlier in the year.

The programme of training which he introduced to 15 Corps was hard, embraced every soldier in every type of unit, and was recalled by those who experienced it as being without mercy. Slim's first target was his own headquarters which, by his own admission, had become 'static and stodgy' during its sojourn in Calcutta. Physical toughening, weapon

* 36 British Division was also called 36 Indian Division so as to confuse the Japanese.

training and practice at cross-country mobility with mules was carried out despite the monsoon rains. Everything was practiced constantly.

To provide a focus for both individual and unit training in Ranchi Slim drafted a summary of the key tactical ideas that had impressed him in Burma, some of which were lessons learned directly from the Japanese, which he then promulgated as a training directive to his Corps. His driving imperative was to devise clear and simple strategies for defeating the Japanese and in so doing started from first principles. He deliberately excluded some issues, such as the potential in Burma for air support to ground formations (such as air-to-ground attack and aerial resupply), on the basis that the aircraft required were not available. His concern at this stage was to define for his troops a set of rules which would enable them, in time, to take on the Japanese on equal terms:

1. The individual soldier must learn, by living, moving and exercising in it, that the jungle is neither impenetrable nor unfriendly. When he has once learned to move and live in it, he can use it for concealment, covered movement, and surprise.

2. Patrolling is the master key to jungle fighting. All units, not only infantry battalions, must learn to patrol in the jungle, boldly, widely, cunningly and offensively.

3. All units must get used to having Japanese parties in their rear, and, when this happens, regard not themselves, but the Japanese, as 'surrounded'.

4. In defence, no attempt should be made to hold long continuous lines. Avenues of approach must be covered and enemy penetration between our posts dealt with at once by mobile local reserves who have completely reconnoitred the country.

5. There should rarely be frontal attacks and never frontal attacks on narrow fronts. Attacks should follow hooks and come in from flank or rear, while pressure holds the enemy in front.

6. Tanks can be used in almost any country except swamp. In close country they must always have infantry with them to defend and reconnoitre for them. They should always be used in the maximum numbers available and capable of being deployed. Whenever possible penny packets must be avoided. 'The more you use, the fewer you lose.'

7. There are no non-combatants in jungle warfare. Every unit and

sub-unit, including medical ones, is responsible for its own all-round
protection, including patrolling, at all times.

8. If the Japanese are allowed to hold the initiative they are
formidable. When we have it, they are confused and easy to
kill. By mobility away from roads, surprise, and offensive action
we must regain and keep the initiative.

By no account could these ideas be regarded as staid, stolid or conservative.
They outlined the key requirements necessary to enable individual soldiers
– in particular junior non-commissioned and commissioned officers – to
master the art of fighting in the jungle against a skilful, determined
and resourceful opponent by day and night. Training was central to
the discipline soldiers needed to control their fear, and that of their
subordinates, in battle; to allow them to think clearly and shoot straight
in a crisis, and to inspire them to maximum physical and mental endeavour. Slim recognized that the psychological dimension of battle against
the Japanese was formidable. The Japanese were not bogey men, as
many in Burma Corps had realized during the retreat, but the myth
of their invincibility had swept the British-Indian Army following the
unprecedented disasters of the loss of Malaya, Singapore and Burma.
The Japanese were, nevertheless, well trained and hardy, prepared to
accept almost any hardship and sacrifice in the pursuit of their goals.
They co-ordinated artillery, armour and air support well with attacks
by infantry, their camouflage and concealment was excellent and they
made the maximum psychological impact through their tactics of dislocation.

Once they had been defined, Slim's aim was ruthlessly to train the
Army to live by these new standards. The principles were to stand the test
of time: 'I do not think I changed them in any essential detail throughout
the rest of the war,' he recalled. It is difficult today to recognize just
how ground breaking these principles were to the British-Indian Army
in 1942. The Army of 1945 took them for granted. They thereafter
provided the basis for the British Army's approach to jungle warfare
in the decades after the war. The fact, however, is that Slim's ideas were
new and largely revolutionary to many elements of the British-Indian
Army in 1942 which, as the year-long British campaign in Arakan was
soon to show, continued to follow an almost bone-headed adherence to
unsuitable tactics.

In turning conventional wisdom on its head in 1942 Slim's flexibility, imagination and penchant for tactical innovation shone through. It was precisely these personal characteristics that were to be instrumental in forging the distinctive approach to warfare that was to bring over-whelming victory to 14 Army during 1944 and 1945. They also reflected Slim's own belief in the principles of the indirect approach where the aim was to seek the psychological domination of the enemy, to avoid unnecessary frontal attacks where more subtle approaches could achieve decisive results at least cost, and to develop in all commanders a desire to out-think and out-smart the enemy at every turn. But this is to anticipate matters. In 1942 the Army was far from able to meet these high designs. Slim set out to change this situation. His tough training regime in 15 Corps was extended to the remainder of Eastern Army. It was continuous, progressive and comprehensive. As he describes:

> There were infantry battle schools, artillery training centres, co-operation courses with the R.A.F., experiments with tanks in the jungle, classes in watermanship and river crossing and a dozen other instructional activities, all in full swing. Our training grew more ambitious until we were staging inter-divisional exercises over wide ranges of country under tough conditions. Units lived for weeks on end in the jungle and learnt its ways. We hoped we had finally dispelled the fatal idea that the Japanese had something we had not.

One consequence of the intensive training to which Slim now subjected the divisions of Eastern Army was the removal and replacement of commanders at all levels who proved unsuitable. Slim ensured that in the selection of his officers those who were yet untried in the rigours of this type of fighting 'won their spurs' before taking over command by under-studying their jobs first. It would have been unfair, he argued, 'either to the men they were to command or to the officers themselves to have thrust them raw into a jungle battle.' Most won their spurs '. . . but some did not. It was as well to find out first.'

This casts an interesting light on Slim's own approach to choosing his staff and subordinate unit commanders. Although he disavowed the practice adopted elsewhere of commanders building up staffs around themselves and taking chosen officers with them on each successive upward posting, Slim nevertheless chose very carefully those who were to work for him. He was often just plain lucky in the appointment of his subordinate commanders, as when he found himself surrounded by old and trusted friends on taking command of Burma Corps. But on that occasion, too, he had no compunction in stealing an old gunner friend, Brigadier Welchman, from 'Punch' Cowan, and adding him to his own staff. When he took command of 15 Corps Slim brought officers with him who had served with him in Burma Corps, although of course this was necessary to build up a newly-formed headquarters. When he was promoted to command Eastern Army on 16 October 1943, he took only his ADC with him, although he nevertheless conducted some ruthless weeding of his new headquarters after he had arrived. Likewise as a corps commander he supported the efforts of his divisional commanders to breathe new life into their headquarters staff by replacing those officers regarded as unsuitable for the peculiar strains of fighting the Japanese in Burma.[10]

The pressure on Wavell during the monsoon of 1942 to take the offensive was intense, and was reflected in a speculative paper he passed to General Morris on 17 September. Entitled 'Operation Fantastical', the paper exhibited the same dangerous penchant for underestimating the strength and capabilities of the Japanese that he had shown during the retreat. 'I have a hunch,' he told Morris, 'which may be quite unjustified, that we may find Japanese opposition very much lower than we expect in Burma if we can only act with boldness and determination. The Jap has never fought defensively and may not be much good at it.'[11] Some idea of the depth of Wavell's delusion about what could be achieved with the resources at hand is provided in the paragraph that followed: 'My scenario is something like this: we occupy Akyab without much trouble. Japanese air reaction is weak and we inflict heavy casualties on his planes ... Our advance to Chindwin produces little reaction and there is evidence that Japanese in Burma are rather disorganised and demoralised.' He concluded: 'Such might well be the picture early in 1943.'[12] Unfortunately, the reality in early 1943 could not have been more different. At the time, no senior commander in India doubted the necessity of mounting offensive operations against the Japanese at the earliest possible opportunity. Wavell's instruction to Morris in this regard reflected equally well the concerns of both Irwin and Slim. 'The first thing I want' noted Wavell to Morris, 'is to create a spirit everywhere from G.H.Q downwards of determination to get as far into Burma this winter as possible, to recapture the whole of Burma without a day's delay that can be avoided; to be profoundly dissatisfied with our present programme and to be determined to exceed it.' Further, in words that Slim could heartily endorse, Wavell added: 'We have got a difficult problem from an orthodox point of view and we shall never solve it by purely orthodox thinking and orthodox methods. We should still be holding Burma ourselves if the Japanese had thought and acted on purely orthodox lines.'

Wavell's original plan was that 6 and 29 British Brigades,* the latter of which had recently been successfully blooded in the amphibious operation to seize Madagascar, would launch an amphibious assault on Akyab to capture the island and seize its airfields. 14 Indian Division would, at the same time, apply pressure on the Japanese by advancing down the Mayu Peninsula from Chittagong. Because this advance was to be merely a diversionary operation there was no need for urgency, and Lloyd was instructed to build a line of communication behind his division all the way down to Foul Point. The key to the whole plan was to ensure that Akyab could be seized before *General Iida* had an opportunity to reinforce it from Burma proper. 14 Indian Division accordingly set out on this task in September, the immediate object of which was to secure the coastal port of Maungdaw and the road across the Mayu Range to Buthidaung. Patrols reached Buthidaung on 15 October and encountered a Japanese unit in the process of disembarking from river vessels. Much to Irwin's chagrin the battalion involved did not engage the enemy but withdrew back to Maungdaw and then to Bawli. An incensed Irwin wrote to Wavell on 29 October 1942 to tell him that he was sacking the commanding officer of this battalion and had arrested a 'V' Force officer whom he accused of spreading panic.[13]

By mid-November, however, Wavell realized that the amphibious assault force and aircraft required to continue the original operation would not be available. In what was to prove an expensive error, Wavell did not then re-evaluate the strategic objective of the plan in the light

---

* 6 British Brigade (Brigadier R.V.C. Cavendish) was from 2 British Division and 29 British Brigade from 26 Indian Division.

of the dramatic reduction in forces now available to him. He decided to press on with the operation in the hope that it would achieve the same object as the original plan. Wavell was increasingly desperate for the comfort that a victory, no matter how minor, would bring. He was also under constant pressure from Churchill to mount a successful offensive against the Japanese. Wavell subconsciously or otherwise transmitted these pressures to Irwin. His thinking was also undoubtedly influenced by the fact that the advance of 14 Indian Division had already received considerable publicity and would not have been easy to halt without severe embarrassment to both London and New Delhi. Slim regarded this pre-operation publicity to be dangerous. Although he agreed that 'we badly needed a victory of some sort', he argued that it would have been 'better to let a victory speak for itself [as] it has a voice that drowns all other sounds.' As soon as the over-hyped advance began to falter, recriminations, cynicism and disillusionment spread quickly.

Following the change of plan, the advance of 14 Indian Division, now in the vanguard of the operation, re-started on 19 November. Irwin instructed Lloyd to seize Foul Point by 15 January, so that 6 British Brigade, the one brigade remaining from the original plan, would then be in a position to launch an assault on Akyab across the Mayu River. Lloyd was also instructed to seize the village of Rathedaung on the east bank of the Mayu to prevent the Japanese from using the river.

Speed, as Wavell acknowledged, was suddenly imperative. If the Japanese had time to reinforce their defences at Akyab and in the Mayu Peninsula the success of the whole venture would be jeopardized. Wavell's biographer insisted that he fully recognized the difficulties that his revised plan entailed. Nevertheless he did not appear to appreciate the extent of the risks associated with continuing the operation with a greatly reduced force, particularly when it included the laborious task of pushing an all-weather road down the Arakan through some of the most inhospitable terrain on earth. Unseasonably bad weather then added to the slowness of the advance. Without the sort of logistical imagination suggested by Slim's plan to 'hop, skip and jump' down the Mayu Peninsula, the only solution was to expend enormous resources to build up, and maintain, the lines of communication. This quickly became the British centre of gravity and, as the Japanese had found earlier in 1942, its principal weakness. Critically, Wavell failed to recognize that while considerable haste was now demanded, his new plan would prove only to be agonizingly slow. Remote from the hard realities of 14 Indian Division's ill-preparedness for war, Wavell's decision to continue the operation led nowhere but ruin.

A second problem only emerged once the advance had got underway. This was that Irwin proved unwilling to take any operational risks with 14 Indian Division. Throughout the campaign he was slow to make use of opportunities for surprise or boldness, eschewing a high-risk approach to war in favour of methodical predictability. Even if he had had sight of Slim's training directive to 15 Corps by this stage, he made no effort to adopt Slim's principles himself or to ensure that the lessons so painfully learned during the retreat were incorporated into the Army's training as a whole. It seemed not to occur to him that the Japanese, by acting quicker than him at every turn, would retain the initiative throughout, despite the overwhelming British numerical superiority both on the ground and in the air. Irwin's constant delays to ensure superiority of numbers at the point of attack meant only that the Japanese, time and again, were given the opportunity to reinforce, to outflank and to prepare thoroughly, and thus to retain the advantage of tempo throughout the campaign.

Lloyd planned to attack the Maungdaw–Buthidaung area on 2 December with four battalions. Irwin's caution, however, led him to direct that the attack should only go ahead once all of Lloyd's division had been deployed into the area. 'I believe it essential to win the first round and without acting as a brake to Lloyd I must satisfy myself that the chances of doing so are adequate', he wrote to Wavell on 14 November.[14] But waiting for Lloyd's division to move up took more time than even he expected. Three weeks later he rather disingenuously blamed the delay on Lloyd's faulty planning. 'I decided to put Lloyd's operation against the Tunnel position back a little over a fortnight,' he wrote to Wavell, 'because I was confident that as planned it would go off at "half cock".'[15]

At the time the opposition to Lloyd's forces was minimal. The Japanese had only two battalions from 33 Division in Akyab at the end of September. One battalion was sent forward to Buthidaung and Maungdaw in late October on news of the British advance and began preparing defensive positions along the Maungdaw–Buthidaung road. But on 16 December, unwilling to commit themselves to a battle against heavy odds and at the end of a long line of communication, they withdrew back down the Mayu Peninsula. In early January 1943 General Iida decided to reinforce Arakan with *55 Division (Lieutenant-General Koga)*. *Iida* knew that, if he could prevent the British securing the Mayu Peninsula, they would tire quickly and make themselves vulnerable to counter-attack. Importantly, it would prevent them from making a successful attempt at Akyab. It would also provide him time to reinforce his meagre forces in Arakan, something that *Iida* was able to afford at this time because he was not pressed elsewhere in Burma.

Lloyd duly occupied an empty Maungdaw on 17 December. Soon after 47 Indian Brigade* advanced down both sides of the Mayu Range, one battalion to the east and two battalions to the west, while 123 Indian Brigade† advanced to capture Rathedaung.‡ The newly formed 55 Indian Brigade remained in reserve at Chittagong. Progress was satisfactory. On Christmas Day a patrol from 123 Indian Brigade arrived opposite Rathedaung and reported it clear of the enemy. By 27 December 47 Indian Brigade had reached Indin on the coastal strip and a patrol reached Foul Point without contacting the enemy. In a serious error of judgement, however, and reflective of the failure of British commanders to seize opportunities when they presented themselves, Rathedaung was not occupied immediately. The Japanese took advantage of this lapse and quickly fed troops into the town. When 123 Indian Brigade attempted to take it in daylight on 28 and 29 December they were repulsed with heavy loss.

At the same time Lloyd had received reports of a significant Japanese presence at Kondan, on the eastern ridge of the Mayu Range. Mindful of Irwin's concern to take no risks with the advance, Lloyd decided to attack and clear the area before continuing 47 Indian Brigade's move towards Foul Point. Unfortunately, the numbers of Japanese reported to be at Kondan had been greatly exaggerated, and when a well-prepared attack was finally made on the village on 4 January it was discovered that the enemy – a platoon at most – had left. The decision to delay the advance for ten days to deal with what turned out to be an empty enemy position was to have dire consequences for the remainder of the campaign. Wavell blamed the delay on 'administrative difficulties',[16] although this was only partly true. The real reason was that Irwin's orders were insufficiently

* Brigadier Wimberley.
† Brigadier Hammond.
‡ Brigadier Hunt.

clear to Lloyd. Lloyd's principal task was to secure Foul Point, without which no attack could be mounted on Akyab, and his orders should have reflected this fact. Irwin, however, had instructed Lloyd to clear the Mayu Peninsula physically and comprehensively of enemy, which meant that the latter was forced to subordinate what should have been his main task to that of chasing an elusive enemy through the jungle vastness of the Mayu Peninsula.

During the time that Lloyd was engaged with the supposed threat from Kondan, *Koga* managed to insert an infantry company into a defensive position along a *chaung* about a mile north of Donbaik, which the British described as the Japanese 'Foremost Defended Locality', subsequently abbreviated to the 'F.D.L. *chaung*'. The *chaung* itself had steep sides and proved to be a natural anti-tank obstacle. *Koga* realized that Akyab was now in considerable danger and decided that he had to hold the position at all costs until reinforcements could be fed into Arakan. Over the ensuing weeks the position developed into a network of well dug and skilfully concealed bunkers stretching from the jungle edge down on to the beach. Bunkers were positioned with interlocking arcs of fire so that they could provide mutual support for each other. A hastily reconnoitred frontal attack by a company failed to break through the ever strengthening defences on 7 January and two successive battalion attacks, on 8 and 9 January respectively, both also failed dismally. The 123 Indian Brigade likewise failed once again to capture Rathedaung.

The Donbaik position proved invincible in 1942, and developed a legendary status for the British and Indian troops of 14 Indian Division, convinced that the bunkers were constructed of some new type of armour plating or concrete. The truth was that the walls and roofs were made simply of logs, but were up to five feet thick and deeply sunk in the ground. They were invariably well camouflaged, so that they often could not be seen until the troops stumbled on them. Irwin wrote to Wavell on 26 March 1943 that his troops had 'been shelling [the enemy bunkers] at point-blank range as well as shooting at them with 0.5 AT rifles, and it appears [that they] may contain some form of armoured plate protection rather than the concrete which was previously suggested. No penetration has yet been claimed. We are examining the possibilities of getting Naval depth charges to hurl at these posts.'[17]

In addition, the positions were held with a tenacity that took the men of 14 Indian Division by surprise. None of their limited training had prepared them for such an immovable foe. British tactics were based on the assumption that an enemy who was overwhelmed would invariably surrender. This might have been the case elsewhere, in North Africa perhaps, but it was not true against the Japanese. In order to take a Japanese position, recalled Geoffrey Evans, 'one had to fight on until the defenders had fired their last round and were down to their last man. And he had to be killed or incapacitated.'[18]

Japanese defensive tactics came as an unpleasant surprise, too. When British and Indian infantry battalions came up against Donbaik, concluded an assessment made in 1945, they all 'made the mistake of advancing through Japanese positions, searching areas only perfunctorily, and then being attacked by surprise, in the rear. They did this not once, but repeatedly.'[19] When bunkers were attacked the Japanese would call down artillery, mortars and machine guns on their own positions irrespective, wrote Slim, 'of any damage they might inflict on their own men. Actually, as the Japanese defenders were mostly in bunkers they suffered little, while our troops, completely in the open, had no protection from this rain of projectiles.' Bunker clearance, involving the burning of surrounding vegetation prior to direct bombardment from artillery and tanks, was perfected only in 1944. John Hedley, writing of practice in 1945, explained that the only way to knock out bunkers was 'to take one bunker at a time, indicate it by smoke – 3" mortar smoke – and then send Mustang or Thunderbolt dive bombers on it. Given good indication one Mustang out of three should get a direct hit, and then you move on to the next bunker. But you must be prepared to take a bunker position slowly or have a fearful loss of life.'[20] Mustangs and Thunderbolts were not available in 1942, however, and Lloyd's troops could not, after three months, and despite supreme efforts, find a way past the Donbaik defences.

The wholly unexpected failure to break through at Donbaik prompted a flurry of meetings between senior commanders. Wavell and Irwin visited Lloyd on 10 January and reiterated the importance of a break through. On the following day all three commanders flew on to Lloyd's headquarters near Maungdaw to discuss the situation with both Lloyd and Wimberley. Irwin believed that there was a simple reason for the set back. He was convinced that Lloyd had applied insufficient pressure on the Japanese position, and that with concentration of force and thorough planning the position would easily be broken. Wavell agreed. Irwin accordingly ordered Lloyd to try again. Like many of his generation, brought up in the hard school of the Western Front, Irwin was convinced that only meticulous preparation and carefully choreographed battlefield planning would bring about success in battle. In part, he was right. But his unwillingness to take any risks with these preparations meant that weeks were required to rehearse the various phases of the plan, and build up sufficient stocks of ammunition and stores to cater for every eventuality. The lack of surprise this entailed, coupled with a rigid inflexibility in procedures once battle was joined, enabled the Japanese to read every British move, and thus pre-empt them with ease.

Following the setback of early January, Wavell penned a letter to Irwin on 15 January in language that only a week later would appear extraordinarily complacent. 'I hope they will manage to put in a properly co-ordinated attack and clear up the Mayu Peninsula and Rathedaung', he wrote. 'But it is no use running our heads against places without proper preparation, since there is no great urgency in the operations now. We ought to be acquiring valuable experience of Japanese methods and the correct way of dealing with them, which may enable us to get on quicker in future.'[21] Wavell was wrong on the first point and misguided on the second. In the first case there was a desperate need for urgency. Unless Irwin was able to break through to Foul Point he would not be in a position to mount an attack on Akyab. The longer the attack was delayed the greater the chance of failure: the Japanese were known to be feeding troops into Arakan and the arrival of the monsoon in May would make an attack on Akyab impossible. On the second point, 15 Corps already possessed considerable knowledge of Japanese methods: these did not need to be re-taught. However, Irwin's deliberate sidelining of Slim prevented valuable lessons from the retreat being incorporated in the planning and conduct of the campaign.

Wavell's apparent lack of concern on 15 January, however, soon gave way to anxiety. Because of the length of time Irwin required to organize and prepare for battle, the next attacks did not actually take place until the third week of January. Wavell blamed the delays primarily on the 'difficulties of communications which made reinforcements and supply very slow', but he was also critical of Irwin's failure to make faster progress. 'It may be that the urgency of the situation was not fully recognised', he wrote in his Despatch, 'and that troops should have been pushed forward in spite of all difficulties to take advantage of the situation.'[22]

But despite Irwin's optimistic belief that the long preparation time would pay off in a successful breakthrough at Donbaik, the attack by two battalions on the FDL *chaung* again failed on 18 and 19 January with heavy loss. This had been preceded by the failure on 13 January of another attempt by 123 Indian Brigade to capture Rathedaung. Irritated but not deterred by this failure Irwin pressed Lloyd to mount another attack. Lloyd, however, now wanted the opportunity to replace the tired and depleted 47 Indian Brigade with the fresh, albeit newly formed and inexperienced 55 Indian Brigade. Irwin acquiesced, and the next attack was now planned for 1 February 1943: 123 Indian Brigade was to attack Rathedaung again on 3 February.

To assist in this next attack Lloyd asked Irwin to release a small number of Valentine tanks from 50 Tank Brigade, which were at the time preparing to accompany the attack on Akyab. Irwin agreed to send a troop of eight. When Slim, who was by now no more than an anxious observer on the sidelines of the Arakan operation, heard of the request he protested that such a small number of tanks would be wholly insufficient. Using small numbers in penny packets was 'against all my experience in the Middle East and Burma', he wrote. 'I argued that a regiment could be deployed and used in depth even on the narrow front chosen for attack.' But Irwin rejected these representations. 'We were overruled', Slim recalled, 'on the grounds that more than a troop could not be deployed and that the delay in getting in a larger number across the *chaungs* was more than could be accepted.'

When it was launched, the fourth attempt to capture the Japanese positions on the *chaung* mirrored in every respect the dismal pattern of its predecessors. Troops advanced frontally on bunkers against which artillery fire appeared to have no effect, and the tanks could not bridge the *chaung*. Following several attempts by infantry over the next three days to invest the Japanese bunkers Brigadier Hunt was forced to admit failure on 4 February. No new way of breaking through the Donbaik position seemed to present itself.

Wavell, nevertheless, had yet to be persuaded that the task was impossible. On 9 February he met Irwin in Calcutta. After considering the problem they acknowledged that it would not be possible to clear the whole of the Mayu Peninsula in time to deliver the assault on Akyab before the first rains of the monsoon fell in mid-May. Nevertheless, Wavell believed that there was sufficient justification to continue the attempt to secure the Mayu Peninsula and he gave Irwin 6 British Brigade for the purpose of mounting a fifth attack. His insistence on securing the Mayu Peninsula at this stage is puzzling. Now that there was no longer any possibility of seizing Akyab the Mayu Peninsula had lost its strategic value. It would have been very vulnerable during the monsoon, being only a short flight away from Japanese aircraft based on Akyab Island and at the end of a long line of communication which would have been difficult to maintain through the wet weather. The truth seems to be that Wavell had become mesmerized by holding ground. There is no doubt that the pressure on him to produce a victory was intense. However, it seems likely that this served to unbalance his military judgement to the extent that he was prepared to fight for the Mayu Peninsula simply so that his map – and that of Churchill's in London – could show a comforting patch of red in the heart of enemy territory. Militarily, however, the policy was impossible to sustain.

Lloyd, nevertheless, attempted to do as he was bidden. 55 Indian Brigade attacked on a narrow front with all available artillery on the early morning of 18 February but was repulsed at a cost of 130 casualties. The troops got in amongst the Japanese positions but were beaten back without being able to penetrate the bunkers. The failure led to 55 Indian Brigade being relieved on 20 February by 71 Indian Brigade* and retiring to Buthidaung to be divisional reserve.

With the failure of this latest attack Irwin now believed that the attempt to break through at Donbaik should halt and that 14 Indian Division should be allowed to withdraw to prepare robust defensive positions before the onset of the monsoon in May.[23] He was now increasingly concerned about the threat to his left flank from a Japanese encircling attack across the Kaladan and Mayu Valleys, which if successful would cut off his forward units on the Mayu Peninsula. Rather prematurely as it transpired Irwin ordered Lloyd to consolidate the positions gained and to hold them until the monsoon made a withdrawal inevitable. He then took these arrangements to Wavell on 23 February in the hope that Wavell would agree and confirm the orders. But he was forcefully rebuffed by the C-in-C. 'I refused to accept this recommendation and to take up a defensive attitude without first obtaining a marked success over the enemy, so that the troops should be confident of their ability to beat

* Part of 26 Indian Division

the Japanese', recalled Wavell in his Despatch. 'I directed General Irwin to use 6th Brigade . . . to assault the Donbaik position in conjunction with the 71st Brigade. My intention was that the attack should be delivered in great strength and depth with the object of swamping the Japanese positions.'[24]

Wavell's choice of words is revealing, if only to indicate how increasingly out of touch he was with the situation in Arakan. Lloyd's troops were in no position to mount a successful morale-restoring attack. Irwin now recognized this truth, and Wavell, who appeared wilfully to ignore the advice of his Army Commander, should have known it, too. Equally, the tactics advocated by Wavell were precisely those which had failed so dismally in bloody and inconclusive attacks during the previous six weeks. They were obviously seriously flawed. The reference to 'swamping' the Japanese recalled the language of the Western Front, spoke in terms of heavy casualties and lacked even the pretence of intelligence or subtlety. Wavell lacked neither of these attributes, and shows just how desperate he had become by early 1943 to achieve a victory at any cost. Through his demand for 'more of the same', Wavell served merely to reinforce failure in Arakan and exacerbated the ever-growing crisis of morale in 14 Indian Division.

Unwilling to argue with Wavell, Irwin duly ordered Lloyd to plan a sixth attack. Lloyd's plan was for 6 British Brigade to attack Donbaik down the coastal plain, 71 Indian Brigade to attack along the Mayu foothills and 47 Indian Brigade along the summit of the Range. But when Lloyd presented this plan to Irwin the latter rejected it as being too similar to the last and thus likely to fail. Irwin's trust in Lloyd, which had never been strong, now began to falter. He wrote to Wavell on 9 March:

> In some ways I have been disappointed because Lloyd has not shown that determination of command which I had expected and is more prone to wait for suggestions or requests from his subordinate commanders than to impose his will on them. He is not sufficiently meticulous in examining plans put up by them or in supervising the detailed conduct of their operations – long distances account for this to a considerable extent. I have warned him to this effect.'[25]

Irwin's solution was to take over the planning for the attack himself.

He told Wavell on 9 March: 'The plan I made was the result of sitting on the top of a hill for an hour overlooking enemy territory ... I have gone for a highly concentrated attack on a very limited objective.'[26] He gave 15 March as the earliest date for the attack. Criticizing Lloyd and his subordinate commanders to Wavell he complained:

> It is a monstrous thought that it should be necessary to undertake in this way, the duties which should be properly carried out by the Divisional, Brigade and Battalion commanders ... I am left in no doubt that we are most weakly served by our relatively senior commanders and by the lack of training and, unpleasant as it is to have to say so, the lack of determination of many of our troops.

Irwin's criticism of his subordinate commanders was only partly fair. After countless fruitless attempts to get the better of the Japanese in the jungle of the Arakan, the officers and men of 14 Indian Division knew that they needed more than 'determination' to break through at Donbaik. They needed, above all, new tactics to meet the challenges posed by Japanese tenacity, proper equipment to allow them to fight and live in the jungle, and more tactical imagination by their leaders to ensure that they were not faced, time after time, with the morale shattering news that the next attack was to be a frontal one against the same Japanese positions that had held off countless 'highly concentrated attacks on limited objectives' before. The truth is that there was a profound lack of confidence in the higher command and leadership of 14 Indian Division.

At this time, and in some desperation, Irwin grudgingly instructed Slim to go to the Arakan from Ranchi to prepare a report on the situation for him. Slim was given strict instructions, however, that he was not to take command. Because of the likelihood that he might have to criticize Irwin's handling of the campaign, these instructions placed Slim in an invidious position from the outset. It is not clear what Irwin's reason's were for such an inspection. He already knew, from many visits of his own, the precise situation in Arakan. The conspiracy theorist might conclude that Irwin was quietly lining Slim up to be the scapegoat for the campaign, knowing that disaster was looming. It is unlikely, however, that any such suspicion bothered Slim. Pleased to be involved at last, Slim flew immediately to Lloyd's HQ, near Maungdaw, on 10 March 1943 and visited units of the Division over the following few days. He was shocked by what he found. He quickly formed the view that Lloyd could not cope with having nine brigades under his command when the norm was three: the situation was clearly preposterous and demanded a corps headquarters between Lloyd and Irwin.*

Likewise it was self-evident that morale was appallingly low. On the battlefield nothing the British did seemed to have any effect on the Japanese. Every attack was repulsed, the Japanese moved where the British could not, seemingly without the same requirement for supplies, and at far greater speed. They were determined in attack and impossible to budge in defence, even when faced with seemingly overwhelming firepower.

Obvious too was the fact that the tactics repeatedly employed at Donbaik were discredited and wasteful. Slim was surprised that this truth was not apparent to Lloyd or Irwin. Virtually all of the maxims framed by Slim following the retreat and employed so vigorously to train 15 Corps had been broken. Every attack had been frontal and no effort had been made to use the jungle to outflank the Japanese positions. Even worse, commanders appeared not to have any idea how to solve the problem, and Lloyd's plan for the sixth attack on Donbaik entailed 'more of the same'. Slim was horrified. Lloyd assured him that there was no alternative to mounting another direct frontal attack because he had no ships for a hook down the coast and his patrols had reported repeatedly that the ridge and its jungle were impassable to a flanking force. Slim wrote:

> He was confident that with this fresh British brigade [6 British Brigade], improved covering fire by artillery and aircraft, and the increased knowledge he had gained of the Japanese defences, he would this time succeed. I told him I thought he was making the error that most of us had made in 1942 in considering any jungle impenetrable and that it was worth making a great

* To 14 Indian Division's original order of battle had been added 4, 23, 36, and 71 Indian Brigades and 6 British Brigade.

effort to get a brigade, or at least part of one, along the spine of the ridge.

Lloyd disagreed with Slim's observations. 'He replied', recalled Slim, 'that he had given a lot of thought to this and had decided it was not feasible and his brigadiers agreed.' Disappointing though Lloyd's response was, there was little that Slim could do. He had no operational authority over Lloyd and had been tasked by Irwin solely to report on his findings to Calcutta. Slim later regretted that he had not ignored Irwin's instructions and compelled Lloyd to take an alternative course of action. When Slim's report to Irwin was delivered, it was polite but frank. Although Slim did not say it at the time, he was clear that the blame for the fiasco pointed unerringly at Irwin himself. Slim's first two observations – that Lloyd had an overburdened chain of command and repeatedly employed poor tactics in the attack – came about as a direct result of Irwin's own policies. The third observation, regarding the collapse of morale, was quite patently the result of the first two. In *Defeat into Victory* Slim wrote:

> In war you have to pay for your mistakes and in Arakan the same
> mistakes had been made again and again until the troops lost heart.
> I got very angry with one or two units that had not behaved well
> and said some hard things to them, but thinking it over I was not
> sure the blame was all theirs.

Following the delivery of his report, Irwin sent Slim on leave, which he took with his wife, Aileen, in India. This period of enforced relaxation was short-lived, however. In an embarrassing *volte-face*, Irwin ordered Slim on 5 April to move to Chittagong and to prepare to take over operational control in Arakan. But again Irwin refused to allow Slim a free rein. 'I was not', wrote Slim, 'even when I assumed operational command, to have administrative control; that would remain with Army Headquarters.' Slim regarded the distinction between the two to be absurd, especially, he wrote, 'as a corps could have relieved the overworked division of much of its administrative burden but the Army Commander was insistent.'

The Japanese counter-attack on the left flank from the Kaladan Valley which Lloyd and Irwin had long feared burst suddenly upon 14 Indian Division on 7 March. Lloyd had told Irwin of his concerns about the security of this flank after the Donbaik fiasco of 18 February, which prompted Irwin's subsequent request to Wavell to withdraw to defensive positions in advance of the monsoon. But Irwin was unable to persuade Wavell that the situation was sufficiently grave to justify a withdrawal. On the very day *Koga* launched his counter-attack, Wavell wrote to Irwin:

> It looks as if the Japanese are going to make some sort of long-range penetration against our LofC from the direction of the Kaladan, but you should be able to deal with this; and a strong blow on the Mayu Peninsula and a real success here will do more than anything to help the situation. I should like to finish up this campaigning season with a real success which will show both our own troops and the Jap that we can and mean to be top dog.[27]

*Koga's* plan was to sweep in from the east behind Lloyd's forward units at Donbaik and to cut the line of communication to Maungdaw. The plan worked perfectly. While three battalions of *Uno Column* continued to hold Donbaik, the *Miyawaki Column* (one battalion plus an additional company, and a mountain artillery battalion) advanced into the Kaladan Valley on 7 March, forcing Lloyd to evacuate the area and withdraw to Htizwe and Buthidaung. On the same day, the *Tanahashi Column* (two battalions and a mountain artillery regiment) attacked 123 Indian Brigade north of Rathedaung and began systematically to work northward through its dispersed units.

By 14 March the situation had become critical, as the Japanese began to uncover Lloyd's left flank. Late on 13 March Lloyd, in desperation, sent 71 Indian Brigade across the Mayu Range to Buthidaung to reinforce 55 Indian Brigade and allow it to cover the withdrawal of 123 Indian Brigade from Rathedaung. With pressure on 55 Indian Brigade increasing, and to allow Lloyd the ability to prepare unhindered for the seventh attack on Donbaik, Irwin created on 15 March a new headquarters ('Mayforce') to take command of all troops east of the Mayu River.*

The sudden transfer of 71 Indian Brigade to Buthidaung now necessitated a change of plan for Lloyd's attack on Donbaik. 6 British Brigade now had six battalions† and two 25-pounder artillery regiments. Lloyd knew that *Koga* had as many as three battalions at Donbaik. Nevertheless, confident that 6 British Brigade would be able to break through where Lloyd's Indian brigades could not, Irwin authorized the attack to take place on 18 March. It was to be preceded by a heavy artillery bombardment.

But the web-like complexity of the interlocking Japanese defences proved too much even for 6 British Brigade to unpick. Yet again the Donbaik position held, and by the morning of 19 March the brigade had suffered more than 300 casualties for no appreciable gain. 'Advancing again', wrote Slim, 'straight in the open, over the dead of previous assaults, they got among and even on the tops of the bunkers; but they could not break in.' Irwin was desperate for a successful attack, and was prepared to accept almost any casualties in order to achieve it. In a letter to Wavell after the attack he complained:

> my parting words to the Brigade and Divisional commanders was to be sure that there were sufficient waves of troops not only to capture each objective, but to swamp anything which might be encountered en route ... Obviously this was not done ... It failed obviously because – although the local commanders think otherwise – there were not enough troops following each other up. It was not, in my mind, the frontages that were wrong, but the depths.[28]

Wavell, too, was bitterly dissatisfied with the result but blamed Irwin, at least in part. Knowing that he had personally planned and supervised the attack, he wrote to his Army Commander on 22 March:

> I was, as you probably realise, most disappointed at the Donbaik

---

* Brigadier Curtis.

† Four of its own battalions plus one each from 47 and 71 Indian Brigade.

attack. It seemed to me to show a complete lack of imagination, and was neither one thing or another. An attack in real depth with determined soldiers like the 6th Brigade would, I am sure, have accomplished something, though it might have cost us casualties.[29]

In his Despatch, however, Wavell repeated Irwin's tortuous explanation for this failure: 'The attack was made with great dash and determination but was not carried out in the strength or depth that I had considered necessary to overrun the enemy position. The losses of the attacking troops were heavy, especially in officers.'[30] Both Irwin and Wavell clearly refused to accept the more obvious but unpalatable truth that frontal attacks of the kind launched repeatedly at Donbaik could never hope to prevail over an enemy so tenacious in defence as the Japanese, particularly with such poorly trained troops as were available to Lloyd. Slim, seemingly alone, was convinced that the original prescription was wrong.

Following this defeat, Irwin and Lloyd met Wavell again at Lloyd's headquarters at Maungdaw on 20 March. The outcome of the meeting was more or less an acceptance of defeat. It was determined that no immediate attempts would be made to capture the Mayu Peninsula and that defensive positions in depth as far back as the Maungdaw–Buthidaung line should be taken up as early as possible in preparation for the monsoon. But there was to be no precipitate withdrawal, and certainly no move back without Irwin's express permission. Lloyd's divisional headquarters at Maungdaw was to be replaced by Lomax's 26 Indian Division in early April. Nevertheless, and despite continued setbacks at Donbaik, the seriousness of the situation on the left flank of 14 Indian Division did not appear to be appreciated by Wavell, even at this late stage. 'I am quite clear that the best, and in fact the only, way to upset the Japanese and take the initiative from him', he wrote to Irwin on 22 March, 'would be by getting the whole of the Mayu Peninsula and thereby controlling the river mouths and threatening Akyab.'[31]

By late March 1943, however, the opportunity for this to happen was remote. Nevertheless, Wavell was still hopeful for a success at Donbaik, but in a letter to Irwin three days later he dropped a strong hint to Wavell that he would support Lloyd's removal from command:

'I feel it is no use ordering it while Lloyd is in command', he wrote, 'since he obviously does not believe in it. But, if Lomax takes over and after examination thinks it can be done, I am quite prepared to support another attempt.'[32]

All the while the threat to Lloyd's left flank continued apace. On the night of 24 March, *Colonel Tanahashi* crossed the Mayu River and by 27 March had reached the mountains east of Indin, where he cut the communications to 47 Indian Brigade. Desperate attempts by the brigade to restore the situation over the ensuing days failed. Fearing that it would be cut off and destroyed piecemeal, Lloyd, on 29 April, ordered the brigade to abandon its positions on the track over the Mayu Range and withdraw to join 6 British Brigade on the coastal strip, after which both brigades were to make their way to safety to the north. Despite the fact that these orders were designed to save 47 Indian Brigade from destruction, they ran counter to Irwin's instructions that there were to be no further withdrawals. On hearing of this order, Irwin promptly sacked Lloyd, took direct control of 14 Indian Division himself, rescinded Lloyd's instructions and called up Lomax to take command. Lloyd's removal was so rapid that he was in New Delhi that evening. On 30 March Irwin sent a message to 47 Indian Brigade saying, '4th Brigade is on the move, stick it out.' He also reiterated the instruction that neither brigade was to withdraw without explicit orders from him.

As if to reinforce the hopeless unreality of his perception of operations, Wavell sent instructions to Irwin on 1 April* which ordered him to regain the initiative and to conduct offensive operations on both sides of the Mayu River. These orders were immediately passed on to Lomax, who arrived at Maungdaw on 3 April, with the added rider from Irwin that the withdrawal of 4 Indian and 6 British Brigades to monsoon positions in the Maungdaw–Buthidaung area was not to begin before 15 April. Curtis was to take command of all troops east of the Range (55 and 71 Indian Brigades) and take up positions covering Buthidaung and the Maungdaw road.

* Received by Irwin on 3 April.

However, on the very day these orders were received *Tanahashi's* column burst out at Indin, and set up a block behind 6 British Brigade. The bold crossing of the Mayu Range, which involved considerable operational and logistical risk, proved, as had such tactics during the retreat in 1942, to have a profound psychological effect. 'Straight over the Mayu Range they came', wrote Slim, 'following or making single file tracks through the jungle and over the precipitous slopes that we had complacently considered impassable.' This crisis forced Lomax to ignore Irwin's instructions on the very day they were issued. Instead he ordered 6 British Brigade to launch an immediate counter-attack on the Japanese block prior to regaining communications with 47 Indian Brigade and then withdrawing northwards. These attacks failed on 5 April, however, and on 6 April the disaster was made complete when the headquarters of 6 British Brigade was overrun and Cavendish and his staff were killed. 47 Indian Brigade, forcibly retained on the Mayu Range by Irwin, were now cut off by *Tanahashi's* encirclement, as Lloyd had feared it would. Unable to break out the brigade commander broke the brigade into small groups, abandoned his heavy weapons and equipment and ordered his men to make their way back to the coast. It ceased thereafter to exist as a fighting formation.

Irwin was outraged by the collapse of the brigade and blamed the disaster on the failure of its soldiers to fight. In a letter to Wavell on 9 April he wrote: 'I believe a great many of them who have come out have done so without their weapons . . . and a captured Jap document indicates that British troops are surrendering readily.' There was some truth in his allegations. The fighting spirit in many units of 14 Indian Division at this time was weak. One of Slim's liaison officers reported: 'the seasoned and highly trained Japanese troops are confronted by a force which, although impressive on paper, is little better, in a large number of cases, than a rather unwilling band of raw levies.'[33] On 2 April a Japanese diary recorded: 'The troops opposing us are British and have no will to fight and are just knocked down in the stride of our attack.'[34] Irwin fumed: 'I'll have courts of inquiry all ready for such cases including the loss of equipment when I get the 14 Division troops out.'[35] The truth was, of course, that had Lloyd's original instructions to withdraw been followed, the brigade would not have been lost. It would even have provided Lloyd the opportunity to create a small reserve, which could have been used to counter other attempts at encirclement. Despite his earlier recognition about the security of his left flank, Irwin seemed not to recognize, in late March, the immediacy of the threat of encirclement to Lloyd's brigades on the coastal strip. Irwin's fixation with retaining ground had contributed directly to the brigade's destruction.

# 4

# Architect of Victory

Slim, newly appointed to take charge of the deteriorating situation in Arakan, entered this cauldron of confusion and uncertainty on 6 April, landing at a forward strip near Lomax's headquarters at Maungdaw. For the first time in the whole sorry Arakan affair he was now in a position to exert a positive influence on the outcome of the campaign. But his involvement was to prove too late to be effective. 'The situation as far as it could be discovered was fantastically bad,' he wrote. It was obvious that the Japanese had run rings around the ponderous British. In a quite remarkable admission, given all that he had gone through during the retreat, Slim confessed: 'For myself, I was in a strange position, which was new to me, and which I did not like. I have rarely been so unhappy on a battlefield. Things had gone wrong, terribly wrong, and we should be hard put to avoid worse. Yet I had no operational control and, even if I had, no troops in hand with whom I could influence events.'

Morale in both Indian and British units had suffered grievously as a result of the abortive attempts to break through in the Mayu Peninsula. The Indian Official Historian recorded:

The Indian brigades, many of whom had been engaged for long and continuous periods, were tired. Battle casualties had not been very severe but malaria and fever had exacted a very heavy toll amongst the troops who had been given practically no anti-malarial training, and for whom very few protective measures were then available. Reinforcements were also arriving untrained and completely unfit to play their part in the current operations.[1]

Even Wavell began to worry about the effect of a widespread collapse of morale. He wrote to Irwin on 9 April:

> I should like to hear from you as soon as possible what our losses have been in personnel and equipment and what the morale of the troops is like, British and Indian. Has there been any surrender without fighting or desertion to the enemy by Indian troops? . . . I am now more worried about the morale aspect both of the troops and to India as a whole, than anything else.[2]

On 20 April Irwin wrote to General Alan Hartley, Wavell's deputy in New Delhi:

> I went down to Maungdaw this morning and took Bill Slim with me and there I found, as I was beginning to fear, among the commanders an attitude of almost complete subordination to the Jap. By and large, the impression firmly fixed in their minds is that they are unable to prevent the Jap reaching the Maungdaw–Buthidaung road . . . As regards the battle, with such very weak material I find it difficult to give you any assurances that we will succeed in keeping the Jap at bay and have in consequence, told Slim to do all the necessary planning and reconnoitring necessary for any withdrawals which may be forced on us.[3]

Irwin's instructions to Slim and Lomax in early April placed both men in difficult positions. Lomax, whose divisional headquarters was completely untried, found himself suddenly responsible for nine brigades and a long line of communication back to Chittagong in the midst of a confusing and fast flowing battle in which the initiative was almost completely in the hands of the Japanese. Slim did not know Lomax and only had a proportion of his own headquarters with him. He was not in command and indeed did not know when Irwin would cede responsibility to him, if ever. Irwin had yet to make up his mind to use Slim. 'So long as the position remains stabilised I do not wish to introduce Slim and his HQ into command', he wrote to Wavell on 9 April, 'but they are now at Chittagong ready to function as soon as I say they are to.'[4]

It had been obvious to Slim from his reconnaissance in April that the position of 14 Indian Division was precarious, to say the least, and in a brief rebellious moment he toyed with the idea of disobeying Irwin and taking operational command immediately. This would at least ensure that the situation did not deteriorate further. Alternatively, he could take the risk of trusting Lomax, and hope that the situation did not deteriorate too rapidly for a recovery of sorts to be made. Slim decided to risk the latter course. Fortunately, over the coming days and weeks Lomax proved more than capable, despite the inexperience and weakness of his divisional headquarters, of creating some measure of order from the crisis: despite the desperate situation he remained imperturbable. Finally, after much unnecessary prevarication, Irwin handed over all responsibility forward of Chittagong to Slim on 14 April. Taking command of the operation, now in its dying weeks, nine months after it had begun, was a chalice to rival that of Burma Corps a year before.

Slim agreed with Irwin that Maungdaw was the most suitable position to sit out the monsoon, but only if it could be defended in strength. He recognized that for this reason *Koga*'s immediate goal would be to secure the Tunnels. With these in their possession Buthidaung would be cut off, Maungdaw threatened and the door to north Arakan locked to the British, making it much more difficult to re-open again at the end of the monsoon. Slim also believed that the primary direction of the Japanese attack would not be along the coastal strip where 6 British Brigade was dug in along the foothills of the Mayu Range, but along the eastern edge of the jungle clad ridges of the Mayu Range to Buthidaung, where the British were weakest. In a letter to Irwin four days after assuming command he wrote:

> The general impression I got was that the Jap is infiltrating small parties Northwards past our people along the MAYU ridge, probably with the view to collecting enough to put down a block on the Maungdaw–Buthidaung Rd. The jungle etc. is not as impassable as was made out: both ourselves and the Jap are moving fairly freely about it in small parties on foot.[5]

Slim's assessment was correct. *Koga*'s plan was to begin an advance on 25 April through the Mayu Valley to secure monsoon positions along the Buthidaung–Maungdaw line with the Tunnels being his immediate object.

At first the Japanese tried uncharacteristically to batter their way up the Mayu Valley on the night of 24 April, but were stopped by 55 Indian Brigade at Kanthe. *Koga* then decided to use *Tanahashi*'s *Column* to secure a corridor north along the eastern edge of the Mayu Range direct to Point 551, which dominated the high ground to the east of the Tunnels. With this important tactical feature in their hands, the British troops east of the range would be forced to withdraw from Buthidaung.

Deciding how best to prevent *Koga* from seizing the Maungdaw–Buthidaung line placed Slim in a quandary. He could only spread his troops thinly, and given the size and nature of the country, the state of his troops and the obvious penchant of the Japanese for swift and destabilising encirclement, Slim concluded that *Koga* would be able to lever him out of any position he decided to create. In order to prevent the Japanese from securing the Maungdaw–Buthidaung area before the monsoon arrived, the first and most obvious choice was to cripple *Koga*'s columns by decisive attacks during their advance north. Only a strong counter-attack, Slim believed, would be sufficient to force the Japanese off balance and allow Lomax the opportunity to regain the initiative.

However, Slim believed that the circumstances were not right for a counter-attack at this time. He knew that *Koga* would protect the flanks of his advance to the Tunnels with forces picketed in strength along the route northward through the hills. Any attack would therefore almost certainly suffer the same fate as those made at Donbaik. By this stage, of course, Slim had only one uncommitted brigade, 36 Indian Brigade, and the remaining formations were weak and tired. An alternative, therefore, to a counter-attack into the flank of *Koga*'s advancing force was needed. Slim devised a plan by which the Japanese, advancing north along the spine of the Mayu Range, would be contained within a 'box' created by Lomax's infantry battalions. Two battalions from 4 Indian and 6 British Brigade would form the western edge, 55 Indian Brigade would garrison the eastern and 71 Indian Brigade with an extra battalion from Maungdaw would form the lid at the Tunnels themselves. With the Japanese safely in the box the lid would then be slammed shut and the enemy within it defeated in detail. The viability of this plan, however, depended upon the sides of the box remaining firm and unyielding.

As Lomax prepared to fight the battle of the Tunnels, Slim turned to the problem of defending eastern Bengal if *Koga* decided to continue his advance towards Chittagong. Rather than create a long linear line of defence, which would consume vast quantities of troops and still fail to cover every possible area of weakness, Slim determined that the best alternative option would be to create 'large, strong, well-stocked and easily maintained pivots of manoeuvre from which striking forces could operate, not to hold or gain ground but to destroy the Japanese forces. Such pivots would have to be so placed that the Japanese would have to attack them in order to open a line of communication for their advance.'

An additional problem, acknowledged Slim, was that Lomax's 'men were still untrained for the jungle and feared it more than they did the enemy.' Consequently, Slim was forced to find areas of terrain in which his advantages in artillery and tanks could be brought to bear. His preferred choice was in the area of Cox's Bazaar, where the wide fields of rice padi made it ideal for tanks and artillery. As it turned out a withdrawal this far north was not after all required, as *Koga* was content to consolidate his positions on the Maungdaw–Buthidaung line. In part, Slim's proposals for such 'pivots of manoeuvre' recalled Alexander's plan before Prome over a year earlier. Irwin, however, would have no truck with such preposterous notions, particularly that of willingly giving up ground, and rejected Slim's proposal out of hand.

Initially, all went well in the attempt to catch *Koga's* columns in the Mayu flytrap. *Tanahashi* walked into the box on 2 May, as Slim had believed he would. But in the event the training, morale and skill of Lomax's troops proved insufficient to maintain the integrity of the box and exhaustion led to the northern part of it being quickly broken. With fresh and determined troops, Slim was certain that the Japanese attempt to seize the Tunnels could have been prevented. 'If our troops were in first class fighting form and health' he told Irwin on 18 April, 'we should have little to worry about.'[6] On paper, Slim accepted, the plan was 'nicely geometrical and simple, but translated into tired troops, many of them badly shaken, holding positions among tangled jungle hills and streams, it was not so tidy, and much less simple. I was more than a little anxious as to the outcome.' Sure enough, by 3 May the lid collapsed completely and the Japanese captured Point 551. Counter-attacks on 4 May failed to release the Japanese hold on the position, which became progressively stronger. On this day also *Tanahashi* crossed the road three miles to the east of the East Tunnel and destroyed the bridge to Letwedet.

Buthidaung was now cut off from Maungdaw. Slim recognized that he now had no chance of retaining the town and on the afternoon of 5 May authorized Lomax to withdraw 55 Indian Brigade when he felt it necessary. Maungdaw, however, was not to be relinquished – yet. By that evening, however, it became apparent that 55 Indian Brigade's position was untenable and Lomax was forced to use 36 Indian Brigade to extricate it *via* the Ngakyedauk Pass to the north during the night of 6 May, after which 36 Indian Brigade also withdrew through the Pass.

The spotlight now focused on Maungdaw. On 7 May, during which time Lomax was already withdrawing 55 Indian Brigade from Buthidaung, Slim prepared Irwin for the loss of the port. He warned of a 'determined Jap attempt to take Maungdaw certain within days . . .' He stressed:

> The most serious danger in the defence of Maungdaw is however the state of the troops. All except part 6 and 4 Brigades are very tired. In several units morale is low and strengths seriously down. Lomax is of opinion that with present troops there is grave danger of collapse in face of determined attack and fears debacle with heavy loss of troops and irreplaceable equipment. I have ordered him to hold out but I agree with him to extent that from purely military view it would be better to withdraw from Maungdaw.[7]

The tiredness of the troops was an issue Slim had raised with Irwin repeatedly before. On 18 April he told him by letter:

> All Brigadiers . . . are worried about the state of the troops. This is the most serious aspect of the whole show . . . The British troops are tired and they are 'browned off' with the operations in ARAKAN as a whole. Their health is deteriorating. The recent rain has added to the malaria and the three battalions and attached troops in 6 Brigade are now evacuating 50 men a day . . . the Indian troops, except 4 Brigade, are tired too, but with them the fault is the inferior quality in physique, training and spirit of the men, especially of the drafts that have joined in ARAKAN.[8]

The one imperative with which Irwin was now fixated was that Maungdaw must not under any circumstances be evacuated. Evacuating the port would give up everything that had been gained during the previous nine months, and underline the immensity of the failure in Arakan. Late on the afternoon of 6 May Irwin, who was at the time with 4 Corps in Assam, sent a signal to Slim giving him instructions to this effect. On 8 May he visited Slim in person and impressed on him the importance of retaining the town. Slim, however, disagreed with Irwin's assessment, and a heated debate followed. Slim believed that Maungdaw had little strategic value and feared that even then the Japanese were engaged in wide outflanking movements to the east to cut the British off from Chittagong. He also regarded Irwin to be dangerously misinformed about the capabilities of Lomax's troops. After considerable argument Irwin finally but reluctantly accepted Slim's point of view, although the affair exacerbated the already fragile relationship between the two men. In a postscript to a letter he sent Slim on 10 May, Irwin rebuked Slim for allowing *Koga* to dominate the battlefield:

> I have just been shown a summary of the battle casualties reported to these HQ for the week ending 8 May. For Arakan they totalled British and Indian all ranks: – 10 killed, 40 wounded, 3 missing and for that loss, 17 battalions have been chased about by possibly 6, a sad but realistic commentary on the present fighting.[9]

The evacuation of the town followed, with *Koga* occupying Buthidaung on 9 May and Maungdaw on the 14th. 'Here we were back where we had started' wrote Slim somewhat despondently, 'a sad ending to our first and much heralded offensive.'

The disaster was now virtually complete, except for one thing: who was to blame? With recrimination looming, Irwin wrote to Hartley on 8 May, seeking to deflect blame from both himself and Wavell for the Arakan debacle. 'We are about to be faced with the difficult problem of how to explain away the loss of Buthidaung and Maungdaw' he wrote, '. . . although the commanders are far from being much good; the cause unquestionably lies in the inability of troops to fight . . . [They are certainly] not yet up to tackling a skilled Jap soldier in country in which he has obviously had much training.'[10] This was a theme he pursued at a press briefing on 9 May. But his intention

ARCHITECT OF VICTORY

was much more sinister: he was preparing to cast Slim as the villain.

On 26 May Irwin peremptorily dismissed Slim from command of 15 Corps. He did so by sending him a telegram bitterly critical of his conduct of the Arakan battles, and instructing him to report to Calcutta forthwith. Irwin then flew off to visit 4 Corps in Imphal, leaving Slim to his fate. What Irwin did not know, however, was that Wavell, recognizing precisely where responsibility for the conduct of operations in Arakan lay, had determined the previous week to replace Irwin at Eastern Army with General Sir George Giffard.[11] Irwin, when he received notice at Imphal of his own removal, at least had the manners to send a signal to Slim: 'You're not sacked, I am.'[12]

For the second time in thirteen months Slim had been given responsibility for a failing operation, and for extricating a bewildered and retreating army from the jaws of impending danger. On both occasions he was constrained by factors far beyond his control and pressed by a succession of crises, with the complication that on the second occasion he was grossly mistreated by the Army Commander who sought to deflect criticism from himself for the conduct of the campaign. Yet the particular strengths of his character that had shone out so strongly during the retreat emerged again in abundance in Arakan. He was able clearly to see the strategic imperatives of the operation. But even more important than this was his rare ability to see how these were affected by the changing circumstances of the battlefield, in a manner seemingly denied to Wavell through distance, and to Irwin because of personality. His remarkable calmness in crisis, despite his own inner fears and anxieties, contributed significantly to a lessening of the storm of panic which erupted at every new and unexpected Japanese move. As Lewin affirms, 'there was always something unflurried about Slim.'[13] Although in every sense a disaster, and one in which for the most part Slim remained, because of the lateness of his appointment, but a frustrated spectator, the Arakan provided further confirmation of Slim's eminent suitability for high command and fully vindicated his approach to war.

The Arakan campaign was a story of a compound failure of strategy and tactics, leadership and morale. British arms had rarely before suffered so comprehensive a defeat. Even the retreat from Burma had the sense of the heroic about it: Arakan, however, could not have been a more profound disaster. In relative terms the number of casualties was not excessive, as Slim wrote:

'Our actual losses in killed, wounded and missing were not high, about two thousand five hundred, and while we had not inflicted as many on the enemy, he had suffered too. Malaria had taken a heavy toll, far above our battle casualties, and we had lost a good deal of equipment. Neither these serious losses nor the abandonment of territory was a damaging as the loss of morale. It was no use disguising the fact that many of the British and Indian units which had fought in Arakan were shaken and depressed ... It was plain that our main task during the respite of the monsoon must be to rebuild that morale.

It was clear to Slim that the basis for the successful application of his tactical principles was the confidence of his troops and that the most inspired of plans would only succeed if soldiers were sufficiently trained, equipped, prepared and led for the tasks expected of them. By the time Irwin had transferred responsibility to Slim in Arakan it was far too late for new tactics to overcome the cumulative effects of ill preparedness and exhaustion. He was equally convinced, as his training programme in 15 Corps had evidenced, that the only way to build this confidence was through rigorous, effective and appropriate training.

Churchill, attending the Trident Conference in Washington, embarrassed and angry by this latest setback, observed bitterly to Alan Brooke on 21 May 1943 that the 'campaign is one of the most disappointing and indeed discreditable which has occurred in this war. A complete outfit of new commanders must be found. Severe discipline must be imposed upon troops whose morale is 'lessened'. The whole British Army in India is being brought into disrepute by the thoroughly bad conduct of these operations.'[14] The only compensation, Churchill noted sarcastically 'was that the relatively small scale of operations kept them from attracting much public notice.'[15] Churchill's confidence in Wavell, and in the Indian Army as a whole, had reached its nadir. Churchill's suspicion of the latter did not help matters, especially when a very large number of the 115,000 troops who had surrendered in Singapore were Indians and a number had subsequently joined the Japanese-sponsored

Indian National Army (INA) under the command of Subhas Chandra
Bose.

It is clear that despite the energetic defence of his official biographer,
much of the blame for the defeat has to be placed at Wavell's feet.
There is no doubt that the campaign was premature and ill conceived,
perhaps indeed, as one of his biographers admits, 'one of Wavell's worst
mistakes.'[16] Nevertheless, the pressure placed on Wavell by Churchill
played a significant factor in pushing the campaign on despite the risks.
In this respect Wavell was justifiably aggrieved by the criticism levelled
against him at the time. 'I received neither encouragement nor help nor
understanding of the difficulties', he complained in his Despatch, 'only
criticism for the failure of a bold attempt to engage the enemy with
inadequate resources, in hazardous circumstances.'[17] Wavell nevertheless
refused to acknowledge that the whole exercise had been a humiliating,
wasteful and purposeless venture. 'The greatest gain from the campaign
was experience, of the enemy's methods and of our own defects in training
and organisation,' he insisted. 'The serious loss was in prestige and morale.
On balance I shall certainly never regret that I ordered the campaign to
take place in spite of lack of resources.'[18]

The fact remained, however, that the stock of the British–Indian Army,
and with it Wavell's reputation and GHQ India's perceived ability to
mount effective military operations, had fallen to an all-time low. It was,
unfortunately, to taint further the image of the British-led Indian Army
for many in both the United Kingdom and the United States.


Between February and May 1943, as Irwin's campaign in Arakan was
heading for disaster, the British Army suffered yet another military defeat.
Yet this one was not as publicly humiliating as the debacle in Arakan and
paradoxically came to be seen by some as a stunning victory. In May 1943
the last stragglers of Brigadier Orde Wingate's 'Chindit' columns returned
across the Chindwin after several weeks behind Japanese lines in central
Burma. Casualties had been high, so much so that Wingate expected to
be court-martialled on his return to India for the loss of a third of his
brigade. Eight hundred of the three thousand men of 77 Indian Brigade
who had set out in February did not return and virtually all of the brigade's
heavy equipment and weapons had been lost. Most troops had marched
eight hundred miles, some as many as a thousand, in an operation which

ultimately had no greater purpose than to test Wingate's theories of long range penetration and irregular warfare.

During Operation Longcloth the brigade, divided into seven infantry columns, had destroyed bridges, stretches of railway lines and harassed and confused the Japanese. But despite the courage and endurance demonstrated by the Chindits, the expedition achieved little of real substance. Nevertheless, General Hartley recognized that the story of a daring raid deep behind enemy lines had considerable publicity value, and arranged for the operation, which had thus far been kept secret, to be announced to the public on 21 May 1943. Hartley could not have foreseen the impact of his decision. Almost overnight, people took heart from this extraordinary tale of derring-do, self-evident courage and human endurance, as much as from the fact that plucky John Bull had cocked-a-snoop at the still exultant Japanese by roaming through his backyard.

Wingate was an eccentric, if single-minded, Royal Artillery officer who had gained experience in irregular operations in both Palestine and Abyssinia. Wavell, appreciating Wingate's enthusiasm and penchant for the unconventional, sent him to Burma in early 1942 to see how guerrilla action could assist the disintegrating defence of the country. Following the retreat Wingate set about persuading GHQ India of the merits of creating dedicated units designed to operate inside enemy territory, disrupting enemy supply lines and communications, in support of an offensive by conventionally trained forces. In July 1942 Wavell promoted Wingate to brigadier and gave him 77 Indian Brigade to train for the purpose of long range penetration, intending to use it in support of offensives he had planned for Eastern Army later in 1942.

Slim had met Wingate first when they had been fighting the Italians in East Africa in 1940. They met again soon after Slim had taken command of Burma Corps in the third week of March 1942, Slim commenting that they 'had several lively discussions . . . on the organisation and practice of guerrilla warfare.' After the first of these meetings Wingate remarked to Michael Calvert that Slim was the 'best man, bar Wavell, east of Suez.'[19] Despite what some detractors have averred, Slim was a firm supporter of irregular warfare, so long as it was closely linked to the activities of the main forces, fitted into the overall strategic plan and did not create divisive and expensive private armies. What he opposed was the vast spawning of a plethora of 'special units' designed only for one type of operation, which were wasteful and did not give, militarily, a worthwhile return for the resources in men, material and time that they consumed. In 1943, however, all the principal commanders in India recognized the value of operations of the kind Wingate espoused. In particular, Wavell's successor as C-in-C, General Sir Claude Auchinleck, had made a name for himself through the sponsorship of long range commando-style groups in North Africa.

Indeed, Slim had originally hoped that 77 Brigade would be used in conjunction with the proposed 15 Corps advance into Arakan. This would have suited him perfectly, as it would have provided him with useful flank protection as well as having a valuable disruptive effect on the Japanese supply lines into Arakan. But it was not to be. Instead, Wavell allocated the brigade to Scoones' 4 Corps for an offensive across the Chindwin in early 1943. The intention was that the brigade would play a minor role in diverting Japanese attention away from the main front by means of sabotage and the disruption of enemy supply lines. In the event, however, this plan also came to naught, and the 4 Corps offensive was called off. There was now no strategic rationale for a deployment into Burma by Wingate's force. Undaunted, Wingate, who had developed an almost fanatical attachment to his developing theories of long range penetration, badgered Wavell to allow him to go anyway. Wavell needed little convincing and, supported firmly by Irwin, agreed to take the risk.[20] The expedition was launched from Imphal on 8 February 1943.

The first phase of Operation Longcloth went well, with the Mandalay–Myitkyina railway being demolished at various points. However, thereafter the Chindits found themselves the hunted rather than the hunters once the initial element of surprise had been lost, and all efforts had then to be focused on avoiding large scale engagements and on preserving the safety of the columns. Large guerrilla groups were relatively easily to locate and attack and two of the original seven columns were lost very early on in the operation to enemy action.[21]

Wingate's theories of long range penetration were based on the premise that his foot and mule-bound troops could be supplied almost exclusively by air, the aircraft being called forward when required by radio. Operation Longcloth provided valuable experience in this regard, although Slim rather disparagingly regarded this to have been 'a costly schooling.' While it is clear that Wingate did not invent the notion of air supply, as some of his supporters have subsequently claimed, his expedition did show the way for the extensive use of air resupply during the two years of campaigning in Assam and Burma which followed. Wingate was to find, however, that supply by air was itself not as easy or problem-free as he had originally assumed. Sufficient transport aircraft had to be made available and in 1943 these were in very short supply.

Equally, local air superiority was required to protect the supply drops, which could take as long as two or three days to complete. Relying on air supply for survival alone left no margin for error if for any reason the drop had to be cancelled and the distance patrols could travel away from the airhead was restricted by the range of the aircraft. Wingate was also to discover that the weakness of his columns in terms of firepower was not compensated by the use of bombers and ground attack aircraft as he had expected. Ground attack aircraft were not as accurate as artillery and could not provide prolonged assistance to troops engaged on the ground without enormous effort, which was often impossible to provide to a Chindit column several hundred miles from the nearest airfield.

The operation did show that even the most impossible terrain was not an obstacle to mobility, a lesson that arguably the Japanese already understood and that they were quick to exploit a year later. Wingate had proved that well led and well trained troops were capable of moving through difficult jungle country and operating in the heart of enemy-held territory. Ordinary troops – British conscripts and young, inexperienced Gurkha recruits and survivors of the original Burma Army, were raised to a peak of physical fitness and military training that surprised many. All in all Wingate's hard training, his unrelenting pursuit of mental and physical robustness in the drive to prepare his men for war, all augured well for the future of the British–Indian Army in its war against the Japanese. Nevertheless, few of the survivors ever saw operational service again because of the effects of the physical deprivations they suffered.

The boost to public and service morale alike made by Hartley's press conference, numbed as they were to news of successive disasters in the region, and following on so closely from the Arakan debacle, was dramatic. For the first time British soldiers had boldly marched deep into Japanese territory, had fought the Japanese on their own territory, and had seemingly triumphed over the Japanese 'superman'. Slim wrote that there:

> was a dramatic quality about this raid which with the undoubted fact that it had penetrated far behind the Japanese lines and returned, lent itself to presentation as a triumph of British jungle fighting over the Japanese ... This not only distracted attention from the failure in

Arakan, but was important in itself for our people at home, for our allies, and above all for our troops on the Burma front . . . For this reason alone, Wingate's raid was worth all the hardship and sacrifice his men endured, and by every means in our power we exploited its propaganda value to the full.

The contrast with Lloyd's futile battering ram in Arakan could not have been starker. 'The two operations were simultaneous', writes Louis Allen in his magisterial account of the Burma campaign. 'But the spirit and energy behind them were totally different, and although First Wingate also ended in defeat, it was a defeat full of promise for the future.' He concluded, 'LONGCLOTH had panache, it had glamour, it had cheek, it had everything the successive Arakan failures lacked. It was the perfect psychological medicine for an Army sadly devoid of confidence in its methods, its purposes and its ability to fulfil them.'[22]

Slim has since been criticized for being too harsh in his assessment of the achievements of Operation Longcloth.[23] But Slim was not unaware of the benefits Wingate's operation provided for the war effort as a whole. Longcloth 'cannot be judged on material results alone . . .' he insisted in *Defeat into Victory*. Louis Allen agrees. A mere statistical analysis of enemy troops killed or miles of railway track destroyed 'is battle accountancy of the wrong kind,' he argues. 'At a moment when a glance at the British performance in Burma could only have induced the utmost gloom in the observer, the Press, sensing there was something vastly different here, of a different moral dimension from what had been happening in Arakan, amplified.' Part of the problem in assessing Operation Longcloth is that by early 1944, when Wingate's second expedition – Operation Thursday – was launched, many, from Wingate himself through to Winston Churchill, had begun to believe the propaganda that had been pumped out two years before. 'Unfortunately', writes Anthony Barker, 'the widely publicised exploits of (the operation) . . . gave an exaggerated impression of the possibilities of this kind of operation . . . and Wingate was depicted as a new "man of destiny". More sober judgement on the operation described it as "an engine without a train".'[24] Certainly the consensus in late May 1943 was that raids, no matter how spectacular, could not win wars. That this was indeed the case seems clear from the fact that no immediate follow-up operations were planned.

There is no doubt that Wingate was a man out of the ordinary. His difficult – even bizarre – personality did not endear him to the Indian military establishment, particularly when his brazen method of demanding what he wanted for his operations so flouted the conventions of military bureaucracy and hierarchy. It seemed then, as now, impossible to be indifferent about Wingate. What one saw as enthusiasm was regarded by another as the meddling of a 'scatterbrain allowed power without any responsibility.'[25] His ideas on irregular warfare were visionary to some and dangerously naive to others, and his unconventional manner was regarded by many as nothing more than inconsiderate rudeness. Consequently, and without doubt unintentionally, Wingate alienated many people who were actually prepared initially to give him a fair wind: in many others he created bitter opponents.

Slim was one of the very few senior commanders in India who was able to differentiate dispassionately between Wingate's difficult personality and his professional worth. There is no doubt that there were many in India Command who had no time for Wingate and who rejected everything he said. Slim was not one of them. He recognized the value of Wingate and acknowledged the sense of many of his ideas. This was in good part because of Slim's own non-conformity. While he never ploughed solitary intellectual furrows in the field of military science, Slim was always an individualist in his thinking and approach to military affairs. This inclination to challenge ideas and not to accept convention for its own sake, together with his innate humanity, meant that Slim did not reject Wingate outright when many others did so. Slim was profoundly interested in *people*, with all the strengths and weaknesses of the human condition, far more than he was interested in rank or status, behind which personal frailties lay obscured. Slim regarded Wingate as no mere upstart but an experienced soldier with innovative and constructive ideas for taking the war to the Japanese. As such he had to be listened to. Wingate also had a remarkable gift for inspirational leadership, which Slim recognized and admired. 'He could ignite other men', Slim writes. 'When he so fiercely advocated some project of his own, you might catch his enthusiasm or you might see palpable flaws in his arguments; you might be angry at his arrogance or outraged at so obvious a belief in the end, his end, justifying any means; but you could not be indifferent. You could not fail to be stimulated either to thought, protest or action by his sombre vehemence and his unrelenting persistence.' Many of those who served with him in Burma remained loyal to his memory – many fanatically so – for the rest of their lives.

But while Slim throughout saw the possibilities that Wingate's ideas could offer the campaign against the Japanese as a whole, he recognized that they were only a part of the solution. He intuitively knew in 1943 what he was going to have to prove in 1944 and 1945, namely that long range penetration operations, even when mounted on a considerable scale, could never constitute the sum total of all that was required to defeat the Japanese in Burma. Slim believed that Wingate often took many of his arguments to illogical extremes, and inferred in *Defeat into Victory* that he was one of those who attempted to sell 'short cuts to victory.' Wingate's belief in his own cause was on occasions at the expense of proper balance in his consideration of strategic problems, a failing that became increasingly pronounced throughout 1943 and 1944. It was the role of long range penetration as a *strategy* of war that was to provide the fundamental tension in Slim's relationship with Wingate throughout this period.*

The years of defeat in the Far East, together with a diminishing regard in London and Washington for the effectiveness of GHQ India in the prosecution of the war, had convinced Churchill and Roosevelt that a radical restructuring of command responsibilities in the region was required if victory was ever to be achieved over the Japanese. Accordingly, at the Trident Conference in May 1943 Roosevelt and Churchill agreed in principle to the establishment later that year of a South East Asia Command (SEAC), separate to India Command, with the task of conducting the war against Japan in south-east Asia. India Command then would be responsible solely for creating a base for operations and for training, equipping, maintaining and moving all SEAC forces in the theatre. At their next meeting, the Quadrant Conference in Quebec in late August 1943, Churchill and Roosevelt appointed Acting-Admiral Lord Louis Mountbatten as the Supreme Allied Commander, SEAC. His deputy was to be the American commander of the Northern Combat Area Command (NCAC), Lieutenant General 'Vinegar Joe' Stilwell.

---

* This issue is developed in Chapter 6 with the account of Wingate's second expedition, Operation Thursday.

At the Casablanca Conference in January 1943 the Combined British and American Chiefs of Staff had proposed an offensive in Burma at the end of the monsoon in November 1943. To be called Operation Anakim, the offensive was to involve operations by 4 Corps from Assam, NCAC forces from Ledo and Chinese forces from Yunnan, together with amphibious operations along the Arakan coastline with the ultimate intention of seizing Rangoon. By the time of the Trident Conference in Washington in May 1943, however, it was recognized that Anakim was too ambitious for the scale of resources that would be available. Trident, therefore, reduced the size and scale of the Anakim proposals, and directed that the operations in Arakan be limited to minor amphibious operations to capture Akyab and Ramree Island. The primary task of Allied forces was to expand the air route from India to China while at the same time beginning the work required to build a road through to China from Ledo.

This decision hinted at the vastly differing strategic ambitions of the United States and the United Kingdom with regard to the necessity for the physical reconquest of Burma. Could the country be isolated and bypassed or did it – or parts of it – need to be physically reconquered? The Americans viewed *northern* Burma as a crucial lifeline in their efforts to sustain China. 'To the Americans', wrote Slim, 'the reconquest of Burma was merely incidental to the reopening of land communications with China', which had been lost with the capture of Rangoon in March 1942. The air bridge that had been established thereafter to supply Chiang Kai-shek over the Himalayan air route known as the 'hump' was extraordinarily expensive to maintain, and the Americans decided to drive through another road to China, from Ledo. In the main the recovery of the remainder of Burma had no strategic interest for the United States during the war.

Although he was not in a position to influence strategic policy Slim's view was that, if Rangoon could be re-taken, the old road could have been quickly re-opened at a fraction of the expense required to build a new one from scratch. 'If it had been left to me', he wrote, 'on military grounds I would have used the immense resources required for this road, not to build a new highway to China, but to bring forward the largest possible combat forces to destroy the Japanese army in Burma.'[26]

Churchill, however, preferred a strategy that saw Burma only as a stepping stone for the recovery of Malaya, Singapore and Sumatra:

I disliked intensely the prospect of a large scale campaign in Northern
Burma. One could not choose a worse place for fighting the Japanese.
Making a road from Ledo to China was also an immense, laborious
task, unlikely to be finished until the need for it had passed . . . We
of course wanted to recapture Burma, but we did not want to have to
do it by land advances from slender communications and across the
most forbidding fighting country imaginable. The south of Burma,
with its port of Rangoon, was far more valuable than the north.[27]

And it was into the south, advancing into south-east Asia by successive
amphibious operations, that Churchill believed the correct strategy to lie.

Accordingly, he argued persuasively throughout 1943 that the Allies'
strategic goal should not be Burma, but Sumatra. Large-scale amphibious
operations to seize Malaya or Sumatra would make Japanese control of
Burma untenable. The idea was to be developed into a plan called
Operation Culverin, which Churchill pressed at every opportunity. A
less ambitious concept was of an amphibious attack on Rangoon, which
would obviate the need for an overland advance into Burma from Assam.
But Churchill was unable to persuade Roosevelt to turn the American
focus away from the imperative to provide support to China, either *via*
the air bridge over the hump, or *via* the Ledo Road. As the Americans
called all the shots in the Far East, Churchill had to acquiesce. By August,
however, it was not strategic divergence that dictated the course of events,
but logistical realities. At the Quadrant Conference it was acknowledged
that the paucity of resources available for opening up a front against Burma
– particularly amphibious equipment – meant that the Anakim proposals
would have to be scaled back even further. Accordingly, it was agreed
that operations in south-east Asia in early 1944 should be limited to an
offensive in northern Arakan in preparation for amphibious operations
to capture Akyab and Ramree in the spring of 1944.

Slim had by now commanded 15 Corps for a year and would have
ordinarily been expected to be considered for advancement. However,
largely due to Irwin's pique, he had been prevented from contributing
to all but the last few weeks of the campaign in Arakan and he now
had to make his mark on an entirely new set of senior commanders.
This was undoubtedly a conspicuous waste of an outstanding talent.

That such a thought passed Slim's mind, however, is doubtful. His sense of duty transcended any bitterness that may have accompanied Irwin's alienation of his experienced corps commander. But 1943 was to see the onset of a whole new series of command relationships in India, which were fundamentally to improve Slim's fortunes.

Wavell, whose stock with Churchill had fallen to an all-time low, was removed from his position of responsibility for the war in the Far East through elevation to the post of Viceroy, a position vacated by the retiring Lord Linlithgow. General Sir Claude Auchinleck, who had originally swapped places with Wavell in June 1941, and whom Churchill had removed from command of the 8th Army in August 1942, took Wavell's place as C-in-C India Command in June 1943, despite the initial reservations of Brooke who believed that the 'Auk' also had irretrievably lost Churchill's confidence.[28] Auchinleck's immediate responsibility was to hold the ring against the Japanese until Mountbatten arrived later in the year; thereafter he was to develop India as a base for the prosecution of the war against Japan by the newly formed South East Asia Command (SEAC).

One particular boon for Slim was the new Army Commander. Slim was to enjoy a warm and productive relationship with Irwin's successor. General Sir George Giffard presented an entirely different personality to Irwin. Supremely confident and self-assured, Giffard exuded calm and professional competence. Slim admits that when he first met him in Calcutta at the end of May Giffard 'had a great effect on me.' In what could be seen as direct criticism of Irwin, Slim remarked that Giffard's great strength lay in his grasp of 'the fundamentals of war – that soldiers must be trained before they can fight, fed before they can march, and relieved before they are worn out.' Similarly, and with what was clearly direct reference to Irwin's command arrangements, Slim noted with satisfaction that 'Giffard understood that front-line commanders should be spared responsibilities in rear, and that soundness of organisation and administration is worth more than specious short-cuts to victory.' Likewise, in relation to his own preference for telling his subordinates *what* to achieve rather than *how* they should achieve it, Slim found in Giffard a man of like temperament. Having 'chosen his subordinates, and given them their tasks, he knew how to leave them without interference, but with the knowledge that, if they needed it, his support was behind them.' Commenting on the Arakan battles of early 1944 Slim gratefully recalled that Giffard 'had the invaluable knack of not interfering, yet making one feel that he was there, calm, helpful, and understanding, if required.'

Lieutenant-General Sir Geoffrey Evans comments:

> From their first meeting, Generals Giffard and Slim had a respect and liking for one another, largely because they shared many of the same characteristics. Both had complete integrity; unassuming, but firm in their opinions, neither enjoyed publicity of a flamboyant nature; they had the same ideas on the exercise of command and the handling of their subordinates; they understood the soldier, his needs and his training; both were readily prepared to give the credit to others that was their due.[29]

Nevertheless, however good his relationship with Slim, Giffard did not have the same effect on everyone else. Stilwell, for example, regarded him to be so uninspiring that he refused to serve under him directly. Mountbatten, as Giffard's immediate commander, did not enjoy the easiest of relations with his land-forces commander, in part because of what Mountbatten grew to perceive as Giffard's lack of foresight and imagination. The difficult relations between the two were undoubtedly caused in part by the twinning of a brilliant, young and impulsive supreme commander (Mountbatten was forty-three) with a more cautious soldier of vastly different age (Giffard was fifty-eight), background and temperament. While thoroughly competent, Giffard was 'never a firebrand and now grown slow and prudent', remarked Mountbatten's official biographer. 'All his instincts told him to defend his prerogatives against the incursions of an inexperienced naval overlord, and, although his courtesy softened the impact, a collision was in the end inevitable.'[30] Slim acknowledged that Giffard was not at his best in the political milieu of New Delhi but insisted that his great virtue was that 'he kept to the fore the element of practical soldiering.' For this reason, Lewin avers, Slim 'always rode comfortably at Giffard's anchor.'[31]

In early June 1943 Slim returned to Ranchi from Arakan and re-assumed command of 15 Corps and responsibility for the defence of Eastern Bengal. While Lomax's 26 Indian Division held the Corps' monsoon positions in Eastern Bengal, Giffard instructed Slim to prepare his Corps to recommence offensive operations in Arakan at the end of the monsoon, in order to pre-empt a possible Japanese attack against Chittagong. In practical terms for Slim this meant continuing the rigorous training programme he had instituted across Eastern Army several months before as well as drawing up a plan for the land advance of 15 Corps into Arakan.

Giffard's instructions gave Slim less than three months to prepare and train his troops for war, all of it during the monsoon. Slim would have three divisions for the task: 26 Indian Division would withdraw to Chittagong to form the corps reserve at the end of the monsoon and be replaced at the front by 5 and 7 Indian Divisions.* Interestingly, Slim now found himself in exactly the same position he had been in a year earlier, namely, examining the various possibilities for an offensive by his corps into Arakan. The eventual plan prepared by Slim and subsequently agreed by Giffard and Auchinleck contained two elements. The first, Operation Cudgel, was to be a land advance by Slim's 15 Corps which would take place whether or not a subsequent amphibious operation (Operation Bullfrog) by 2 British Division was mounted against Akyab. The object of Cudgel was to capture the Maungdaw–Buthidaung road by January 1944 and exploit to the area of Indian–Rathedaung by mid-March. The inter-divisional boundary was to be the crest of the Mayu Range which would be inclusive to 5 Indian Division. The problem, of course, was the same one with which he had been faced a year before, namely the military impoverishment of any plan which had at its heart a 'straightforward advance overland'.

Given the calamitous events of 14 Indian Division's recent experience in Arakan, the task set for Slim would ordinarily have appeared impossible. Slim, however, was convinced that defeating the Japanese was not just possible, but that given the right tools – well-trained, well-led and well-motivated soldiers – he could do so decisively. For his part, Irwin, now back in the United Kingdom, remained deeply pessimistic about the chances of Eastern Army ever succeeding in battle against the Japanese, and told Mountbatten in September that the morale of the British–Indian Army was so low that the Japanese could not be prevented from marching on Delhi should they wish to do so.[32] Reading the lessons of the retreat and of the abortive Arakan campaign rather differently to Irwin, Slim was convinced that the Japanese were not invincible, but he knew also that

* Commanded by Major-Generals' H.R.Briggs and F.W. Messervy respectively.

the peculiar conditions of 1942 and 1943 had not allowed any scope for British success. These ranged from inadequate training for jungle fighting; the process of 'milking' experienced personnel and using them to form the basis of new units, which prevented units from developing battle experience; limited mobility off-road, and the lack of close co-ordination of air and ground troops in battle. At the very least the recently concluded Arakan debacle had taught the British–Indian Army crucial lessons about how to fight the Japanese.

During this period Slim developed four principles upon which planning for future operations against the Japanese were to be based. These were that the ultimate intention must be an offensive one, that the main idea on which the plan was based must be simple and that it must be held in view throughout, that everything else must give way to it, and it must have an element of surprise. But in translating these principles into action Slim faced three fundamental difficulties, each of which of itself was sufficient to cripple his offensive aspirations. The first related to the protection of his Corps' vulnerable left flank as it advanced into Arakan. To overcome this Giffard promised to supply Slim with two brigades of Major-General Woolner's 81 West African Division when it arrived in India in August 1943.[33] These brigades would maintain a parallel advance down the Kaladan Valley not only to protect the left flank of 5 and 7 Indian Division from a wide Japanese envelopment, but also to threaten the Japanese lines of communication into Arakan. Slim proposed that Woolner's division be exclusively supplied by air, to remove the prospect of having a vulnerable land-based line of communication deep in the Arakanese hills. For the size of force involved this was a novel innovation in the theatre, but the way had clearly been forged by Wingate's first expedition. Giffard readily agreed, and it became part of the plan Giffard submitted to Auchinleck in September 1943.

The second problem concerned the best way to overcome the devastating Japanese tactics of envelopment and infiltration. Slim's solution developed in detail through the monsoon and became an integral part of the training programmes for both 5 and 7 Indian Divisions. His plan was at the same time both simple and bold, and was little changed from the proposals he had made to Irwin a few months earlier. It involved two separate ideas. The first was that of a defensive area or 'box' – reminiscent of infantry squares of an earlier era – which was to be formed by units when they had been surrounded by the enemy. If units withdrew immediately into a defensive posture when surrounded, and then aggressively struck back to counter-attack the enemy, much like a snake when threatened by a predator, units would thus become 'pivots of manoeuvre' against which the Japanese could themselves be attacked and cut off. During the advance all troops – from fighting formations to supporting units of every description without exception – would be trained to turn themselves instantly into self-sufficient strongholds and to stand fast if bypassed and be supplied by air if necessary. Then, by aggressive counter-action the Japanese would have their own supply lines cut in turn. This ability to stand and fight in strongholds would provide the second element, namely an anvil against which the hammer of the army or corps reserves could smash in counter-attack and thus complete the destruction of the enemy that the strongholds had begun.

Slim knew from first-hand experience that the Japanese had one fatal weakness. They were often too pig-headed in the attack to realize when they had failed and when they should withdraw. Obedience to their strict military code and a concern not to dishonour the memory of their ancestors or to sully their families with the shame of defeat, made Japanese soldiers fanatically brave, and determined to do what they perceived as their duty to the utmost, even if this sometimes meant hammering away in ultimately fruitless attacks, at great expense, simply because that was what they had been ordered to do. Heroic *banzai* charges rarely defeated a staunch defender, as 48 Indian Brigade had shown so decisively at Kokkogwa. 'Their will to win was formidable,' recalled Anthony Barker. 'Against an enemy of insufficient resolve this fanaticism was often enough to carry the day, but against stiffer opposition it often meant that troops were thrown mindlessly into the fray even when it should have been obvious that the battle was lost.'[34] Slim's reasoning was that if the numerous and scattered British positions could form themselves quickly into air-supplied and impregnable bastions the Japanese would throw themselves fruitlessly against them, and would do so until they fell exhausted under the hammer that he planned to bring down upon them from the north.

The final problem Slim faced was the need for an effective method for attacking Japanese defensive positions. He appreciated only too clearly that one of the fatal errors of the first Arakan campaign had been unimaginative attacks on narrow frontages. He also appreciated the tremendous strength of Japanese defensive positions and the impossibility of defeating them through means of conventional frontal attacks, no matter how well co-ordinated they were between air, artillery and infantry, or how well supported by firepower. At this stage he emphasized to his divisional and brigade commanders that frontal attacks were to be avoided in favour of attacks from the flanks and the rear, and that the best means of overcoming Japanese positions was by adopting the envelopment tactics so decisively exploited to date by the Japanese themselves. This would have the effect of cutting off the defenders' supply lines and thereby placing pressure on them where they least expected it. In time, experience in Arakan taught that the best method of attacking a Japanese defensive position was to capture ground behind the main enemy position that was so vital to the enemy – preferably on a line of communication – so that he was forced to counter-attack immediately to recover it, and at considerable cost.

It should be noted that the notion that attacks should be anything other than frontal and conventional in their execution – with artillery and tanks first neutralizing and then infantry occupying – did not at first receive universal acceptance, even amongst soldiers of considerable military experience. Indeed some received it in the same negative fashion in which Lloyd had received Slim's advice to seek more innovative means to attack Donbaik a year before. In part the conventional approach was by far the easiest and least problematic, but for this reason was that expected by the Japanese. Envelopment and infiltration were, for many in the British–Indian Army in 1943, unconventional and even unsound notions. At the very least they entailed risk, unacceptably high levels of low-level command initiative given the inexperience of the junior non-commissioned and commissioned officer cadres of the Indian Army, high levels of individual and collective training and an acceptance of operating without clearly defined supply lines. Yet Slim was convinced that his ideas were correct. In time his directions for the conduct of operations during the forthcoming campaign in Arakan were to be fully vindicated and became 14 Army's standard procedure for the remainder of the campaign in Burma.

Such tactics demanded a number of basic prerequisites. The first was for battalion, brigade and divisional commanders of high quality, men who would hold their nerve in times of acute crisis, and who could inspire their soldiers to give of their last ounce of commitment and energy. In this regard Slim benefited considerably from the calibre of his two key divisional commanders. Although significantly different in temperament, both Briggs and Messervy were thoroughly professional and skilled commanders. Equally, they were beloved of their soldiers. Harold Briggs, who after the war rose to fame as one of the architects of victory in the long insurgency against communist guerrilla movement in post-war Malaya, was perhaps the less dynamic of the two. His future corps commander, Lieutenant-General Sir Philip Christison, described him as 'stolid, methodical, slow to think, express himself and act, but extremely sound and conventional.'[35] Frank Messervy, an Indian Army cavalryman by background, was by contrast a powder keg of enthusiasm and dash, with an abundance of ideas and energy tempered by a commitment to thorough planning and detailed training. Both men were flexible and imaginative in their thinking, which enabled them to contribute significantly to the bold new approach to warfighting advocated by their corps commander.

The second requirement, in combat and support units alike, was for well-trained, motivated and confident troops. Units that were able to infiltrate through and around Japanese positions at night, separated from their regular supply chain, and able to form quick defensive 'boxes' when threatened in turn by Japanese infiltration, needed to be exceptionally confident in their fighting skills, their tactics and their leaders. Such could be achieved only as the result of hard and realistic training. Even administrative and support units had to be able to stand fast in the event of encirclement and defend their perimeter against attack. It was to training to meet these demands that 5 and 7 Indian Divisions turned their full effort during the monsoon.

Responsibility for preparing the Army for war lay with Auchinleck. In 1943 he initiated a massive programme of intensive training throughout the whole of the Army in India.[36] This covered the whole spectrum of officer selection and training, the length, quality and subject matter of training for Indian recruits, the training in jungle warfare given to British reinforcements, both of individuals and whole units, and the collective training given to battalions and brigades prior to their transfer to Eastern Army.

These measures had an immediate and dramatic effect on the fighting efficiency of Eastern Army.[37] The ill-fated 14 Indian Division, together with 39 Indian Division, which contained many of Slim's old units from 1 Burma Division, and which had for a time come under Slim's command at Ranchi, were both transformed into training divisions in India. The work of these training divisions was to have a profound and positive effect on the quality of individual reinforcements, units and formations destined for the battle area as they were first comprehensively inducted into jungle warfare before they made their way to the front. By the time Mountbatten arrived in early October, new life was cascading through the veins of what was shortly to become 14 Army.[38] Slim was regularly to repeat 14 Army's debt of gratitude to Auchinleck in *Defeat into Victory* and was several years later to write to him: 'I think I personally owe more to you than any other Commander for the way in which . . . you supported the Forces in the Field and kept us supplied with well trained reinforcements.'[39]

However, the requirement to train 5 and 7 Indian Divisions for an offensive late in 1943 necessitated the full gamut of collective training to be conducted during the wettest and most difficult time of the year – the monsoon. This in itself was no easy task. Indeed, there were many in India who professed it impossible to train or fight during this time of year. When Mountbatten arrived to take command of SEAC, he directed – to the amazement of some – that operations were to continue throughout the monsoon. But he received the immediate and unequivocal support of Slim. For two successive monsoons (1942 and 1943) Slim had successfully prepared 15 Corps for war despite the constant downpour and without much of the wet weather equipment many thought necessary. He knew that while large scale fighting would never be possible in Arakan during the monsoon, small-scale operations and training certainly were. 'I had been told by a lot of people', Slim told assembled troops of 11 East African Division on 25 January 1945, 'that it was impossible to operate in the monsoon. However, I had done two monsoons myself, and I was sure that really good troops would be able to move and fight even in the appalling conditions of the monsoon.'[40]

Slim's training regime for 15 Corps during the 1943 monsoon built upon the principles he had so clearly enunciated in his Training Directive of 1942. Of his two formations, Frank Messervy's 7 Indian Division had by far the greater opportunity for training and preparation. When battle was joined the following January this disparity showed. Training in 7 Indian Division had begun, and was conducted with the utmost seriousness and rigour, from as early as March 1943. 'Every man . . . was, in fact, rigorously trained to be a fighting man', wrote Henry Maule, Messevy's biographer. 'Only a handful of unarmed Indian followers, traditional to the Indian Army, were allowed to be classified as "non-combatant" . . . Messervy saw to it that every unit had its own jungle lane or lanes set out with dummy Japs to be attacked with the utmost ferocity ... Every man was put through battle inoculation, crawling along a shallow trench or across open paddy while ... machine guns fired a few inches above.'[41]

Live training with artillery, mortars and medium machine guns was carried out and in March 1943 battalions took part in a divisional exercise. As Michael Roberts, the divisional historian, recalled:

> Realistic, and at times exciting, these manoeuvres were to prove of immense value. Time and again problems and situations arose which were to be reproduced within the year in real battle. For the first time operations were being carried out on a large scale in forest, and the outstanding lesson was perhaps the ease with which surprise could be achieved. Officers and men learnt to expect the unexpected and to realize that, given good battle procedure, the worst threat could be held at bay long enough to enable a plan to be made to deal with it and perhaps even to turn the tables by an unexpected counter thrust. Day patrolling, wide encirclement, unexpected encounters on jungle tracks, all combined to build up in everyone's mind a picture of war in a country of forest and few roads, where infantry use the tracks made by elephant and deer, and battle often opens at fifty yards range.[42]

When units of 7 Indian Division deployed to Arakan from June 1943 in preparation for the relief of 26 Indian Division, Messervy placed the greatest stress on determined patrolling against Japanese forward positions. 'Not only would this help build up a picture of what the Japs were doing,' explained Henry Maule, 'but it would also give officers and men the confidence so desperately needed in the weird gloom. Thus inoculated they would then take part in ambushes and fighting patrols of platoon or greater strength. Morale gained by training was to be confirmed into even higher morale gained by fighting.'[43]

Five Indian Division returned to India from Iraq in June 1943, after which it began began intensive jungle training, discarding its trucks for mules and preparing to fight a considerably different type of war than that for which it had trained in the Middle East, and against a vastly different enemy. It deployed to Arakan in November 1943. Under Slim's careful tutelage the division prepared for war. Antony Brett-James, who wrote both a personal account of his experiences in Burma and the official history of the division, recalled that he:

saw Slim for the first time when he still commanded the Fifteenth
Indian Corps. The Division held a "War game" . . . at which syndicates
of officers planned the future campaign in Arakan round a large scale
model. Slim summed up at the close of each day, and I was mightily
impressed by his penetrating criticisms and appreciation of the detailed
tactics, and by his calm drive and humour; he showed insight into the
Japanese mind and methods, and seemed to hold no illusions about
what would face us in Arakan, yet he was able to look bravely and
with certainty into the New Year, despite every past disaster in Burma.
I sensed a nature as robust and tenacious as his own physique; in place
of flash, superficiality, polish or elegance, waxed a purposeful, business
like, imperturbable and seasoned personality.[44]

Briggs directed that every member of the Division learn by memory his
'Five Commandments':

1. Be determined to kill every Jap you meet, and then some [more].
2. Be determined not to let the Jap frighten you with ruses and induce
you to disclose your positions and waste ammunition. Ambush him
and do unto him as he would unto you.
3. Be determined to hold fast when ordered, whatever happens. The
Jap will then have to give you the target you want, while our reserves
are on the way to help you.
4. Be determined to carry out to the letter every task given to you,
whether on patrol, in attack or defence. No half measures. Plan for
all eventualities, after anticipating enemy reactions. Plans cannot be
too thorough. Be observant and suspicious.
5. Be determined – even fanatical.[45]

'The jungle called for better junior leadership than any other theatre
of war', recorded Brett-James. 'Mental and bodily endurance would be
essential. Individual fieldcraft, observation and concealment had to be
learned and practised. Japanese characteristics and methods were studied
with care; the troops were trained in fire discipline and control to avoid
shooting at mere noises; they were taught to treat the jungle as a friend,
able to supply them with shelter and food. Aggressive tactics was to be
the basis of our tactics.'[46]

The third requirement of Slim's approach to war was for an efficient air transport system. The success of Slim's 'pivot' idea depended entirely upon the ability of the defended bastions to be supplied from the air with everything they required for their defence. This in turn required not just a substantial transport aircraft fleet but local air superiority as well. Air supply 'was of course not a new conception,' Slim recalled in a lecture he gave after the war. 'On the Indian Frontier in 1928 we were using it, I used it in Iraq in 1941, we talked about it in Burma in 1942, in 1943 the Wingate raid used it, but it was not until 1944 that the aircraft were available to allow us to use it on an effective scale.' Until he had the aircraft he had no choice but to ignore them for planning purposes. Yet he was constantly exercised in 1942 and 1943 about the possibilities aircraft could offer, and would gladly have availed himself of the advantages they brought had they been available in sufficient quantities for both the retreat and the first Arakan campaign.[47]

Once the decision had been taken to support 81 West African Division exclusively by air, Eastern Army built up the aircraft and air supply organization during the 1943 monsoon sufficient to supply a division continuously in the jungle for a prolonged period. More importantly perhaps, both Slim and Giffard worked hard during this period to inculcate in the minds of all troops a sense of what Slim described as 'airmindedness'. In this they were remarkably successful. In time all who served in Burma came to regard the supply of units from the air as no more unusual than resupply by rail or road. Commanders also came to regard the support provided by ground attack aircraft and bombers as indispensable – and as readily used – as they had traditionally regarded the use of mortars and artillery.

Critical to an appreciation of the importance Slim placed on the full use of air power was the degree of integration he insisted upon between the land and air forces, first in 15 Corps, and then later in 14 Army as a whole. The bitter experience of the retreat confirmed to him the key importance well integrated air power played in land operations: indeed, he came to believe there was no such a thing as an exclusively 'land' campaign. By 1943 – if not much earlier – he was convinced that all successful operations in modern warfare were in fact 'air-land' operations in which military forces in both environments had to work seamlessly, at tactical, operational and strategic levels, in pursuit of a common objective.

He suffered from none of the debilitating prejudices that had so often stifled the growth of effective communication between Services in the past. When he arrived in Barrackpore on 3 June 1942 to command 15 Corps, Slim discovered that he had been co-located with the Air Officer Commanding Bengal and Burma, Air Vice-Marshal Bill Williams. 'He should . . . by rights, have been with Eastern Army who were responsible for the same areas as he was, not with 15 Corps,' Slim recalled. 'However, the arrangement suited us admirably . . .'. The air element assigned to 15 Corps was 224 Group, RAF based in Chittagong. We 'at once began' Slim comments, 'the close and friendly co-operation that lasted between the corps and the group until the end of the war.' He insisted, for instance, that officers shared the same mess irrespective of service. The same pattern repeated itself when Slim was given command of 14 Army in October 1943. Fourteen Army, Baldwin's 3rd Tactical Airforce and Brigadier-General Old's Troop Carrier Command 'worked to a considerable extent as a joint headquarters . . . [growing] into a very close brotherhood, depending on one another, trusting one another, and taking as much pride in each other's triumphs as we did in our own.'

By the time the first rains swept in from the Bay of Bengal in late May 1943 to make north Arakan virtually unnavigable except by boat, the Japanese, exhausted by their bold exertions against 26 Indian Division, contented themselves with consolidating their positions along the Maungdaw–Buthidaung road. Indeed, very little Japanese activity took place during the monsoon months that followed. Slim, however, saw the period of impending stalemate in north Arakan as a priceless opportunity to develop the fighting abilities of his troops. On 14 June 1943 he laid down that the 'policy of formations in contact with the enemy will be aggressive defence', and that 'contact with the enemy will be maintained continuously and the monsoon period will be used for gaining the upper hand of the Japanese in patrol and minor enterprises.' Slim's purpose was to develop confidence in his fighting troops that they could fight and prevail against the Japanese in battle. Battle skills were infinitely better practised for real than artificially in training, and aggressive patrolling allowed the development of the all-important low-level soldiering skills which Slim so urgently sought in his soldiers.

The aim of such activity was, in Slim's words, 'to convince the doubters that our object, the destruction of the Japanese Army in battle, was practicable. We had to a great extent frightened ourselves by our stories of the superman.' Superiority over the Japanese had to be demonstrated publicly, and although Wavell had attempted to do this in Arakan, it had proved premature and ill-conceived. The solution lay in mounting extensive patrol activity against the Japanese to develop the troops' confidence. For the most part these small-scale operations were successful and by them both 7 and 26 Indian Division gained the initiative in northern Arakan during the monsoon. 'By the end of November', wrote Slim, 'our forward troops had gone a long way towards getting that individual feeling of superiority and that first essential in the fighting man – the desire to close with his enemy.' The next step was to escalate these actions and a series of carefully stage-managed minor offensive operations to drive in the Japanese outposts forward of the Maungdaw–Buthidaung road were mounted during November and December 1943. These were also very successful. Battalions attacked enemy platoon positions while brigades attacked companies. Slim was the first to admit that this approach was akin to using a hammer to crack a nut, but he was satisfied that the results, not least in terms of the morale of his troops when they saw for the first time the defeat of the once-exultant Japanese, fully vindicated his approach. He knew, as did a growing proportion of his Army, that victory against the Japanese was no longer the inconceivable notion it had been only seven months earlier. Although the evidence still remained a trickle, Slim was confident that the forthcoming year would see the turn of the tide.

# 5

# Army Commander

Slim hated Barrackpore. It was from here between June and August 1942 that he had first commanded 15 Corps, but he considered it too close to Calcutta and its sordid slums depressed him. Even though by his own admission it was a good communications centre, and thus an ideal location for a joint land/air headquarters, it was still a long way from the front line: Scoones' 4 Corps at Imphal was 400 air miles north-east in Assam. But on 16 October 1943 he found himself back in the garrison town, called back from Chittagong where he had moved his forward 15 Corps HQ, to take Giffard's place as the GOC-in-C of Eastern Army.* The geographical distance between himself and his two corps led him to decide immediately to transfer his complete headquarters two hundred miles north-east to the town of Comilla, which lay midway between Calcutta and Imphal.[1] The town was only forty-five minutes by air from Imphal in good weather, and allowed Slim to visit regularly in a battered old Anson aircraft provided for him by the Royal Air Force. As the threat to Assam grew in the early months of 1944 the proximity of Slim to Scoones became extremely important.[2] Giffard was elevated in turn to the command of 11 Army Group, commanding all land forces in SEAC and becoming the Supreme Commander's land force adviser. Eastern Army had its responsibilities for Bihar, Orissa and most of

* The story of Slim's appointment is at Appendix 2.

Bengal removed, leaving Slim with responsibility solely for the security of India and the conduct of land operations against the Japanese east of the Meghna River.

The strongest possible vindication of Slim's approach to war came within a week of his taking command. Admiral Mountbatten, the newly arrived Supreme Commander, paid a fleeting visit to the joint 14 Army/ 3 Tactical Air Force Headquarters in Barrackpore on the afternoon of 22 October 1943 on his way back from visiting Chiang Kai-shek in Chungking, and the two men met for the first time. Slim invited him to address the eighty or so officers of his and Baldwin's joint HQ gathered to meet him. In a profound way the occasion proved to be a meeting of minds and began a relationship that was to be dramatically fruitful over the following twenty months. Many years later Mountbatten recalled that 'something happened that first meeting – somehow we clicked . . . and we developed a friendship – a life long friendship so that although we were never actually next to each other in the Command, because I always had an Army Group Commander in Chief or a Land Force Commander in Chief between Bill Slim and me, we always saw eye to eye.'[3]

In his diary for that day Mountbatten recorded: 'I . . . staggered them by saying that I understood that it was the custom to stop fighting during the monsoon in Burma, but that I was against this custom and hoped that they would support me and keep the battle going to the best of their ability, whatever the weather conditions were. I hope this policy, spoken on the spur of the moment, may perhaps yield great results later on, but that remains to be seen.'[4] Mountbatten told them that there was to be no more retreat, that troops that had been cut off by the Japanese would be supplied by air and that he would set up a group of medical experts with the aim of drastically cutting the number of men taken ill by tropical disease.

But Mountbatten's extempore speech was not enthusiastically received by all who heard it that day. Brigadier Cobb, Giffard's Director of Plans at 11 Army Group, who was accompanying Mountbatten, told him rather candidly afterwards that,

> although it had been a stirring and inspiring talk it had been criticised by those he spoke to afterwards on the grounds that I did not understand the situation properly and would soon find out that

the monsoon made an offensive out of the question during the five months it prevailed. Further they could not see how troops could be ordered to stand fast and face the infiltrating Japanese if they were cut off from their supplies and no transport aircraft were available . . . In fact . . . they were shaken by my quick decision based on inadequate understanding of the conditions in Burma.[5]

Giffard, on hearing of Mountbatten's speech, for his part 'dismissed it as a piece of empty braggadocio' based on Mountbatten's ignorance of the realities of war in Burma.[6] Perhaps Mountbatten recognized some incredulity in his listeners. When they were alone Mountbatten said to Slim, 'That didn't go very well did it?' 'No, they're not used to revolutionary ideas but I like it,' Slim replied. 'When the time comes I'll back you to the hilt.'[7]

The somewhat hostile reception afforded to Mountbatten was understandable. Slim had been in the headquarters for less than a week, and for many of his new staff officers, all of whom he had inherited from Giffard,* he was still an unknown quantity. Certainly, many did not yet understand the extent or the implications of the ideas that he had been developing and promoting in 15 Corps, nor that Slim had already established in practice what Mountbatten now proposed in theory.

The fact was that while Mountbatten thought many of these ideas to be new, and perhaps of his own invention, following the pessimistic assessments given to him by Irwin and Wingate in London in September, Slim recognized them from the development of his own approach to battle over the previous two years.[8] Lewin, when preparing Slim's official biography in 1975, saw this clearly. In correspondence with Lewin, Mountbatten had sought to take more of the credit for the innovations brought about in 14 Army than Lewin knew to be justified. Replying to one such letter Lewin argued that:

whatever the rest of the doubting Thomases at Barrackpore thought of your ideas, I must retain the point that many of them – standing fast, air supply, monsoon fighting etc – were already present in Slim's mind ... According to my interpretation, he welcomed you and thereafter served you loyally because he was delighted to discover a commander at last who not only shared his ideas but also had the

* Except for his ADC, whom he brought with him from 15 Corps.

dynamism and determination – and power – to see that they were put into practice.[9]

Lewin was right. By happy coincidence Mountbatten's bright ideas for reviving what he had been led to believe was a flagging war effort in the Far East were in actual fact all issues with which Slim was himself in the process of re-educating and re-training his Army.

Little of the planning effort expended during 1943 bore any fruit. By December 1943, following the Tehran Conference, only four operations in SEAC were scheduled for 1944, all of which were to be under the command of Slim. Churchill's hopes for an amphibious strategy (Operation Culverin) had come to nought, sunk on the rocks of an Allied strategy that placed the defeat of Germany foremost. This demanded all available landing craft and amphibious vessels to be concentrated in Europe for the invasion of France. In the Far East, the strategic priority, pressed on an unwilling British by Roosevelt, was for the continued sustenance of China through the expansion of land and air lines of communication from India. Land operations were to be mounted in Burma merely to allow the construction of the new 'Burma Road' from Ledo to Myitkyina. Of the offensive plans that remained, the first was to be by 15 Corps in Arakan – Operation Cudgel. Slim intended to include a much reduced amphibious operation against Akyab at the same time by 36 Indian Division under the title of Operation Bulldozer. The second was to be an advance by Scoones' 4 Corps in Imphal to the Chindwin, the third an advance by Stilwell's forces to Myitkyina and finally, to assist Stilwell, a second, more ambitious long range penetration operation by Wingate, to be called Operation Thursday.

The prospect of launching an offensive into Burma posed two critical problems for the new Army Commander. The most immediate difficulty lay in developing the confidence of his Army so that it would be able to take on the Japanese in battle, and win. The second was to overcome the enormous physical problems posed by geography and climate. Neither issue was new to Slim, nor indeed to Giffard. Nevertheless, considered together, in their scale and complexity they posed conceivably the greatest problem ever faced by a British commander in war. The omens did not look good. To meet this challenge Slim had nothing but defeat upon which to build. But it was the imagination and inspiration brought by Slim's approach to these two issues that was fundamentally to reverse British fortunes in the Far East in 1944 and 1945.

Morale had undoubtedly improved across the Army as a whole in the four months or so since May 1943 when it had been, as Slim acknowledged, at 'a dangerously low ebb.' The change was due in the main to the concerted efforts of Giffard, Slim and Scoones to train, re-equip and re-motivate the troops of Eastern Army, and of Auchinleck to focus the resources of India Command towards the fundamental need to train for war. News of Wingate's expedition earlier in the year had also provided a significant boost, but this contributed to the process of invigoration sweeping through the Army rather than being its cause. But the situation was still far from satisfactory.

As an experienced soldier Slim knew that high morale was critical if soldiers were to confront and overcome the terrors, deprivations and uncertainties of battle. High morale required that soldiers had confidence in themselves, the loyalty of their NCO's and officers, their training, their equipment and their generals. They needed to know that their commanders had their best interests at heart, that they would not be needlessly sacrificed, that their physical and material wants would be met as far as was possible in the circumstances, and that they would be trusted with information about the purpose of any sacrifice they might be called upon to make. This confidence had to extend not just to the fighting men but to those in support functions to the rear as well.

Slim had long been exercised about the power of morale in war. When commander of 10 Indian Division in Iraq in early 1941 he had gathered his commanders together at Lake Habbaniyah and lectured them on their need as leaders to motivate their men and to build up a desire in them to overcome in battle, whatever the odds. Slim stressed neither strategy nor tactics as the fundamentals of successful soldiering, but the resolution and spirit of each fighting man. John Masters recalled the lecture, in which Slim told his audience:

We make the best plans we can and train our wills to hold steadfastly to them in the face of adversity, and yet to be flexible to change them when events show them to be unsound, or to take advantage of an opportunity that unfolds during the battle itself. We have already trained our men to the highest possible level of skill with their weapons and in their use of minor tactics. But in the end every important battle develops to a point where there is no real control by senior commanders. Each soldier feels himself to be alone. Discipline may have got him to the place where he is, and discipline may hold him there – for a time. Co-operation with other men in the same situation can help him to move forward. Self-preservation will make him defend himself to the death, if there is no other way. But what makes him go on, alone, determined to break the will of the enemy opposite him, is morale. Pride in himself as an independent thinking man, who knows why he's there, and what he's doing. Absolute confidence that the best has been done for him, and that his fate is now in his own hands. The dominant feeling on the battlefield is loneliness ... and morale, only morale, individual morale as a foundation under training and discipline, will bring victory.[10]

The rebuilding of the confidence of an army, sufficient to take it from defeat into victory, was one of Slim's greatest triumphs. But in the dark days of 1943 such victory was by no means certain, and even to the most perspicacious of observers it still lay a long way off. As Slim wrote, the

practical realities of campaigning in Eastern India and Burma, its huge distances, appalling weather and difficult terrain, the tortuous lines of communication, the low priority the theatre had within Allied strategy as a whole, the rampant diseases of every kind, the strange jungle environment – and the seemingly unbeatable Japanese – combined to create a sense of hardship which could not fail to depress morale. The epithet 'The Forgotten Army' was taken up by the troops and before it became a statement of pride it reflected the fears and frustrations of soldiers thousands of miles from home whose hardships and deprivations were not widely appreciated.

His problem was as much logistical as it was about developing successful stratagems for defeating the Japanese in battle.

Indeed, the difficulties involved in fighting in Burma with an Army based in India and separated by long and difficult lines of communication were such that in Slim's mind they threatened the possibility of an offensive. In 1945 14 Army 'had a ration strength of 750,000 – the population of a great city – scattered along a 700-mile front in area as big as

Poland with the poorest of communications and most meagre of resources,'
he recalled in a lecture given in 1946. 'Before we could get on with our real
job – fighting – we had to feed, clothe, house, and all the time we were
doing it, equip, doctor, police, pay and transport by road, ship, rail and air
all of those men. All that and jungle too!'[11] Slim's new command stretched
from China to the Bay of Bengal, covering 'some of the least suitable
campaigning country in the world . . . [with] some of the world's worst
country, breeding the world's worst diseases, and having for half the year
at least the world's worst climate.' A strategy for defeating the Japanese
in Burma depended principally on Slim's ability to get sufficient forces
into Manipur and North Arakan, and to maintain them there. 'Supply',
he acknowledged, 'was, of course, largely a matter of communications.'
Both geography and climate conspired to complicate this, as did 14 Army's
low priority for stores and the bureaucratic peacetime procedures that still
burdened the procurement system.

By the time he had taken command of 14 Army, Slim had developed
a programme to rebuild the fighting spirit of his troops, based on three
enduring principles of action. These dealt with spiritual, intellectual and
material factors. 'Spiritual first,' he wrote later in *Defeat into Victory*,
'because only spiritual foundations can stand real strain. Next intellectual, because men are swayed by reason as well as feeling. Material
last – important, but last – because the very highest kinds of morale are
often met when material conditions are lowest.'

By the 'spiritual' principle he meant that there must be a great and noble
object, its achievement must be vital, the method of achievement must be
active and aggressive and each man must feel that what he is and what he
does matters directly towards the attainment of the object. It was critical,
he argued, that all troops, of whatever rank, background and nationality,
believed in the cause they were fighting for. The cause itself had to be just.
'We fought for the clean, the decent, the free things of life,' Slim wrote.
'We fought only because the powers of evil had attacked these things.' By
the 'intellectual' foundation he meant that soldiers had to be convinced
that the object could be attained. The principal task was to destroy the
notion that the Japanese soldier was invincible. Equally, each soldier had
also to know that the organization to which he belonged was an efficient
one. He knew that the physical care of a soldier in the field has a direct
bearing on his performance in battle: lack of food, water, medical support
or contact with home works to weaken the resolve, over time, of even the

stoutest man. By the 'material' foundation Slim meant that each man had to feel that he would get a fair deal from his commanders and from the army generally, that he would, as far as humanly possible, be given the best weapons and equipment for his task and that his living and working conditions would be made as good as they could be.

Slim's agenda, therefore, was one of radical change for his 14th Army. Within the constraints of the limited resources available to him, and in conjunction with Auchinleck who was endeavouring simultaneously to revitalize India Command, Slim sought to rebuild the spirit of the Army. No one was exempt. The first priority was for an administrative plan to overcome the difficulties of geography, for which Slim gave responsibility to an old friend. Major-General Alf Snelling,* who had worked for him as his Principal Administrative Officer in 10 Indian Division in Iraq, was called in by Slim to be his Major-General in charge of administration. His BGS, Brigadier Steve Irwin, whom Slim had inherited from Giffard, co-ordinated the running of his HQ while Snelling became, by default, his senior staff officer. 'For an Army engaged in a campaign in Burma this was logical', explained Slim, 'as administrative possibilities and impossibilities would loom large, larger than strategical and tactical alternatives.'

Problems with the lines of communication appeared almost intractable. Both 4 and 15 Corps were painfully isolated from the rest of India. The lack of roads in Bengal forced a dependence upon a rickety system of railways between Calcutta and the north-east frontier of India. These were themselves hampered by a break in gauge and by the fact that there was no bridge over the Brahmaputra river (both railway carriages and wheeled vehicles crossed the river by ferry at Jogighopa). Wheeled vehicles had to be transported by rail 235 miles from Calcutta to Siliguri before they could join the road to Assam, which ran on to the Brahmaputra. A fleet of river steamers and barges plied between the ports on the Brahmaputra, but the capacity of the river route had been greatly reduced by the despatch of boats to other theatres of war, and to the behaviour of the river itself: its level fluctuated by as much as six metres and its course changed every monsoon with the result that jetties, roads and rail spurs at river ports were frequently washed away or left high and dry and had to be entirely reconstructed. East of the river the road and a single-track metre gauge line

---

* Nicknamed by some 'the Grocer'.

ran to Dimapur, over 600 miles from Calcutta, and from there to Ledo, the base for the 'Hump' airlift to China, 200 hundred miles further on.

The area east of the Brahmaputra was one of the most backward in India. Its railways were designed solely to meet the seasonal tea and jute industries and had a peacetime daily capacity of 600 tons. While by strenuous effort the capacity had increased to 2,800 tons per day by October 1943, this was still inadequate to meet all the requirements of 4 Corps, Stilwell's Northern Combat Area Command (NCAC) and the Hump airlift.

Steps were taken in 1942 and 1943 not only to improve India as a base for future operations in Assam and Burma, but also to improve as quickly as possible the existing state of the lines of communication to the front. The first was Auckinleck's problem, the second was Slim's. Both were daunting tasks. To improve the line of communication into Manipur necessitated the construction, much of it by hand using Indian labour, of hundreds of miles of roads, pipelines and airfields. The condition of the existing roads was poor. Few were all-weather and the machinery to improve them did not exist on a scale to make a difference in the short term. In Arakan, to support the build up of 15 Corps, due to a lack of road making stone in the region, thousands of bricks had to be baked alongside the road that ran forward of Cox's Bazar to make it usable in all weathers. The manpower demands of such a long and difficult line of communication were considerable. To 'maintain a division 15,000 strong deployed forward', records Major-General Julian Thompson, in his study of logistics in war, 'required 36,700 men, of whom 5,000 were in the transport and supplies branch. The Arakan was no better. Fifty per cent of the tonnage which left Chittagong for the forward areas was absorbed by the line of communication personnel and services before the corps areas was reached.'[12]

Slim discovered that the purchasing procedures for his Army remained mired in the petty bureaucracy of peacetime India. The result was unnecessary paperwork and delay. Within days of taking command he represented these problems, with Snelling, to Auckinleck. Auchinleck immediately agreed to change these processes, and within months the effect of a more responsive procurement system was being felt by 14 Army. The availability of equipment and their delivery over the vast distances of the line of communication – particularly to Assam – posed special problems. In almost every area – ammunition, rations, vehicles, radios, medical equipment and stores of every kind – 14 Army was seriously deficient. Stocks of rifle and artillery ammunition, for example, were between 25 and 45 per cent below requirement. Slim's approach to the problem of administration was to develop self-reliance from within rather than to wait for help from outside. His staff in 14 Army were second-to-none, he declared in a lecture to the Press Club in 1946, because 'it realised that it existed to keep the fighting troops supplied and second, because it regarded any difficulty whether of man or nature as a challenge and a challenge to be taken up.'[13]

Although delivered in the exuberant afterglow of victory, Slim's comments pointed up clearly the enormous difficulties that had to be overcome before sustained operations – offensive or defensive – could be mounted against the Japanese. Food in particular proved to be a serious headache. In late 1943 14 Army's wide variety of races, religions and castes meant that it also had about thirty different ration scales. Only limited quantities of food could be obtained from local sources, which meant that the bulk of all rations – both fresh and dry – had to come up the already overburdened line of communication from Calcutta. The lack of cold storage created great deficiencies in the procurement of meat and there were no alternatives to the monotonous diet of bully beef. The same deficiencies occurred in the provision of milk and milk products, and vegetables. Consequently, 14 Army was forced to develop innovative ways of feeding itself. In this respect Snelling worked wonders. One of his solutions was to fly in Chinese to start a duck farm to produce eggs. 'Eventually', comments Julian Thompson, 'in a reversion to the logistic methods of earlier wars, sheep and goats were kept at Imphal, where there was plenty of rice straw available for feedstuff, and 18,000 acres of vegetables were cultivated.'[14]

Likewise in 1943 the medical services were undermanned and unable to cope with the scale and diversity of the diseases in the region – which ranged from malarial mosquitoes, the bacteria and amoebae of dysentery, and scrub typhus mites. Malaria in particular was a scourge and there was extensive parasitic infection in the troops. 'A Battalion had been turning over in 6 weeks', recalled Lieutenant-General Sir Philip Christison in his memoirs.[15] 'In 1944, for every man evacuated with wounds we have one hundred and twenty evacuated sick,' wrote Slim. 'The annual malaria rate alone was eighty-four percent per annum of the total strength of the Army.' In 1944 the British–Indian army suffered 250,000 casualties from malaria and dysentery[16] and a further 2,400 casualties from scrub typhus, of which 20 per cent were fatal.[17]

Slim's solution was to reorganize the medical services in the forward area. Men who contracted malaria were no longer sent to hospitals in India, thus reducing the pressure on transport and on the individual who was otherwise forced to undergo an uncomfortable and often hazardous journey to the rear. Forward treatment meant that now a man who contracted the disease would be in a Malaria Forward Treatment Unit within twenty-four hours and could be back in his unit in weeks rather than months. The application of robust military discipline helped ensure that anti-malarial instructions were obeyed. Commanding officers of units that did not have over 95 per cent of the men test positive for taking their daily dose of mepacrine were sacked. Through these measures the annual malaria rate fell to 13 per cent by 1945. Whole units were de-wormed. Surgeons operated also in 'forward areas, performing major operations within a few hours of a man being wounded,'[18] and nurses were sent as far forward as possible. These measures not only saved many lives but had a dramatic effect on morale.

Welfare provision improved dramatically in the first six months following Slim's assumption of command, the consequence of the determined efforts of Mountbatten, Giffard and Slim to improve conditions for the men of South East Asia Command. The delivery of mail, the introduction by Mountbatten of a theatre newspaper, and improvements to rations and accommodation were all key elements in this programme of change. Slim made a particular effort to ensure that the many thousands of troops in support functions and on the lines of communication who were not involved in the fighting but who were essential to the maintenance of the combatant units, benefitted from these changes and were made to feel part of the Army as a whole. Slim brooked no combat-arm snobbery in his Army. All men, however menial the tasks they performed, were vital for victory.

Information and honesty were key ingredients of Slim's approach to the problems faced by 14 Army. He was convinced that the Army as a whole had to understand the reasons for delays and deficiencies, and collectively develop new and innovative ways of solving them. He talked frankly to his troops at every opportunity, and he encouraged his commanders to do likewise. This was done not in any contrived or artificial manner but by 'informal contacts between troops and commanders.' While there was nothing new in this, Slim gave it renewed priority. 'It was the way we had held the troops together in the worst days of the 1942 retreat,' he recalled; 'we remained an army then only because the men saw and knew their commanders.' Information rooms were set up in units to keep the men informed not only of the progress of operations but of other items of interest to them. Slim was determined from the outset to explain the difficulties he faced in getting supplies to his troops, giving them the reasons for equipment shortages and keeping them informed about efforts made on their behalf to improve the situation. He knew that whatever he had been promised in the way of increased resources from the United Kingdom, 14 Army would remain, for a long time yet, desperately short. 'In my more gloomy moments' he wrote, 'I even doubted if we should ever climb up the priority list.' He impressed upon his troops the realities of a global war effort, that defeating the Germans had to take first priority but that despite every difficulty he and his commanders would endeavour to obtain everything that the Army needed. If this were not possible then they would all have to improvise. Slim commented that 'it is not so much asking men to fight or work with inadequate or obsolete equipment that lowers morale but the belief that those responsible are accepting such a state of affairs. If men realize that everyone above them and behind them is flat out to get the things required for them, they will do wonders, as my men did, with the meagre resources they have instead of sitting down moaning for better.' 'No boats?' asked Slim rhetorically to the Press Club in 1946. 'We'll build 'em! No vegetables, we'll grow 'em! No eggs? Duck farms! No parachutes? We'll use gully!* No road metal? Bake our own bricks and lay 'm! No air strips? Put down bithess!† Malaria, we'll stop it! Medium guns busting? Saw off three feet of the barrel and go on shooting! Their motto, "God helps those who help themselves." '19

By 1945 14 Army was not recognizable from that which it had been two years before. George MacDonald Fraser's infantry section in a British battalion advancing through central Burma in 1945, typified the new spirit which infused Slim's army:

Nine section *was* morale, they and the barking Sergeant Hutton, and tall Long John, the courteous, soft-spoken company commander whose modest demeanour concealed a Berserker, and the tough, black-browed colonel . . . and all the rest of that lean and hungry battalion. To say nothing of the Gurkhas along the wire, grinning and chirruping, and the fearsome Baluchi hillmen looking like the

* Woven jute.

† Hessian strips soaked in bitumen. See Chapter 8 for an example of the use of bithess.

Forty Thieves. And the green and gold dragon flag of the regiment planted down by the lake, and the black cat insignia of the oldest division in the Army.* You felt you were in good company; Jap wasn't going to stop this lot.[20]

The first test of 14 Army and its new commander was the offensive by 15 Corps against the Japanese in Arakan in late 1943 – Operation Cudgel – and the battles that then ensued for control of the Maungdaw–Buthidaung road. This was the offensive for which Slim had long trained but for which, due to his elevation to 14 Army, he was unable to command directly. Lieutenant-General Philip Christison,† a colleague of Slim's from Camberley Staff College days, took his place in command of 15 Corps on 15 November 1943, and adopted without change the five-phase plan that Slim had prepared for the operation. The plan was for 15 Corps to advance to the Maungdaw–Buthidaung road while 36 Indian Division launched an amphibious assault against Akyab (Operation Bulldozer).‡ Fifteen Corps would then attack the defensive line the Japanese had built during the monsoon, and which the Japanese had named the 'Golden Fortress'. This formidable barrier stretched across the Mayu Range, following the route of the Maungdaw–Buthidaung road from Point 124, north of Razabil, west of the Bawli Road, on to Point 1301 through Letwedet and then on to the east of the Kalapanzin river. The whole defensive system was of considerable strength and was based around three powerful bastions. The first was in the centre at the Tunnels, another guarded the western approach at Razabil and the third guarded the eastern approach at Letwedet. The defences comprised networks of deep, well-constructed and well-camouflaged bunkers that were largely impervious to mortar and light artillery fire. The result, explained the 7 Indian Division historian, when added to 'the fanatical courage of the Japanese soldier, ordered to defend to the last man and last round . . . one has all the ingredients of the impregnable position.'[21]

5 Indian Division was tasked with seizing the Razabil bastion after

---

* 'Punch' Cowan's 17 Indian Division.

† He had previously commanded 33 Corps in India.

‡ This was a replacement for the more ambitious Operation Bullfrog, cancelled in December 1943, which had envisioned an attack against Akyab by 2 British Division.

which 7 Indian Division was to capture Buthidaung and attack the
Letwedet bastion from the rear. When these bastions had been seized
both divisions would simultaneously attack the central bastion, at the
Tunnels, from opposite sides. At the same time 81 West African Division
would advance as far as Kyauktaw, after which it would cut the enemy's
main line of communication between Kaladin and the Kalapanzin Valley.
Until Operation Cudgel could be launched, Christison was ordered to
continue minor operations to drive in the forward Japanese outposts,
forward of Razabil and Letwedet, and on the Teknaf Peninsula opposite
Maungdaw.

In order to create a line of communication over the Mayu Range to
supply 7 Indian Division a road had to be constructed on the track that led
for five miles through dense jungle over the Ngakyedauk Pass. This crossed
the Mayu Range some five miles north of the Maungdaw–Buthidaung
road. Converting the track over a precipitous pass with a 1,000-foot
rise and fall in three miles into a road by December 1943 was an
extraordinary engineering achievement. Where the Pass emerged into
the valley at Sinzweya an administration area was laid out to support 7
Indian Division's advance. It was here at Sinzweya, quickly nicknamed
the 'Admin Box', that the initial battle for northern Arakan would be
fought.

5 Indian Division completed taking over its new areas of responsibility
during the first week of November 1943. 7 Indian Division then crossed
over to the eastern side of the Mayu Range and took up widely dispersed positions on either side of the Kalapanzin river in preparation
for the forthcoming offensive against Buthidaung and Letwedet. By
December 123 Brigade* (of 5 Indian Division) was in close contact
with the Japanese outposts forward of Razabil, while to the east of
the range 89 and 33 Brigades† (of 7 Indian Division) were in contact
with Japanese positions forward of Letwedet. The 114 Brigade‡ was
east of the Kalapanzin, while 81 West African Division had reached
Kaladan.

In mid-January 1944, with his corps now concentrated, Christison

---

* Brigadier T.I.W. Winterton. Winterton had been Alexander's Chief of Staff in the
Burma Army.

† Brigadiers Crowther and Loftus-Tottenham respectively.

‡ Brigadier Michael Roberts.

launched his offensive. The first phase, Briggs' attack on the Japanese positions forward of Razabil, was given the rather unfortunate title of Operation Jericho. Unlike its Biblical namesake, the attackers were unable to engineer the collapse of the Japanese defences. In spite of all Slim's strictures to the contrary, and to his immense frustration, Briggs' plan involved a frontal assault by 161 Brigade.* Unsurprisingly, the attacks failed to dislodge the Japanese who demonstrated to Briggs something of the skill and tenacity with which they had repeatedly repelled the assaults on Donbaik exactly a year before. The lead battalion of the brigade attacked the Japanese hilltop position continuously for six days, but was unable to batter its way through the deeply dug and mutually supporting trench system. The brigade was weakened by having no armour or medium artillery in support. The only consolation was that by the middle of the month Briggs occupied Maungdaw, which allowed a seaborne line of communication to be opened up from Chittagong.

Falling into the same trap as Lloyd at Donbaik, Christison believed that the failure of Jericho was caused by the lack of artillery and air support and that with more *weight* of fire the Japanese positions could be overrun. By the third week of January the 25th Dragoons and the Corps Artillery Group had arrived and Christison accordingly ordered Briggs again to seize the Razabil fortress by what he described as an 'all-out' attack. This – Operation Jonathan – was of a considerably greater magnitude than Jericho. Briggs' plan for the new attack, however, was as unimaginative as the first. It entailed another frontal offensive by 161 Brigade against the Razabil Fortress and two of its surrounding hill features, known respectively as Tortoise and Scorpion.

The attacks once again proved abortive. A preliminary bombardment by aircraft of the United States Strategic Air Force opened the attack on 26 January 1944, but the ninety tons of high explosive dropped on the Japanese positions proved to be startlingly ineffective. Infantry then advanced under the cover of a creeping artillery and tank barrage fired directly into Japanese bunkers which had been exposed from their jungle camouflage by the aerial bombardment. However, in spite of the weight of support provided, the infantry yet again failed to penetrate any but the bunkers on the forward slopes of the positions. The Japanese positions proved virtually impregnable to frontal assault. Even 3.7-inch anti-aircraft

* Brigadier D.F.W. Warren.

guns fired in the ground role at point-blank range made very little impression on the log bunkers, a finding that merely repeated the lessons of Donbaik. The Japanese defended tenaciously and intelligently. Small groups hidden in the jungle forward of each locality counter-attacked the flanks of the attackers. Casualties in 161 Brigade mounted quickly and little of substance was achieved. 'Bunkers, wire, bamboo stakes . . . and withering fire', recorded the divisional historian, 'had brought our ambitious offensive to a halt.'[22]

Briggs' plan for and conduct of Operation Jericho and Jonathan was an undoubted set back for Slim. He was disappointed that the attacks ran counter to the ideas he had carefully developed in 15 Corps since June 1942. It was especially galling that Briggs had repeated many of the costly mistakes of Donbaik. It was a commonplace to him that frontal attacks, even when co-ordinated with aerial bombardment, artillery, and then pressed home by determined tank and infantry assault would prove fruitless, and 'did not shift the Japanese, borrowed deep into the hills, with their cunningly sited, wonderfully concealed, and mutually supporting machine guns.' He had said precisely this for nearly two years. As many others had shown before – invariably to their cost – it was easy to underestimate the Japanese. Briggs had now fallen into this trap.

Slim had no involvement in the planning for or conduct of either Jericho or Jonathan. Nor did he expect to. His approach to command was to explain to his subordinate commanders what had to be done, rather than to prescribe the precise details of how to do it, and then to let them draw up plans within the overall operational principles he had laid down. He especially eschewed the dangerous meddling in subordinate's plans of the likes of Irwin. Accordingly, this was Christison's battle and Slim was determined that responsibility for overseeing the battle plan lay not with himself but with the commander of 15 Corps. In the event, Slim did not publicly criticize Christison or Briggs for these failures at Razabil. Despite the fact that they did not conform to his tactical strictures or his principles for battle he commented merely that 'This was the first time we had assaulted an elaborate, carefully prepared position that the Japanese meant to hold to the last, and we expected it to be tough. It was.' He recognized that for both Christison and Briggs the battle for Razabil constituted their baptism of fire against the Japanese and was prepared to give them a second chance. As Gallabat had shown, Slim had himself been allowed to learn from his mistakes, and subsequently he deliberately adopted a policy of allowing commanders to do likewise so long as they proved that they were able to learn from them. In this case Slim was convinced that with the bitter experience of failure behind them, both Christison and Briggs would be better commanders and tacticians as a result.

He was right. Briggs' plan for the second series of assaults against Razabil in March 1944 was dramatically different. Attacks were made not against ground which the enemy had chosen to defend but against ground which was, or could be made, so vital to the enemy that the Japanese were forced to counter-attack in response. Encirclements, hooks from left or right flank, and guile – the message that Slim had been preaching since the retreat – replaced futile and expensive frontal assaults.

In contrast to the slow-learning Briggs, Messervy needed no persuading that Slim's approach to battle was the correct one. He already had a reputation as a bold and imaginative tactician from his command of his division in North Africa. Two weeks *before* Briggs mounted his abortive attacks against Razabil, Messervy had told his brigade and battalion commanders that the only way to attack Japanese positions was by infiltration rather than frontal attack. 'All experience in the Arakan has demonstrated the utter futility of a formal infantry attack supported by artillery concentrations or barrage against Japanese organised jungle positions,' he insisted. 'Normally, one appreciates that superior fire power and superior numbers are dominating assets,' he continued. 'Here this is NOT so; we shall get into trouble and have unnecessary casualties and set-backs if we fail to realise this clearly . . . The right answer to capturing Japanese positions and killing Japanese in this type of country and in these tactical circumstances is quite simple. It is infiltration and encirclement for which the country is extraordinarily suitable.'[23]

Messervy began issuing directives for his commanders, in which he carefully developed these ideas, towards the end of 1943. He emphasized the importance of avoiding stereotypical attacks, and to plan in advance using both guile and boldness. 'We want to be much more subtle and tricky,' he ordered on 28 October 1943. 'We must be constantly "putting a fast one" on the little yellow blighter – outwit him, out think him, out fight him and lick him.'[24] Two weeks later he argued that, although the conventional frontal attack seemed more attractive and straightforward, it was by far the most dangerous against the Japanese and the least likely to succeed in the difficult jungle country of Arakan. The only sure way of surprising and defeating the formidable defences of the Golden Fortress was by mounting brigade-sized infiltration attacks against his flank and rear, even though these would involve movement through difficult and unknown country. Messervy concluded: 'We will undoubtedly have a Neapolitan sandwich of British–Jap–British–Jap, but it will be one made by ourselves, and with the initiative in our hands will soon be transformed to British–Jap–British.'[25] Prophetic words indeed.


Having failed to penetrate the Razabil position, Christison switched the corps main effort across the Mayu Range at the end of January, leaving 5 Indian Division to maintain pressure on Razabil. Armour and artillery was transferred across the Ngakyedauk Pass to prepare 7 Indian Division for its attack on Buthidaung and Letwedet. 9 Brigade* of 5 Indian Division was also moved eastwards so as to free up 89 Brigade for the assault against Buthidaung. By early February Messervy's headquarters was located at Laung Chaung, a few miles to the north of Sinzweya. 33 Brigade was holding the front from the Mayu foothills to the Kalapanzin River, including two hills astride the Maungdaw–Buthidaung road – ABLE to the north and CAIN to the south – which had been captured from the Japanese in mid-January after fierce fighting. Messervy's plan was for 33 Brigade to cut the Maungdaw–Buthidaung road south of Letwedet village and then to form a corridor to allow 89 Brigade, together with the tanks of 25th Dragoons, to seize Buthidaung. At the same time 114 Brigade to the east of the Kalapanzin would deploy to cut off the east and rear of Buthidaung in order to prevent the withdrawal or reinforcement of the garrison. With Buthidaung captured, the division could then turn due west, and apply its whole effort to breaking down the Letwedet bastion.

Throughout January, as Briggs fruitlessly battered at the gates of Razabil, it became increasingly obvious to both Slim and Christison that the Japanese were planning to launch a counter-attack against 15 Corps. Slim had long supposed that the Japanese would seek to do this and expected that a counter-attack would involve at the very least an outflanking movement around the left of 7 Indian Division. It might

---

* Brigadier G.C. Evans. Evans had just been appointed to command 9 Brigade and had been in Arakan for two days.

even be something more ambitious, perhaps with the aim of reaching Chittagong. Slim was aware that the Japanese had significantly strengthened their forces in Burma, from four divisions early in 1943 to seven by November, and others were thought to be following. 'Kawabe . . . was not likely to have his army practically doubled for purely defensive purposes,' he reasoned. 'It would be unlike the Japanese to reinforce anywhere on that scale unless they intended seriously to attack.'

If the Japanese did attack, Slim planned to put into effect his 'hammer and anvil' plan. Under no circumstances were troops to withdraw. Units would form strong defensive boxes – his 'pivots of manoeuvre' (or 'hedgehogs' as Christison was to describe them) – and would hold firm, being supplied by air where necessary. They would thus create the anvil against which the hammer of 26 Indian Division would smash down on the Japanese from the north. The 'boxes' would also, once the first Japanese assaults had been stayed, take the offensive against the attacker at the earliest opportunity. Mountbatten, Giffard and Christison were all firmly in agreement with this plan.* Detailed preparations had been undertaken by HQ 14 Army to supply the boxes by air, should this be required, building on the few months of experience already garnered of supply dropping to the two brigades of 81 West African Division in the Kaladan Valley. 'The complete maintenance for over a division for several days, everything it would require, from pills to projectiles, from bully beef to boots, was laid out, packed for dropping, at the air strips', wrote Slim. 'We were as ready as we could be.'

Messervy had planned to launch his attack on Buthidaung on 7 February. On the 4th, however, Slim, ill with dysentery, was watching a flame-thrower demonstration at his headquarters at Comilla when he received a message that the Japanese attack had fallen on the rear of 7 Indian Division. Protected by the usual heavy mist which shrouded the Arakanese river valleys in the early morning at this time of year, a Japanese force of uncertain strength had emerged unexpectedly from the jungle and rushed Taung Bazar, six miles to the rear of Messervy's headquarters. Except for the final part of the Japanese column, containing food, ammunition and a complete medical unit which had been intercepted

---

* Christison was to go so far as to claim in his unpublished memoirs, written in his old age, that the idea for this plan was his, and that Slim was persuaded of its merits and authorized its implementation. This, of course, is pure fiction.

and destroyed, the force moved undetected through 7 Indian Division's left flank. No warning had been received and 89 Brigade, positioned north of Sinzweya and the area of the Ngakyedauk Chaung, and in its first day of rest from battle for three months, was immediately engaged. Despite his expectation that the Japanese would launch an attack, *Sakurai's* sudden assault took Slim by surprise. He had expected at least a day or two's notice of an impending offensive. Nor was the scale and depth of the offensive anticipated. He was not the only one to be taken back by the speed and audacity of the attack. 'I must freely admit that I had no inkling', conceded Christison, 'that the Japanese plan . . . envisaged the complete surrounding of 15 Corps, the cutting of its communications and an attack on Corps HQ.'[26]

The Japanese strategic intent was to mount an offensive in north Arakan of sufficient severity to make the British believe that this would be their main offensive effort against India. In reality, *Hanaya* planned to advance no further north than Goppe Bazaar. His key assumption was that when faced by the threat in Arakan, the British would immediately despatch their Army and Army Group reserves to the threatened region, leaving Imphal weakened and vulnerable to attack. Once the British had committed their reserves to support 15 Corps, the principal attack would then be launched against the 4 Corps positions in Manipur. The Arakan operation, planned by *Major General Sakurai Tokutaro* and appropriately called '*Ha-Go*' ('headlong attack'), involved some 3,500 troops in three parts. The first was the infiltration, by 'nocturnal as well as speedy and daring movements',[27] of a regimental infantry group under *Colonel Tanahashi*, together with artillery and engineers, along the east bank of the Kalapanzin through and around 114 Brigade, to capture Taung Bazaar. *Tanahashi* was then to wheel south-west to fall on the rear of 7 Indian Division, cutting the Ngakyedauk Pass and capturing the base at Sinzweya, from which he was to replenish himself. The second element involved a force of battalion size, under *Colonel Kubo*, striking west across the Mayu Range from Taung Bazar to block the road running north from Maungdaw to Bawli Bazar, thereby isolating 5 Indian Division. Finally, two remaining battalions under *Colonel Doi* were to maintain pressure across the whole of 7 Indian Division's front forward of the Maungdaw–Buthidaung road.

The twin characteristics of *Ha-Go* were to be bluff and deception. The Japanese assumed that, once attacked from the rear or from a flank, the British would, as they had done in the past, be frightened into a panicked defence of their lines of communication. The dislocation caused by *Tanahashi*'s unexpected descent on 7 Indian Division would, it was believed, force Messervy to retire in confusion back across the Mayu Range, during which the division would be destroyed. 5 Indian Division would then also be isolated and destroyed, a process which would be made all the quicker if Briggs attempted to escape northwards in the direction of Chittagong, where he would be blocked by *Kubo Force*. 'As they have previously suffered defeat,' *Sakurai* declared encouragingly in his order of the day on 4 February 1944, 'should a portion of them waver, the whole of them will get confused and victory is certain.'[28] It was expected that 15 Corps would be routed in 10 days. The Japanese had every reason to be confident. They had never before suffered a serious reverse at the hands of the British. *Sakurai*'s plan was characteristically bold, used surprise to the full, and was led by the man who had succeeded so brilliantly against 14 Indian Division the previous year. Morale was high. Confident of a quick victory they equipped themselves with rations for only seven days.

But in their complacency lay the seeds of their destruction. In making such confident assumptions about the projected course of the battle the Japanese committed the error that had led in part to the humiliating British defeats of previous years: they grossly underestimated their enemy. They knew nothing of the new commander of 14 Army or of the vigorous work he had undertaken to transform the training and motivation of his forces. No longer were the British cowed by threats of encirclement, or frightened by the bogey of the invincible Japanese 'superman'. Nor too were the Japanese faced by enemy commanders at every level who lacked the confidence and tactical expertise to maintain control of fast moving, savage and confusing battles against quick-witted and resourceful opponents. By February 1944 the troops of 15 Corps were confident and aggressive. It was the failure to recognize that they were now fighting a new enemy, one imbued with high morale, offensive spirit, trained to exacting standards and supported by robust new supply arrangements in the form of air supply that led directly to the Japanese defeat.

Three days of confused fighting followed *Tanahashi*'s surprise attack on Taung Bazar and his subsequent drive south-west to Sinzweya and the Ngakyedauk Pass. Moving north on 4 February to ascertain the extent of *Tanahashi*'s force, the two battalions of 89 Brigade became embroiled in intense but broken fighting against overwhelming odds as *Tanahashi* infiltrated his units southwards through the jungle. In attempting to stem the Japanese infiltration they provided the first shock to *Tanahashi*'s force, and gave the first indication that the task the Japanese had set themselves would not be as simple as they had led themselves to believe. Although unable to deny all approaches to *Tanahashi*'s force, the brigade put up a determined and unexpectedly strong resistance, causing the Japanese to waste time, energy and lives.

Nevertheless, *Tanahashi*'s troops pushed on and in the early morning mist of 6 February a force of about 500 stumbled into Messervy's divisional headquarters at Laung Chaung. Messervy had determined to obey Slim's and his own instructions to the letter by standing firm regardless of the consequences but his 120-strong headquarters was not made for defence and after being overrun he was forced to withdraw to the Admin Box at Sinzweya, which he reached in the early afternoon.* Over the following days troops cut off in small groups across the area made their way back through the jungle to Sinzweya.

Shortly after noon on 6 February Slim told Christison that he believed the attack on Taung Bazar to be the long-awaited Japanese offensive, and he therefore placed the whole of 26 Indian Division, the Army Reserve, at Christison's disposal. Mountbatten made arrangements to provide the aircraft necessary for the airlift of supplies to 7 Indian Division, and Giffard had arranged, two days before, for the concentration at Chittagong of 36 Indian Division, part of the Army Group Reserve, to be speeded up.† The two brigades of 36 Indian Division had been specially trained for amphibious operations and were tasked with mounting an assault on Akyab – Operation Bulldozer – designed to support the advance of 15 Corps. Christison ordered Lomax to move two brigades to Bawli Bazaar immediately and then to launch a counter-offensive against the Japanese in the Kalapanzin valley, hammering them against the anvil that was being

---

* This is from Evans' account (p. 127). Others state that Messervy did not reach Sinzweya until the afternoon of 7 February after spending twenty-four hours in the jungle.

† The 11 Army Group reserve was 33 Corps, commanded by Christison up until November 1943, and thereafter by Lieutenant-General Montagu Stopford. It had three partly-trained divisions, a commando brigade and the units allotted to Wingate's 'Special Force'.

formed by the defensive boxes of the surrounded 7 Indian Division. The Japanese hope that Slim and Giffard would divert their reserves to Arakan was realized far more quickly than they had expected and in consequence dramatically exacerbated – in their view – the vulnerability of 4 Corps in Manipur. But it was the only one of their ambitions that would be realized during their offensive.

In the 7 Indian Division area – some seven miles wide by four miles deep – order, certainty and purpose lay behind initial confusion. In accordance with their training and the plans of the Army Commander, units stood resolutely firm, digging themselves into positions of all-round defence when they found themselves to be surrounded, and not withdrawing in panic as *Sakurai* had expected. Within days a number of 'boxes' had been formed which, as the battle for north Arakan developed over the coming weeks, became the focus for 7 Indian Division's defence. From these positions, as Slim had planned, they fought off their attackers. On 7 February Slim ordered that 7 Indian Division be put on air supply, and because of the high degree of preparation that had taken place, was able to turn it on immediately. 'Air supply for 15 Corps was on,' wrote Slim, 'and, as long as needed, never faltered.'

Two days after *Tanahashi* fell on Taung Bazar, *Doi Force* began fierce attacks on 33 Brigade along the original positions on the Maungdaw–Buthidaung line in an attempt to drive their way north from the area of Letwedet and to link up with their compatriots in the north. But here too Japanese expectations were confounded. Over the next two days of fierce hand-to-hand fighting, instead of overrunning 33 Brigade as they confidently expected, they succeeded only in capturing a mortar position, the mortars of which were successfully recovered a few days later. By this stage 89 Brigade had done all it could to lessen the impact of *Tanahashi*'s assault in the north and was ordered, as best it could, to fall back to cover the rear of 33 Brigade, while troops in isolated positions were ordered to make their way into the Admin Box at Sinzweya to bolster the garrison.

The Admin Box was the weak link in 7 Indian Division's defences. It had been deemed to be sufficiently to the rear to avoid the effects of any Japanese counter-offensive. Accordingly it was not designed for defence, and formed a bowl at the foot of the Ngakyedauk Pass about 1,200 yards in length. For the most part it was devoid of vegetation and was surrounded on all sides by jungle-clad hills. It was thus remarkably vulnerable to direct observation, fire and encirclement. Nevertheless, it was critical to the viability of 15 Corps' defence as it provided the door to the Ngakyedauk Pass and contained the vast cache of stores built up to support Messervy's offensive. If it were captured it would have fueled *Tanahashi* almost indefinitely. To complicate matters it was manned, initially at least, largely by administrative and logistical personnel. However, in spite of these weaknesses it unwittingly became the centre piece of 7 Indian Division's defence. On 6 February, therefore, Christison ordered HQ 9 Brigade to take control of its defence, and to defend it at all costs. Despite its motley garrison the Admin Box, as Slim affirms 'held against the odds.' That it was able to do so was vindication in part of Slim's insistence that all troops – not just those in the combat arms – were to be trained to stand and fight. The first Japanese attack on the Admin Box fell on the evening of 6 February and was repulsed by the soldiers of a mule company.

By 8 February the extent of the Japanese encirclement had become apparent. The Japanese were in control of the Ngakyedauk Pass and had thus effectively cut off 7 Indian Division from the remainder of 15 Corps. Additionally, *Kubo Force* had managed to reach – and block – the road between Maungdaw and Bawli Bazaar. The Japanese were able also to concentrate a significant air effort over Arakan. For the first six days of *Ha-Go Sakurai* was supported by forty-five aircraft of *7 Air Brigade*, and in the first ten days some 350 sorties were flown, largely against 7 Indian Division. For a further eighteen days the Admin Box remained surrounded and under constant attack by infantry, artillery and air. Although there were insufficient troops fully to man the perimeter, the defenders, key among which were the tanks of 25th Dragoons, beat off successive attempts to overrun the Box. A new phenomenon also appeared: despite the ferocity of the fighting and the daily increase in casualties morale did not diminish. Christison even asserted that morale increased as the siege of Sinzweya developed. By the end even non-combatants were confident enough to join in the defence and even went on patrol.[29] This was 7 Indian Division's baptism of fire in Burma. It was not found wanting. Caught 'as they were widely deployed for offensive action', records the divisional historian, 'surprised and surrounded, all communications cut, and their divisional headquarters overrun, it says much for the fortitude of the troops, the sound doctrine and skill of leaders and the confidence born of high morale and *esprit de corps* that at the end of four days it was the enemy who was beginning to have qualms as to the outcome.'[30] 'It was good to see how the attitude had altered from that of 1943' wrote Slim. 'Now confidence and the offensive spirit reigned in everyone.'

Within a week of the opening of their offensive the Japanese began to feel the effect of the huge risks they had taken. The decision to enhance mobility by travelling lightly made them vulnerable to starvation and disease if they failed to capture British stores. This was the fate that befell both *Tanahashi* and *Kubo*. By 12 February their supply situation was critical. The act of passing *Sakurai's* force through 7 Indian Division meant that subsequent resupply to both *Tanahashi* and *Kubo* had to run the gauntlet of the aggressive defence adopted by those units of 7 Indian Division not trapped in Sinzweya. This quickly reduced resupply to a trickle. By the second week of the siege 7 Indian Division was killing hundreds of Japanese every day, and it was increasingly apparent to Slim that *Sakurai's* position was hopeless. Lomax's division had quickly recaptured Taung Bazar and had begun to press down from the north, with 71 Brigade to the east of the Kalapanzin and 4 Brigade* to the west. To the west 123 Brigade of 5 Indian Division was fighting through the Ngakyedauk Pass. To the south, the Japanese maintained heavy pressure on 33 Brigade's positions throughout the period, particularly on 'Able', but repeated attacks made no progress and were repulsed with heavy loss to the enemy.

But, as Slim had foreseen, the Japanese refused to accept failure, and continued to throw themselves profitlessly against the British boxes which, after the first supply drops on 11 February, began to increase in strength rather than become weaker. Messervy's prediction that the new tactics would result in the enemy being sandwiched between the combined might of 5, 26 and 17 Indian Divisions was now fulfilled. By 13 February Slim knew that he would win the battle. Disastrously for the Japanese, *Hanaya* did not. He failed to realize that the opportunity for breakthrough diminished with every day that passed without the capture of British stores. No amount of fanatical bravery could make up for the lack of supplies reaching *Tanahashi* and *Kubo Force* which, now trapped, rapidly grew weaker. The diary of a wounded Japanese officer dated 13 February 1944, later found on his dead body, complained: 'Planes are bringing whiskey, beer, butter,

---

* Brigadier A.W. Lowther.

cheese, jam, corned beef and eggs in great quantities to the enemy. I am starving.'[31]

Instead of withdrawing his troops *Hanaya* allowed *Sakurai* to continue to battle fruitlessly against 7 Indian Division until death, starvation and, in a few instances, despair, suicide or surrender overtook them. On 14 February, simultaneous attacks were ordered by *Tanahashi* in the north against the Ngakyedauk Chaung, and in the south against the positions held so determinedly by 33 Brigade. The northern attack fell only on the Admin Box, however, and was repulsed.

Between 17 and 24 February the final battle for the Boxes was fought. On the night of 15 February HQ 89 Brigade with a battalion moved into the Admin Box to bolster the defences on the eastern sector and during the day that followed patrols of 4 Brigade reached the Laung Chaung where Messervy's headquarters had been two weeks before. 33 Brigade began going over to the offensive across much of its sector and 114 Brigade established contact with troops of 71 Brigade. On 23 February 123 Brigade secured the Ngakyedauk Pass from the west and met up with 89 Brigade, and on the following day the Admin Box was relieved. Immediately, the 500 casualties from Sinzweya were evacuated, the pass was opened and air supply to 7 Indian Division ceased. The relief of Sinzweya signified the end of the Japanese offensive. Weak and starving, the few survivors of what had begun as a bold and promising enterprise struggled through the jungle to the relative safety of the Golden Fortress. The only Japanese success was against 81 West African Division. Following a rapid advance down the Kaladan Valley, Woolner's units were counter-attacked by four battalions of *54 Division* and pushed back to the area of Kaladan Village.

Slim wrote with satisfaction:

> The hammer and the anvil met squarely and the Japanese between disintegrated. *Kubo Force*, among the cliffs and caves of the Mayu range, was destroyed to the last man in a snarling, tearing dog-fight that lasted days, with no quarter given or expected. Of *Sakurai's* seven thousand men who had penetrated our lines, over five thousand bodies were found and counted, many more lay undiscovered in the jungle; hundreds died of exhaustion before they reached safety; few survived.

It was the first major Japanese defeat in Burma and as such represented a turning point in British fortunes. It gave an enormous boost to the morale of the Army as a whole. For the first time the Japanese had been significantly bettered in battle by opponents they had come to despise. Slim's defensive concept provided the framework for the success of 7 Indian Division and the thwarting of Japanese plans, and the merciless training regime he had imposed on 15 Corps nearly two years earlier gave it the substance. Mountbatten's willingness and ability to provide the aircraft necessary for the air dropping operation, the respective leadership of Messervy, Briggs, Lomax and their brigade and battalion commanders, together with the renewed fighting spirit and efficiency of the troops, were also crucial determinants of victory.

During the twenty-one days of the main action over 1,600 tons of supplies were dropped to the besieged troops with the loss of only one aircraft. But air supply was not solely responsible for the success of 7 Indian Division in first halting, and then routing, the Japanese. The air supply of 7 Indian Division began only after *Sakurai*'s assault had been stayed and his ambitions denied, by which time the Japanese were well on the way to defeat. The first air drop on the Admin Box took place on 11 February. The new policy of standing firm and fighting back, the staunchness and aggressiveness of 15 Corps, especially 89th, 33rd and 9th Brigades, was responsible for *Sakurai*'s defeat. So long as the units of 7 Indian Division held firm, and 5 and 26 Indian Divisions pressed on from the outside, cutting *Sakurai*'s own line of communication, thus inhibiting their own resupply, the Japanese position was untenable. The air supply operation was a remarkable feat, but proved to be more important in enabling the British quickly to resume the offensive when the time came than in bringing about the Japanese defeat in the first place.

A major development in the use of air power during the Arakan battles was the evacuation of wounded by light aeroplane directly from the battlefield. Seriously wounded troops were flown out of the 114 Brigade Box at Kwazon by American pilots flying light aeroplanes. A makeshift airstrip was constructed in 11 days and in the week following 16 February 'some 240 seriously wounded were flown out . . . including many from the 33rd and some from the 89th Brigade, brought across the river under escort of strong fighting patrols.'[32] One hospital during fighting later in the Burma campaign, recounted Slim, received 'over eleven thousand British casualties straight, in their filthy blood-soaked battledress, from the front line. The total deaths in that hospital were twenty three. Air evacuation', he concluded, 'did more to save lives than any other agency.' During Wingate's second expedition it was not uncommon for badly wounded men to be 'on their way to hospital, in an aircraft, ten minutes after being hit.'[33] By contrast, men who had been wounded during Operation Longcloth had to be abandoned to their fate. The knowledge that they would receive the best care possible if wounded and not be left to the tender mercies of the Japanese was of very great importance to the troops and contributed significantly to the raising of morale across the Army during 1944 and 1945.

The destruction of *Hanaya*'s offensive meant that Slim could now return his thoughts to Operation Cudgel. The importance of seizing the Maungdaw–Buthidaung road, and thus the Golden Fortress, remained. But he was faced with two problems. First, the delay to Messervy's offensive by a month because of *Ha-Go* meant that it would not now be possible to mount an amphibious attack against Akyab before the monsoon arrived in May. This freed up 36 British Division, which Giffard accordingly allotted to Slim on 10 February. Slim's priority now was to capture the Golden Fortress. He intended thereafter to abandon all positions east of the Mayu Range and to maintain only a strong garrison in Maungdaw during the monsoon. Akyab would have to wait until a later date. Slim's second problem was that he knew that the Japanese were about to take the offensive on the main front in Assam. He had assumed as early as October 1943 that the Japanese would attack 4 Corps: the question was when? As early as 13 February Slim was convinced that *Ha-Go* was intended merely as a strategic feint to draw in British reserves to Arakan prior to launching the main Japanese attack against Imphal. Accordingly, on 5 March Slim ordered that once Razabil and Buthidaung had been captured, 5 and 26 Indian Divisions were to be withdrawn, 5 Indian Division to Imphal to act as 4 Corps reserve, and 7 Indian Division to Chittagong for a rest and to form the Army reserve. 25 Indian Division, commanded by Major General 'Taffy' Davies, would come forward from India to take over the left flank of 15 Corps from Briggs' division and 36 Indian Division would take the right from Messervy. These two fresh divisions would then have responsibility for the final phase of Operation Cudgel, the attack on the heart of the Golden Fortress at the Tunnels.

Fifteen Corps resumed the offensive on 5 March 1944. To the east of the Mayu Range Messervy's aggressive pursuit of the remnants of *Sakurai Force* led to the seizure of Buthidaung on 11 March. To the west of the range Briggs tried again to reduce the Razabil fortress. His approach was now markedly different than before, and was characterized by both stealth and guile. 'The plan was ... to close a tight ring around the fortress by surprise, to bring 161 Brigade in from the foothills to the south, and to sever the enemy's lines of communication,' recorded the divisional historian. 'The success of a scheme designed to bypass the fortress and appear on dominating features, so isolating it from the rear, depended on accurate preliminary reconnaissance both of the route and final positions. Officers of 161 Brigade spent several days behind the Japanese lines, making these reconnaissances. And their daring and careful observation was amply repaid when the operation began.'[34] The operation was a resounding success. After two months of frontal attacks the Japanese were entirely surprised by the skilled night insertion of the brigade behind their position and Razabil fell in fighting between 9 and 12 March 1944.

New tactics accompanied Briggs' successful new approach to the problem of reducing Japanese defences. Firepower was employed selectively and intelligently, rather than as a battering ram. Short rapid surprise artillery concentrations to help the infantry onto their objectives were employed in place of the lengthy bombardments which had consistently failed to make any real impact on Japanese positions in the past. Bunkers were exposed from the surrounding jungle by light artillery and then demolished with direct sniping by tanks. Cannon fire from ground-attack aircraft proved to be of the greatest value. While the infantry were closing in, dummy attacks were made to keep the defenders' heads down during the few vital minutes required to allow the attacker into the enemy's trenches. Tanks were also used to get behind enemy positions to snipe against the reverse slope bunkers so that they could be neutralized and destroyed.

Using these methods the Western Tunnel was seized by 36 British Division on 27 March and the Eastern Tunnel was taken after fierce fighting on 6 April. The final Japanese position was Point 551, the loss of which had prevented Slim's chances of retaining the Maungdaw–Buthidaung road exactly a year before. 'It was under attack throughout April, during which 26 Indian Division delivered three separate assaults on it. Its capture on 3 May, at the fourth attempt,' he recalled 'was the toughest fighting of the whole Tunnels battle.'

At the time the success of 15 Corps – first in stopping *Ha-Go* and then in capturing the Golden Fortress – was trumpeted by HQ SEAC and India Command as great victories. Were they? Calvert rather dismissively comments that during Operation Cudgel the Japanese were vastly out-numbered by the British, the inference being that Slim overreacted to the threat in Arakan by using a sledge hammer to crack a nut, and that such preponderance of strength made a British victory inevitable.[35] In total numbers, measured across the campaign as a whole, Calvert's claim is true. Nevertheless, pure statistics disguise the true picture on the battlefield. At the decisive point – the eastern exit of the Ngakyedauk Pass – where the Japanese concentrated their forces to achieve overwhelming superiority in early February 1944, the Japanese were beaten off by the dispersed and unprepared troops of 7 Indian Division, many of them administrative units, all of whom were nevertheless determined to stand their ground and fight. The Japanese were unable to break into the scattered but defiant brigade positions even when they enjoyed a substantial local superiority in both ground troops and aircraft. Where and when it was needed, the British did not enjoy a superiority of numbers over the enemy: the reverse in fact was the case. But these troops were imbued with a fighting spirit yet unseen in the campaign to date. It was this fighting spirit in support troops – men who never expected to be in the front line of the battle – which so emphatically emphasized the change which had come over the British–Indian Army since the dark days of May 1943. There is no doubt that 7 Indian Division's victory was genuine and well deserved.

Second, Calvert's criticism fails to acknowledge Slim's plan for the battle. Slim was determined to smash *Sakurai's* force resoundingly, and was prepared to take significant risks with his reserves in order to achieve this. Fifteen Corps was faced by the whole of *55 Division* and two extra battalions, with another one – *54 Division* – also moving in. Slim reasoned that 'apart from the fact that we should need a preponderance in strength if we were to attack, I had no intention, if I could avoid it, of pitting my army division for division against the Japanese on their own ground.' Fourteen Army needed a victory. 'I hoped that the Arakan campaign would be the first step towards building up a tradition of success', he argued later, 'and I did not intend to take more risks than I had to at this early stage. Later we would take on twice or thrice our number in Japanese divisions – but not yet. At this time all my plans were based on ensuring a superiority in numbers and force at the decisive points.'

It is arguable that Slim was too sanguine about the threat to Imphal and that he should not have risked using his reserve in Arakan when it was evident that an offensive against Manipur was in the offing. In retrospect, Slim admitted that it was a close run thing. However, at the time he judged the risk to be acceptable. If generalship is judged on the management of risk, Slim's response to *Ha-Go* is difficult to fault. He knew that, although *Ha-Go* was likely to be but a strong feint, he had nevertheless to crush it decisively. This left him with little choice but to use everything he had to smash *Hanaya*'s offensive, remove the Japanese threat to Eastern Bengal for good and thereafter to switch his effort to the defeat of the Japanese army on the Chindwin. Not to have used his reserve to defeat *Ha-Go* would have put at risk the chance he had decisively to defeat *Sakurai*. An equally important consideration was that a failure to destroy *Ha-Go* would have meant defaulting on his promises to 15 Corps, and would have done irreparable damage to the confidence of his troops.

Slim was clear that the success of Operation Cudgel was a considerable achievement. If not a battle on the scale of many others during the Second World War, it was a turning point as significant as El Alamein and Stalingrad. The enemy had been turned away from the gate of India and had been resoundingly defeated. 'For the first time', he asserted, 'a British force had met, held and decisively defeated a major Japanese attack, and followed this up by driving the enemy out of the strongest possible natural positions that they had been preparing for months and were determined to hold at all costs.'

The Japanese had, nevertheless, thwarted the plan to advance to Rathedaung and had removed the possibility of an amphibious assault on Akyab by 36 Indian Division. They had also forced Slim and Giffard respectively to concentrate Army and Army Group reserves to Arakan, leaving Manipur dangerously weak. However, these were insignificant achievements compared to the far-reaching success of 15 Corps in smashing *Ha-Go*, capturing the Golden Fortress and inflicting massive and irreplaceable casualties on the Japanese. The victory provided an enormous tonic for British morale. Equally importantly, as Henry Maule avers, it shook the confidence 'of an arrogant enemy exulting in his omnipotence.

The fact that Messervy's men had taken fifty Jap prisoners, something previously unheard of in Burma, proved this point emphatically.'[36] 'It was a victory', Slim insisted, 'about which there could be no argument, and its effect, not only on the troops engaged but on the whole Fourteenth Army, was immense. The legend of Japanese invincibility in the jungle, so long fostered by so many who should have known better, was smashed.' With the long struggle for the Imphal Plain yet to come, it was a victory that could not have come at a more opportune time.

It was also a battle which fully vindicated Slim's approach to war. Hard and realistic training had created a soldier able to cope with the demands of the jungle battlefield, and against a tenacious enemy. Firm bases, air supply and the movement of reserves to counter the otherwise debilitating effects of infiltration and encirclement proved outstandingly successful. Slim had designed a pattern for victory, and 15 Corps had given the British their first success against the Japanese in the war. It was the perfect foundation upon which 14 Army as a whole could build as the threat to Manipur drew nigh.

# 6

# Operation U-GO

On 17 January 1944 Churchill confided to General Ismay, his chief of staff, his belief that the threat of a Japanese invasion of India had passed.[1] The picture from Comilla, however, was far different. By January 1944 it had become apparent to Slim that a Japanese offensive against Manipur was imminent. Patrol activity, information from 'V' Force agents along the Chindwin, secret signal intelligence and aerial reconnaissance all pointed unerringly towards this certainty.[2] What Churchill could not see from London was the threat to the security of Burma that the Japanese perceived to emanate from Imphal. The Japanese had determined as early as September 1943 to launch a massive and decisive pre-emptive strike against the town to remove this threat. To be called Operation *U-Go*, the offensive, based on the now low Japanese estimation of British military prowess, was confidently expected to be over in a month. In order to draw away Slim's reserves it was planned to mount an offensive by *Lieutenant General Sakurai Shozo's 28 Army* (Operation *Ha-Go*) in Arakan two or three weeks before.

Slim's sources of information were such that by the end of the month he knew that 4 Corps faced attack by the whole of the newly formed *15 Army*, commanded by the fifty-six-year-old Lieutenant-General *Mutaguchi Renya*.* He was even able to put a date on

* *Mutaguchi* took command of *15 Army* from *Iida* in March 1943.

the start of the offensive: 15 March 1944. It was also clear that the Japanese attack would be conducted in great strength with three divisions (*15, 31* and *33*), an *INA Division* of seven thousand[3] and a Tank Regiment: in total some 84,000 fighting troops. It appeared to Slim that the Japanese intended to capture Imphal as the first step in a campaign to break into the Brahmaputra Valley to cut the line of communication to the northern front at Ledo. Slim's initial assessment was that *Mutaguchi* would attempt to isolate and destroy his two frontline divisions in Manipur and cut the Imphal–Dimapur road at Kohima to prevent reinforcements reaching Imphal. If successful *U-Go* would prevent any further allied operations from either Imphal or Ledo against Burma or in support of China, probably for the remainder of the war.

The knowledge of an imminent Japanese offensive posed Slim a number of immediate difficulties. The first was that the focus of his attention at this time remained the desperate battles in Arakan. The second was that his forces in Manipur were building themselves up slowly to mount their own limited offensive into Burma, and were not configured or prepared to receive an attack. Lieutenant-General Geoffrey Scoones' 4 Corps (17, 20 and 23 Indian Divisions) provided the forward defence of India along the eastern frontier with Burma.[4] Major-General Ouvry Roberts' 23 Indian Division was in reserve with 254 Tank Brigade[5] on the Imphal plain. 17 and 20 Indian Divisions, however, were based well forward of Imphal in two widely dispersed areas of operation on a front which, running parallel to the Chindwin river, stretched for some 250 miles from the Chin Hills in the south to the Naga Hills in the north.

Since December 1943 the primary task of 4 Corps had been to dominate the hill country east and south of the Imphal plain in order to prepare for the offensive across the Chindwin that was planned for the spring of 1944. Scoones' headquarters was in Imphal where, in anticipation of the forthcoming offensive, it was joined by an increasing array of supply dumps, hospitals, workshops and airfields. The offensive was intended as a limited affair, designed to support both the insertion of Wingate's Special Force into central Burma and the advance towards Myitkyina from Ledo of Stilwell's Chinese forces. Consequently 20 Indian Division at Tamu was preparing to advance across the Chindwin, and to support this 4 Corps had built up extensive supply and administrative bases along the line of communication to Imphal and thence to the sprawling base at Dimapur. A large forward base, sufficient to supply two divisions, had been established close to the front at Moreh. Because of these arrangements 4 Corps was ill-positioned and vulnerable if the Japanese were to attack.

Forty miles long and twenty miles deep, the Imphal plain was ideally suited for air and land operations against Burma, a fact readily recognized by the Japanese. However, its location and topography made Imphal difficult to supply. Indeed, the logistical problems associated with maintaining 4 Corps in Imphal arguably posed Slim's single greatest difficulty at this time. There were but two roads between Manipur and the rest of Assam, only one of which was all-weather and useable for heavy traffic, although single-lane for much of it. This road travelled a difficult, mountainous route for 138 miles from Dimapur to Imphal *via* the mountain village of Kohima in the Naga Hills. Although the only viable road into Imphal, it ran parallel for much of its route with the Chindwin, which made it vulnerable to being cut at any point. The second route – the Silchar track – was but an animal track that ran due west from Imphal *via* Bishenpur for 130 miles to Silchar in Assam.

The limited volume of these routes restricted the number of fighting units that could be sustained on the Imphal plain at any one time to the three divisions of 4 Corps. Equally, the rate at which reinforcements could be fed into the plain was limited. Building up the strength necessary to mount an offensive into Burma, or indeed to defend Imphal should it come under attack, was problematic. In order to prepare for 4 Corps' forthcoming offensive a massive upgrading of this line of communication was required, as its peacetime capacity was a mere 600 tons per day, a fraction of that required. By November 1943 this capacity had been increased to 3,070 tons and by June 1944 it had struggled up to 4,690 tons per day. By March 1945, after herculean efforts to improve its capacity, it was carrying 8,630 tons per day. Slim was later to wish that he had taken the risk of moving an extra division into the Imphal plain in advance of the expected Japanese offensive despite the logistical difficulties that this would have entailed. None of this was made easier by the fact that supplies for what he described as his 'Cinderella' army, 'receiving only what its richer sisters in Africa and Europe could spare', remained desperately short throughout the war.[6] As an example of Burma's relative priority in the minds of allied strategy-makers, Mountbatten recalled how on one occasion the 'order was received to send back 5.5-inch ammunition to the European theatre at a time when it appeared to be the only real answer to the Japanese fox-hole.'[7]

Slim's second difficulty was caused by the fact that, by sending his reserves to Arakan, he had reduced his flexibility to reinforce 4 Corps quickly. On 6 March Slim ordered 5 Indian Division to make its way to Imphal during the period 13 March and 14 April as planned, and for 7 Indian Division then to be withdrawn from Arakan and placed in 14 Army reserve. These moves could not be completed quickly, however. The lack of a land link between Arakan and Manipur meant that troops had to be laboriously transported by road and rail back through Chittagong and thence into Manipur *via* the Brahmaputra Valley and Dimapur. In the event the speed and power of *Ha-Go* ruled Slim's plans obsolete.

The experienced and self-confident 17 Indian Division, containing the predominantly Gurkha 48[*] and 63 Brigades,[†] had moved to Tiddim, 163 miles south of Imphal in the Chin Hills, in November 1943. The division was still under the able command of 'Punch' Cowan. Tiddim was connected to Imphal by a road which remained, even after many months of painful upgrading work by Cowan's troops during 1943, little more than a donkey track for much of its route. This provided a serious problem for the division's maintenance. Worse still, it ran parallel with the Chindwin front for its whole length and was vulnerable to being cut with comparative ease at any point. This weakness was to be exploited to the full in Japanese planning. 20 Indian Division (32,[‡] 80[**] and 100[††] Brigades) arrived in Manipur in November 1943, and was centred on Tamu, thirty miles south-east of Imphal. The journey to Tamu from Imphal followed a metalled road for twenty-five miles to the key airfield at Palel, on the edge of the Imphal plain, after which it rose steeply to Shenam at the western edge of the six-thousand-foot mountains that separated the Imphal plain from the Kabaw Valley. Shenam was the

[*] Brigadier R.T. Cameron.
[†] Brigadier A.E. Cumming, then G.W.S. Burton.
[‡] Brigadier D.A.L. Mackenzie.
[**] Brigadier Sam Greaves.
[††] Brigadier W.A.L. James.

final obstacle the Japanese would have to overcome in an attack on Imphal from the south-east. The position ran between Shenam Saddle and Nippon Hill three-and-a-half miles further east. From Nippon Hill the road then ran for a further twenty-five miles to Tamu. From Tamu, the Chindwin lay a further seventy miles to the east along the same unmade road by which Slim had brought Burma Corps in May 1942. 20 Indian Division was not yet battle-tried but it was well-trained and well-led. Its commander, Major-General Douglas Gracey, was highly capable and respected. He 'had no great gifts of oratory or capacity for the grand gesture', recalled Harry Seaman, the author of an authoritative account of the momentous battle at Sangshak, 'but his troops came to feel great affection for his steely determination coupled with total dedication to their welfare.'[8]

Scoones' third division – 23 Indian Division (1,[*] 37[†] and 49[‡] Brigades) – had guarded Imphal since the start of the campaign in 1942. Major-General Reginald Savory had handed over command in 1943 to the forty-one-year-old Major-General Ouvry Roberts. Roberts, a Royal Engineer, had been Slim's chief staff officer in 10 Indian Division in Iraq and was highly regarded by all who served with and under him. Prior to taking over the division in July 1943, Roberts had been the successful BGS of 4 Corps, handing over responsibility for that job to the equally well regarded Geoffrey Evans.

It was no coincidence that one of the pre-eminent characteristics of all three divisional commanders was the high priority each placed upon hard, realistic training. In this they each proved to be a mirror of the Army Commander. Indeed, Gracey's training policy for 20 Indian Division, promulgated on 13 April 1942 while Burcorps was extricating itself from Burma and only days after 20 Indian Division had been formed, was a model of sound, practical common sense that was to require no revision in the years that followed.[9] Likewise, Roberts, when he was BGS of 4 Corps, established a highly successful 4 Corps Training School at Shillong, the capital of Assam, in 1943.[10]

During late 1943 and early 1944 the tempo of operations for both

[*] Brigadier R.C. McCay.

[†] Brigadier H.V. Collingridge. On 5 June Collingridge was replaced by John Marindin.

[‡] Brigadier F.A. Esse.

17 and 20 Indian Division intensified. Both divisions were tasked with continuous and intensive patrolling in order to maintain contact with the Japanese and to obtain intelligence of their moves and intentions. While neither side gained a decisive advantage in these operations they nevertheless acted to raise the confidence of the troops. This period proved also to be an important learning experience for 4 Corps, and especially for those units which had no direct experience to date of the Japanese.[11]

Since assuming command of 14 Army Slim had been troubled as to how best he should take the war to the Japanese, particularly if they did not plan to venture outside Burma. If allied policy were to change, and a land offensive was eventually required, it would involve elements of 14 Army launching itself across the Chindwin, and sustaining offensive operations deep into Burma thereafter. Slim knew that if he were forced to mount such an operation in his present state he would have to do so at an overwhelming disadvantage. With his precarious line of communication running back from the Chindwin to Dimapur through Tamu, Imphal and Kohima, he would have great difficulty in building up a force strong enough first to cross the Chindwin unmolested, to sustain his forces on the eastern shore and then to overcome the might of the Japanese Burma Area Army in decisive battle. His army would have to advance at the end of ever-increasing and tenuous lines of communication and with forces that would barely match his opponents in terms of numbers and materiel. In short, without first reducing the military effectiveness of the Japanese in Burma, Slim knew that he would have great difficulty in mounting a successful offensive at all.

From the moment he knew that *15 Army* was to attack Manipur, Slim determined to use the Japanese offensive to his own strategic advantage. The prospect of a massive Japanese attack against Imphal suggested a simple solution to Slim's quandary. It might be possible, he thought, to seek the degradation of the Japanese in Burma by enticing *15 Army* into a major battle in India in circumstances favourable to 14 Army. Slim could thus exploit his growing strength in aircraft, armour and artillery while simultaneously exploiting the enemy's weaknesses in logistics and resupply, problems that would be compounded by the onset of the monsoon at the end of May. Slim had first mapped out this approach in the context of the first abortive campaign in Arakan in early 1943. 'The surest way of quick success in Burma', he wrote, 'is not to hammer our way with small forces through jungle where the Japanese has every advantage, but to make him occupy as much area as possible, string himself out until he is weak, and then, when we have got him stretched, come at him from the sea and air.' 'I was tired of fighting the Japanese when they had a good line of communications behind them and I had an exorable [*sic*] one,' he reasoned in 1944. 'This time I would reverse the procedure.' If they could first be comprehensively defeated, the way would then be open for Slim to launch his own offensive into Burma should it be required.

During January and February 1944, building upon what he knew of Japanese intentions, Slim translated this concept into a plan. *Mutaguchi* was to be allowed to advance deep into Manipur, while 4 Corps withdrew from the forward positions it had been consolidating since late 1943 to occupy positions around the periphery of the Imphal plain which would then hold fast against the Japanese attack. Key points, including Imphal town itself and the six airfields on the plain, would be transformed into self-supporting bastions capable of defending themselves unaided for at least 10 days. Allowing the Japanese to advance directly onto Imphal would serve to extend their lines of communication back through difficult country to the Chindwin, where they would lie prey to the exertions of the Allied air forces and, when the monsoon fell, the depredations of the weather. In a lecture given in 1946 he explained: 'It was no good in 1944 pushing a small force into Central Burma where, with a great river and 150 miles of jungle hills behind it, it would meet double its number of enemy. We therefore decided to pull in to the Imphal area and meet the Japanese offensive there where, for the first time, he would have all those disadvantages.'[12] By contrast, 4 Corps would, by withdrawing, enjoy vastly reduced lines of communication and benefit from concentration. Slim's primary concern was to ensure that he had overwhelming force at the point of main effort. As 'much as our troops had improved in training and morale,' he wrote, 'I did not want the first big clashes to be on equal terms, division for division. I wanted superior strength at the decisive point for the opening of the struggle.' By pulling 4 Corps back towards Imphal Slim's intention was to grasp the initiative, not relinquish it, but doing so would deliberately send a different message to the Japanese. Pulling back his forces from their forward positions to the Imphal plain would be precisely what *Mutaguchi* expected, and would reinforce Japanese expectations of an early and easy victory. The Japanese assumed that the British would have no stomach for a fight and would crumble quickly under pressure. Slim's hope, however, was that once concentrated, with a clear superiority in armour, artillery and air power, 4 Corps would be able to create a defensive area far too strong for *Mutaguchi* to break.

Slim knew that, in addition to their penchant for pressing ultimately fruitless attacks, another weakness would allow the Japanese to fall into his trap. As he had observed, Japanese commanders often took considerable logistical risks, particularly when they believed themselves to be faced by a weak opponent. In part this was because of their willingness to consider what conventional military wisdom might have regarded as difficult or unachievable. But partly, too, it was because the Japanese were fearful of failure. Every possible effort was made to achieve battlefield success, and few commanders regarded logistical constraints as an excuse for failure. *Mutaguchi* was one such. Headstrong, opinionated and forthright, *Mutaguchi* was a commander renowned for both the fierceness of his temper and for his reluctance to accept criticism or unpalatable advice. It was a dangerous combination for the commander of such a risk-laden venture. Slim's plan was based on the hope that *Mutaguchi* would be so mesmerised by the prospect of capturing Imphal that he would take extraordinary efforts to break in, and that in doing so would push his units beyond their capability. The inability to disengage from an action in which the advantage had clearly turned to their opponents was a fundamental weakness in the Japanese military psyche that Slim was determined to exploit. He was about to have his chance.

The risks inherent in Slim's plan were significant, however. Not only were withdrawals difficult to manage but failure would have had a deleterious effect on the morale of his troops, which he and his commanders had built up so painstakingly over the previous months. A withdrawal would also have a correspondingly negative effect politically on friends and allies. He knew well from his own experience that there was no guarantee that 4 Corps would be able successfully to withdraw at the required moment, particularly if it was in contact with the enemy. There was no guarantee either that the defences of the Imphal plain would be sufficient to defeat every attempt by the enemy to break in,

The fruit of victory. On a hastily bulldozed field at Imphal on 15 December 1944, at a time when his troops were aggressively pursuing the defeated Japanese through the jungle-clad mountain vastness to the Chindwin and beyond, Slim was knighted with the KCB by the Viceroy of India, Lord Wavell. Slim's three Corps Commanders (Christison, Scoones and Stopford) each received the KBE.

Two extremely rare photographs of Slim and Wingate together. It is possible that both were snapped on the same day at Lalaghat airfield in Assam on Sunday 5 March 1944, prior to the departure of the first air-landed Chindit troops of Operation Thursday. To the right of Slim in the bottom photograph is Brigadier General Old of the USAAF.

Possibly the only photograph in existence of Slim with Mountbatten (left) and Leese (right). It seems probable that it was taken at a staff conference in Delhi on Wednesday 30 May 1945, only a week after Leese had been forced to reinstate Slim as Commander of 14 Army.

Slim broadcasting to his troops courtesy of the BBC, following a ceremony in April 1945 to mark the capture of Mandalay and the end of the decisive battle of Meiktila, described by Kimura, commander of the Japanese Burma Area Army as 'the master-stroke of Allied strategy.'

At his investiture, Slim gave one of the strangest parade-ground commands of his life, and one of the rarest in the history of the British Army: 'Lieutenant Generals, by the right, quick march!' From left to right, Lieutenant General Sir William Slim (14 Army), Lieutenant General Sir Phillip Christison (15 Corps), Lieutenant General Sir Geoffrey Scoones (4 Corps) and Lieutenant General Sir Montagu Stopford (33 Corps).

A picture of the perfect Army-Airforce co-operation that existed in India and Burma throughout 1944 and 1945. Slim, at his forward HQ on 5 February 1945, with Air Vice Marshal Vincent RAF (standing right) and Air Marshal Coryton (Commander RAF, Bengal and Burma standing left), just ten days before Slim's assault across the Irrawaddy at Pakokku and the audacious thrust at Meiktila. This was also the very day that Mountbatten ordered Leese to liberate Burma 'at the earliest date', something that Slim at the time was well on his way to securing.

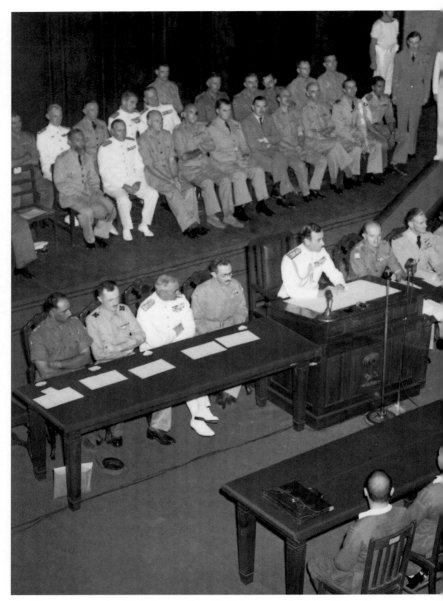

'In Singapore on the 12th September 1945 I sat on the left of the Supreme Commander, Admiral Mountbatten...while the formal unconditional surrender of all Japanese forces, land, sea and air, in South-East Asia was made to him...The war was over.' (*Defeat into Victory*).

Despite the formality of the Mandalay victory parade, here was 'Uncle Bill' as his soldiers remembered him, and doing what he enjoyed most: chatting with one of the soldiers who had helped him secure one of the most dramatic British victories of the war.

or that he could reinforce 4 Corps quickly when required. Replying to a letter from Mountbatten on 5 March Slim wrote, 'I think we are in for something . . . serious on 4 Corps front, where our dispositions are not quite so favourable for meeting it. I hope, however, that the 3rd Indian Division* will have a very great effect on the Jap's plans, but I am very anxious to reinforce that front if I possibly can.'[13] If the Imphal defences were strong enough and if Slim could maintain a steady flow of reinforcements and supplies into Imphal by some means, the Japanese would merely exhaust their strength in ultimately fruitless attempts to overwhelm the defenders. These were big 'ifs'. To be successful Slim's scheme would require careful planning, a finely honed assessment of his own troops' capabilities and the ability to juggle limited resources between competing priorities at a moment's notice. What was certain was that the battle would be a long, bloody confrontation where the victor would require perseverance, moral and material strength and nerves of steel in abundance.

There were some indeed who opposed Slim's plans. It was an understandably altogether too sensitive concept for many at the time. 'I was not surprised', Slim wrote, 'to find it hard to convince many, especially highly placed civil officials, that it was possible to fight defensively and even to retreat, yet keep the initiative.' By withdrawing he lay open to the charge that he had lost his nerve and lacked the courage to stand and fight the Japanese. This accusation, in the face of the humiliations of 1942 and 1943, would have deeply hurt a less robust commander. Rather than suffer the indignity of retreat, Slim was encouraged by some not to withdraw but to anticipate the enemy by launching his own pre-emptive attack across the Chindwin. Such suggestions were quickly dismissed. 'Had I accepted their advice,' Slim noted, 'the enemy could easily have concentrated, along good communications, a force greatly in excess of any we could maintain east of the Chindwin. We should have fought superior numbers with the dangerous crossing of a great river behind us and with our communications running back through a hundred and twenty miles of the worst country imaginable.' 'I noted' remarked Slim rather caustically, 'that the further back these generals came from, the keener they were on my "flinging" divisions across the Chindwin.' It was not ground that mattered', he argued consistently, 'but the opportunity

* The cover name for Wingate's 'Special Force'.

to engage, on ground of my own choosing, the might of *15 Army*. That done,' he argued, 'territory could easily be reoccupied.'

Slim's motives for defining his battle plan for Imphal and Kohima, were not merely to repel the Japanese offensive, but to destroy utterly *15 Army* as a fighting force. His aim was neither the general protection of Eastern India or the defence of Imphal *per se* but the removal of *Mutaguchi*'s ability thereafter to defend Burma against a strong British counter-offensive. Imphal was Slim's chosen killing ground for the destruction of the Japanese legions. To be successful his strategy required *Mutaguchi* to be drawn into his trap, and then locked in a death-embrace until his army had been destroyed. If *15 Army* were repulsed from the gates of India without being smashed, Imphal's safety may well have been secured, but Slim's strategy would not have succeeded and *15 Army* would have lived on to fight another day.

Although he did so from a different perspective, Scoones came rapidly to the same conclusion as Slim with regard to what needed to be done to receive the impending offensive. Whereas Slim wanted to create the conditions necessary to support an advance by 14 Army into Burma against a substantially weaker foe, Scoones was pre-eminently concerned with preserving his corps and re-deploying them to meet, and defeat, the Japanese offensive. He reasoned that both 17 and 20 Indian Divisions, unable by dint of geography to provide each other mutual support, would be easy prey to Japanese encirclement and defeat if they remained in their current locations. Nor would it be possible for them to withdraw into defensive boxes to be sustained by air as would be the case in Arakan because the allies simply did not possess the number of aircraft required for such an enormous undertaking. The concentration of 4 Corps to defend Imphal was the only solution, and the only place that offered Scoones the chance of doing this was the periphery of the plain. It would also allow Scoones the opportunity to use to best effect the advantage he enjoyed in armour and air power. For this reason he concurred with Slim: 4 Corps had to be withdrawn from its current positions and re-deployed to defend Imphal.

Accordingly, Scoones and Slim determined to get both divisions back at the first definite sign of a Japanese offensive. Whatever the difference in origin, the minds of both men worked in harmony to reach a common goal, the analysis of one fitting comfortably with that of the other. They met regularly.[14] When Scoones came up with his plan for the defence of

Imphal in early February 1944 Slim was able to give it his immediate
approval. When he sanctioned the final plan on 7 March and forwarded
it on to Giffard, he did so in the knowledge that it had been constructed
fully in accord with his own strategy.

So far, so good. However, in what was to prove to be an unfortunate
misappreciation of Japanese capabilities, Scoones made the assumption
that the Japanese would attack along two major arterial routes into the
plain leading through Tiddim and Tamu, with no more than a regiment
being tasked with the seizure of Kohima. His plan was that at the first sign
of the Japanese offensive 17 Indian Division would withdraw unmolested
from Tiddim and then leave one brigade on the southern edge of the
plain at Bishenpur. The second brigade would join 23 Indian Division to
form a powerful corps reserve, containing armour, artillery and aircraft.[15]
20 Indian Division would hold the vital Shenam Pass, against which
Scoones expected the greatest weight of the Japanese offensive to fall.
Should the enemy attempt to break into the plain, 23 Indian Division
would counter-attack vigorously. Scoones reasoned that as he did not
have the troops available to guard every stretch of his enormous front
it was better to place the major part of his forces on these routes
while leaving sufficient forces on hand to counter-attack the Japanese
breakthroughs wherever they appeared. This was a better alternative, he
decided, than attempting to defend every part of a huge sector and thus
being weak everywhere, and having only a limited reserve available to
deal with crises as and when they arose. Accordingly huge stretches of
territory, much of it apparently impenetrable jungle or impossible hill
country, were deprived of real defences and as a result the eighty miles
or so of rugged country between Litan and Kohima through Ukhrul
came to be defended by only a few weak battalions.

However reasonable Scoones' assessment appeared in conventional
terms, it nevertheless proved to be unfortunate in the light of what was
already known about Japanese methods. It assumed that 4 Corps would
have a strong reserve able to deal with any unforeseen eventuality. This
could not, in every instance, be guaranteed, however. It also betrayed
something of a naivety about Japanese tactics. As was by now very clear,
the Japanese rarely took the obvious route or a conventional course
of action. *U-Go* was to be no different. *Mutaguchi* had no intention

of fighting according to the conventional norms that framed Scoones'
appreciation of the situation. He intended instead to seize Imphal by a
combination of guile and extreme physical endurance, seeking to achieve
the same advantages that surprise and dislocation had brought successive
Japanese commanders in their encounters with the British Army in the
past. Scoones was not sufficiently alert to the possibilities for surprise
posed by the Japanese approach to war, a problem exacerbated by the
fact that this was his first field command of a formation in action since the
First World War.[16] In agreeing to Scoones' plan when it was presented
to him on 6 March Slim was also to fall into *Mutaguchi's* trap, namely
failing to appreciate the defensive weakness of the vast length of the
hilly jungle terrain that lay between the Chindwin and the mountain
village of Kohima.

*Mutaguchi's* plan was daring, inventive and aggressive. He correctly
assumed that Scoones would attempt to hold Tiddim and Tamu in
strength. He decided, therefore, to reinforce Scoones' assessment by
appearing to direct his attack through these areas, while in fact reserv-
ing his most dangerous thrust for a direction that would be wholly
unexpected by Scoones. *U-Go* was to comprise four parts, launched in
two phases. In the first phase, half of *Lieutenant-General Yanagida's*
*33 Division* was to isolate Cowan at Tiddim by cutting the road to
Imphal. Blocks were to be placed at Tongzang, forty miles north of
Tiddim, and at Milestone 100, the first to prevent 17 Indian Division's
escape from Tiddim and the second to prevent reinforcements from
Imphal coming to Cowan's rescue. The second phase of *U-Go* was to
begin a week later, on 15 March. The first part of this phase involved
the remainder of *33 Division*, under the command of *Major-General
Yamamoto*,\* advancing up the Kabaw Valley against 20 Indian Division,
thus threatening Imphal from the south-east along the axis Tamu, Moreh,
Shenam and Palel. *Mutaguchi* correctly assumed that Scoones would then
commit his reserves to his Tiddim and south-eastern sectors as a result
of these attacks.

Just as Scoones struggled to address the problems in the very two
areas where he had always expected an attack to fall, *Mutaguchi* planned
to launch his two most powerful attacks in the eastern and northern

---

\* *31* and *33 Divisions* (but not *15 Division*) had, in addition to the divisional commander
(a Lieutenant-General) a Major-General as commander of the divisional infantry.

sectors. Two regiments of *Lieutenant-General Yamauchi's 15 Division*, amounting to some 6,000 men in six battalions, with eighteen guns and several thousand horses and bullocks, were to advance in secret through the wild and difficult country between the Chindwin and the north-east of Imphal, following the line Ukhrul, Sangshak and Litan. *Yamauchi* was thereafter to block the road to Kohima north of Imphal in the area of Kanglatongbi, cross over to the west of the road, and then fall on Imphal from the north-west, an area from which *Mutaguchi* knew Scoones would be least expecting an attack. At the same time the whole of *Lieutenant-General Sato's 31 Division* – some 20,000 men – was to be launched against the hilltop village of Kohima, on the strategic artery linking Imphal with Dimapur and the Brahmaputra Valley. *Sato's* orders were to prevent reinforcements coming to the aid of Imphal from the north. One combined arms column of *31 Division*, comprising infantry, artillery and engineers – some 4,000 men – under the command of the Infantry Group commander, *Major-General Miyazaki Shigesaburo*, was to advance on Kohima *via* Ukhrul and the Imphal–Kohima road. The other two columns were to head straight for Kohima, 120 miles from the Chindwin through the wild and mountainous jungle country of the Somra Tracts.

It was a bold and daring plan, but it was also based on an out-of-date assessment of British strengths and intentions. It also relied, as Slim expected it would, on the acceptance of a considerable logistical risk. So confident was *Mutaguchi* of capturing Imphal within a month that he ordered his units to carry with them no more than twenty days' worth of supplies.[17] It was this overconfidence that was to negate his initial advantages and that was to lead *15 Army*, in time, to disaster.

There was one serious threat, however, to Slim's achievement of his vision for a 14 Army *götterdämmerung* on the plains of Imphal. This was the competing strategic ambition of Orde Wingate, whom GHQ India's brilliant media exercise had successfully transformed into the victor of Operation Longcloth. While the relevance of Wingate to the overall situation diminished as the Japanese threat to India developed during the early months of 1944, and as his influence at court waned commensurately, Wingate nevertheless continued to provide the only serious alternative to Slim's plan for taking on *Mutaguchi*. The propaganda exercise following Operation Longcloth in May 1943 had at least one significant spin-off: it persuaded Churchill that in Wingate a David had been raised up to smite the Japanese Goliath. Following the expedition Wingate had sent a private and unexpurgated copy of his report to the Secretary of State for India, Leo Amery, who in turn gave it to Churchill. This was undoubtedly what Wingate desired but it is unlikely that even he could have foreseen the consequences of such deliberate flouting of military convention. Without verifying the contents, or checking to see whether anyone in India had an alternative view, Churchill grasped the straw Wingate offered to him. In an infamous memorandum on 24 July 1943 to Ismay, he exulted:

> See now how all these difficulties [in Burma] are mounting up, and what a vast expenditure of force is required for these trumpery gains. All the commanders on the spot seem to be competing with one another to magnify their demands and obstacles they have to overcome. All this shows how necessary it is to decide on a commander ... I consider Wingate should command the Army against Burma. He is a man of genius and audacity, and has rightly been discerned by all eyes as a figure above the ordinary level. There is no doubt that in the welter of inefficiency and lassitude which has characterised our operations on the Indian Front this man, his force and his achievements, stand out, and no mere question of seniority must obstruct the advance of real personalities to their proper stations in war.[18]

At Churchill's invitation Wingate accompanied the British delegation to the Quadrant Conference in Quebec in July and August 1943 and found himself, to his great surprise, propelled by the absence of any representative from GHQ India to the unexpected position of Far Eastern 'expert'. Far from admitting the truth, Wingate's natural egotism drove him to accept this mantle gratefully as if it had been conferred on him by divine prerogative, and thereafter to believe his elevation to sainthood. Before the *Queen Mary* had arrived in Canada, Wingate had persuaded Churchill and the British Chiefs of Staff that a large scale Chindit operation should precede any future advance by the main force into Burma.

Churchill and the British Chiefs of Staff, desperate to hear of any solution to the apparent impasse in Burma, fell ready victims to Wingate's flawless delivery, brilliant exaggerations and simplistic explanations as to why India Command had failed so dismally in the past and why a dramatic new approach – air-landed Long Range Penetration Groups (LRPGs) – would bring quick and decisive victories against the Japanese. Unwittingly Wingate in fact told Churchill precisely what the Prime Minister wanted to hear: that the British–Indian army was inept, its leaders fumbling, its strategies visionless and its tactics and procedures byzantine. Worse, he told Churchill that the current regime in New Delhi was not just immune to change but bitterly opposed to it.

The truth, however, was dramatically different. Although only time was to prove it, Wingate's vision was largely ephemeral. Fortunately, Churchill was persuaded not to pursue the idea of elevating Wingate to high command, a proposal which, if adopted, would have caused incalculable damage to the allied war effort as a whole in the region. Churchill was, nevertheless, determined to pursue Wingate's ideas for a season, if only to shake GHQ India from what he unfairly regarded to be its death-like lethargy. Time would show that the only result of Churchill's pursuit of the Wingatean chimera was a massive expenditure of scarce and irreplaceable resources.

Auchinleck desperately tried to counter what he considered to be some of Wingate's wilder proposals, but not being in Quebec left him at a distinct disadvantage. In a calm and considered telegram to the Combined Chiefs of Staff on 19 August 1943 he rejected Wingate's argument that LRP forces could provide significant results against well organized Japanese conventional forces, although he acknowledged that a two-brigade LRP force could achieve much good. Auchinleck was not opposed to the notion of LRP per se: indeed, it is arguable that he knew more about its potentialities than many others, as he had sponsored extensive activity of this kind in North Africa. But Wingate's standing at Quebec, and conversely Auchinleck's own personal ill favour with Churchill, guaranteed the almost out of hand dismissal of Auchinleck's arguments. The Americans, too, were won over at Quebec, seeing in Wingate tangible evidence at least of one Briton who was willing to engage with the enemy. In the excitement of the moment the conference authorized Wingate to be given six brigades (23 infantry battalions)[19] and a vast American-supplied air armada.[20] What is more, Churchill told Wingate to bypass the military chain of command and to contact him direct if ever he felt that his plans were being met with obstruction or prevarication.

But when Wingate returned in victor's triumph to India in September 1943 it was to a less than enthusiastic reception. The concern about Wingate's plans and his exposure at Quebec concerned not just many British officers: Stilwell was aghast that a small number of American troops, 'Galahad Force', were to be placed under his command.* 'After a long struggle', he fumed to his diary, 'we get a handful of US troops and by God they tell us they are going to operate under Wingate! We don't know how to handle them but that exhibitionist does! He has done nothing but make an abortive jaunt to Katha, cutting some railroad that our people had already cut, got caught east of the Irrawaddy and come out with a loss of 40 per cent. Now he's the expert.'[21] Wingate's 'genius' was not as widely recognized at the time as Wingate's supporters like to imagine.[22] It is true, of course, that Wingate encountered gratuitous and ill-informed opposition from some in the Indian military establishment, but to claim that his opponents were lily-livered 'curry colonels' who had not an ounce of offensive spirit in their bodies and who resolutely opposed anyone who did, as some continue to do, is a travesty of the truth.[23] Whatever people thought of Wingate personally, opposition to him stemmed largely, as one of his biographers acknowledges, not out of 'jealousy, malice and folly alone' but from an 'appalled conviction that the decision for a second Chindit expedition was a colossal military blunder which must be prevented at all costs.'[24] General Sir Henry Pownall, Mountbatten's Chief of Staff, confided to his diary on 17 October 1943:

One thing I am sure is going to give trouble. That is the man Wingate . . . He has extraordinarily narrow views, runs in blinkers and can see no good except in his own chosen path . . . In fact he is distinctly *un*stable. He has succeeded in selling himself to the P.M. who has that remarkable flair for choosing oddities just because they are oddities (he, being one himself, has a sympathetic feeling) . . . In many ways Wingate is very good and can be made useful provided he is kept in order. But he is resentful of anything that is normal, deliberately runs counter to authority, demands first priority for

* 5307 Composite Unit, commonly known as 'Merrill's Marauders'.

his affairs and if he isn't getting it (and he is very touchy) threatens to wire direct to the Prime Minister.[25]

Wingate didn't help himself by the way he exploited the fruits of his victory at Quebec. His brusque approach to bringing about what he believed he had been promised created more enemies than friends, even amongst those who were prepared to help him.[26] 'To those who suffered his open insults,' writes John Connell in his biography of Wavell, 'Wingate appeared – whatever his unquestioned talents as a commander – a churlish bully, resentful of imagined snubs and rebuffs in the past, and eager now to demonstrate his recently acquired authority.'[27] Even his biographer admits that 'The character of Orde Wingate was one of close concentration, of fixed purpose, of few, ardent and narrow passions ... Many who admired him and gave him devoted service found little to love in him.'[28] Like his mis-appreciation of Auchinleck, Wingate was never to understand that people did not oppose the concept of guerrilla action against the Japanese *per se*. Auchinleck, Giffard and Slim and the majority of their respective staffs recognised the immense value that such operations could provide. What they objected to was Wingate's arrogant assumption that nothing else in the region mattered, and they were repelled by the offensive methods he used to obtain what he wanted. The Official History, traduced by Wingate supporters for its supposedly biased treatment of Wingate, was nevertheless correct in its assertion that Wingate's 'consuming fire of earnestness were such that, in a theatre where resources were limited, he relentlessly set about acquiring anything which he thought would further his own plans.'[29]

The principal reason why Wingate faced increasing opposition was because his view of the military situation differed in very large measure from that of most others. Indeed, by March 1944 Wingate's strategic vision for operations against the Japanese in Burma had become anomalous. His view of a powerful LRP force operating deep behind enemy lines to assist the advance of a main force into Burma, laudable enough in mid-1943 when so few alternatives offered themselves for launching offensive action against the Japanese, had been bypassed by a number of new strategic realities in south-east Asia. It was Wingate's great loss that he failed to detect in the *new* India of autumn 1943 that the strategic environment had changed significantly to that of only four months earlier, when he had stumbled exhausted back across the Chindwin at the end of his epic first expedition. Auchinleck's arrival as C-in-C India Command in June 1943 had significantly energized the preparation and training of the Indian Army for war, and the development of India as a base for operations against the Japanese. The appointment of Mountbatten as Supremo gave, for the first time, direction and focus to the conduct and planning of operations against the Japanese. The creation of 14 Army in October provided the beginning of an impressively fine-tuned fighting organization and the appointment of Slim to lead it provided a commander of note and vision who had the increasing confidence of his superior and subordinate commanders. By August 1943 the long road of defeat had ended. By the end of that year in tactics, training and *esprit d'corps* 14 Army was vastly superior to the demoralized troops of Eastern Army who had been defeated in Arakan only seven months before and a substantial reason for this improvement was the personality and drive of Slim himself.

In addition, Allied plans for a large scale offensive into or around Burma had been shelved while it had become increasingly apparent that a Japanese offensive into India was imminent.

By the start of 1944 two competing concepts of operations had emerged as to how best to mount an overland campaign against the Japanese in Burma. For the most part, as we have seen, an overland offensive into Burma was not attractive to Allied strategists during 1943 and 1944 but at Corps and Army level some thought had been given to this vexed question. While these two concepts were never formally set against each other, they nevertheless represented dichotomous approaches to the question of how to launch a land offensive into Burma. The first was that espoused by Wingate and endorsed in outline at Quebec, and the second was that developed by Slim in the later months of 1943 and the early weeks of 1944. Although the Quadrant Conference was not presented with Wingate's full-fledged views on the strategic use of LRPs to defeat the Japanese – these ideas were not fully developed in Wingate's mind until December 1943 – Quebec nevertheless was responsible for providing sponsorship for the LRP idea. Slim's plan stood in distinct contrast to Wingate's vision. Instead of going *into* Burma, as Wingate proposed, there to deal a death blow to *15 Army*, Slim believed, as we have seen, that the best course of action would be to withdraw his forward divisions and concentrate on the Imphal plain.

By February 1944 Slim, Giffard and Mountbatten were convinced

that whereas Special Force could offer useful service to the east of the
Chindwin it would be but one element in the overall plan for offensive
operations against the Japanese during 1944. The usefulness of LRP forces
in *support* of a conventional advance was widely accepted, but the idea
that LRPs should take on the *primary* offensive role found no support
amongst most senior commanders in the theatre. Wingate, however,
refused to accept that Special Force would play anything but a pivotal
role in operations in Burma during 1944. He had, by this time, become
firmly entrenched in this view. His ideas about the utility of LRPs
had undergone radical change since August 1943 and he increasingly
believed that the actions of Special Force *alone* would be the critical
determinants of the whole campaign, and that all other activities would
be secondary to it. He went so far as to doubt whether conventional
forces even had a role in a future campaign to eject the Japanese from
Burma. On 10 February 1944 he argued in a paper to Mountbatten that
14 Army could never hope to be in a position to fight over the mountains
bordering the Chindwin and that only his Special Force had the training
and wherewithal to take the war to the Japanese in Burma.* Further, he
believed that LRP formations 'would supersede conventional formations
with such impedimenta as tanks, artillery and motorised transport.' He
argued that the seizure of a town in central Burma by LRP forces, such
as Indaw, should be the first of a series of stepping stones which could
take the Allies directly to Bangkok, Saigon and thence up the coast of
China. When Special Force had seized one stepping stone they could
then be consolidated by conventional divisions following up behind.[30]

Slim had noted the change in Wingate's ideas when he had conducted
preliminary discussions with Wingate on 3 December 1943 to prepare
plans for Operation Thursday.[31] 'His original idea', recalled Slim, 'had
been that of a force, which, penetrating behind the enemy lines, would
operate in comparatively small, lightly equipped columns to harry his
communications and rear establishments while our main forces struck
the decisive blows elsewhere. From this, as he increasingly appreciated
the possibilities of air supply and transportation, he had gradually
swung to the view that the main force should be the penetrating one,
the subsidiary forces those that would remain comparatively static.'
Such an idea was, as Slim explained to an old friend in 1952, 'a

---

* An unfortunate prediction, as 14 Army was to do precisely this later in 1944.

nonsense'.[32] Wingate's developing ideas entailed, Slim told the British Official Historian in 1958,

> a much larger LRP force – several divisions in fact – and a heavier scale of equipment ... The more this idea of a massive new model LRP force gained on Wingate, the more he demanded and schemed to increase his command, to raise the scale of its armament and enlarge its own air force ... At the time of his second expedition, he realised that such grandiose ideas were not practical as we had not the aircraft they would require, and he accepted, though with reluctance and not very genuinely, the role I gave him of 'Strategic Cavalry'. But he worked and schemed unceasingly to build up a great LRP force which would absorb a large part of the standard formations and would be very different from the original LRP columns.[33]

The problem of such a proposal, to Slim, stood out starkly: Wingate's new ideas played directly to the enemy's strengths, and as a strategic concept stood at absolute variance to that proposed by Slim. Wingate's idea would have meant placing his forces precisely where the Japanese were strongest and where his own line of communication would be by air and thus extremely tenuous. By placing Special Force in the heart of the enemy's own territory, where the advantage of communication and supply lay firmly with the Japanese, Slim knew that Wingate could never hope to achieve the decisive advantage he sought. His aircraft-supplied troops, light in artillery and bereft of armour, would exhaust themselves quickly, particularly if they were used for conventional rather than guerrilla purposes. 'The strategic idea that a penetration formation, operating behind the enemy, could be the decisive force was by no means new or unsound ...' wrote Slim, 'but what would have been unsound was to attempt it with his present force and with his present air resources.' It would be far better, Slim reasoned, to force the Japanese into this situation of vulnerability instead. This, in a nutshell, was the difference between Slim and Wingate's conception of offensive operations in early 1944. The history of operations in 1944 was to prove resoundingly that it was Slim's operational concept that was the correct one.

Because of his view that Special Force could win the war for the Allies in Burma, Wingate began to demand that his operation be given the overwhelming priority in SEAC. At his meeting with Slim on 3 December 1943 Wingate insisted that Slim give him Lomax's 26 Indian Division, at the time 14 Army's only reserve, to bolster his forces. When Slim refused Wingate threatened to refer the matter to Churchill. Slim declined to be bullied and Wingate finally backed down. It was to prove to be but one occasion in the long and tortuous process of planning and preparation for Operation Thursday, in which Mountbatten and Slim attempted to temper the Wingate volcano lest it erupt and result in a missile from Wingate to Churchill. This was a very real fear. Although Slim at no time felt threatened by Wingate, the danger of an unchecked missive from Wingate to Churchill could have had a disastrous effect on the whole military planning and preparation of SEAC. Pownall noted in his diary for 28 January regarding demands from Wingate for more troops:

> This will bring the PM straight down on to Giffard and Slim, for he has already expressed his doubts as to the quality of the military advice that Mountbatten has been receiving. He will jump at any chance of breaking another general or two and will then push very hard, and maybe successfully, to get Wingate installed in command of 14th Army – which would be a most dangerous affair.[34]

The problem for Wingate was that, by early 1944, the strategic imperative for LRP action had diminished greatly. Slim, however, recognizing the political importance of Special Force, as well as acknowledging the usefulness of guerrilla activity as a whole in support of conventional forces, worked hard to give Wingate a meaningful role. He decided that Special Force would offer best value by cutting the lines of communication to the Japanese *18 Division* facing Stilwell's Chinese divisions at Ledo. Special Force was not to engage in conventional warfare, but rather in guerrilla-type actions against roads, railways, supply dumps and the like, in order to create the greatest possible confusion and disturbance for the Japanese in northern Burma. If they were successful their action might persuade the Chinese armies in Yunnan, facing *56 Division*, to launch their own offensive into Burma. Stilwell had been ordered by Mountbatten on 14 January 1944 to advance to the area Mogaung–Myitkyina to assist in the development of the China road that was to run from Ledo to Kunming.

This was not what Wingate wanted, but he nevertheless eventually agreed to Slim's proposal. 'It's quite true of course that the reduction in scope of the operations as a whole has reduced the usefulness of the L.R.P.G.s,' recorded Pownall in his diary entry for 6 January 1944; 'they won't have to go so deep, and if they do they won't get the support which Wingate wants. But they can still do useful things within the framework of what we *are* going to do. The total results may disappoint Wingate, but so they will a lot of people.'[35]

Wingate's fervent yet inflexible advocacy of the LRP idea locked him into a doctrinal straightjacket that removed the flexibility of mind necessary to view the changing strategic landscape as a whole, and reduced his utility in the higher command of the war in the theatre.[36] This reality Slim saw clearly. It exasperated him to see Wingate stumble blindly forward into the trap dug for him by the advocacy of a single ideal which was increasingly separated from strategic reality.

Slim experienced at least two confrontations with Wingate during the preparations to receive *U-Go*. At a meeting on 19 January 1944 Slim promised Wingate that if the strategic situation allowed he would give Special Force an extra four battalions from his reserve – 26 Indian Division – to garrison the strongholds. Wingate left the meeting with the impression that these units would be forthcoming when he called for them; but this was not what Slim had agreed. When, on 25 January, Wingate discovered that his understanding of the allocation of garrison units differed to Slim's, he in a fury wrote impassioned letters to both Mountbatten (26 January) and Giffard (27 January) accusing Slim of not having his heart in the operation, and threatening to resign. In this Wingate overreached himself. By demanding that Slim provide these units he was making the unwarranted assumption that Special Force was SEAC's strategic priority. This was far from the case. Slim's offer of four battalions from his reserve had been given in the context of 14 Army operations as a whole. He knew that if the impending Japanese offensive proved to be overwhelming he would need to keep his reserve intact for use in the decisive battle. Wingate, however, believing that Indaw would prove to be the decisive battle of the campaign, continued to demand that Slim honour his 'promise' to allocate to him these battalions. Slim had decided that, should the situation prevent him from giving Wingate units from the 14 Army reserve, Wingate would have to make do for garrison defence with the units of 3 West African Brigade. *Mutaguchi*'s offensive into Manipur was to prove Slim's assessment of the situation to be correct. In the end Slim gave Wingate a battalion of Gurkhas but he had to rely on 3 West African Brigade for the remainder of the garrison troops he demanded.

The second confrontation with Wingate concerned Slim's plan to employ some of the units earmarked for Wingate's use in the defence of Kohima. The plan to allow two to three months before the fly-in of the second wave allowed Slim to use 14 and 23 Brigades, if necessary, in an emergency elsewhere during this time. Quite naturally with the impending onslaught by *15 Army*, Slim planned to do so, as it would have made no sense to leave these brigades idle while Manipur remained in peril. Wingate, however, assumed from the outset that 14 and 23 were *his* brigades, to do as he willed. He was outraged, therefore, when on 9 March he discovered that Slim proposed to use both brigades to relieve some of the pressure he anticipated at Imphal when the *15 Army* storm erupted around them, and he immediately flew to Comilla to protest. 'He had not paused to consider', notes Bidwell, 'that for [once] he and his superior were in agreement, for both men, for a brief moment, perceived that the Chindit effort might be better employed in cutting Mutaguchi's supply lines than in awaiting Stilwell's advance.'[37] 'With tact and restraint', records Evans, 'Slim pointed out to Wingate that it had never been the intention to use the reserve brigades in the heart of Burma until two or three months after the initial fly-in, so that to employ them in the Imphal battle at this stage would not affect the operation.'[38] Slim agreed nevertheless to release 14 Brigade to Wingate once the situation at Kohima had stabilized, and was true to his word, giving the brigade to Wingate two weeks later, followed by 3 West African Brigade.

Wingate has had many posthumous apologists. In many cases their *apologia* has been based on a belief that the efforts and tribulations of the Chindits during both Longcloth and Thursday have been undermined by criticism levelled against their leader. This is, however, to misconstrue the argument. Wingate has had, it is true, his detractors and opponents, many of whom were antagonistic to him because of the *way* he behaved, not *what* he achieved. Slim's perspective – that Wingate's strategic assessment of the Burma problem was faulty – has been ignored by the Wingate camp, a point seen clearly by Lewin. Whatever one may say about Wingate as a person or as a leader of men, he argues, 'the central fact ... still remains indisputable: he and his Army Commander were thinking about different battles.'[39]

Despite what Slim perceived to be Wingate's doctrinal waywardness, Slim did not dislike Wingate, nor does the historical record show that Slim did anything but support the operations entrusted to Wingate by Quebec. Indeed, Slim appreciated the merit of many of Wingate's ideas. In particular, Slim recognized in Wingate the driving ambition to seek out new, inventive and if necessary unconventional ways to defeat the exultant Japanese, but became frustrated with the lack of balance this often brought to Wingate's judgement. Pownall went further: he was afraid that Wingate would be found out to be a fraud. On 19 February 1944 he confided to his diary: 'I shouldn't be at all surprised if within the next three months it is proved that Wingate is bogus; at any rate he is a nasty piece of work.'[40] But Slim stayed away from a debate which was clearly not his. It is an extraordinary distortion of the truth to claim, as some have done, that Slim opposed Wingate's ideas *in toto* and that he resented Wingate's influence in the corridors of power, or feared for his own position as commander of 14 Army. Slim was very aware of the political imperatives supporting Wingate, most if not all of which were outside his own command responsibility and thus his orbit of influence, and he expended no energy in what would be rather fruitless attempts to denigrate and resist Wingate.[41] In any case this was simply not his way. Consequently he sought not to hinder or frustrate Wingate, but to channel his unruly subordinate's undoubted energies into objectives designed to meet 14 Army's operational tasks without prejudice to the demands made by Quebec.

Despite the fact that Wingate quite obviously resented these restraints both men worked out a reasonably amicable relationship during the planning and preparation for Operation Thursday. Sykes claims that Slim and Wingate 'were not made for each other. Their relations were to be strained and variable.'[42] This is an exaggeration. The truth is that Wingate got on with preciously few people, but Slim was one of the few senior officers with whom he could work. Slim recalled,

> On the whole, Wingate and I agreed better than most people expected, perhaps because we had known one another before, or perhaps because we had each in our own way arrived at the same conclusions on certain major issues, the potentialities of air

supply, the possibility of taking Burma from the north, and in our estimates of the strengths and weaknesses of the Japanese. Of course we differed on many things. It was impossible not to differ from a man who so fanatically pursued his own purposes without regard to any other consideration or person.

Interestingly, Wingate also recognized that in Slim he had an ally of sorts. The last time Slim met him before his death on 24 March 1944 Wingate told Slim that '"You are the only senior officer in South East Asia who doesn't wish me dead!"'[43]

The battles of what became widely know as the 'bloody plain' are difficult to follow. No less a soldier than Wavell found the scattered battlefield hard to fathom. Writing to Brooke following a visit to Slim in July 1944 he confessed that the conduct of the battle was a mystery to him: it seemed to have been strangely fought in 'penny packets'.[44] Acknowledging this difficulty when writing *Defeat into Victory*, Slim guided his readers through the complicated series of engagements using the analogy of the spokes on a wheel. The first spoke was the road northwards from Imphal to Kohima. The second spoke followed the line of the Iril River Valley, the third the track north east to Ukhrul while the fourth represented the road to Tamu. The fifth spoke was the Tiddim road and the sixth was the track running west from Bishenpur to Silchar.

Slim's strategy was now to be tested to the full by *Mutaguchi*'s onslaught. Three potential disasters faced him in those anxious first three weeks of the battle from mid-March to early April 1944, any one of which could have resulted in defeat for 14 Army. The first threat to Slim's plan appeared a week before the Japanese offensive was expected to begin. Unbeknown to either Slim or Scoones, the date fixed in both of their minds for the start of the Japanese offensive – 15 March – was the date on which *Mutaguchi* intended to launch *15* and *31 Divisions* across the Chindwin to start the *second* phase of *U-Go*. They had no inkling of the fact that operations against 17 Indian Division were to begin a full week before, on 7 March, when units of *33 Division* were to march across the hills from Yazagyo on the Chindwin to cut the all-important road from Tiddim to Imphal. These operations began as planned. On 8

March other units secretly crossed the Manipur river below Tiddim and began moving upstream on the west bank of the river in order to place a block at Milestone 100 to complete the outflanking of Cowan's division. Nevertheless, despite the secrecy in which these moves were conducted, Cowan quickly became aware of them through his patrols and from V Force. All this information was quickly fed back to 4 Corps.

Slim's approval of Scoones' plan on 7 March had been accompanied by the proviso that Scoones himself was to make the decision as to when exactly 17 and 20 Indian Divisions were to withdraw. Slim was concerned lest Cowan or Gracey withdrew their divisions prematurely, before an all-out Japanese offensive had been confirmed. Leaving the decision to Scoones, however, was to prove a mistake of considerable magnitude, and one which he was to rue as it very nearly cost the loss of Cowan's division.

While it was increasingly obvious to Cowan that the Japanese opening moves had begun, Scoones discounted the possibility that this was the start of the decisive move against Imphal. Not anticipating a Japanese move until 15 March at the earliest, Scoones did not believe that the time was right to order a withdrawal. Nevertheless, as each day passed a picture began to be built up by 17 Indian Division of Japanese activity to the west of the Manipur River. Increasingly concerned that his warnings to HQ 4 Corps were falling on deaf ears, Cowan began actively to prepare to withdraw his division. He ordered the backloading of extraneous personnel and stores from Tiddim to Imphal, and started the preparation of the divisional area into defensive boxes. From his experience of 1942 he knew that *33 Division* would attempt to cut off his line of withdrawal by blocking the Tiddim road. Thus surrounded his units would fall prey to a slow defeat in detail. He needed no convincing that he had to make all speed back to the Imphal plain before his division was cut off completely. On 13 March, worried that he had not yet received orders from Scoones to withdraw, Cowan decided to act alone and ordered the withdrawal of his division, thereby disobeying Scoones' explicit instructions to the contrary. At 2040 hours that day Scoones called Cowan by telephone and gave the long-awaited and undeniably late order to withdraw his division. Scoones then informed Slim by signal of the situation.[45]

Most subsequent accounts blame Cowan for not reacting quickly enough to Scoones' instructions.[46] Scoones himself was somewhat disingenuous on this point, and suggested that it was Cowan, not he, who was to blame for the slowness of the withdrawal from Tiddim. Scoones' account was the one that went into the Official History in due course. But the records of both 17 Indian Division and of 4 Corps show unequivocally that this perception is false. Delaying the withdrawal of 17 Indian Division was caused not by Cowan's failure to act swiftly in response to Scoones' order of 13 March, but by Scoones' failure to allow Cowan to withdraw early enough in the first place. Cowan, after successfully saving his division, and mauling *Yanagida*'s regiments in the process, received no recognition for this feat.

Slim undoubtedly made a mistake in leaving the final decision to withdraw 17 Indian Division to Scoones, and he admitted his culpability in full. 'To put the responsibility on local commanders was neither fair nor wise,' he concluded. 'I was in a better position to judge when a real offensive was coming for I had all their information, and, in addition, intelligence from other sources.' Further, there 'was thus a real risk, that I did not appreciate, of the withdrawal being started too late. Instead of being carried out without interference, it might degenerate into a series of fights to break through involving our reserves and disorganising the whole plan of battle.' Slim's defence of Scoones here is tortuous. Slim had already delegated responsibility for initiating the withdrawal to Scoones, but Scoones had clearly failed to judge the correct time to pull Cowan back from Tiddim. Cowan himself, the local commander, was well placed to judge this moment and did so correctly. The issue was not the level at which responsibility to withdraw was delegated, but the person to whom Slim entrusted this responsibility. In the event Cowan rose to the occasion and Scoones did not.

When Scoones recognized, on 12 March, the predicament facing Cowan he ordered the corps machine-gun battalion to make all haste to the Manipur river bridge at Tongzang.* A day later, on 13 March, he followed this up with an order to Collingridge's 37 Brigade – part of his corps reserve – to deploy down the Tiddim Road early on 14 March. In fact, Scoones was pre-empted in this by twelve hours. Ouvry Roberts, noting with alarm the events at Tiddim, ordered Collingridge of his own accord to deploy to assist Cowan, clearly suggesting that he thought Scoones was acting too slowly.[47] Scoones decided on 14 March to despatch 49 Brigade to the Tiddim road as well. These two brigades,

* Milestone 126.

however, constituted the whole of Scoones' infantry reserve, and their deployment to the Tiddim road unhinged at one stroke Scoones' plans for the defence of Imphal. He realized that if 17 Indian Division could not get back to Imphal the whole plan for the defence of Manipur would collapse. With 17 Indian Division about to be embroiled in a fight for its life, and with a major part of this reserve assisting Cowan, Scoones' cupboard was suddenly bare. There existed an urgent imperative for reinforcements to be moved into Imphal at short notice to replace those of 23 Indian Division now moving to positions on the Tiddim road. How was this to be done? 5 Indian Division was not scheduled to arrive in Imphal from Arakan until mid-April, which would be far too late to alleviate the current crisis. The situation could not have been worse, and although it was arguably Scoones' fault, the responsibility for sorting it out lay with Slim.

During the following three weeks Cowan's 16,000 troops, 2,500 vehicles and 3,500 mules fought their way northwards, while elements of 37 Brigade fought southwards from Milestone 100. Troops of both divisions now found themselves interspersed along the road with the Japanese, who attempted constantly to encircle and cut off. 'The situation on the Tiddim road was now for a time as it had once been on the Arakan coast', recalled Slim, 'a Neapolitan ice of layers of our troops alternating with Japanese ... But in both training and morale our men were much better fitted to deal with such a confused and harassing business than they had been in 1943.' Air support, both in terms of air supply in the closing days of the withdrawal, and of ground attack throughout it by 221 Group RAF, proved to be of considerable value to 17 Indian Division. After fighting through the final Japanese block at Milestone 72, 17 Indian Division reached Imphal by 4 April, after which the division's 1,200 wounded were flown out to India.

Despite the confusion evident at the start of the battle and the casualties suffered by 17 Indian Division, Cowan's fighting withdrawal from Tiddim, under constant pressure from the Japanese, was highly successful. *Yanagida* had been unable to isolate or outfight Cowan's Gurkhas, and both brigades managed to reach the safety of the Imphal plain and thereafter to play a full part during the ensuing months in Scoones' defence of the plain. Substantial delay had been imposed upon *33 Division*, and the heavy casualties it suffered severely reduced its ability thereafter to break through to Imphal.

The second near-disaster to confront Slim occurred to the east of Imphal in the second week of the Japanese offensive. Scoones' initial plan was to withdraw 20 Indian Division to defend the Tamu road between Moreh in the east and Shenam in the west, along which three defensive boxes had been prepared. From 9 March the backloading began from 20 Indian Division's forward area of the engineers, logisticians and non-combatants who had been preparing for the anticipated advance across the Chindwin.

The first attacks began in earnest on the evening of 14 March with infantry and tanks trying to break through the 100 Brigade defences at Witok, sixteen miles south of Tamu on the track to Kalemyo. On the following night the main crossings of the Chindwin River by some 45,000 troops of *15* and *31 Divisions* began. The flimsy reconnaissance screen along the west bank of the river was quickly brushed aside and the Japanese wasted no time in pushing into the mountains on the way to their objectives on the Imphal road and Kohima. On 16 March Gracey was ordered to withdraw to occupy his defensive positions on the Shenam–Moreh road. 100 Brigade successfully prevented *Yamamoto* from breaking through at Witok, and succeeded in withdrawing to Moreh by 19 March. By 20 March 32 Brigade halted a Japanese armoured advance along the track to Kalewa some two or three miles south of Tamu. It, too, withdrew successfully to Moreh on 21 March. Meanwhile, 80 Brigade, which was watching the Thaungdut area on the Chindwin further north, withdrew successfully to positions along the Palel–Tamu road. These operations went largely according to plan. But the orderliness of Gracey's withdrawal to the Tamu road positions hid a fundamental problem. While Gracey was successfully holding off *Yamamoto*, *Mutaguchi* was in the process of passing a large and powerful force through the jungle to the north far away from the fixed defences of the Tamu road.

Before long information began to reach Imphal that Japanese troops were advancing in force on Ukhrul and Sangshak. Inexplicably, however, this information appeared not to ring any warning bells in HQ 4 Corps, which was preoccupied with the developing threat in the Tamu area where the main Japanese thrust was confidently predicted. It was, perhaps understandably, unwilling to consider information that appeared to tell a different story. Whatever the reason, no warnings of an impending onslaught were transmitted to Brigadier Hope-Thompson, whose two battalions of 50 Indian Parachute Brigade were in the process of taking over the locations hastily vacated by 49 Brigade, recently despatched to the Tiddim road.[48]

Even worse, because a major attack had not been expected in this sector, the area boasted no defences worthy of the name. The result was that the eastern approach to Imphal lay open, and virtually undefended. Nevertheless Hope-Thompson had managed, by 22 March, to concentrate his two ill-prepared battalions on a stony and virtually waterless hill at Sangshak, where for the ensuing four days he beat off fierce Japanese attacks by *Miyazaki's 58 Regiment. Miyazaki's* real objective was Kohima, but he was determined to brush aside the defences he found at Sangshak, despite the fact that he knew Sangshak to lie not in his, but in *15 Division's* area of responsibility.

Lacking even basic direction from HQ 4 Corps, with little or no information about the enemy, and without ammunition and stores of even the most basic kind, including barbed wire for the construction of defensive positions, Hope-Thompson's men found themselves alone and faced by heavy odds. The long-term prognosis was never in doubt and the frantic and heroic self-sacrifice of the brigade proved insufficient to stop the Japanese tidal wave overwhelming it by 26 March.[49]

While 50 Parachute Brigade was virtually destroyed in the four days of the Sangshak battle, considerable benefit fell to 4 Corps by their sacrifice.[50] The battle cost *Miyazaki* 600 casualties and his advance was held up for a week, causing serious delay to *Sato's* plan for the attack on Kohima and giving Slim and Scoones valuable breathing space to reorganize and reinforce the Imphal positions. This was a serious setback to *Mutaguchi's* hopes of capturing all of his objectives within three weeks. It was the first sign that *Mutaguchi's* plan was turning awry: the British at first seemed intent on flight, but here was stubborn – even fanatical – resistance, and it took the Japanese by surprise.

Why did HQ 4 Corps – under the direction of Scoones – fail to react sufficiently to the threats against both Tiddim and Sangshak? By all accounts Corps Headquarters appeared overwhelmed by the emerging crisis and had difficulty making sense out of the mass of information it received. In Imphal, Slim recalls, the fog of war descended immediately. To an extent this situation was understandable and to be expected.

Indeed, in *Defeat into Victory* he commented that, in the circumstances, Scoones and his staff did an admirable job. 'In Imphal I was impressed by the steadiness of commanders and troops', he wrote. 'Scoones, in control of the tactical battle on the whole Assam front, had been faced with a difficult and momentous decision . . . He was deluged with reports and rumours of Japanese columns which seemed to flit in and out of the jungle, now here, now there; little was definite and nothing was certain.' Later, Slim took pains to stress the confused and unconventional nature of the fighting as a whole and in so doing sought perhaps to protect his subordinate from criticism.

> At no time and in no place was the situation, either to commanders or troops, [clear] . . . In to Scoones's headquarters, from every point of the compass, day and night, streamed signals, messages, and reports, announcing successes, set-backs, appealing for reinforcements, demanding more ammunition, asking urgently for wounded to be evacuated, begging for air support. His was the task of meeting or withstanding these appeals, of deciding which at the moment was the place to which his by no means over-generous reserves should be allotted. It was impossible for him to satisfy all his commanders. It needed a tough, cool, and well-balanced commander to meet, week after week, this strain. Luckily Scoones was tough, cool and well-balanced.

Others, however, have been less generous about Scoones' performance and that of his headquarters, particularly in those early weeks of the battle when failure at either Tiddim or Sangshak could have resulted in overwhelming and ignominious failure for 14 Army. Seaman, for instance, regards him to have been both temperamentally unfit for the task ahead of him and tired. After almost four unbroken years in harsh physical conditions, he argues, Scoones was quickly overwhelmed by the pressures and complexities of *Mutaguchi*'s offensive.[51] This is certainly an exaggeration although it does contain an element of truth. Ouvry Roberts' view was that, however wise and analytical, Scoones was temperamentally unable to act quickly.[52] The combination of an overloaded and possibly tired commander, an inexperienced headquarters staff together with the surprise engendered by the unconventionality of the Japanese attack undoubtedly resulted in a significant reduction in the effectiveness of HQ 4 Corps during the early stages of this most crucial of battles.

The bitter struggle at Sangshak led Scoones belatedly to an awareness of the danger posed to Imphal from the north-east. On 25 March Brigadier Bayley, Scoones' new BGS vice Geoffrey Evans, who had been sent to command 9 Brigade in Arakan, sent an urgent signal to Gracey warning him that he might have to relinquish one of his brigades in order to bolster the weak sector to the north, through which, if 50 Indian Parachute Brigade gave way at Sangshak, the whole approach to Imphal lay open.[53] Gracey, taken unawares by the proposition, did not receive it warmly. His division had successfully completed a difficult withdrawal to its new positions between Moreh and Shenam, and he did not view kindly the prospect of another, particularly one that appeared to be the result of poor forward planning, and he complained bitterly to Scoones by letter on 26 March:

> This division has fought magnificently so far and all the troops have been fully aware of the necessity of withdrawing to their present position, with the Army Commander's [Slim's] assurance that behind them is a pile-up of reserves rapidly being reinforced to deal with the situation behind them. Our morale is sky high, as we have beaten the enemy and given him a real bloody nose everywhere. Everyone is prepared to hang on where they are now like grim death. It is their Verdun. It will be most shattering to morale if they are now asked to assist in the Imphal Plain and they will feel that someone has let them down.[54]

Gracey was particularly reluctant to abandon Moreh, but the Sangshak disaster left Scoones with little choice as 20 Indian Division was in danger of being outflanked by *15 Division*'s assault on Imphal from the north-east. If *Yamauchi* were successful in penetrating the Imphal plain the whole defence of Imphal would unravel and Gracey's defences at Shenam would become irrelevant. Scoones undoubtedly made the right decision. If he is to be criticized it is for failing to keep Gracey informed about the overall situation from the outset.

Gracey had no option but to withdraw further west towards Shenam.

After destroying virtually everything that remained, 32 Brigade withdrew from Moreh, with the Japanese at their heels, at the end of the month. Eighty and 100 Brigades occupied positions between Shenam and Tengoupal, about nine miles from Palel, while 32 Brigade was withdrawn into Corps Reserve. 20 Indian Division now held a twenty-five-mile front from Tengnoupal through Shenam to Shuganu, fifteen miles south-west of Palel. Gracey's new plan was to defend a number of fortified boxes on the high ground on Shenam Ridge and keep the road to Shenam and thence Palel open, rather than to hold the whole of his twenty-five-mile front in its entirety. Intensive patrolling covered the gaps.

# 7

# The Bloody Plain

If the first two mistakes to mark the opening of the momentous and protracted battle for Imphal were Scoones' late order to Cowan to withdraw from Tiddim, and then his failure to anticipate the thrust by *15 Division* through Ukhrul, Litan and Sangshak, the third blunder was to prove almost calamitous to the fortunes of 14 Army in Manipur. This involved a misapprehension by both Slim and Scoones of the importance to the forthcoming battle of the mountain village of Kohima or, to be more precise, the Kohima Ridge, around which the road between Dimapur and Imphal looped and across which the village was spread. The village, sitting at five thousand feet above sea level in the mountains north of Imphal, guards the route from Dimapur to Imphal. If Kohima were captured, Imphal would be cut off from the rest of India by land. While both Slim and Scoones had always assumed that the Japanese would attempt to seize Kohima, they believed that this would be done only in conjunction with, and as a precursor to, the capture of Dimapur. Dimapur consisted of a huge supply dump on the line of communication to both Ledo and Imphal, and was the hub around which the wheel of Allied activity revolved. There was no doubt in Slim's mind that it was the obvious strategic prize. If Dimapur fell, Manipur would be indefensible. Its loss 'would have pushed into the far distance our hopes of relieving Imphal,' he explained, 'laid bare to the enemy, the Brahmaputra Valley with its string of airfields, cut off Stilwell's Ledo Chinese, and stopped all supply to China.'

Slim's logic appeared unarguable. But there was one problem with his analysis about which he was to remain dangerously unaware until the beginning of April: the Japanese had decided to seize not Dimapur, but to go for Kohima instead with the whole of *31 Division*. While *Mutaguchi* also recognized the strategic importance of Dimapur he was unable to persuade his superiors of the need to place its capture before Kohima and Imphal. *Kawabe*, commander of the Burma Area Army, believed that his subordinate's desire to attack Dimapur was but a product of dangerous egotism and refused to sanction any move further west than Kohima. Slim subsequently ridiculed *Sato*'s seemingly pig-headed attacks on Kohima to the exclusion of all else, but *Sato* was doing simply what *Mutaguchi*, reluctantly and against his better judgement, had ordered him to do.[1] To compound the problem – of believing Dimapur rather than Kohima to be the Japanese objective – Slim now, rather surprisingly, fell into the fatal trap of underestimating the Japanese. 'I had been confident that the most the enemy could bring and maintain through such country would be one regimental group,' he admitted. He did not consider that a whole division would be directed to capture the village and block the vital Imphal to Dimapur road. 'In that, I had badly underestimated the Japanese capacity for large-scale, long-range infiltration, and for their readiness to accept odds in a gamble on supply.'

The severity of the threat facing Kohima was not appreciated until it was nearly too late. Slim claims that he had realized within a week of the start of the offensive that the situation at Kohima was likely to be more dangerous than he had anticipated. It seems clear, however, that even by early April Slim was still not aware that the bulk of *31 Division* was pushing on to the town. If he had known that this was the case by 22 or 23 March, he would undoubtedly have defended the village appropriately to prevent its capture by the Japanese. By a stroke of good fortune, a copy of *Miyazaki*'s battle plans had fallen into the hands of 50 Parachute Brigade during the Sangshak battle, pointing to Kohima as the objective for the whole of *31 Division*. But it does not appear to have found its way into Slim's hands, despite superhuman efforts by Hope-Thompson to get the information safely to 4 Corps. Slim remained, therefore, ignorant of this fact until the last minute.[2]

Slim's fears for the security of Dimapur were magnified suddenly by

Cowan's unexpected withdrawal from Tiddim in contact with the enemy on 13 March, and the loss to Scoones over the following days of the major part of his Corps reserve. With 17 Indian Division potentially no longer available to defend Imphal, Scoones' reserve already engaged and Dimapur threatened, Slim knew that the only way he could prevent Imphal from being overwhelmed was by the rapid and substantial reinforcement of 4 Corps. In this sudden, dramatic and entirely unexpected turn of events *Mutaguchi* came close to achieving all his objectives well in advance of his own timetable. Had he been successful it would undoubtedly have resulted in one of the most serious reverses of British arms during the war. Slim was already aware of the need to reinforce Imphal and had already planned to bring in 5 Indian Division from Arakan when the situation on that front had stabilized. He had also approached Giffard for extra reinforcements for Dimapur. But the urgency of the new situation meant that speed was now vital. The only way that troops could be delivered to the threatened areas in Assam in days rather than weeks and months was by aircraft. Slim, however, had no transport aircraft at all, although within SEAC considerable numbers of American aircraft were involved in the Hump airlift.* It was these aircraft that offered themselves as the solution to Slim's sudden predicament. On the morning of 14 March Slim and Baldwin met Mountbatten at Comilla airport, explained the grave and unexpected situation facing 4 Corps, and asked that some of these aircraft be diverted to reinforce Imphal. 'If we lost the Imphal–Kohima battle', Slim reasoned, 'the Hump route would be closed. It seemed obvious therefore that it would be madness not to divert some of the China airlift to the vital needs of the Fourteenth Army.'

Realizing the critical nature of the sudden emergency, Mountbatten immediately and on his own initiative agreed to do what Slim had requested and to divert to 14 Army the aircraft required. He had, in fact, no authority to do anything of the kind, responsibility for tasking these aircraft remaining with the US Chiefs of Staff in Washington, and he had been instructed by Roosevelt not to divert these aircraft to any other use. But with no time to lose he decided to divert the aircraft first and ask permission later. On the same day – 14 March – Mountbatten

* By September 1943 the USA had provided fifteen Squadrons (230 x DC3) for the Hump air lift, flying from airfields in north-east Assam, as part of Air Marshal Baldwin's 3rd Tactical Air Force.

instructed Giffard to waste no time in reinforcing 14 Army with elements
of the Army Group reserve – Lieutenant-General Montagu Stopford's
33 Corps. That evening Slim quantified his requirement for aircraft,
signalling to Mountbatten that he needed 260 Dakota sorties to get
each of the three brigades (9, 123 and 161) of 5 Indian Division to
Imphal in time to prevent a possible disaster. When, on the next day –
15 March – he discovered during a visit to Imphal that Scoones had been
forced to send 49 Brigade to the Tiddim Road in addition to 37 Brigade,
the urgency of the situation was reinforced. Slim therefore sent another
message to Mountbatten asking urgently for twenty-five to thirty C47s for
the period 18 March to 20 April. Mountbatten immediately agreed. Slim
then proceeded on 17 March to give orders for the air move of 5 Indian
Division to begin. A day later, from Dohazari airfield near Chittagong,
the battalions of 123 Brigade began the fly-in. Flying two sorties a day,
the division was flown to Assam in the period through to 29 March.

By dint of commendable forward planning, HQ 14 Army had, months
previously, prepared detailed loading tables to transport the whole of a
division by Dakota in an emergency. Suddenly this foresight paid off, and
the first operation of its kind in history seamlessly to transport by air a
whole division from one battlefield to another was completed without a
hitch. For the vast majority of the soldiers involved it was their first ever
flight in an aircraft.[3]

Mountbatten's courage in unilaterally taking aircraft from the Hump
to meet the needs of the current emergency when he had no authority to
do so was a critical factor in the successful defence of Imphal. Washington
could do little but retrospectively agree Mountbatten's *fait accompli* on
17 April, authorizing the diversion as a temporary measure to overcome
the crisis of the moment. Retaining these aircraft to maintain the airlift
into Imphal in order to sustain 4 Corps, as opposed to the fly-in of
5 and 7 Indian Divisions as rapid reinforcements, was an altogether
different problem. On 23 March Slim wrote to Giffard stressing the
need to increase the air supply to 14 Army in the event of Imphal
being cut off. With land routes cut, an air bridge was the only way
in which 4 Corps could be supplied.[4] Slim warned Giffard that if the
aircraft supporting 4 Corps were withdrawn he could not be responsible
for the consequences. Mountbatten needed no second urging, appealing
immediately to Washington for another seventy aircraft to supply 4 Corps
while it lay besieged. This was no easy thing for the Chiefs of Staff to agree,

as there was intense pressure on the limited number of transport aircraft across all theatres of war at the time. But Mountbatten refused to budge. Churchill signalled Mountbatten giving his support: 'Chiefs of Staff and I are backing you to the full, I have telegraphed the President [that] in my view nothing matters but the battle – be sure you win.' Mountbatten won the argument and the return of the aircraft was deferred until 15 June.

Even before Slim had come to him on 14 March with his urgent request for air transport Mountbatten had been exercised by the need to increase the flow of reinforcements to Imphal. Privately he believed that Giffard was not doing enough to ensure that Slim had the resources he required to fight the forthcoming battle.[5]

On 5 March Slim asked Giffard for a division to defend Dimapur and to provide rapid reinforcement for Kohima and Imphal should it be required. The obvious solution was to send forward the bulk of Stopford's 33 Corps from India. Giffard was concerned, however, that moving an additional division from India would place an intolerable burden on the Assam railway. A compromise was reached. Slim was given the two battalions of 50 Indian Parachute Brigade and Giffard promised 2 British Division* from 11 Army Group reserve should it became necessary. Slim admitted later that this 'was by no means what I asked for' although he recognized Giffard's concerns about exacerbating the already significant supply problem on the Imphal plain.[6]

Shortly afterwards Giffard agreed to give him Wingate's 23 (Long-Range Penetration) Brigade,† which was still in India. 'He agreed to rail it to Jorhat', Slim recalled, 'where I could place it as a mobile force to cover the railway to Ledo, and, if necessary, use it against the flank of an attack on Dimapur.' On 18 March Slim asked for HQ 33 Corps and confirmed his request for 2 British Division to go to Chittagong to replace 5 Indian Division. Giffard 'at once agreed', Slim noted. Giffard also accepted Slim's request for 14 (LRP) Brigade and decided that once the airlift of the latter to Imphal was complete 7 Indian Division would then also be airlifted to Manipur. But with the rapid deterioration of the situation in Manipur, Slim requested on 27 March that 2 British Division be sent not to Arakan, but to Dimapur instead. This brought its own problems, as the earliest it could arrive was the first week of April.

* Major-General Grover.
† Brigadier Lancelot Perowne.

The aircraft secured by Mountbatten to support 4 Corps were unable to begin their airlift into Imphal until mid-April. Scoones therefore took the precaution of cutting the ration scale by a third and flying out thousands of non-combatants to India by returning aircraft.* Baldwin's 3rd Tactical Air Force began Operation Stamina on 18 April but it took some time to build up to the daily requirement of 540 tons. Nevertheless, across the period of the siege the airlift was a remarkable success. By 30 June the operation had flown in 19,000 reinforcements, 14,317,000 pounds of rations, 1,303 tons of grain for animals, 835,000 gallons of fuel and lubricants, 12,000 bags of mail and 43,475,760 cigarettes.[7] At its height in the second half of April the airlift employed 404 aircraft from fifteen squadrons.

By contrast, as Slim had predicted, the Japanese supply situation became increasingly precarious. In his assessments of British reactions to *Ha-Go*, *Mutaguchi* could have had no inkling of the dramatic power air transport would give to Slim to move troops around the battlefield. Certainly he could not have expected the rapid transfer of two whole divisions from Arakan to Imphal and Kohima to meet the threat posed by the sudden onset of *U-Go*.

Giffard, Slim and Scoones met together in Imphal on 20 March to consider the impending crisis. As yet, they did not know the true scale of the imminent threat to Kohima. Even without this knowledge the situation was grave. 17 Indian Division and the major part of 23 Indian Division were fully engaged on the Tiddim road. 20 Indian Division was withdrawing in contact with the enemy to Moreh, and the unprepared and weakened 50 Parachute Brigade had suddenly and unexpectedly been confronted by large numbers of enemy in the Ukhrul area the day before. In addition enemy forces were known to be moving on Kohima and it was assumed that the Japanese were likewise closing in on Silchar to the south-west.

Certain that Scoones now had enough on his plate with the defence of Imphal Slim gave temporary responsibility for the defence of Dimapur and Kohima to Major-General Ranking, commander of 202 Line of Communication Area. Ranking was to transfer responsibility to Stopford

* 43,000 non-combatants and 13,000 casualties were evacuated from Imphal during the battle.

when the latter arrived with 33 Corps in early April.* On 22 March Slim ordered a scratch garrison under Colonel H.U. Richards to Kohima to act as a forward defence for Dimapur. On the same day Slim briefed Stopford at Comilla. When, exactly a week later, Warren's 161 Brigade arrived from Arakan Slim sent it directly to Kohima to assist in the defence of the village.[8] Slim told Warren that he expected the Japanese to arrive at Kohima by 3 April and Dimapur by 10 April, by which time only one brigade of 2 British Division would have arrived to support the defence of the area.

Stopford's plan was to concentrate his corps as it arrived at Jorhat† ready to launch a counter-stroke against Dimapur if in the meantime the base had been occupied or was under attack by the Japanese. One brigade of 2 British Division would be despatched as soon as it arrived to hold the Nichugard Pass, eight miles south-east of Dimapur on the road to Kohima, to support 161 Brigade already defending the village. Finally, 23 LRP Brigade, which was expected to arrive on 12 April, would be used to strike south on Kohima and to the east of it to disrupt and cut the Japanese line of communication back to the Chindwin.

On 29 March *31 Division* cut the Imphal–Kohima road at Milestone 72.[9] The race to feed units into Dimapur before the arrival of *31 Division* was now one of dramatic urgency. Giffard's slowness in bringing 33 Corps forward to the Brahmaputra Valley now threatened to have dangerous repercussions for Slim. 'Even when these moves were in hand my anxiety was hardly lessened,' he recalled. 'They would take time – and time was short. It was a race between the Japanese onrush and the arrival of our reinforcements.' Characteristically, Slim accepted responsibility for mistakes that were not of his making.

> As I struggled hard to redress my errors and to speed by rail and air these reinforcements I knew that all depended on the steadfastness of the troops already meeting the first impetus of the attack. If they could hold until help arrived, all would be well; if not, we were near disaster. Happily for the result of the battle – and for me – I was,

* When fully constituted 33 Corps was to consist of 5 and 7 Indian Divisions (flown in from Arakan) and 2 British Division.
† 65 miles NNE of Dimapur.

like other generals before me, to be saved from the consequences of
my mistakes by the resourcefulness of my subordinate commanders
and the stubborn valour of my troops.

With Stopford's troops still several days away the question of how
to defend Kohima and Dimapur became critical. There was no simple solution, as the sum total of experienced combat troops available
before Grover's 2 British Division arrived was Warren's two-battalion
brigade. On 29 March Slim met to discuss the issue first in Imphal
with Scoones and Stopford and then later in the day, after a short
flight from Imphal, with Ranking at Dimapur. Stopford, as incoming
Corps commander, was concerned that if 161 Brigade was surrounded
and isolated at Kohima before Grover's division arrived there would
be nothing with which to defend Dimapur. Slim agreed that this was
a serious risk but argued that a well-defended Kohima would invariably force *Sato* to deal with it prior to proceeding to Dimapur, thus
giving valuable breathing space to Stopford to move the remainder of
33 Corps into position. A compromise of sorts was reached, but as
with most compromises some degree of clarity as to the main intention
was lost.

Following these two meetings Slim issued his orders to Ranking
in writing. Ranking was to prepare Dimapur for defence and hold
it when attacked; to reinforce Kohima and hold it to the last; and
to prepare for the reception of the 33 Corps reinforcements on their
way. Ranking interpreted in these orders no instructions to evacuate 161
Brigade from Kohima. Indeed, Warren's troops, on Slim's orders, were
arriving that very day. Meanwhile Stopford concentrated on moving his
Corps HQ to Jorhat, where it was established on 3 April. That night,
the day before Ranking formally transferred command, Stopford made
what proved to be a serious error of judgement. Still firmly of the
belief that the Japanese objective was Dimapur, and in response to
erroneous intelligence that Japanese units were at that very moment
in the process of outflanking Kohima, Stopford ordered Ranking to
withdraw 161 Brigade from Kohima immediately. All involved in the
defence of Kohima – Warren, Colonel Richards, and the civilian District
Commissioner – were aghast at the decision. Despite Ranking's protest,
that evening two battalions had fallen back to Nichugard. Ranking, sure
that Stopford was making a mistake, went over the head of his new

superior officer and called Slim directly by telephone to petition him to leave Warren at Kohima. Slim, perhaps unwilling to overrule Stopford, and in any case as convinced as Stopford that Dimapur was the Japanese objective, confirmed Stopford's order. The compromise reached on 30 March had not lead to a clear understanding of whether, with the limited troops available, it was better to defend Kohima or Dimapur and 161 Brigade, which had been in the process of organising the desperately needed defence of the village, left Kohima virtually undefended only one day before Japanese attacks began. Had they remained where they were the trauma of the siege that followed would have been much reduced and the stranglehold which *Sato* was able to maintain on the vital road to Imphal for two long months would have been significantly weaker than it turned out to be.

In *Defeat into Victory* Slim inexplicably blamed Ranking rather than Stopford for this error:

> In taking this action Ranking was, I think, influenced understandably by the stress I had laid on his primary task – the defence of the Dimapur base. The reports [of a Japanese envelopment of Kohima] proved untrue, and the withdrawal of the brigade was an unfortunate mistake. Had it remained south of Kohima, Warren would almost certainly have at least delayed the Japanese advance on Kohima for several days. That would have put a very different aspect on the battle which followed.

Quite. But the decision to withdraw 161 Brigade was made first by Stopford, and then endorsed by Slim himself on 3 April, *not* by Ranking, who opposed it vigorously. Evans suggests that the problem lay in the imprecision in the wording of Slim's instructions to Ranking on 30 March.[10] But this was only a manifestation of the real problem, which was to deem the defence of Kohima of limited consequence relative to that of Dimapur. When reality dawned, and Slim realized that *31 Division*'s objective was the weakly defended Kohima ridge and not Dimapur as he had expected, he admitted that the shock was considerable. 'I have spent some uncomfortable hours at the beginnings of battles', he wrote, 'but few more anxious than those of the Kohima battle.'

On the morning of 4 April, within hours of this blunder taking place, the Japanese attacked the southern edge of Kohima ridge* after a march of some 160 miles in twenty days over terrain which both Scoones and Slim had considered impassable to large bodies of troops. It was a remarkable feat and in its execution Ranking and Warren's worst fears had been realized. In desperation 161 Brigade immediately began to retrace its steps. By the following morning – 5 April 1944 – the leading battalion of 161 Brigade† had managed to rejoin the Kohima garrison as *Sato* launched further attacks on the ill-prepared defenders. Over the next few days the full weight of *31 Division* was brought to bear against the Kohima ridge. The puny garrison now consisted of some 2,500 men, of whom 1,000 were non-combatants. Worse still, and to Warren's surprise when he first arrived on 29 March, no systematic defence of the village had been prepared. Consequently the motley garrison was forced to dig in and defend itself where it could. The remainder of 161 Brigade was unable to get back into Kohima so Warren set up a defensive box at Jotsoma, two miles to the west, where he could use his artillery to support the Kohima defenders.

The first phase of the battle of Kohima thus began. For the next two weeks of vicious fighting *Sato* sought to crush the defenders. The Japanese 'mortared and shelled the garrison every evening at dusk', wrote Louis Allen. 'When it grew dark, they sent in wave after wave of infantry. Inevitably, the defenders gave ground, and the Japanese remorselessly began to crawl and bomb and bayonet their way along Kohima Ridge . . . The actions were hand-to-hand combat, fierce and ruthless, by filthy, bedraggled, worn-out men, whose lungs were rarely free of the noxious smell of decaying corpses inside and outside the perimeter.'[11]

By 9 April the depleted garrison was concentrated in a tight perimeter on Garrison Hill and after more than a week of ferocious hand-to-hand fighting the Japanese managed to divide that in two on 18 April. Just when the position began to look untenable 2 British Division began to advance from Dimapur and 161 Brigade was able to move out of its box at Jotsoma and relieve the exhausted defenders on 20 April. The ferocity of the battle that had taken place was clear to the relieving force. 'If Garrison Hill was indescribable for its filth and horror and smell', recalled the Brigade Major of 161 Brigade, David Wilson, 'the

* General Purpose Transport or 'GPT' hill.
† 500 men of the 4th Battalion Royal West Kents.

sight of its defenders was almost worse. They looked like aged blood stained scarecrows dropping with fatigue, the only thing clean about them was their weapons and they smelt of blood, sweat and death.'[12] 'Kohima had been changed beyond recognition,' records Slim. 'Most of its buildings were in ruins, walls still standing were pockmarked with shell bursts or bullet holes, the trees were stripped of leaves and parachutes hung limply from the few branches that remained. It was the nearest thing to a battlefield of the First World War in the whole Burma campaign.'

Slim admits that as a consequence of these three near-disasters the first week of April was 'an anxious one. Thanks to my mistakes the battle had not started well; at any time crisis might have slipped into disaster – and still might.' Even though the Japanese were doing what Slim expected them to do this knowledge was cold comfort, as they clearly retained the tactical advantage on three different sectors of the front during this time. Indeed, to *Mutaguchi* everything appeared to be going his way. By early April *15 Army* had successfully pushed 4 Corps onto its heels, and had cut all land links to the rest of India. It seemed to *Mutaguchi* only a matter of weeks before Scoones would be starved into submission, unless of course the demoralized British and Indian troops capitulated first. However, by the second week of April Slim had cause to relax somewhat. The successful concentration of 4 Corps on the Imphal plain by 4 April, the rapid insertion of 5 Indian Division and the arrival of 33 Corps by the end of the first week of April meant that the immediate danger was over. These were the first signs that Slim's great gamble would pay off. Despite the poor start to the battle in the Tiddim, Ukhrul and Kohima areas, 4 Corps had not been defeated and the makeshift defences at Sangshak, Kohima and the fighting withdrawal up the Tiddim road had inflicted grievous and irreplaceable casualties on the enemy. Slim's cautious optimism at the beginning of April grew stronger as the month progressed. By mid-April his command of the situation had been unequivocally reasserted. Slim's belief in the fundamental correctness of his approach, his steadiness and that of his principal subordinates in the face of impending disaster and the stout fighting qualities of his troops did much to stabilize the situation in 14 Army's favour during the first critical weeks of the battle.

Nevertheless, the stabilization of the front heralded merely the beginning of the end of Slim's difficulties. While the immediate crisis was over,

Slim now had to prevent *Sato* capturing Kohima and Dimapur; *Yamauchi* from penetrating Imphal from the north; *Yamamoto* from penetrating Gracey's defences at Shenam, and *Yanagida* from breaking through at Bishenpur in the south. He also had to ensure that 4 Corps was resupplied. Nor, too, were his other fronts devoid of concern at this time. On the Ledo front Stilwell was making heavy weather of his task to replicate *Sato*'s achievement in reverse by seizing Myitkyina. After securing the Hukawng Valley on 7 March he still had over 150 miles to go over some of the world's most atrocious terrain before his objective was reached, let alone captured. In Arakan *General Hanaya's 28 Army* remained full of fight and attempted to recapture Buthidaung in early May, only to be driven back with heavy loss by Christison.

Through all of these tribulations Slim stood like a rock, firm and unyielding in his refusal to be cowed by *Mutaguchi*'s onslaught, and quietly confident that the measures he had put in place to smash *U-Go* would bear eventual – and satisfactory – fruit. To those who were close to him at this time his resilience and fortitude under pressure struck them forcibly. Ouvry Roberts recalled that he 'never showed any anxiety or strain – he'd drive up in his jeep with a smile on his face – he'd jump out and say "Hello Ouvry, how's things?" Then he'd ask me to introduce him to the officers who were there to meet him – many of whom he'd know, and he'd chat to them – ask them questions, try and see and hear as much as he could for himself, assess morale for himself and in this way he really would know what the situation was.'[13] 'Slim was imperturbable in the worst of circumstances,' reflected Anthony Brett-James. 'The confidence that he showed in his troops aroused their confidence in him as their commander.'[14] In the moral power thus exerted lay the developing confidence of his army.

In order to cut Japanese communications to *18 Division* Wingate's plan for Operation Thursday was to concentrate his effort in an area within a circle of forty miles radius from Indaw, from where the railway went north to Myitkyina, and roads led west to the Chindwin. The operational concept agreed by Slim and Wingate at Ranchi on 19 January 1944 centred upon the creation of strongholds capable of self-defence, in areas inaccessible to Japanese armour and artillery, to provide bases for guerrilla raids against the Japanese lines of communication.[15] They would be properly garrisoned and would contain an airstrip so that supplies could be flown in and casualties flown out, as well as ground and anti-aircraft artillery, the lack of which proved to be a severe deficiency during Operation Longcloth.

The operation was to be in two phases. During the first phase three brigades would walk and fly to four strongholds in the Indaw area. After two to three months these brigades would be replaced *in situ* by the three relief brigades. Because of the lack of sufficient air transport resources, 16 Brigade* would have to march the 360 miles from Ledo in early February 1944 to its stronghold at Aberdeen, twenty-seven miles north-west of Indaw, while 77 Brigade† would fly to two strongholds in the Kyaukke Valley – Broadway, thirty-five miles east-north-east of Indaw and Piccadilly, forty miles north-east – flying in from Assam on 5 March 1944. The 111 Brigade‡ would fly to Chowringhee, thirty-five miles east of Indaw, beginning on 6 March 1944. In the second phase 14,** 23†† and 3 West African Brigades would relieve the original brigades.

Shortly before the operation to lift 77 Brigade was due to begin on 5 March, an aerial photograph of Piccadilly showed that the landing site was obstructed with logs. The photograph was immediately shown to Wingate and Slim. Wingate concluded that the Japanese had ambushed Piccadilly and that the whole operation had been compromised and should therefore be called off. Slim disagreed, however, as did Michael Calvert, commander of 77 Brigade. Slim was certain that not all of the landing sites could have been compromised. He knew that Stilwell needed the help Special Force was to bring, and that 16 Brigade on its insertion march could not simply be abandoned. He knew also that morale among Special Force – now at fever pitch – would not recover if the operation were cancelled. Accordingly, he made the decision to continue the operation, Piccadilly was abandoned and the troops switched to Broadway instead.[16]

Of the sixty-one gliders which set off for Broadway that night only thirty-five landed at their destination. Nevertheless, some four hundred

* Brigadier Bernard Fergusson, later Earl Ballantrae.

† Brigadier Michael Calvert.

‡ Brigadier Lentaigne, who was to become Wingate's successor after Wingate's death on 24 March 1944.

** Brigadier Brodie.

†† Brigadier Perowne.

men landed during the night, together with enough mechanical equipment to enable an airstrip capable of taking Dakotas to be constructed. On the following three nights, 272 aircraft sorties landed at Broadway completing the fly-in of the whole 77 Brigade. There was no interference from the Japanese throughout the entire operation. Within a week both 77 and 111 Brigades, totalling 9,000 men, 1,350 animals and 250 tons of stores, an anti-aircraft and a 25-pounder gun battery, were landed by 650 Dakota and glider sorties into the heart of Burma. With 16 Brigade this gave Wingate 12,000 men, 'well placed,' as he put it, recalled Slim, 'in the enemy's guts.' There was very little interference from the Japanese air force which had been reduced by this time to approximately ninety aircraft in the whole of Burma. Surprise low-level air attacks were made on a number of enemy airfields which further reduced the Japanese ability to counter allied activity both in the air and on the ground over the period of the fly-in. By 15 March a block was established at Henu, known as White City after the parachutes that littered the site. Throughout the remainder of the month, and in April, Special Force mounted attacks throughout the area, cutting the railway to Myitkyina, and dominating a thirty-mile-long corridor astride the railway.

The landings took the Japanese by surprise. The first news of the landings reached 15 Army HQ on 9 March, but it took some time for the size and significance of the invasion to sink in. Nevertheless once this had been appreciated a force which within four weeks was of divisional size was formed to counter the landings. Once deployed, Wingate began to press for Special Force to support 14 Army directly by attacking *Mutaguchi*'s rear. He proposed as much in a paper on 13 March 1944. Wingate told Calvert: 'We have got to help 14th Army. We are all, including Stilwell, under 14th Army command, and in spite of my complaints at times, they have been very helpful on the whole, even if they did doubt the practicability of this operation. Now they are converted.'[17] Slim accepted Wingate's argument that 14 Brigade could offer some usefulness in attacking for a time the lines of communication to 31 and 15 Divisions. Slim's instructions on 20 March to redeploy 14 Brigade in support of 14 Army, after supporting 16 Brigade's attack on Indaw, was manna from heaven for Wingate.[18] While this was a change from Wingate's original instructions, Slim believed that the threat to Imphal was such that he felt justified in temporarily redeploying one of Wingate's brigades to meet the new threat.[19] For his part, Wingate believed that redeploying his force to assist 14 Army would help prove his principal theory, namely that LRP action alone would degrade *15 Army*'s lines of communication to such an extent that it would be the decisive factor in bringing about the defeat of the enemy. When this had been proven, as he was sure it would be, Wingate believed that Special Force would be substantially reinforced and perhaps even given the lead in defeating *15 Army*. The flaw in this logic was that *15 Army* had taken such logistic risks that it planned to be virtually self-sufficient until it had captured British stocks in Manipur, and thus were remarkably resilient to attacks on their long line of communication. Action to interdict the Japanese supply chain in the early weeks of an offensive therefore had a marginal impact on Japanese operations.

Other problems began to waylay Wingate's original plans. One was the exhaustion of the 4,000 men and 500 mules of Fergusson's 16 Brigade who were forced, due to a lack of air transport, to march 360 miles to the area of Nab-Indaw and Banmauk. The brigade left Ledo on 5 February, but because of the difficulty of the terrain the brigade was already ten days behind schedule by 28 March. They were unable to carry with them the heavy weapons and ammunition required to survive a large-scale contact with the Japanese. To compound their exhaustion Slim was convinced that Wingate underestimated Japanese tenacity in battle and believed that Special Force would find opposition to be stiffer than they expected. Additionally, Wingate now found himself using his brigades in a conventional role, for which they were not suited or trained. For instance, 77 Brigade was ordered to build Broadway into 'a small fortress in open country astride the railway' and to hold it indefinitely.[20] This contravened Wingate's original argument that strongholds were to be bases for rest and supply, protected by 'floater' columns, and sited in country 'so inaccessible that only lightly equipped enemy infantry can penetrate to it ... We can transport our defensive stores there by air: the enemy cannot.'[21] Likewise, the stronghold at White City was placed in an area which made it vulnerable to Japanese armour and artillery.[22] As Raymond Callahan records, in his history of the war in Burma, 'the attempt to hold territory was not what the LRP brigades had been designed for, and was bound to deprive them of the assets of dispersion and mobility that had been their strength, and ultimately their salvation, during Chindit I.'[23]

Failure and tragedy balanced the success of the airborne insertion. On 24 March Wingate was killed in an air crash in the hills west of Imphal.

The nature of the operation changed immediately. 'Without his presence to animate it', wrote Slim, 'Special Force would no longer be the same to others or to itself. He had created, inspired, defended it and given it confidence; it was the offspring of his vivid imagination and ruthless energy. It had no other parent.' Slim's wording of this eulogy is interesting. It reflects Sykes' assertion that the Chindit ideal died with Wingate. Sykes argues that this was because they no longer enjoyed 'Wingate's inventive mind to devise a role for them in new circumstances,' indicating perhaps that the Chindit role actually had little to justify it outside of Wingate's personal advocacy.[24] It is impossible not to conclude that Operation Thursday was the product not of strategic necessity but of the determined promotion of one man. With his death, the idea evaporated.

Because of the gradual reduction in effectiveness of the Chindits as they were worn down by casualties and exhaustion, Lentaigne, Wingate's successor and formerly commander of 111 Brigade, proposed that he redeploy his brigades northward more directly to assist Stilwell's efforts in the battle for Mogaung and Myitkyina. His plan was to create another block fifty miles north of White City, near the railway in the Hopin area, to be called Blackpool, after which the exhausted 16 Brigade was to be evacuated by air and the remaining strongholds abandoned. His aim was to concentrate his remaining units (77, 111, 14 and 3 West African brigades) to attack Mogaung from the south while Stilwell's forces attacked from the north. Slim agreed to all these plans, as did Stilwell, after some persuasion. Stilwell believed that Special Force could do more harm in and around Indaw than moving north, but when he realized the difficulties involved for the Chindits remaining in that area for too long he agreed to Lentaigne's plan.

On 9 April a meeting between Mountbatten, Slim and Lentaigne confirmed that Special Force would be firmly committed to assisting Stilwell. Only six days before Slim had agreed at a meeting at Jorhat with Lentaigne, Mountbatten, Stilwell, Baldwin, Boatner (Stilwell's deputy) and Stopford, that 14 and 111 Brigades would focus on *15 Army*'s lines of communication on the Chindwin. He was now persuaded, however, that the Chindits as a whole, except for 23 Brigade which was assisting 33 Corps in the battle for Kohima, should go back to their original role of supporting Stilwell's advance on Myitkyina. Slim was later to consider that his decision on 9 April was a mistake. 'Imphal was the decisive battle,' he wrote; 'it was there only that vital injury could be inflicted on the Japanese

Army, and I should have concentrated all available forces to that end. I fear I fell into the error of so many Japanese, and persisted in a plan which should have been changed.' As a result, concludes Callahan, Operation Thursday, despite 'an epic of courage and endurance, became irrelevant to the decisive battles taking place around Imphal and Kohima.'[25]

The 111th Brigade accordingly occupied Blackpool on 7 May, and 16 Brigade was flown back to India. By this stage Special Force was down to about 6,000 men. A few days later the remaining brigades moved north to Blackpool, this being abandoned after constant Japanese attacks at the end of the month. Bad weather, a lack of air transport and difficult country all combined to slow down the move north of the remainder of Special Force. When it was realized that Blackpool could not be held, an area around Indawgyi Lake was secured to evacuate the wounded.

The Chindits came under Stilwell's operational control from 16/17 May, after which they ceased to engage in the guerrilla-style operations originally envisaged for them. However, it is wrong to blame this change of tactics on either Lentaigne or Slim, as some in indignation have done. The Chindits by this time no longer operated as guerrillas, and Wingate himself had employed his columns in conventional operations, such as his ill-fated instructions to the exhausted and ill-equipped 16 Brigade to launch an unsupported attack on Indaw at the end of their long infiltration march. Self-evidently the theories of guerrilla warfare and LRP activity that had been developed in great detail *before* Operation Thursday were forced through circumstance to be adapted to the battlefield realities that were faced once Special Force had deployed.

Although Imphal was now besieged Slim was not unduly concerned about the ultimate outcome. *Mutaguchi* was conforming to his plan, and he was confident that Scoones had the wherewithal to withstand any attempt to break through. He was less sanguine about Kohima, however, and decided that, with his limited resources, his priority must be the destruction of *31 Division* rather than the immediate relief of Imphal. He determined that responsibility for relieving Imphal was to rest with 33 Corps and was to take place only after *31 Division* had been defeated at Kohima. While this was taking place 4 Corps was to deny penetration of the plain by *15* and *33 Divisions* and to counter-attack once Scoones was certain that the Japanese offensive was faltering.

With the siege of Kohima lifted the task of ejecting *31 Division* from the Kohima ridge began. Stopford's task was not an easy one. 'It was clear from the beginning' remarked Slim, 'that the battle would be prolonged and savage.' The harshness of the terrain, the tenacity of *Sato*'s troops, the ferocity of the fighting and the relative inexperience of many of Stopford's new units combined to slow down the speed of 33 Corps' advance. While there is evidence that Slim was occasionally exasperated with the slowness of Grover's 2 British Division* Slim was nevertheless concerned not to hasten 33 Corps as a whole beyond its capability and to build up its strength so that it enjoyed a decisive superiority over the Japanese. This was not something that could be achieved quickly. In the meantime the Japanese proved as stubborn and fanatical as ever and simply refused to be budged from their positions. Although ejected from Kohima ridge on 13 May it was to take a further month of hard fighting before *Sato*'s units began to withdraw from the Naga Hills, their mission unfulfilled. Every inch had to be fought for. Fighting was constant, close-range and ferocious, with the brunt being taken by the infantry, although gunner Forward Observation Officers and tank commanders also suffered heavy casualties. 'Each Japanese position had to be individually dealt with,' recalled David Wilson, 'and this was a very slow business. We were slowly strangling them with our air and artillery power, but starving or not, 31 Division was not in any mood to give in.'[26]

The prolonged and bloody experience at Kohima was replicated across the battlefield. On the Iril Valley and Ukhrul spokes north and north east of Imphal, *15 Division* cut the road between Imphal and Kohima on 30 March, thus threatening the virtually open door to Imphal from the north.† Everywhere imagining that the British were in panicked flight, *Yamauchi* urged each of his battalions to attack without hesitation at every opportunity. Scoones rushed 63 Brigade, just back from the withdrawal from Tiddim, forward to Sengmai, ten miles north of Imphal on the Kohima road, to plug the gap, as well as Brigg's 5 Indian Division, when it had completed its fly-in from Arakan. A grim struggle developed during the first half of April for the imposing heights of Nungshigum Hill, which at 4,000 feet dominates the northern end of the plain and was a mere four

---

* 4, 5 and 6 Brigades.

† Allen says that they didn't reach the Imphal–Kohima road at Kanglatongbi, where there was a Mission church, until 3 April.

miles from Kangla airfield and six miles from Scoones' HQ. *Yamauchi's 51 Regiment* was eventually repulsed with severe losses, and the Japanese were turned away from the northern gate to Imphal.

Angry at *Yamauchi's* repulse at Nungshigum, *Mutaguchi* ordered *Sato* to send a regiment south from Kohima to assist *15 Division's* attack on Imphal. A copy of these orders fortuitously fell into Slim's hands on 20 April. Slim, in what the historian Arthur Swinson describes as 'a brilliant stroke of perception', immediately ordered Stopford to put such pressure on *Sato* that he could not possibly obey *Mutaguchi's* order.[27] This move proved to be remarkably successful, for by 25 April *Sato* concluded that he could not break into Kohima if he had also to diminish his forces there to assist in the attack on Imphal. Consequently and increasingly convinced that his superior did not understand the nature of the battle he was fighting, *Sato* refused to obey *Mutaguchi's* order, and began signalling *HQ 15 Army* that his division was rapidly approaching exhaustion. While this act of disobedience undoubtedly assisted the defence of Imphal, it nevertheless made Stopford's job at Kohima all the more difficult and served to delay the opening of the road to Imphal.

Meanwhile, on the south-eastern spoke the Japanese managed to seize Nippon Hill on 2 April, initiating a long slow fight for the vital Shenam position. For seven weeks Gracey's two brigades faced the furious assault of *Yamamoto's* battalions, desperate to break through to Palel and beyond. On the Tiddim spoke to the south 32 Brigade was placed at Bishenpur, eighteen miles south of Imphal, on the ridge astride the track running westward to Silchar in Assam. Its task was to block any advance by *Yanagida's* battalions towards Imphal. The Japanese immediately sought to outflank these positions to the west.[28] Throughout April and May fierce fighting took place for possession of the track to the west of Bishenpur. The fighting was often at close range and because of limited ammunition and the nature of the ground 17 Indian Division enjoyed very little close support by artillery. By the end of the month Cowan had clear possession of the road on the ridge and had begun to push the Japanese away from the track, and despite desperate attempts *Yanagida* was unable to force 32 Brigade from overall control of the ridge. Attempts to infiltrate through to the villages south and south-west of Bishenpur during May also failed, although they demanded considerable effort, including counter-attacks by 63 Brigade, to expel the Japanese.

With *Yamauchi's* offensive to the north of Imphal blunted, and mindful of the need to re-open the road to Kohima, Slim gave orders to Scoones on 10 April to turn to the offensive. Scoones' plan was for 5 Indian Division to advance to the north on either side of the road to Kohima beyond Kanglatongbi, fourteen miles north of Imphal, and for 23 Indian Division to chase *15 Division* in the direction of Litan and Ukhrul. Elsewhere Scoones planned to continue to hold the Bishenpur front with 17 Indian Division (now rejoined by 63 Brigade) and to launch a limited counter-attack against *33 Division*'s line of communication on the Tiddim road. 20 Indian Division would continue to absorb *Yamamoto*'s punches against the Shenam defences while Stilwell was instructed to push on for Myitkyina and Special Force was ordered to continue to block Japanese communications in north Burma.

In mid-May Cameron's two battalions were secretly inserted, after an eleven-day approach march, on the road near Torbung and Milestone 32. The intention was that once this anvil had been formed, Burton's 63 Brigade would smash down on it from the north, destroying any of *Yanagida*'s battalions caught between. The Japanese response to this provocation was hornet-like, and from May 20 they swarmed around the block furiously, losing in the process over 600 killed, a large number of vehicles and five tanks. 63 Brigade, however, was unable to break through from the north, with the result that Cameron was forced to remove his block on 24 May and fight his way back to the British positions at Bishenpur.

The offensive by Roberts' 1 and 37 Brigades to open the Ukhrul road to Kasom succeeded by 20 April in ejecting *15 Division* from the area. With the road open, 1 Brigade then continued its pursuit and harassment of *Yamauchi*'s HQ. By early May Ouvry Roberts had driven *15 Division* twenty miles east to Litan and scattered its units through the remote jungle vastness. Roberts' success against *Yamauchi* in fact disguised a growing number of problems with *15 Division*. Although it had succeeded in making good progress, and in the first two weeks of April posed a significant threat to the northern approach to Imphal, the division was rapidly weakening. *Yamauchi* was terminally ill with tuberculosis and his relationship with *Mutaguchi* was also deteriorating.

Meanwhile Briggs' 5 Indian Division, reinforced by Crowther's 89 Brigade from Arakan on 7 May, began moving gradually against the enemy up the Iril Valley from Nungshigum and on the Mapao Ridge. The Japanese had constructed three roadblocks at Sengmai and defensive positions in the adjacent hills. Crowther secretly infiltrated a whole battalion through the Japanese front lines on 15 May to form a block to their rear. The main attacks by 89 Brigade on the surrounding heights made little headway, but the block worked superbly and the Japanese launched constant, furious and unavailing assaults upon it. Briggs was able to reinforce the block and by 20 May the enemy were forced to give up the struggle and evacuate their forward positions while 123 Brigade applied pressure against the blocks on the road. By 21 May the vast dump at Kanglatongbi which had fallen into Japanese hands on 9 April was recovered.

With the tide clearly turning in his favour on the Ukhrul spoke, Scoones was faced with no let up of pressure on the Shenam spoke, and decided to replace Gracey's two exhausted brigades with 23 Indian Division, the exchange taking place between 13 and 16 May. 37 Brigade, reinforced with two extra battalions, now moved into the Shenam positions.[29] By this time British and Japanese positions snaked through the hills, made devoid of vegetation by many weeks of shelling. Only yards apart in places, the ground lay littered with the decomposing bodies of British, Indian and Japanese alike. The Japanese, desperate to break through, launched repeated assaults on the British positions. Some positions changed ownership several times as the battle raged across the mountains. When the monsoon arrived, 'conditions changed to provide further horrors', wrote Louis Allen. 'The troops were almost submerged in rain and, at 4,000 feet, in clouds for weeks on end, so that visibility was reduced to 100 yards, and the sun itself became invisible. Trenches collapsed in the incessant downpour, dugouts were ankle-deep in mud.'[30] But despite the ebb and flow of battle, Roberts' troops held firm and at no time did *Yamamoto* break through the Shenam position to threaten Palel or Imphal.[31]

By the middle of May Slim acknowledged that his worst anxieties were over. Progress, although slow, was tangible nevertheless and the Japanese offensive was everywhere showing signs of faltering. Anxieties of a different nature then presented themselves. Slim commented wryly that now that the worst threat had past the number of visitors to 14 Army increased, but that most remained gloomy, urging him to 'relieve Imphal before it is too late'. Slim's sanguinity about Imphal was regarded with suspicion by some in Kandy, London and Washington.[32] Some even accused him of being insufficiently aggressive. Mountbatten tells the story of Pownall, his chief of staff, who at this time was unable to sleep because of worry about the fate of the surrounded 4 Corps.[33] Mountbatten did not share Pownall's fears, but Pownall was representative of 'those, who, crediting from a distance the alarmist reports that always circulate at such moments', recalled Slim, 'urged me at all costs to "break through and relieve Imphal".' Pressure was put on Mountbatten from London to make the opening of the Kohima road and thus the relief of Imphal his priority. When Mountbatten approached Giffard to enquire as to the earliest date the road could be opened, Giffard refused to be hustled. 'Neither General Giffard nor I was as anxious as they appeared about Imphal's power to hold out,' wrote Slim; 'we knew that 4 Corps would shortly take the offensive.' 'It is not the easiest task of a superior commander to stand between such pressure and his subordinate commanders,' he reflected, 'but at times it is his duty. General Giffard, who understood the situation well, increased my debt to him by the firmness with which he did this now.'

Slim was determined to stick to his guns. His primary objective was not the relief of Imphal – this would occur in due course anyway – but rather the destruction of 15 Army. Slim could see clearly that Mutaguchi was now playing directly into his hands. In early May the Japanese were suffering fearsome casualties all across the front, losing experienced fighting men who could not be replaced. All the while 14 Army was growing rapidly stronger in experience, reinforcements and supplies. With only six weeks before the monsoon broke, it was in Slim's interest not to force the Japanese into an early retirement. He had three reasons for believing in the essential correctness of his strategy. In the first place, at no time after 4 April was Slim concerned that Imphal would fall. Four Corps had stayed Mutaguchi's initial onslaught, and Imphal was defended sufficiently strongly for Slim to be confident that Scoones had the resources to deal with any eventuality. The only urgency was to ensure that Imphal did not run out of supplies. The airlift would improve that situation in part but the impending monsoon meant that the flying programme would be severely disrupted. Accordingly, in early May, Slim determined that Scoones would have to re-open the road to Kohima by the third week of June to prevent the possibility of the 55,000 men and 11,000 animals remaining in the pocket from running critically short of essential supplies. The truth is that, although

Scoones was forced to reduce the ration scale during the siege, supplies never fell to critical levels and indeed, in some instances, surpluses were built up.

Second, the last thing Slim wanted was two offensives: one from Dimapur and the other from Imphal. It would have been impossible to sustain logistically, as the supplies required for an Imphal-based offensive would have had to be flown in by air. Third, an offensive from Imphal solely to open up the Kohima road could have meant a weakening in Imphal's northernmost defences. Slim was particularly concerned lest a too-rapid advance by 5 Indian Division created a gap in these defences which could be exploited by a surprise Japanese counter-offensive. He was later to regard this view to have been too cautious, but at this juncture it was a very real issue. Slim's greatest concern was that a dual offensive would dangerously diminish his ability to inflict grievous injuries on *Mutaguchi*, and it was this above everything else that he was determined to achieve.

To his credit, Mountbatten, thus persuaded, backed his subordinates to the hilt, and directed that the road be opened by mid-July. 'I was grateful to him for not being stampeded by more nervous people into setting too early a date,' Slim recalled. 'I intended that the road should be open well before mid-July, but I was now more interested in destroying Japanese divisions than in "relieving" Imphal.'

By early June 1944 it was evident to Slim that the Japanese offensive was near collapse. Despite desperate attempts, *Yamamoto* had failed to evict 23 Indian Division from the Shenam ridge. With casualties mounting with every attack he could do little else during the latter half of June but attempt to hold the ground that he had managed to seize, as the lifeblood drained from his exhausted division. Likewise at Kohima, exhausted, without adequate reinforcements or resupply, and increasingly alienated from *Mutaguchi*, *Sato* had finally recognized the inevitable and ordered the withdrawal of *31 Division* through the jungle towards Ukhrul, in direct and wilful disobedience of *Mutaguchi*'s orders. This was by no means a headlong flight for safety, however. *31 Division*, desperately short of supplies and suffering fearsome casualties, fought an organized and tenacious retreat over the ensuing six weeks. In the south, determined not to relax its pressure, *Yanagida*'s two weak regiments* attempted one last effort in late May to break through the Bishenpur defences. Unable to advance and unwilling to withdraw, the attacking Japanese were trapped and systematically destroyed. This fighting matched anything at Shenam or Kohima for its intensity. By this time, wrote Slim, *Yanagida*'s 'division as a whole had suffered 3,500 casualties (including 1,200 killed). And only two battalion commanders in the entire division were unwounded.' By 30 June *33 Division* had lost 12,000 men, 70 per cent of its strength.

Angered by *Yanagida*'s inability to break through at Bishenpur, *Mutaguchi* accused him of timidity and at the end of May replaced him with *General Tanaka*. Japanese command relationships, weak from the outset of the campaign, now began to unravel, and in June *Mutaguchi* dismissed both *Yamauchi* and *Sato*. Unwilling to accept publicly the possibility of failure, *Tanaka* promulgated a Special Order on 2 June which perhaps reflected his own pessimism about his chances of attaining his goal, ordering his men to fight on until either they were overtaken by either victory or annihilation. Such determination against all odds deeply impressed Slim. 'Whatever one may think of the military wisdom of thus pursuing a hopeless object,' he commented, 'there can be no question of the supreme courage and hardihood of the Japanese soldiers who made the attempts. I know of no army that could have equalled them.' This stubbornness, however, as Slim had calculated, and as events were beginning at last to show right across the Manipur front, was also to prove their downfall. 'The Japs,' he wrote in a report to Mountbatten on 13 September 1944, 'by constantly attacking and reinforcing failure, played into our hands, and it was at this period that around Imphal he was gradually worn down.'[34]

In obedience to *Tanaka*'s orders, *33 Division* held on desperately, although the difficulties faced by his exhausted troops were made considerably worse by the fury of the monsoon. To the north of Imphal the Japanese fought hard for every position. By mid-June, after a month of fighting, the forward troops of 9 Brigade now leading the 4 Corps advance up the road to Tiddim had only reached a point some sixteen miles north of Imphal. Slim wrote:

> The whole countryside lent itself to delaying tactics, and the Japanese, skilfully dug in astride the road and the hills overlooking it, were

* *214* and *215 Regiments*.

determined to make the best use of this advantage. Each hill had to be taken separately. Guns had to be brought up to fire point-blank to destroy the heavily timbered and earth bunkers. To make matters worse, the weather was atrocious. The rain teemed down almost incessantly ... With head-on attacks and hooks into the jungle to get behind the Japanese positions, the division pushed slowly northwards, killing large numbers of the enemy and incurring many casualties in the process.

From 4 June, after sixty-four days of fighting described by Major-General Grover as equal to anything he had experienced as a young officer on the Somme or at Passchendaele, 2 British Division, led by 6 Brigade*, began methodically to clear the road from the Kohima end.[35] On 22 June it joined hands with 9 Brigade advancing from Imphal, and the road was opened. That night the first convoy in three months drove through to Imphal.

Japanese tenacity and dogged bravery could not stave off the inevitable. By 8 July *Mutaguchi* accepted that the offensive against Bishenpur had failed, and the remnants of *33 Division* were ordered to withdraw to Tiddim. On 20 July, formalizing what was already happening to his shattered army, *Mutaguchi* ordered a general retreat across the Chindwin. Slim sought now to pursue *Mutaguchi* with such vigour that *15 Army*'s defeat was turned into a rout. Mountbatten's orders to Giffard allowed Slim to push *Mutaguchi* hard. Accordingly Slim ordered Scoones and Stopford to place unremitting pressure on the retreating Japanese in order to destroy *31* and *15 Divisions* before they managed to reach the relative safety of the Chindwin.

From Kohima, 7 Indian Division chased *31 Division* through the Naga Hills and 23 (LRP) Brigade harassed the flank of the division as it attempted to escape. On 7 June 80 Brigade of 20 Indian Division† on the Ukhrul spoke began to cut the line of communications and withdrawal routes for both *15* and *31 Divisions*. 100 Brigade, moving east along the Ukhrul road, met up with its sister brigade in early July near Litan.

---

* Brigadier W.G. Smith.
† 32 Brigade remained attached to 17 Indian Division at Tiddim.

The conditions made progress difficult and slow for 14 Army, however. Disease and malnutrition had weakened many and exhaustion was widespread. The extreme ruggedness of the terrain made progress difficult and slow. Many of Scoones' troops had fought continuously in appalling conditions for eight months. The monsoon rains, which had arrived in their full fury by the middle of May, made life miserable for all. But conditions were infinitely more desperate for the retreating Japanese. While they fought every step of the way back across the Naga and Chin Hills, starvation, exhaustion and the savage monsoon rains daily extracted their toll, many hundreds dying on the way. The absurdly optimistic risks taken at the outset of the campaign, which provided support for an offensive lasting only twenty days, now began to demand their deadly payment. Continuing to display his ignorance of the conditions in which his soldiers had fought *Mutaguchi*, in one final explosion of martial fervour, exhorted his troops: 'If your hands are broken, fight with your feet . . . if there is no breath in your body, fight with your ghost. Lack of weapons is no excuse for defeat.' Such exhortations might feed the soul but they did nothing to fill the belly, and it was food above anything else that the starving remnants of *Mutaguchi*'s once proud army now desperately craved. Disease, starvation and despair were accompanied in places by cannibalism. The pursuing British troops came across countless putrefying bodies, skeletons and abandoned weapons and material littering the jungle paths that led back through the hills to the Chindwin.

By the last day of the month Slim's great test was over. Roberts had captured Tamu, Gracey's division was in the hills east of Ukhrul overlooking the Kabaw Valley and 5 Indian Division was methodically pushing aside *Tanaka*'s remaining rearguards on the Tiddim road. Slim's gamble had paid off. Japanese rearguards continued to fight their way slowly for several months, particularly down the Tiddim road, but *U-Go* had been defeated and *15 Army* comprehensively smashed, just as Slim had set out to do. Scoones, together with his headquarters, 17 and 23 Indian Divisions and 50 Parachute Brigade returned to India to rest. The battle had provided the largest, most prolonged and most intense engagement with a Japanese army yet seen in the war. 'It is the most important defeat the Japs have ever suffered in their military career,' wrote Mountbatten exultantly to his wife on 22 June 1944, 'because the numbers involved are so much greater than any Pacific Island operation.'[36] It was a significant victory, however, not just because of the numbers involved. Importantly, it created the conditions, as Slim always intended it should, for an offensive by 14 Army into Burma. *Fifteen Army*'s command structure had disintegrated, and *Mutaguchi* himself was removed in December.* Of the 65,000 fighting troops who set off across the Chindwin in early March 1944, 30,000 were killed in battle and a further 23,000 were wounded.† Only 600 allowed themselves to be taken prisoner. Some 17,000 pack animals perished during the operation and not a single piece of heavy weaponry made it back to Burma. When considered with his defeat of *Hanaya's 55 Division* in Arakan, Slim's substantial – even extraordinary achievement – can be seen. Not only had he destroyed five divisions and inflicted some 90,000 casualties on the enemy, something that would have been considered inconceivable only five months before, but in so doing he had severely degraded the fighting power of the Burma Area Army. He had also decisively removed any remaining notions of Japanese superiority on the battlefield. The cost? Fourteen Army had suffered 24,000 casualties in Arakan, Kohima and Imphal, many of whom recovered under 14 Army's medical care.[7]

More than anything else the battle vindicated Slim's strategy for defeating the Japanese. He had single-mindedly developed his plan, in parallel with the building up of his Army, in the face of extraordinary material difficulty and, in some cases, opposition. He had withstood pressure during the battle to follow a different route. In the case of Wingate, Slim suffered from the political machinations of a pretender to 14 Army's strategic crown. He had proven himself to be the rightful owner. Strongly pragmatic and realistic, his judgements remained deeply rooted in an intimate knowledge of the Japanese way of war. He *knew* what he had to do to defeat *Mutaguchi*, and he accordingly developed a plan of battle to turn that theory into reality. It was Slim's strategy that delivered victory over *15 Army* to the allies, not Wingate's grandiose airborne extravaganza into enemy-held Burma, although this is not to demean the heroic nature of that extraordinary venture.

---

* He was replaced by *Lieutenant-General Katamura*.

† *15 Army* consisted of 115,000 troops, 50,000 of whom were support, line of communication and administrative troops. Of this latter number, 15,000 were lost. *Fifteen Army* overall, therefore lost 65,000 of its original number during the fighting in Manipur.

With considerable deftness Slim successfully mastered the not inconsiderable risk his plan entailed. Withdrawing 4 Corps onto the Imphal plain, transferring first 5 Indian Division and then 7 Indian Division by air to the Assamese battlefield and relying on air-supply to maintain the besieged 4 Corps were all phenomenal risks and yet undoubtedly shifted the balance of the battle in 14 Army's favour. He had far fewer resources than he really needed to undertake the massive tasks he set for himself in Manipur, and the huge logistical risks he took were in direct contravention of the advice he had once been given never to commit himself until he had everything he needed.[38] His ability to do so much with so little was, as General Nye asserted, a measure of his true greatness as a commander.[39] His self-belief allowed him to deflect the fears of those less certain than himself, especially those few who misinterpreted his risk-taking at the start of *U-Go* as recklessness.

His deep understanding and appreciation of the power of air-supply and battlefield air support showed him to be one of the most far thinking senior commanders of his era. Indeed, in Air Marshal Sir John Baldwin's opinion, 'Slim was quicker to grasp the potentialities and value of air support in the jungles of Burma than most Air Force officers. Particularly did he understand what the air required and was always ready to understand their difficulties and limitations.'[40] And by firmness of conviction and strength of character he was able to bind to his cause the two most important senior commanders in the theatre, Mountbatten and Giffard. Unsure perhaps of Slim when first appointed, Giffard quickly came to be a strong ally. Mountbatten, likewise, developed a bond with Slim that transcended the necessities of war such that Slim's advice, more than any else, was sought directly and regularly, as between one confidant to another. It was this relationship far more than any other, even that with Giffard, which was to prove to be *the* relationship of the war in the Far East, and which was to reap considerable profit for the Allied cause during 1944 and 1945. It was indisputably Slim's concept of battle, and Slim's plan for the destruction of *15 Army*, that Mountbatten adopted as his own and represented upwards to Churchill and Roosevelt. This relationship was to follow the same pattern in the coming year as Slim led 14 Army into Burma.

From the training and creation of a fighting spirit second-to-none he had imbued 14 Army with a knowledge of its own greatness and the determination and will to win so necessary for victory in any army.

The troops of 14 Army – Indian, British and African alike * – might still claim that they were the 'Forgotten Army', but there was no doubt about the strength and depth of the hard won *esprit d'corps* that now lay at the heart of each of the fighting divisions, administrative units and air force units that supported the army; a sense of moral power which was to prove a critical element in 14 Army's success in the coming year. Slim had stared disaster in its face during those first desperate weeks of the Imphal–Kohima battle and by his calm and careful handling of the various crises as they arrived brought about their successful resolution. The pressures of this battlefield were compounded by the peculiar difficulties of dealing with both Wingate and Stilwell, a pricklier pair of subordinates one could not wish for. The unique pressures of the retreat in 1942 had made Slim and Stilwell firm friends despite the obvious incompatibilities of their personalities: the gift in 1942 of an American M1 Carbine from Stilwell accompanied Slim throughout the remainder of the war. Slim's own confidence had grown dramatically during these long months, and with this came a certain deftness of touch in his handling of his army that was to grow to full maturity in the encounter battles in Burma proper during 1945. Crucially also, he had earned and retained the respect and confidence of his corps and divisional commanders. He made mistakes, but was the first to admit them, concentrating his effort on solving problems rather than apportioning blame. His calmness in crisis was legendary, and the quiet, determined way in which he directed operations while under a multitude of pressures earned him not just the confidence of his army, but also their affection as well. By the end of these battles General Slim had become 'Uncle Bill', a sobriquet soon in universal currency in 14 Army, and which was to remain with him for the rest of his days.

On 15 December 1944 Wavell knighted Slim at Imphal on behalf of King George V, alongside his three corps commanders, Christison, Stopford and Scoones. Together they had inflicted upon the Japanese the greatest defeat in their country's history. In so doing 14 Army had also completely changed the strategic landscape in South East Asia Command as at last the possibility of an Allied offensive into Burma presented itself.

---

* Fourteen Army was the largest army fielded by the United Kindom and the Empire during the war. In 1945 it had 530,000 troops on its strength, of which 17% were African, 19% were British and 64% were Indian.

# 8

# The Masterstroke

The Allies had not sought the battle of Imphal and Kohima. Despite the stunning victory that it gave them, the Chiefs of Staff in both London and Washington remained ignorant for some months not just of the scale of the Japanese defeat but also of its implications for the conduct of the war in the Far East. Brooke, the CIGS, was still fearful in June of a disaster in Assam. Even if Slim were eventually successful at Imphal and Kohima, Brooke could see no virtue in launching an offensive into Burma. In Churchill's celebrated phrase, it would be akin to 'jumping into the sea to catch a shark'.[1] Consequently, because both battle and victory had taken them by surprise, the Allies were slow to decide how to exploit the new strategic realities in the theatre. The one man who appeared alone to understand what the defeat of *15 Army* now meant for Japanese hegemony in Burma was Slim. He now realized that he had the opportunity not just to expel the residue of *15 Army* from Burma, but to pursue the Japanese back into the heart of Burma itself. Indeed, were he to do this, he became increasingly convinced that bigger prizes were possible, perhaps even the seizure of Rangoon itself. The taste of victory in both Assam and Arakan had injected into 14 Army a new-found confidence based on the irrefutable evidence that the Japanese could be beaten. 'Our troops had proved themselves in battle the superiors of the Japanese', commented Slim with satisfaction; 'they had seen them run'. By mid-1944 Slim was convinced that an aggressive policy of pursuit into Burma to exploit these victories was not just desirable but necessary.

However, few of his superiors saw Slim's vision as clearly as he did. During May 1944 Mountbatten badgered the Combined Chiefs of Staff for a decision as to what to do next, and when they did provide orders on 3 June 1944 the issue of an overland advance into Burma was fudged. So far as Washington and London were concerned the imperative remained the continued maintenance of China in support of Pacific operations. There were to be no extra resources for an amphibious assault on Burma's seaward flank. Mountbatten was nevertheless ordered 'to press advantages against the enemy by exerting maximum effort ground and air particularly during the current monsoon season.' These orders didn't tell him to invade Burma, but they did give him *carte blanche* to pursue his enemy. Mountbatten accordingly, on 9 June 1944, ordered Giffard to exploit across the Chindwin in the Yuwa–Tamanthi area after the monsoon.

Here lay not the full-blooded orders for the invasion of Burma that Slim might have hoped for but instructions merely to push *Mutaguchi*'s stumbling remnants back across the Chindwin. There is no evidence to suggest that during 1944 London ever expected Slim to do anything more than this. On 2 July, however, Slim met Mountbatten and persuaded him that were 14 Army to mount an offensive into Burma proper it could do so with no more resources than those that would anyway be allocated to the defence of India. Furthermore, he believed that an offensive could begin as early as 1 November.* But while Mountbatten was personally persuaded that a successful offensive could be mounted, at least to Shwebo or even Mandalay, Giffard was more cautious, sharing neither Mountbatten nor Slim's optimism. In a note to Mountbatten on 14 July he acknowledged the need to launch a vigorous pursuit of *Mutaguchi*'s retreating army, but suggested that the only hope of successful penetration of the Chindwin barrier would be by an airborne operation to cut the Japanese line of communication in the area of Yeu–Shwebo. It would not be possible, he argued, to mount a predominantly land-based offensive, nor indeed to do this during the monsoon. Mountbatten was furious at what he saw as Giffard's negativity. Undoubtedly Slim was also disappointed, but characteristically no hint of direct criticism can be found in *Defeat into Victory*. There was no need. Mountbatten had already, by this stage,

---

* The offensive actually began on 15 November.

decided to remove and replace Giffard, on the grounds that the Army Group Commander rarely found himself in step with Mountbatten's plans and aspirations and indeed often publicly opposed them. Mountbatten believed Giffard to be a profoundly negative influence, a hindrance rather than a help to the development of an aggressive strategy for operations in the theatre.

Keen to engage the Chiefs of Staff on the subject of the recapture of Burma, Mountbatten, on 23 July 1944, submitted two plans to London for approval. Both plans were designed to be conducted either on their own, independently of each other or together. The first plan, Operation Capital, was to take Slim and Stilwell's forces from Imphal and Lashio respectively deep into Burma, to a line running from the confluence of the Irrawaddy and Chindwin rivers at Pakokku through to Mandalay and then on to Lashio. The second, Operation Dracula, entailed an amphibious assault on Rangoon in early 1945 followed by an advance north to Mandalay. London's reaction to 'Capital' was one of hesitation. Seemingly unaware of the spectacular success of Slim's Assam campaign, few were willing to commit to the prospect of waging an offensive in a country which held so many bitter memories and which would self-evidently consume vast quantities of scarce resources. The Chiefs of Staff were taken by 'Dracula', however, as it meant not having to wage an expensive land campaign from the north. They concluded that, while Slim's forces must on all accounts remain on the offensive, 14 Army was to limit itself to holding operations until such time as Dracula could be launched at Rangoon.[2]

Despite this judgement, Slim was determined to press ahead with his own plans and the Chiefs of Staff's instructions to Mountbatten on 3 June 1944 gave him the opportunity he required. He was realistic enough to accept that he would never have the resources required to mount a two-corps offensive over nearly 1,000 miles of impossible terrain and across two of the world's largest rivers, at a time when the invasion of France loomed large in the Allies' consciousness. At the same time, however, a strategic re-prioritization to allow an amphibious assault on the south-eastern seaboard of Burma on the 'Dracula' model, Slim knew, was also highly unlikely. Despite its obvious disadvantages Slim became convinced that the only sure way of defeating the Japanese in Burma was by land, and that he would have to do it with the resources at hand. 'I believed', he wrote, 'more firmly than ever, in spite of the doubts of so many, that, if we were to regain Burma, it must be by an overland advance from the north.'

Furthermore, Slim believed firmly that if he didn't make the running in preparing a plan to defeat the Japanese in Burma, no one would, and a great opportunity decisively to defeat the whole of the Japanese war machine in Burma would thus be squandered. The difficulty in the aftermath of Imphal lay in bringing this vision to fruition, in the face of the animosity in London and Washington to such proposals and the instructions he had already received merely to pursue *15 Army* to the Chindwin. Yet Slim's clear vision throughout 1944 was undoubtedly not just to destroy *Mutaguchi*'s army, but to launch an offensive into Burma that would succeed in driving the Japanese into the sea. This vision was Slim's alone. 'No other senior commander in South-East Asia envisaged it,' noted his biographer, Ronald Lewin: 'Slim was the artist whose inner eye conceived it and whose master hand gave it visible form.'[3] It is difficult not to conclude that Slim succeeded in weaving his own strategic ambitions into the limited orders he received from Giffard and that as the months went by he allowed the momentum of successful 14 Army operations to apply their own *post facto* legitimacy to plans that were his own rather than those of his superiors. It seems clear that Mountbatten and Giffard, as well as the Chiefs of Staff, accepted Slim's successive *fait accomplis* not just because they worked, but because they themselves had nothing to offer as alternatives.

By September 1944 the climate had improved sufficiently for Mountbatten to secure from the Octagon Conference, meeting in Quebec, an extension of the earlier mandate. On 16 September he was given authority to capture all of Burma, provided that operations to achieve this did not prejudice the security of the air-supply route to China. This was much needed confirmation for Slim of the direction he was already taking. Following on from Mountbatten's orders of 9 June 1944, Giffard, on 24 July, ordered Slim to initiate planning for Operation Capital on the basis that, should it receive ultimate sanction, the offensive could be put into effect in December. On the very day he received these orders Slim was able to tell Giffard that these plans were already underway: indeed, an advance could start on 15 November, using air transport to resupply forward units. Giffard, stated Slim modestly, 'agreed to my continued preparation on these lines.' To enable him to concentrate solely on this task Giffard relieved Slim of responsibility for both Arakan (which was transferred to Christison) and the vast line of communication area for which he had been, until then, responsible.

Many in his own army needed persuading that such an objective was attainable. Brigadier Bernard Fergusson, lately returned from his adventures with Wingate's second expedition, recalled that a 14 Army planning conference at Dehra Dun in July 1944, presided over by Slim, heard 'a lot of talk, much of which sounded to me almost defeatist.' He went on: 'I remember but will not reveal the identity of a divisional commander who said – and not without support from others – that to prevent the Japanese cutting the road behind one a force of at least a brigade would be needed every X miles; there were only Y brigades in the 14th Army; it was Z hundred miles to Rangoon – *ergo*, it would be impossible to capture Rangoon overland.'[4]

Slim was not put off by such pessimistic mutterings. The potentialities of his grand design, despite the obvious risks, some of which had been articulated at Dehra Dun, made him determined to succeed. He knew that the huge logistical nightmare associated with relying on land-based lines of communication could in large part be overcome by the use of air-supply, a factor that had played a significant part in all his operations to date. He knew also that the Japanese had received a defeat the like of which would make it difficult for them to recover quickly. 'A second great defeat for that army, properly exploited, would disrupt it and leave, not Mandalay but all Burma at our mercy,' he reasoned. 'It, therefore, became my aim to force another major battle on the enemy at the earliest feasible moment.' He found himself faced with his second great chance and he was determined to seize it.

The Dehra Dun conference exemplified the way in which Slim engaged his commanders in the process of planning for operations. Planning was an activity that involved the whole intellectual horsepower of his staff. As the historian Duncan Anderson records: 'Commanders' conferences were not unlike post-graduate university seminars, with Slim as Chairman, guiding but not dominating discussion.'[5] 'He was neither Napoleonic nor egocentric in his approach,' records his biographer, Ronald Lewin. 'Disapproving of "soviets" or any hint of "government by committee" he was nevertheless a natural democrat, sparing no pains to elicit from his subordinates a full spectrum of opinions about any important problem.'[6] 'He put forward what he had to put forward in a straight-forward manner, clearly and precisely,' recalled Ouvry Roberts. 'And at the same time, although he had his own definite ideas, he was very ready to listen to any idea people put forward.'[7] Bill Hasted, his Chief Engineer, recalled that the HQ 14 Army's senior officers' mess 'was extremely close-knit, with absolutely no rivalries. In it "Uncle Bill" was just what his affectionate nickname implied. We all spoke freely what was on our minds. We had no secrets from one another, and Uncle Bill joined wholeheartedly in the conversation on whatever subject.'[8] 'For all the thrust and stubbornness of his chin, which was not deceptive', recalled Anthony Brett-James, 'he was most approachable, and a ready listener to the ideas of his officers. If he was prepared to shoulder blame with equanimity, he was also quick to pass on credit to his subordinates rather than accept it for himself.'[9]

Consequently, Slim was the first to agree that the plan eventually arrived at for the advance into Burma was the product of his headquarters as a whole. Slim accepted good ideas wherever they originated. One example was in the make-up of the formations that would lead the advance into Burma. To match the new style of fighting Slim expected once the Chindwin and Irrawaddy had been crossed, Slim appointed Frank Messervy to command 4 Corps in October 1944 *vice* Scoones. His dash and drive in Arakan had impressed Slim greatly. Messervy 'had the temperament, sanguine, inspiring, and not too calculating of odds that I thought would be required for the tasks I designed for 4 Corps,' Slim recalled. It was a good choice. Messervy was also a bold thinker, and suggested, among other things, that one brigade of 17 Indian Division be mechanized and another made air transportable to exploit the new terrain 14 Army would meet once the Chindwin had been breached. Slim agreed and converted 5 Indian Division to the new organization as well. Messervy's idea proved to be critical to the success of both the seizure of Meiktila in February and the epic dash to Rangoon in April.

Slim's plan for Operation Capital necessitated the re-training and restructuring of his army. Once over the Irrawaddy, the army would have to fight in a very different style to that which had won it the great jungle-based victories at Imphal and Kohima. Slim wrote:

For two years our formations had fought in jungles and amongst hills, they were now about to break out into open country with unobstructed views and freedom of movement away from tracks. Not only would the laborious tactics of the jungle have to be replaced by speed, mechanisation, and mobility, but also commanders and troops would have to adjust their mentality to the changed conditions. This was especially so in the case of armour and artillery. Instead of one or two tanks, surrounded by infantry, carefully nosing forward along a narrow jungle track, we might hope to use powerful, rapidly moving, armoured formations on extended fronts. Artillery would fire at longer ranges, change position more frequently, and have to be ready to answer calls from the air more quickly.

During September and October 1944 considerable re-training took place in 14 Army to prepare for the mobile, armour-based operations required once the Chindwin had been crossed, when all-arms co-operation between air, mechanized infantry, armour and artillery would provide the basic theme of Slim's offensive.

Mountbatten's long-sought opportunity to remove Giffard came in October, when at Chinese insistence Stilwell returned to the United States. This created the opportunity for Mountbatten to create an Allied Land Forces Command to take responsibility for 14 Army, NCAC,* 15 Corps and the extensive Line of Communication Command. Lieutenant-General Sir Oliver Leese, lately commander of 8 Army in Italy, took over the post on 12 November, setting up his headquarters in Slim's vacated premises in Barrackpore. From the outset Slim and Leese did not get on well with each other. In part this was because Slim was cross about Giffard's departure. Despite Giffard's failings, the most obvious of which was his inability, deliberate or otherwise, to accept Mountbatten's position as 'Supremo', Slim had built a watertight relationship with the Army Group Commander and resented the imposition of an outsider. Giffard 'had seen us through our efforts to become an army', Slim recalled afterwards, 'and through our first and most desperate battles. Fourteenth Army owed much to his integrity, his judgement, his sound administration, his support in our darkest hours, and to the universal confidence he inspired among us. We saw him go with grief.'

Slim's relationship with Leese, by contrast, remained throughout formal and polite rather than friendly. Their first meeting at Government House in Calcutta, soon after Leese's arrival in Delhi, was difficult. On 15

---

* After Stilwell's departure the NCAC was commanded by the American Lieutenant-General Dan I. Sultan and consisted of 36 British Division (Maj-Gen. F.W. Festing), 1 and 6 Chinese Armies and the American 'Mars' Brigade. 36 British Division transferred to 14 Army on 1 April 1945.

November 1944 Leese wrote to his wife: 'I got a good impression of
Slim – though I think he bellyaches. He was slightly defensive about the
Indian Army, the difficulties of Burma and the need to understand how
to fight the Jap. I said how glad I was to come to his great 14th Army.
He showed no sign of wanting to have me! But I feel somehow that all
will be well. He is very proud of his Army and well he may be – I think
he is sound in his tactics.'[10] For his part Slim wrote in *Defeat into Victory*
that he found it 'easy to serve under Leese. His military judgment was
eminently sound.' But he criticized the staff whom Leese had 'brought
with him and which replaced most of our old friends at General Giffard's
headquarters [because they] had a good deal of desert sand in its shoes and
[were] rather inclined at first to thrust Eighth Army down our throats.'
While Leese recognized the strength of Slim's victory at Imphal/Kohima
he did not consider it to be on the par of those achieved in North Africa
and Italy and was sceptical about Slim's all-round military prowess and
the experience of his senior commanders. In a letter to Brooke on 15
December 1944 Leese proffered the opinion that there was 'a good deal
of ignorance in Senior Officers [in 14 Army] about the employment of
modern arms and equipment. It is for this reason that I am so anxious to
get officers with experience in Europe. Otherwise when we come to fight
on the beaches and in the plains by Mandalay we may get into unnecessary
tangles.' This underestimation of the ability of Slim's army, at a time when
it was already successfully pushing hard out of the Chindwin bridgeheads,
was undeserved. While there is no evidence that it was ever articulated to
Slim in such bald and uncompromising terms, Leese's condescension to 14
Army and its commanders, mirrored by the staff he had imported from
Italy, was obvious for all to see, and bitterly resented.

Leese was a man of his own opinions, a successful and well-regarded
Army commander who quite understandably believed that his task was
not merely to support Slim, as Giffard tended to do, but to *exercise*
command itself. This was to be expected. But Leese consistently failed to
understand that the pattern for victory in Burma had already been mapped
out, and that the principal pieces of the jigsaw had largely been put in place.
Now was not the time for bright new ideas, or for a fresh approach by a
dynamic new commander eager to impress, but rather for the careful, quiet
articulation of plans and preparations that had been years in gestation and
which were fundamentally not of his own making. But this approach was
in every sense out of kilter with Leese's bright, exuberant character, and

it clashed badly with the command relationships that had built up over time, and so successfully, by 14 Army, 11 Army Group and SEAC. That 14 Army had become, as John Masters described it, 'an extension of Slim's own personality', only compounded Leese's difficulties.[11]

Leese, to his immense irritation and frustration, found himself cut out of Slim's decision cycle, and despite his subordinate role, Slim saw to it that Leese was never able to dominate it as he wished. On 27 February 1945, for example, Slim noted with some glee that Leese had ordered him to destroy the Japanese forces in the Mandalay area and to seize Rangoon before the monsoon. Seemingly unknown to Leese, these merely repeated the orders that Slim had already given to 14 Army the previous December, and consequently, Slim noted, 'no changes in our plans or dispositions were necessary.' Leese also found himself cut out of Slim's relationship with Mountbatten. He resented their friendship and twice wrote to his wife to complain that Mountbatten, whom he described as 'crooked as a corkscrew', undermined his authority by dealing directly with Slim. 'Slim and most of the others are really strangers and we have very little in common', he reported.[12] On 2 June 1945 he wrote with some bitterness to his wife: 'It has never been easy with him. He really resented my coming out here at all and has made things difficult all along for me and my staff. He is almost a megalomaniac and compares himself very favourably with [Montgomery?] in his own estimation. He can never resist having a dig at any other HQ's. As a result you can imagine that it has not been all "fun and games" – dealing with Slim on one level and Mountbatten on another.'[13]


Mountbatten and Slim's determination relentlessly to pursue *Mutaguchi* across the Chindwin during the monsoon paid off. On 6 August 1944 – his 53rd birthday – Slim ordered Stopford, who now had responsibility for all operations east of the Manipur River, to direct his pursuit against Kalewa *via* both Tamu and Tiddim, and against Sittaung. 11 East African Division (21, 25 and 26 Brigades)* led the advance from Tamu towards both Sittaung and Kalemyo. They methodically pushed their way against last-ditch opposition to the Chindwin. The process was slow and difficult because of continuing Japanese resistance, the appalling weather

---

* 11 East Africa Division moved to Imphal in July.

and difficult terrain. Men, mules and elephants struggled down jungle tracks after the retreating Japanese, crossing swollen rivers and re-building collapsed tracks and roads. In the air the overstretched air forces pushed through minimal visibility to deliver their precious loads by parachute and free-drop to the troops below them. Malaria continued to ravage the army and even Slim, to his intense embarrassment, contracted the disease after disobeying his own strict orders to cover up after sunset, and he found himself hospitalized in Shillong for a time.[14]

During the advance it became apparent that the scale of the Japanese defeat was far greater than expected. The detritus of a fleeing army was strewn across the jungle hills, bodies and equipment littering the escape routes east, bringing to the fore what Slim described as 'the full horror of retreat in the monsoon, the ultimate beastliness of war.' Sittaung was occupied on 4 September and by 10 September the Chindwin was crossed and a small bridgehead secured. By mid-November Kalemyo was also secured by troops from 11 East Africa Division and those of 5 Indian Division, which had pushed methodically southwards down the Tiddim road. Tiddim was occupied on 17 October.

5 Indian Division's task on the Tiddim front was made immeasurably easier by the activities of the semi-irregular Lushai Brigade. This British-officered force of Indian soldiers and Chin levies proved to be very successful in harassing the flanks of the retreating Japanese. Slim regarded the brigade's exploits to be the epitome of successful long-range guerrilla operations, perhaps even more important than those of Wingate's Special Force. 'As an example of effective Long-Range Penetration through "impossible" country its operation had never been surpassed', he wrote in a summary of the campaign published in Australia in 1950.[15] Kalewa, on the Chindwin, was captured by 11 East African Division on 2 December 1944, proving, despite the immense difficulties posed by climate and terrain, Giffard's earlier pessimism to have been ill placed. 'I had asked for the impossible', Slim remarked, 'and got it.'

During the pursuit to the Chindwin Slim had been exercised about how he could engage and defeat *Kimura**, in open battle once the Chindwin had been breached. His fundamental imperative was to destroy the Japanese army in Burma. Capturing territory was incidental, and would follow on

---

* *General Kimura* replaced *General Kawabe* as commander of the Japanese Burma Area Army in October 1944.

naturally from the former. 'It was not Mandalay or Meiktila that we were after but the Japanese army,' he commented, 'and that thought had to be firmly implanted in the mind of every man of the Fourteenth Army.' Slim's eyes had long been focused on the vast Shwebo plain on the west bank of the Irrawaddy as ideal terrain for the battle he sought, a battle of manoeuvre in which his artillery, armour and air support would have devastating effect on the Japanese, 'where tanks would operate in quantities instead of by twos or threes, where guns must be capable of fire and movement, where infantry must manoeuvre fast and far.' It would also help that the Japanese would be forced to fight with their backs to the Irrawaddy.

The Shwebo plain was 400 miles from the nearest railhead, and 250 miles of that was a simple earth road impassable in the monsoon. Slim's two corps were outnumbered by *Kimura*'s forces which, chastened but far from beaten, amounted to five-and-a-half divisions, an independent mixed brigade, a tank regiment, nearly 40,000 line of communication troops and two Indian National Army divisions. *Honda's 33 Army**\* was based on Bhamo opposing the Chinese and *15 Army*†, now commanded by *General Katamura*, defended the Irrawaddy. 'These were not the odds I should have liked,' Slim commented. 'A year ago I would not have looked at the proposal. But 14 Army's advantage in the air, in armour, in greater mobility in the open, and the spirit of his troops gave him the confidence to press ahead despite what otherwise would have appeared to be unacceptable odds.

Slim's assessment was that the battered remnants of *15 Army* would hold a defensive line in the formidable jungle-clad mountains of the Zibyu Taungdan range. This range of hills lay about twenty-five miles to the east of the Chindwin and ran parallel to it for a distance of 120 miles. Slim's plan was to punch through these hills with Messervy's 4 Corps on the left and General Stopford's 33 Corps on the right, both corps converging on the Yeu–Shwebo area‡. Four Corps was to break out of the Sittaung bridgehead and, following an easterly course, force its way

---

\* *18* and *56 Division* (together with a brigade each from *49 Division* and *2 Division*) numbering 25,500 troops.

† *15 Army* contained *15, 53 Division, 31* and *33 Divisions*.

‡ Messervy took over 4 Corps from General Scoones on 8 December 1944. Four Corps contained 7 and 19 Indian Divisions and 255 Tank Brigade with Sherman tanks, while 33 Corps contained 2 British Division, 20 Indian Division, 268 Brigade and 254 Tank Brigade, with Stuarts and Lee-Grants.

through the mountains, seize Pinlebu and thereafter change direction to capture Shwebo from the north. Stopford's 33 Corps, meanwhile, was tasked to advance from Kalewa on a broad front, following the general south-easterly route of the Chindwin towards Ye-U and Monywa.

In planning the offensive Slim was concerned to tell Messervy and Stopford *what* to do, while allowing them virtually complete freedom to decide *how* they carried out his instructions. Choosing one's subordinates well and then delegating responsibility to them was a strong characteristic of Slim's leadership.[16] In Burma this approach to command made especial sense, for two reasons. First, the obvious geographical difficulties in the theatre made regular communication difficult. Fourteen Army, Slim noted, 'fought on a front of seven hundred miles, in four groups, separated by great distances, with no lateral communications between them and beyond tactical support of one another.' Second, Slim was convinced that his commanders could best achieve his requirements without him breathing down their necks while they were conducting operations.

'My corps and divisions were called upon to act with at least as much freedom as armies and corps in other theatres,' he recalled. 'Commanders at all levels had to act more on their own; they were given greater latitude to work out their own plans to achieve what they knew was the Army Commander's intention. In time they developed to a marked degree a flexibility of mind and a firmness of decision that enabled them to act swiftly to take advantage of sudden information or changing circumstances without reference to their superiors. They were encouraged, as Stopford put it, 'to shoot a goal when the reference wasn't looking.' This acting without orders, in anticipation of orders, or without waiting for approval, yet always within the overall intention, must become second nature in any form of warfare where formations do not fight closely *en cadre*,' Slim later wrote, 'and must go down to the smallest units. It requires in the higher command a corresponding flexibility of mind, confidence in its subordinates, and the power to make its intentions clear right through the force.'

As a result of this freedom a deep mutual trust built up between Slim and his corps and divisional commanders. Commanders had to be self-reliant and not dependent upon higher headquarters for direction at times when decisions needed to be made on the spot. Geoffrey Evans, who as GOC of first 5 and then 7 Indian Divisions had direct experience of Slim's style of command, believed that this approach allowed commanders 'to adapt their tactics according to the country . . . and to make the most of what was given to them; encouraged to use their initiative, they did so without fear. And such was Slim's confidence in them that once plans were made and orders issued, he left them to fight the battle in their own way, making himself and his staff always available to help.'[17] 'Slim was wonderful to serve under,' recalled Frank Messervy. Having 'discussed the thing with you he would make some suggestions. He would then leave it to you. Just give you encouragement.'[18]

Wasting no time 14 Army crossed the Chindwin as soon as it was reached. Slim urged Messervy to advance as quickly as possible and to take risks that would months ago have been unthinkable, in order to maintain the momentum of the advance. Four Corps was led by Major-General Peter Rees's 19 Indian Division.[19] Advancing out of Sittaung on 4 December the division headed for Pinlebu, sixty miles to the east. Rees, driving his units on, made rapid progress through the Zibyu Taungdam. Less than two weeks after the advance had begun he had joined his division up with Festing's 36 British Division at Rail Indaw, ninety miles east of Sittaung, part of General Sultan's successful drive south from Lashio against 33 Army. Surprisingly, Japanese resistance was far less intense than had been expected. Nevertheless, Rees' advance was an extraordinary effort given the appalling nature of the terrain. Roads had to be hacked out of the virgin jungle by troops using what tools they could carry.

Further south a brigade of 20 Indian Division led the 33 Corps advance, crossing the Chindwin at Mawlaik north of Kalewa, while 11 East African Division fought hard to extend the Kalewa bridgehead. By 10 December in an extraordinary logistical and engineering achievement the largest Bailey bridge then in existence – 1,154 feet long – had been thrown across the river. On 18 December the remainder of 20 Indian Division followed through the bridgehead.

Within days of the start of 4 Corps' advance, however, Slim accepted that his initial plan to trap *Kimura* on the Shwebo plain in front of the Irrawaddy would not work. The weakness of the opposition facing 19 Indian Division forced him to recognize that *Kimura* had withdrawn the bulk of his forces east of the Irrawaddy, with the obvious intention of fighting behind, rather than in front of, the river. If this were to happen 14 Army would be stretched out from Tamu and vulnerable to counter-attack just when it was attempting to cross one of the most formidable river barriers imaginable. Slim's original expectation that *Kimura* would be content to meet 14 Army on terms distinctly disadvantageous to himself was, perhaps, unduly optimistic. In any case, *Kimura*'s withdrawal behind the Irrawaddy dashed this expectation resoundingly.

Seeking an alternative strategy, where he could engage *Kimura* in decisive battle while retaining the advantages of firepower and surprise, Slim's eyes turned to the towns of Meiktila and Thazi, lying approximately seventy miles south of Mandalay. These towns were the key nodal pints on *Kimura*'s line of communication, supporting both *33* and *15 Army*, and were in every sense the 'beating heart' of the Burma Area Army. The railway and main road from Rangoon ran through Meiktila before bending north on their way to Mandalay, and the town formed a natural location for supply and ammunition dumps, airfields and hospitals. If Slim could cut off both *Honda* and *Katamura*'s corps from this vital logistical centre, the Japanese ability to resist 33 Corps' inexorable pressure in the north around Mandalay would be fatally weakened. Slim recognized that without Meiktila *Kimura* could not hope to sustain a prolonged battle for Mandalay. Indeed, it might even prove to be the decisive act in the destruction of the whole of *Kimura*'s army.

Within days Slim and his staff had come up with a plan, which he dubbed Operation 'Extended Capital'. The idea was to make *Kimura* believe that nothing had changed, and that Slim would attempt to cross both 33 and 4 Corps over the Irrawaddy north-west of Mandalay. Slim's revised plan, however, was that while 33 Corps would continue to cross the Irrawaddy to the north of Mandalay as originally planned 4 Corps* would instead cross the river in great secrecy far to the south before striking hard with armour, motorized artillery and infantry at Meiktila. The northern advance by 33 Corps (strengthened by 19 Indian Division and 268 Tank Brigade) would be a deception to hide the decisive strike by 4 Corps to the south. If Slim could attract the greatest possible number of enemy divisions towards the northern crossing points he could minimize opposition to the real focus of his attack in the south. This would provide Slim with, as he put it, 'not only the major battle I desired, but the chance to repeat our old hammer and anvil tactics: 33 Corps the hammer from the

---

* Reconfigured for the operation to comprise 7 and 17 Indian Divisions, 28 East African Brigade and 255 Tank Brigade.

north against the anvil of 4 Corps at Meiktila – and the Japanese between.'
Had the aircraft been available, Slim would have employed airborne forces
to capture Meiktila, but in the circumstances this was not possible.

Slim explained his revised plan to Messervy and Stopford on 18
December and on 19 December issued his plan. On 17 December he
had sent a summary of his intentions to Leese, and on 20 December
he sent a full copy of the plan to HQ ALFSEA. On 26 December Slim
moved his formations in accordance with his new plan, 268 Brigade and 19
Indian Division transferring from 4 to 33 Corps. The speed at which Slim
made these changes left little time for wide consultation. Slim regarded
his change of plan to be within the wider remit he had been given, and
thus decided to inform Leese of what he intended rather than seeking
his permission. But Slim's decision not to involve him in the process
of decision making for this most crucial of operations undoubtedly
irritated Leese and did nothing to improve the already fragile relationship
between the two men. Had his relationship with Leese been stronger
Slim would have almost certainly, despite the difficulties of distance and
communication, talked it through with him, as he would have done with
Giffard. Perhaps Slim believed that bringing Leese into the planning for
Operation Extended Capital might actually jeopardize his grand design,
because Leese might have wanted to cancel, change or veto any element
not to his liking. It seems likely that Leese would have wanted in some
way to stamp his authority on the plan, and it may have been this that
Slim was keen to avoid. Rather than risk disappointment perhaps, Slim
acted first and informed Leese afterwards, by which time the change had
become a *fait accompli*.

Confident in their commander, Messervy and Stopford quickly translated Slim's revised plan into action. Indeed, the 33 Corps advance
continued unabated during this period. The leading troops of 2 British
Division, together with the Lee-Grant and Stuart tanks of 254 Tank
Brigade, passed through Pyingaing on 23 December. Japanese rearguards
attempted to hold up the advance through ambushes and mining. Ye-u
and its airfield were captured on 2 January 1945 and by 5 January the
division had established a firm bridgehead over the Mu River. 2 British
and 19 Indian Divisions now began a race for Shwebo, with *15 Division*
streaming before it in full retreat to the Irrawaddy. Shwebo was captured
on 9 January jointly by units of both divisions. Rees' 19 Indian Division
had reached the Shwebo area by 5 January, established bridgeheads over

the Irrawaddy at Thabeikkyin and Kyaukyaung and began to advance southward on the east bank of the river towards Mandalay.

The administrative effort to supply two Corps well forward of their supply bases in inhospitable terrain was formidable. Thirty-three Corps had to push rapidly forward in the north while 4 Corps, with its armour, moved in secret down 330 miles of rough dirt track from Tamu to the area of Pakokku before conducting an opposed crossing of one of the world's mightiest rivers. 'We were, in fact, defying some of the principles of war in undertaking the reconquest of Burma from the north to the south – as the strategic situation compelled us to do – instead of in the reverse direction,' wrote Leese in May 1945. 'Thus our main line of communication ran at right-angles to the enemy, while we were operating in reverse to, and against the trend of the main river and road arteries of the country. The distances were very great, existing communications were poor, and both climate and terrain were unfavourable.'[20]

The physical restraint of operating in difficult terrain at long distances from railheads meant that Slim was able to sustain over the Chindwin no more than four and two-thirds divisions and two tank brigades. However, the decisive advantage the Allies enjoyed in the air meant that he could rely on air transport to maintain his forward units, so long as the requisite numbers of aircraft remained available. With the vast experience of the Sinzweya Pocket, Operation Thursday and Operation Stamina, the air supply organization supporting 14 Army had become the model of its kind. During 11 East African Division's pursuit down the Kabaw Valley during the monsoon of 1944 it was supplied exclusively by air.

Having sufficient aircraft available was a constant problem. Slim's plans were dealt a devastating blow on the morning of 10 December 1944 when he awoke at Imphal to the sound of mass aircraft activity at the nearby airfield. Slim quickly discovered that seventy-five of his precious USAAF DC3s were being diverted to meet a developing crisis in China. Slim immediately told Mountbatten that without these aircraft the success of Operation Capital could not be guaranteed. Mountbatten fought hard to have the aircraft returned, and on 21 January two of the three squadrons Slim had lost were returned to him. Aircraft range, however, soon became an issue of strategic importance. Once the Chindwin had been crossed, the forward supply bases in Chittagong and Agartala, north of Comilla, which had played a crucial role in the survival of the Imphal pocket, became too far distant from the Chindwin to enable supply aircraft to fly economically. Consequently the capture of airfields along the route of Slim's advance was essential to provide the very minimum of support his forces required to sustain offensive operations. The initial objectives for 'Capital', therefore, were the airfields in the area of Ye-U and Shwebo.

The closest possible form of co-operation between 14 Army and the staff of Baldwin's air forces was built up in 1944, and the benefit was reaped in abundance during the campaign of 1945. When Slim moved his HQ to Imphal in October 1944 he co-located it with the HQ of Vincent's 221 Group. Henceforth both headquarters 'lived side by side, worked and moved as one' to become an effective joint HQ. The Allied air forces ranged all over Burma 'on a plan' wrote Slim, 'designed almost entirely to help Fourteenth Army.' Throughout Operation Extended Capital the Allied air forces flew some 7,000 sorties a day to sustain and support the land offensive. By April 1945 nearly 90 per cent of 14 Army's supplies were provided by air. Indeed, Slim regarded 'Extended Capital' not to be a 14 Army offensive at all, but a joint air-land campaign in which land and air elements were equal partners. Slim could rightly claim that operations by 14 Army throughout 1944 and 1945 provided a distinctive contribution 'towards a new kind of warfare.' Slim's judgement was unequivocal. 'Throughout the entire campaign 14th Army had proved right in our reliance on the air forces . . .' he wrote, 'first to gain control of the air, and then to supply, transport and support us. The campaign had been an air one, as well as a land one. Without the victory of the air forces there would have been no victory for the army.' When, in September 1944 Churchill extolled in Parliament 14 Army's success at Imphal Slim wrote to Giffard saying that he was disappointed that no reference had been 'made to the magnificent work which was carried out during the recent campaign by the Third Tactical Air Force.'[21]

But while air transport answered some of Slim's most pressing needs, the land-based line of communication also required substantial work to ensure that 14 Army could operate far ahead of its bases in Assam.* Road building and upgrading was essential, but limited resources restricted what could be done. This constant crisis of resources, however, had a positive effect on

---

* The line of communication from Dimapur to Meiktila from the north-west ran for 506 miles through Imphal, Tamu, Kalewa, Shwebo and Mandalay.

the men of 14 Army. It forced them to become self-reliant and innovative. 'With us', Slim recalled, 'necessity was the mother of invention. We lacked so much in equipment and supplies that, if we were not to give up offensive operations altogether, we had either to manage without or improvise for ourselves . . . my soldiers forced the opposed crossing of great rivers using inadequate equipment, stretched brittle communication links to fantastic lengths, marched over the most heart breaking country on reduced rations, fought disease with discipline to beat it.' Slim's chief engineer, Bill Hasted, invented a means of hardening road surfaces by laying on them strips of hessian soaked in tar, called 'bithess'. 'For over a hundred miles this novel surface proved able to take a thousand vehicles a day when the monsoon came.' Hasted, likewise, felled forests alongside the Chindwin at Kalewa to make barges able to take ten tons each, in order to make best use of the Chindwin as a supply artery. Three of these tied together could carry a Sherman tank. Outboard engines were flown in, boat wrecks were repaired and even sunken vessels on the river bed were recovered, repaired and pressed into service.

Four Corps began its march south on 19 January and despite the difficulties of the terrain moved quickly. Slim had given Messervy 15 February as the last acceptable date for crossing the Irrawaddy. Elaborate deception measures were adopted to ensure that Messervy's move through the jungle to Pakokku remained concealed from the Japanese, and to reinforce in *Kimura*'s mind the certain belief that 4 Corps remained with 33 Corps on the Shwebo plain. While the real 4 Corps had to keep radio silence during its move southwards, a dummy corps headquarters was established in Tamu, using the same radio frequencies, through which all communications from 19 Indian Division to 33 Corps had to pass. Despite the inconvenience this caused for commanders this complicated deception was spectacularly successful.

The Japanese did not believe that a large-scale advance through the Gangaw Valley was feasible and never seriously considered it as a possibility. In order to help reinforce these perceptions, Messervy, when his advance reached the town of Gangaw, arranged with Slim for the town's defences to be overwhelmingly attacked on 10 January by the Strategic Air Force with follow-up occupation by the Lushai Brigade, rather than using his divisions for the purpose. Unobserved and unhindered Messervy's forward units reached Pauk, forty miles from Pakokku, in late January. *Kimura*, while aware of some activity on his southern flank, regarded this to be nothing more than demonstrations by minor forces designed to draw him south, and he was not to be tempted into doing something so foolish. All the while he continued to reinforce the Irrawaddy in the Mandalay area, bringing in all available forces from across Burma, so that by February he had a force equivalent to eight Japanese and one-and-a-third INA divisions. He was confident that these would be more than sufficient to defeat the expected five divisions of 14 Army in what he was now calling the decisive 'Battle of the Irrawaddy Shore'. His failure to appreciate the overall subtlety of Slim's approach, the dynamism and mobility of his army, together with the extraordinary power and flexibility afforded to Slim by virtue of air transport and air superiority, proved to be the major strands in his undoing.

Although considerably reduced in strength to allow Slim the greatest concentration of effort in Burma proper, simultaneous operations were undertaken by Christison's 15 Corps to secure the Arakan coastline, which contained much sought-after airfields. At the end of February 1945 the airfields on the islands of Ramree and Cheduba, which were crucial to the maintenance of operations in central Burma, were captured.

The advantage was now Slim's: only six weeks after he had changed his plan, 14 Army was before the Irrawaddy on a 200-mile front with 4 Corps about to cross the river in the area of Pakokku. The advance of 14 Army had been so rapid that Mountbatten reported to London on 23 February 1945 that 'Dracula' was no longer required as Slim appeared likely to seize Rangoon before the onset of the monsoon in May. With 33 Corps placing growing pressure on the Japanese in the region of Mandalay, the timing of the main crossings became increasingly crucial. Too soon and *Kimura* would recognize the threat to his southern flank and deploy his reserves to counter it: too late and the pressure on 33 Corps might be sufficient to halt its advance on Mandalay.

In early February Stopford made successive and determined efforts from the north to capture Mandalay, reinforcing the impression that this was Slim's point of main effort. *Katamura* threw *15, 53* and elements of both *31* and *33 Divisions* into the attack at the 19 Indian Division bridge-head at Thabeikkyin and *Kimura*, agreeing with *Katamura*'s assessment that this was the likely location of 14 Army's principal attack, gave *Katamura* additional artillery and some of his remaining tanks. However, it was to no avail: as the bridgehead strengthened the Japanese were slowly pushed back. Meanwhile, Gracey's 20 Indian Division approached Monywa and took the town after hard fighting in mid-January. On 8 February Slim moved his and Vincent's joint headquarters to the town that he had vacated in May 1942. Other troops from 20 Indian Division arrived at Myinmu and began to cross on the night of 12 February. The Japanese were slow to oppose this incursion but when they did it was with desperate fury, waves of attacks taking place during the ensuing fortnight against the two bridgeheads, many during daylight.

The real focus of Slim's offensive, of course, lay far to the south. The first crossings by Geoffrey Evans' 7 Indian Division began at Nyaungu on the night of 13 February, although it took four days to establish a bridgehead, 6,000 yards wide by 4,000 yards deep. Messervy's plan was that 'Punch' Cowan's 17 Indian Division, together with the Sherman tanks of 255 Tank Brigade, would then pass rapidly across the river to seize Meiktila. Elaborate deception measures were adopted to cover the Nyaungu crossings. Twenty-eight East African Brigade pretended to parry south to recover the Chauk and Yenangyaung oil fields, dummy parachute drops were made east of Chauk to reinforce this picture and 17 Indian Division applied heavy pressure on Pakokku to make out that crossings were also intended there. These deception schemes were undoubtedly successful and acted to hide from Japanese comprehension, until it was too late, the reality of Slim's strategy. A captured Japanese intelligence officer later explained that they did not believe that there was more than one division in the area, and that it was directed down the west bank towards Yenangyaung.

It was at this stage in the campaign that a young British lance-corporal, George MacDonald Fraser, recalled Slim arriving to talk to his unit, the Border Regiment:

> The biggest boost to morale was the burly man who came to talk to the assembled battalion by the lake shore – I'm not sure when, but it was unforgettable. Slim was like that: the only man I've ever seen who had a force that came out of him, a strength of personality that I've puzzled over since . . . His appearance was plain enough: large, heavily built, grim-faced with that hard mouth and bulldog

chin; the rakish Gurkha hat was at odds with the slung carbine and untidy trouser bottoms ... Nor was he an orator ... His delivery was blunt, matter-of-fact, without gestures or mannerisms, only a lack of them. He knew how to make an entrance – or rather, he probably didn't, and it came naturally ... Slim emerged from under the trees by the lake shore, there was no nonsense of 'gather round' or jumping on boxes; he just stood with his thumb hooked in his carbine sling and talked about how we had caught Jap off-balance and were going to annihilate him in the open; there was no exhortation or ringing clichés, no jokes or self-conscious use of barrack-room slang – when he called the Japs 'bastards' it was casual and without heat. He was telling us informally what would be, in the reflective way of intimate conversation. And we believed every word – and it all came true. I think it was that sense of being close to us, as though he were chatting offhand to an understanding nephew (not for nothing was he 'Uncle Bill') that was his great gift ... You knew, when he talked of smashing the Jap, that to him it meant not only arrows on a map but clearing bunkers and going in under shell-fire; that he had the head of a general with the heart of a private soldier.[22]

Slim may have looked unconcerned, but this was a period of acute anxiety for him. The administrative risks he had taken now looked alarmingly great. All but one of his divisions (5 Indian Division) was engaged; as the tempo increased so too did 14 Army's expenditure of petrol and ammunition, increasing the strain on the already stretched line of communication. 'Throughout the battle', Slim recorded, 'we were never without acute anxiety on the supply and transport side ... time and time again, and just in time, the bare essentials for their operations reached those who so critically needed them. Very rarely had any formation more than its basic needs.' The strain was apparent only to those who knew him best. It was the only time, recalled Vincent, that he ever saw Slim tense. He 'was a little quieter than usual', he recalled, 'and one was conscious that there was a bit of worry going on.'[23]

His problems were compounded by the fact that on 23 February Chiang Kai-shek suddenly demanded the redeployment to China of all US and Chinese forces in the NCAC, and that US transport squadrons should fly them out. If *Kimura* withdrew the forces that he had facing the NCAC and threw them into the battle about Mandalay instead, at a time when he faced the loss of more of his precious aircraft, 14 Army operations would undoubtedly have halted completely. But the threat was lifted in part by the US Chiefs of Staff agreeing after representation from Mountbatten and the British Chiefs of Staff to 'leave the bulk of their transport squadrons in Burma until either we had taken Rangoon or until 1 June, whichever was the earlier.'

Meanwhile, the decisive struggle for Meiktila was taking place. Cowan advanced out of Nyaungu on 21 February. The Japanese commander of the Meiktila area, *Major-General Kasuya*, had some 12,000 troops as well as 1,500 miscellaneous base troops and hospital patients at his disposal for the defence of the town, and every man able to carry a weapon was pressed into service. Messervy's aim was to make a dash to seize the town as quickly as possible, with the road to be cleared subsequently by 7 Indian Division once the security of the Irrawaddy bridgehead was firm. Cowan's plan was to use his armour to punch through the Japanese lines to seize an airfield at Thabutkon, twelve miles east of Meiktila, to allow for the fly-in of 99 Brigade, while Taungtha and Mahlaing were either captured or screened by his other two brigades. The whole division with the armour would then assault Meiktila.

While 63 Brigade brushed aside light opposition to move up closer to the town's western defences, 48 Brigade began moving north-east as 255 Tank Brigade, with two infantry battalions and a self-propelled 25-pounder battery under command, moved to a position east of Meiktila. Cowan's armour, deployed in wide flanking aggressive actions, caught the Japanese defenders in the open and inflicted on them heavy casualties. With the jungle now behind them, 17 Indian Division's tanks, mechanized artillery and mechanized infantry found the flat lands beyond the Irrawaddy well suited to the tactics of encircling and cutting off Japanese positions. The Japanese had no answer to either 14 Army's use of armour or to the effectiveness of the all-arms tactics in which it was employed. When Meiktila was reached, an immediate attack was put in, with all available artillery and air support. The attack penetrated well, but resistance was fierce and fanatical. Yet again, the Japanese soldier showed his penchant for fighting to the death. During 2 and 3 March 63 and 48 Indian Brigades together with 255 Tank Brigade, closed in from differing points of the compass, squeezing and destroying the Japanese between them. By 6p.m. on 3 March Meiktila had fallen. During 4 and 5 March even the most fanatical of resistance was brushed aside as surrounding villages were cleared and the main airfield secured.

*Kimura* was shocked, as Slim knew he would be, by the sudden and unexpected loss of Meiktila. He at once sought to crush 17 Indian Division and recapture the town. *Kimura* ordered *Honda* immediately to turn south, and for three weeks from mid-March the Japanese mounted a series of ferocious counter-attacks against 17 Indian Division. Once in Meiktila, Cowan's policy was one of 'aggressive defence'. Combined arms groups of infantry, mechanized artillery and armour, supported from the air by attack aircraft, were sent out every day to hunt, ambush and destroy approaching Japanese columns in a radius of twenty miles of the town. The pressure on Meiktila built up, however. Soon the land line of communication back to Nyaungu was cut, and the Japanese tried hard to seize the airfield. The situation was sufficiently disconcerting for Slim to decide to commit his last remaining reserve, 5 Indian Division,* which arrived onto one of the Meiktila airfields, under enemy fire, on 17 March. This was a huge risk for Slim, but he knew that if he did not secure victory in this battle he would have to concede the campaign. Slim's gamble paid off. By 29 March the Japanese were beaten back, losing their guns and significant casualties in the process. The river port of Myingyan on the Chindwin was captured after a fierce fight, and its rapid commissioning as a working port substantially reduced the pressure on Messervy's land line of communication. Before long it was receiving 200 tons of desperately needed supplies every day.

Slim's relief at the securing of the Meiktila battlefield was palpable, and he gave thanks where it was due. He was in no doubt that Cowan's success first in seizing Meiktila, then in holding the town against increasingly frantic Japanese counter-attacks, secured the success of Operation Extended Capital. The battle was, he reflected, 'a magnificent feat of arms . . . [which] sealed the fate of the Japanese in Burma.' This was no overstatement. Four Corps' thrust against Meiktila was Slim's decisive stroke, on which the success of his entire strategy rested, and for which he had subordinated everything else. Now, the huge risks he had taken had come good. The Japanese also were in no doubt about the significance of Slim's victory,

---

* Now commanded by Major-General Warren. Warren had replaced Geoffrey Evans who moved on to command 7 Indian Division. Warren was killed shortly after, and was replaced by Bob Mansergh, who had briefly been GOC of 11 East Africa Division. Brigadier Dimoline from 28 East Africa Brigade replaced Mansergh in 11 East Africa Division.

*Kimura* admitting that it was 'the masterpiece of Allied strategy' in the battle for Burma.[24] The historian Louis Allen regarded it to be 'Slim's greatest triumph', a feat which allowed him to place 'his hand firmly on the jugular of the Japanese' and which put 'the final reconquest of Burma within Slim's grasp.'[25]

Slim now needed to attack *Kimura* hard in order to prevent him from turning against the 4 Corps anvil forming around Meiktila. When this anvil was firm Slim intended to allow 33 Corps – the hammer – to fall on *Kimura* hard from the north. The first part of this hammer – 19 Indian Division (62, 64 and 98 Brigades) – broke out of its bridgehead forty miles north of Mandalay on 26 February. By 4 March the division was in tankable country twenty miles north of Mandalay, reaching the northern outskirts of Mandalay three days later. The two strong points in Mandalay – Mandalay Hill and Fort Dufferin – were vigorously defended and required considerable effort to overcome, but were captured by 20 March. While Mandalay was being invested, 62 Brigade struck secretly eastward at Maymyo where they fell upon the town, taking the garrison completely by surprise.

The second part of the 33 Corps advance – 20 Indian and 2 British Divisions – broke out of their respective bridgeheads to the west of Mandalay in early March. The Japanese were everywhere pushed back, losing heavily in men and artillery. Slim deduced that *Kimura* would attempt to hold a line running south-west from Kyaukse to Chauk, with *15 Army* holding the right, *33 Army* the centre, and *28 Army* the left. He knew that, despite Japanese efforts to stiffen the line, it would still be weak. Accordingly he aimed to concentrate at weak points in the line, and strike decisively at the Japanese command and communication network so as to remove the last vestiges of control Japanese commanders had over the course of the battle. Supported strongly by 221 Group RAF, Gracey's 20 Indian Division led the charge. 32 and 80 Brigades sliced through the Japanese opposition to converge on Kyaukse, while 100 Brigade carried out a wide encircling movement to seize Wundin, on the main railway sixty miles south of Mandalay on 21 March, although stubborn resistance prevented Kyaukse from falling until the end of the month. Throughout this period his planning cycle remained well ahead of *Kimura's*. 'No sooner was a plan made to meet a given situation than, due to a fresh move by Slim, it was out-of-date before it could be executed, and a new one had to be hurriedly prepared with a conglomeration of widely scattered units and formations,' wrote Evans. 'Because of the kaleidoscopic changes in the situation, breakdowns in communication and the fact that Burma Area Army Headquarters was often out of touch with reality, many of the attacks to restore the position were uncoordinated.'[26] *15* and *31 Divisions* now retreated in disarray, breaking into little groups of fugitives seeking refuge in the Shan Hills to the east.

Slim's prize – Rangoon – now lay before him. Leaving the remnants of *Kimura*'s army to fall back to the west and south-west, Slim drove 4 and 33 Corps on throughout April in a desperate race to reach the coast before the monsoon rains made the roads unpassable. In a brilliantly paced campaign against the rapidly disintegrating – but still fanatical – Japanese army, Rangoon was captured only a week after the first rains fell. Messervy's Corps had the lead. Punching forward as fast as their fuel would allow, isolating and bypassing significant opposition, his armour raced from airstrip to airstrip, where engineers prepared for the fly-in of aircraft under the noses of the enemy. Fearing that the Japanese might have garrisoned Rangoon to defend it to the last Slim had earlier persuaded Mountbatten to revive Operation Dracula and launch an attack from the sea to coincide with the armoured onrush from the north. In fact, the retreating Japanese had evacuated Rangoon and 26 Indian Division, landing from the sea, captured the city without a fight.

In May 1945 the war was far from over. Three more months of hard fighting were to follow as the troops of 14 Army fought back the tenacious Japanese rearguards over the Karen Hills and Sittang River towards Thailand. Nevertheless the capture of Rangoon set the seal on a brilliantly fought campaign that brought about the defeat of the Japanese in Burma. It was a campaign that the strategists had never planned in the first place and its overwhelming success, like that at Imphal/Kohima the year before, came as something as a surprise to those both in London and Washington who continued to underestimate both 14 Army and its commander. Slim's unhesitating switch of plan to Extended Capital in mid-December 1944, his acceptance of the administrative and tactical risks that this entailed and his command of every nuance of the 1945 offensive as it unfolded showed him to be the consummate master of war. The success

of the campaign led Ronald Lewin appositely to ascribe to Slim every
characteristic of 'a complete general'. 'Deception and surprise,' he wrote,
'flexibility, concentration on the objective, calculated risks, the solution
of grave administrative problems, imagination, sang-froid, invigorating
leadership – all the clichés of the military textbooks were simultaneously
and harmoniously brought to life as Slim, with an absolute assurance,
conceived and accomplished his masterpiece.'[27]

The evidence of his conduct of operations in Burma shows clearly that
Slim's approach to war was built firmly on the principles that framed the
'indirect approach'. A central tenet of this approach was the argument
that the true aim in war was not necessarily the physical destruction
of the enemy but the breaking of his will to fight. This would not, of
course, mean an avoidance of hard fighting and expenditure of blood and
resources, but one was the end of strategy and the other was the means.
While there is no evidence that Slim passed any public judgement in favour
of the arguments of the so-called 'English' school which propounded this
idea during the inter-war years, his approach to the conduct war in 1944
and 1945 demonstrates a strong common ancestry with these ideas. Slim's
approach to war fighting came not from any spiritual attraction to an idea,
or any intellectual dalliance with theory, but rather by the demands of
intelligent soldiering. This insisted that an enemy's strengths were to be
avoided in favour of the exploitation of his weaknesses, and that surprise,
which of course is merely one version of psychological dislocation, was the
oxygen that fuelled every plan and every operation. Just as Slim's conduct
of operations mirrored in close detail the tenets of the 'indirect approach'
they also provided a clear foreshadowing of the principles of 'manoeuvre
warfare'. These ideas *inter alia* are that warfare must jointly combine
sea, air and land power in the planning and conduct of operations; that
combat power should be applied to exploit enemy weaknesses rather than
his strength; that the principal focus of commanders should be the enemy
rather than the ground; that the enemy's will to win must be attacked constantly and that the tempo of friendly operations must dominate and overwhelm those of the enemy. In all these areas Slim's foreshadowing is clear.

Slim would not have achieved his success in 1945 without, among other
things, the understanding and support of Mountbatten and the superb
co-operation of the Allied air forces in theatre. Likewise, Sultan's advance
from Lashio, in which Festing's 36 British Division distinguished itself,
kept *Honda* occupied in the north at a time when Stopford was attempting

to cross the Irrawaddy north of Mandalay. Commanders at every level, imbued with a knowledge of their superiority over the Japanese, kept their men and their material going despite the difficulties of distance, terrain, climate and exhaustion. Ultimately, however, none of these would have even been called into play had not Slim refused to be put off from his grand design to launch aggressive offensive operations against the Japanese in Burma in 1945. When it happened, 14 Army's advance in strength into Burma came about not by virtue of allied policy, but because of Slim's single-minded determination to pursue the Japanese to their destruction and to exploit the opportunity for so doing that he himself had created at Imphal/Kohima. The invasion of Burma took place according to his plan and his purposes. And in all things Slim succeeded spectacularly, repaying with considerable interest the trust and confidence Mountbatten had placed in him.

Slim was unable, however, to savour the full sweetness of his victory. On 7 May 1945 Leese flew to Slim's headquarters at Meiktila and told him that he did not intend that Slim should command 14 Army for Operation Zipper, the amphibious invasion of Malaya. Leese's relationship with Slim had been uncomfortable from the outset, and it was only natural that Leese should want, at the earliest opportunity, and particularly with a major shift in operational emphasis looming, to replace Slim with someone whose personal allegiance would be easier to gain. It proved, however, to be a serious error of judgement. Leese had advised Mountbatten on 3 May that he believed Slim to be tired, needful of a rest and, because of his lack of experience in amphibious warfare, not best suited to the challenges posed by forthcoming operations in south-east Asia. His preferred choice was Christison, currently commanding 15 Corps. Mountbatten, while surprised by Leese's claim that Slim was 'tired' nevertheless agreed that Slim could be asked his opinion, but stressed that no decision was to be made without his personal sanction. Mountbatten insisted, according to his new Chief of Staff, Lieutenant-General Frederick Browning, in a letter to the CIGS, that 'he could not countenance any changes which might carry the slightest indication that Slim was being removed from his command. He informed Oliver', continued Browning, 'that he should handle the matter extremely carefully; that he had the highest opinion of, and confidence in, Slim; and that he would not consider anything which might affect Slim's future, the operations of the theatre or the morale of 14 Army.'[28]

For reasons that still remain unclear, Leese ignored these instructions. He immediately despatched one of his senior staff officers, Major-General George Walsh, a man known for his lack of tact, to explore with Slim the possibility that Slim relinquish command on the ground that as Slim had been in constant action since 1941 he must be tired and needful of a rest. Slim was outraged with what he saw to be an underhand attempt to engineer his removal and insisted to Walsh that if the Commander-in-Chief ALFSEA had lost confidence in him then Leese should at least have the courtesy to discuss the issue with him face-to-face.[29] Leese accordingly made arrangements to fly to Slim's headquarters in Meiktila on the afternoon of 7 May.

Mountbatten's instructions had either not been clear or else Leese was so determined to remove Slim from command of 14 Army that he was prepared simply to ignore them. Following his meeting in Kandy with Mountbatten on 5 May, Leese flew directly to Christison's headquarters at Akyab, from where he wrote that night to Brooke, bypassing Mountbatten completely, suggesting Slim's removal and replacement by Christison. Leese suggested to Brooke that Slim remained to oversee operations and administration within Burma. 'I feel that if our propaganda is good, Slim can be built up as the conqueror of Burma and is the right man to set Burma on a sound footing for the future,' he wrote.[30] The next morning, 6 May, he told Christison, a full day before Leese was due to meet Slim:

Now, Dickie has suggested that I send Slim on indefinite leave, and I have done so. He has already left 14th Army. A new Army is to be formed for the invasion of Malaya and the recapture of Singapore. For prestige reasons it is to be known as 14 Army and the present 14 Army is to be called 12 Army and it will clear up Burma. Stopford is to command it. You, with your combined operations experience, are to take over 14 Army.[31]

Leese met Slim as planned on 7 May. Leese told him that he would not be required for operations in south-east Asia once Burma had fallen, and offered him the command of 12 Army, which would garrison Burma. Slim at once refused, regarding the offer to be an insult, and told Leese that he would prefer to resign and return to the United Kingdom. While Leese was later to deny that this was his intention, Slim considered himself to be sacked.[32] Leese then flew to Quetta in India. With masterful self-discipline Slim told no one but his closest staff. He gathered his senior staff together at 10 a.m. on 9 May and gave them the news. 'I can't tell you what a painful announcement this is for me to make', he told them, 'when, as you all will guess, I have only one ambition and that is to go on commanding 14 Army, of which I am extremely proud, until the Jap is finally beaten flat. But that is not to be.'[33] Without exception the response of his staff was one of incredulity and even anger that the architect of victory in Assam and Burma should be cast aside at the moment of his greatest triumph. Sensing their reaction to Leese's decision, Slim insisted that there was to be 'no adverse criticism of it and no action on anyone's part in sympathy for me.' Slim repeated these instructions during the following days and made no attempt to represent his case to any higher authority.[34] This was not sufficient to prevent waves of bitter antipathy breaking out against those that had allowed this situation to occur. 'Sacked on the very day he'd achieved victory'; 'Oliver Twist and Mountbatten must be out of their minds ... stark, raving mad'; 'I never trusted that affected, silk-handkerchief-waving Guardsman'.[35] Between 10 and 12 May Slim visited Aileen in Shillong (the capital of Assam) and on 13 May he returned to Meiktila to give the news to his faithful corps commanders, Messervy and Stopford. The following day he confirmed in writing to both Auchinleck and Leese his intention to retire. In the meantime Slim prepared to leave 14 Army and Christison, after receiving the congratulations of his staff in 15 Corps, arranged to take it over and began preparing for Operation Zipper. The message that Slim had been sacked spread like wildfire throughout 14 Army and further afield through India Command.

Unbeknown to Slim, a storm of considerable magnitude was even then raging in Kandy and London. Brooke, who had heard nothing from Mountbatten regarding Slim's future except glowing reports as to the conduct of the campaign in Burma, had been surprised by Leese's initial signal. At the very least changes in senior appointments in theatre were to come, in the first instance, from Mountbatten. He penned a reply to Leese on 18 May saying as much and emphasizing that he could not countenance Slim's removal unless he and Mountbatten could produce the strongest reasons for so doing. A separate signal was sent on the same day to Mountbatten. 'Immediately your signal was sent to Leese asking for an explanation why these proposals had not come from the Supreme Commander, we sent for him to come to Kandy to present his explanation,' continued Browning, writing to the CIGS. 'In the meantime ... we heard that Slim had informed his own staff that he was leaving and within a few days it was all over 14 Army that Slim had been sacked.'[36] Auchinleck was in London at the time, and played a part in unstitching Leese's plan. At lunch with Churchill at Chequers on 20 May he described Slim as the best general the Indian Army had, adding that he hoped that eventually Slim would succeed himself as Commander-in-Chief India. Two days later he repeated these thoughts at lunch with Brooke, at which Slim was the main topic of conversation.[37]

Leese then flew to Kandy to explain himself to Browning and Mountbatten. He readily accepted that he had made a mistake and agreed to backtrack. On 22 May Leese was forced to signal news of the about face, which he did with good grace. Slim was to retain command of 14 Army for Operation Zipper and Stopford was to command 12 Army. In the ensuing month Leese's own future was determined. On 19 June 1945 Brooke wrote to Mountbatten to the effect that 'Oliver Leese has proved himself unsuited for his present employment', and suggested that Slim should take his place as commander-in-chief of Allied Land Forces South East Asia (ALFSEA). 'He has the advantage of knowing all the conditions of the theatre,' he wrote. Mountbatten agreed, replying that such a move 'would suit me admirably.' The decision was made.

Leese's humiliation was made complete when on 1 July Mountbatten wrote to him while Leese was on leave in Kashmir informing him that he was to be replaced as Commander ALFSEA by Slim and that he was to return at once to the United Kingdom.[38] 'I made a silly error of judgement,' Leese admitted to his wife in a letter on 3 July 1945, but was convinced 'that Mountbatten meant anyhow to get rid of me ... I am very glad to leave here. It has been a horrid party with Mountbatten and Slim.'[39] Leese duly returned to the United Kingdom in discredit, the victim of his own ill-conceived machinations. Slim had now returned to the United Kingdom with Aileen on a period of well-deserved leave, to a country he had not seen since 1941. The nation was only just awaking to a knowledge of what 14 Army had achieved in Burma, although arguably Slim's army never received the public acknowledgement they deserved. Although no itinerary had been planned, Slim found himself rightly feted as the man who had wrung victory from defeat in the hardest of battlefields against the hardest of enemies. He was promoted to full General on 1 July, attended civic functions in his honour across the country and met Churchill, to whom, three years later, he would work as Chief of the Imperial Staff.*

Until June 1945, Slim had been virtually unknown outside of 14 Army and SEAC. Credit for the succession of victories in Assam and Burma since July 1944 had gone to others, especially Mountbatten and Leese, and the wartime press in the United Kingdom knew little of him. Although Slim's centrality to victory was well known to those who served with and under him, his name did not figure in the government-sponsored adulation of other senior commanders, such as Montgomery and Alexander, at the end of the war. This recognition was to come, albeit slowly, and was only formalized in the publication of the fourth volume of the official history, *The War Against Japan*, in 1965. This concluded that 'the foresight which saw both the opportunities and the dangers and the initiative in seizing the former and forestalling the latter, stemmed from one man – Slim.'

It was while returning to the Far East to take up his new appointment as Commander-in-Chief ALFSEA alongside Mountbatten in Kandy in August that Slim heard the news that the atom bomb had been dropped on Japan, heralding the end of the war. On 12 September he sat in Singapore with Mountbatten to receive the unconditional surrender of all Japanese forces in south-east Asia. Disobeying General MacArthur's stricture that Japanese officers were not to be forced to surrender their swords, Slim insisted that in south-east Asia all Japanese officers were to surrender their swords to British officers of similar or higher rank. 'Field-Marshal Tarauchi's sword is in Admiral Mountbatten's hands', Slim wrote in 1956; 'General Kimura's is now on my mantelpiece, where I always intended that one day it should be.'

Slim's long war in Burma had come to an end, the vanquished now the victor. The journey had been long. It had begun in March 1942 when as an unknown Major-General in the Indian Army he had taken command of 1 Burma Corps at the start of the British Army's longest ever retreat. He had, through skill and stiff-jawed determination, prevented defeat from descending into rout and had marched his troops back into India. His journey had taken him to command of 15 Corps, where he set in motion

---

* Slim replaced Field Marshal Bernard Law Montgomery as CIGS on 1 November 1948. This is another story outside the scope of this book, but told in Ronald Lewin's biography *Slim: The Standard Bearer* (London, 1976).

the re-training of the whole Army, to command of 14 Army on the eve of
the Japanese invasion of India in the spring of 1944. He had moulded the
Japanese offensive to suit his own plans, and step by step, he decisively
broke the Japanese in the hills of eastern Assam and the Imphal plain.
He did not do this alone, of course, and the various contributions of
Auchinleck, Mountbatten, Giffard, Wingate and Scoones at one level,
to say nothing of the sacrifices of the ordinary fighting men – Indian,
British and African – at the other, were critical elements in the overall
success of 14 Army. But there is also no doubt that without Slim the
long battles in the hills around Imphal and Kohima would never have
been won.

Most commanders would then have sat on their laurels. Not so Slim.
He was convinced that real victory against 15 Army required an aggressive
pursuit, not just to the Chindwin but into the heart of Burma itself.
Single-handedly he worked to put in place all the ingredients of a bold
offensive to seize Mandalay at a time when every inclination in London
and Washington was to seek an amphibious solution to the problem of
Burma and thus avoid the entanglements of a land offensive. Slim believed,
however, that it could be done. Virtually alone he drove his plans forward,
winning agreement and acceptance to his ideas as he went, particularly
with Mountbatten, and went on to execute in Burma in 1945 one of the
most brilliant expositions of the strategic art that warfare has ever seen.
He did this in the face of difficulties of every sort and degree. 'Slim's
revitalisation of the Army had proved him to be a general of administrative
genius,' argues the historian Duncan Anderson: 'his conduct of the Burma
retreat, the first and second Arakan, and Imphal–Kohima, had shown
him to be a brilliant defensive general; and now, the Mandalay-Meiktila
operation had placed him in the same class as Guderian, Manstein and
Patton as an offensive commander.'[40] His troops already knew of his
greatness, of course and were, as Mountbatten put it, his devoted slaves.[41]
His modesty and self-deprecation led Brigadier Bernard Fergusson, one
of Wingate's protégés, to argue that Slim was unlike any other British
higher commander to emerge in the Second World War, 'the only one
at the highest level in that war that . . . by his own example inspired and
restored its self-respect and confidence to an army in whose defeat he had
shared.'[42] 'Among other things', Fergusson concluded,' he was the only
Indian Army general of my acquaintance that ever got himself across
to British troops. Monosyllables do not usually carry a cadence; but to

thousands of British troops, as well as to Indians and to his own beloved Gurkhas, there will always be a special magic in the words "Bill Slim."'

'"Bill" Slim was to us,' averred Antony Brett-James, 'a homely sort of general: on his jaw was carved the resolution of an army, in his stern eyes and tight mouth reside all the determination and unremitting courage of a great force. His manner held much of the bulldog, gruff and to the point, believing in every one of us, and as proud of the "Forgotten Army" as we were. I believe that his name will descend into history as a badge of honour as great as that of the "Old Contemptibles."'

To the men who fought with him there was never any question: his was the victory in Burma. It was a victory that placed Slim at the heart of modern military strategy and provides sufficient justification for Mountbatten's claim that, despite the reputation of others, such as Montgomery of Alamein, it was Slim who should rightly be regarded as the greatest British general of the Second World War.

# APPENDICES

# APPENDIX 1

# The Appointment of Slim to
# Burma Corps – March 1942

The common account of Slim's selection to command Burma Corps in March 1942 has it that Alexander asked for him by name when he assumed command of Burma Army on 5 March 1942. The Indian Official Historian comments that, following Alexander's arrival in Burma, GHQ India was 'requested to supply a Corps commander and a skeleton Corps Headquarters.'[1] The assumption is that Scott or Cowan, who knew Slim well, persuaded Alexander to ask for him by name. It appears that this particular story began in the Indian Official History in 1952, which itself was based on a record of the campaign prepared by GHQ India in 1942. The story was repeated by the British Official Historian in 1958[2] and found its way into virtually all subsequent accounts of Slim's appointment, including Slim's official biography.[3] Alexander himself somewhat disingenuously remarks in his memoirs, published in 1962, that he asked for General Slim to command the corps he was forming. 'I could not have asked for a finer man', he records.[4]

The truth, however, is somewhat different. The decision to send a corps commander to Burma in fact pre-dated the decision to send Alexander to replace Hutton as GOC. Alexander agreed to appoint Slim only because Wavell had offered him a corps commander in the first place, not because Alexander had asked for one, of his own initiative. In a cable Hutton sent to Java on 13 February, he asked Wavell for a corps commander. At the time considerable reinforcements for Burma were expected, including 14 Indian Infantry Division, then assembling in India. Hutton recognized that with these reinforcements his span of command would grow commensurately.[5] The aspiration to send 14 Indian Division was short-lived, but Wavell nevertheless recognized the value such an appointment would bring to Burma Army, and repeated the request to London. Wavell went so far as to list some of the candidates, one of whom was Lieutenant-General T.W. Corbett, at the time the commander of 4 Indian Corps in Iraq.[6]

General Brooke immediately cabled Hartley, acting C-in-C India in New Delhi while Wavell was in Java, for his opinion. Hartley replied with the suggestion that Slim, then commanding 10 Indian Infantry Division in Iraq, under Corbett's command, would be a suitable candidate. Accordingly the CIGS, on 21 February, only eight days after Hutton had first made his request, and two days *after* he had appointed Alexander, replied to Wavell to say that he was satisfied that Corbett was first class and that he could be released once 4 Indian Corps had completed its task in Iraq. 'Otherwise,' he noted, 'Slim should go as recommended by CinC India.'[7] Brooke's intention was clearly to provide a suitable corps commander: a replacement CGS for Hutton was an altogether different matter. On 19 February, when Alexander was appointed Commander Burma Army, Brooke commented: 'Shall try leaving Hutton as Chief General Staff; if this does not work shall have to carry out a change. Only hope Alexander arrives out in time, as situation in Burma is becoming critical. Troops don't seem to be fighting well there either which is most depressing.'[8]

The VCIGS, Major-General Nye, was in all likelihood responsible for persuading General Brooke to agree to Slim's name going forward for this appointment.[9] Nye had known Slim well from their days at Staff College together and had been impressed by the diffident but highly competent Gurkha. Whilst it was a happy coincidence that Nye was in a position to influence General Brooke's decision, it is clear that Slim's nomination did not come in the first instance from Whitehall, but from Hartley in New Delhi.

Slim records that the Army Commander in Iraq* telephoned him from his HQ in Baghdad on or about 4 March 1942 to tell him that he had

---

* Lieutenant-General E.P. Quinan.

been given another job, but interestingly the nature of the job was not intimated to Slim until after his return from the reconnaissance to Burma with General Morris. This appears to have been because Wavell, who had resumed the appointment of C-in-C India, was himself unsure of whether Alexander needed a Corps commander or a new CGS, to take over from Hutton.

On 8 March Wavell signalled Alexander:

> Slim is on his way, but I don't know yet when he will arrive. With the forces now in Burma I doubt whether we can justify a major general as CGS permanently, and I shall probably want Slim for a Lieutenant General's appointment in the very near future. Do you consider the present CGS [Hutton] good enough or would you like him changed? I will send you Slim temporarily if you want him: I don't think he can be spared as a permanency.[10]

This was undoubtedly the message Morris was instructed to repeat to Alexander verbally when they met at Maymyo during the reconnaissance with Slim. Slim was available either as CGS *vice* Hutton (in the rank of Major-General) or as corps commander (in the rank of Lieutenant-General). Morris reported back to Wavell that the most pressing task for Slim was the command of the new Corps in Burma and that this was how Alexander wished to employ him. Wavell immediately instructed Slim to take on the task.[11]

# APPENDIX 2

# The Appointment of Slim to Eastern Army – October 1943

The new Supreme Commander SEAC, Admiral Lord Louis Mountbatten, arrived in New Delhi on 7 October 1943, and stayed with Auchinleck until Monday 11 October when he moved into his own official residence, Faridkot House. On 15 October Mountbatten left New Delhi to fly to Chungking to visit Chiang Kai-shek, the day before Slim reported to Barrackpore as acting commander of Eastern Army. During his first few days in New Delhi he discussed the permanent appointment of commander 14 Army with Auchinleck. The post would arguably be the most critical of the whole theatre as it would be responsible for commanding all land-based warfighting operations against the Japanese and would be required in due course to advance into Burma. Auchinleck had raised the issue with CIGS on 4 October, and had proposed that Slim be given the post in an acting capacity.

Initially Auchinleck wanted to move Slim from 15 Corps to be his CGS *vice* Morris, so that he could have an Indian Army CGS. He suggested this option to Brooke on 18 October. Mountbatten, however, who met Slim for the first time on 22 October at Barrackpore, on his return from Chungking, was strongly opposed to moving Slim from 14 Army. The following day he wrote to Brooke:

I understand that it has been agreed that Slim should continue in

command of 14th Army which he has temporarily taken over, that
Scoons [sic] should continue in command of the 4th Corps and that
Christison should take over the 15th Corps from Slim, but I now
understand that this is back in the melting pot as Auchinleck wants
an Indian Army officer to relieve Morris as CGS. I have told him
that I naturally do not wish to stand in his way in this matter and
must leave it to you. But I cannot help feeling uneasy at any further
changes in the military commands so shortly before the opening of
the campaign.[1]

As far as Brooke was concerned there could be no argument. On 30
October 1943 he wrote to Auchinleck:

I consider that in view of operations it would be best for the present
to leave Slim to command the 14th Army and Morris as CGS.
Slim's experience should be a great asset in SE Asia and it will
give him as well as Scoones great opportunities in high command,
whilst avoiding undesirable changes on an operational front. I agree
Christison to command 15 Corps.[2]

Mountbatten had agreed with Slim's provisional appointment, but insisted
that he would only confirm the permanent appointment after he had
met Slim personally. Giffard then drafted a detailed note on Slim for
Mountbatten to read during his long flight over the Himalayas to China,
which substantiated the case for Slim's appointment.

When Mountbatten met Slim for the first time at Barrackpore on 22
October, he recalled, in correspondence with Slim's official biographer
many years later, that:

I fell for Slim the very moment I met him at his headquarters in
Belvedere at Barrackpore, when he was ... acting Army Commander. I had been given his background but it was left to me to
judge what he was like. I immediately offered him command of the
eastern Army and we agreed the name should be changed ... Slim
was obviously delighted but said, 'Won't you have to ask General
Giffard first?' I said 'No' as I was the Supreme Commander and
Giffard was my subordinate.

Mountbatten recalled that when he told Giffard that he 'had given Slim command of the new Army he [Giffard] demurred and said he would have to think it over. I suggested he should telegraph to the CIGS asking whether he had to obey my orders or was permitted to protest. At this he gave in and I maintained my ascendancy over him from that moment though I don't suppose he liked it.'[3] In a diary note he made for the period Saturday 30 October to Friday 5 November 43 Mountbatten recorded: 'After considerable struggle I have succeeded in getting Lieutenant General Slim appointed in command of the 14th Army.'[4]

Thus, in both his diary and letter to Lewin, Mountbatten suggests that the decision to appoint Slim was his alone, insinuates that Giffard objected to Slim's appointment *per se*, and suggests that he had to drive through Slim's appointment against all opposition. Subsequent historians have accepted his account without demur.[5] Some have even concluded that Giffard was not convinced of Slim's suitability for the job. But this was not the case.

What was Mountbatten's supposed problem with Giffard? In short, Giffard objected not to the nomination of Slim himself, to which he had already subscribed and which the CIGS himself had already sanctioned, but to the way in which Mountbatten had confirmed the appointment directly with Slim on 22 October. Giffard was an honest if slightly formal officer, acutely aware of the rules and obligations of the Military Secretary's Branch, and did not take kindly to Mountbatten's cavalier approach to such sensitive issues as promotions and appointments in the Army, even if these were exceptional circumstances.[6] He was also acutely aware that Mountbatten had yet formally to take over command of SEAC: this was planned to take place in mid-November. Giffard had assumed that Mountbatten would first return to New Delhi to discuss his impressions of Slim with both himself and Auchinleck, and that if Mountbatten was amenable to the appointment having now met Slim in person, Giffard himself, as the Army Group Commander and Slim's immediate superior, would confirm the appointment and formally tell Slim. He certainly did not consider it Mountbatten's business casually to confirm Slim's appointment direct to his face, after the shortest of meetings, and regarded it as the worst of form. Mountbatten shrugged off such criticism, and told Giffard that he was empowered to do what he wanted.

Although Mountbatten was formally correct – he did have the power to hire and fire – his role in the affair of Slim's appointment was merely to endorse (or not) the appointment of Slim as commander of Eastern Army. Despite his later inventions, this is precisely what Mountbatten did at the time. When he met Slim at Barrackpore he was genuinely taken by Slim's character and agreed, after only a very short interval, and in typically impetuous fashion, that Auchinleck and Brooke between them had made the wisest of choices. For the second time, therefore, and within nineteen months, persons other than those actually responsible had attempted to claim the credit for Slim's selection to high command.* Mountbatten received a telegram from GHQ India on Saturday 13 November from the Military Secretary confirming the appointments of Giffard, Slim and Christison and in the case of the first two officers, backdating their seniority to 15 October 1943.[7]

* See Appendix 1.

# NOTES

# Introduction

1. Philip Ziegler, Mountbatten (London, Guild Publishing, 1955), p. 295.
2. M.R. Roberts, *William Joseph Slim* (National Dictionary of Biography, 1972), p. 957. Brigadier Roberts commanded 114 Indian Brigade in 7 Indian Division in 1943 and 1944 and went on to become one of the official historians of the campaign.
3. Geoffrey Evans, 'Field Marshal The Viscount Slim' in Field Marshal Michael Carver, *The War Lords: Military Commanders of the Twentieth Century* (London, Weidenfeld and Nicholson, 1976), p. 377.
4. Geoffrey Evans, *Slim as Military Commander* (London, Batsford, 1969), p. 27.
5. Ronald Lewin, *Slim: The Standard Bearer* (London, Leo Cooper, 1976), p. 58.
6. As an indication of how slow promotion was in the peacetime Army, when Slim was appointed Commander of Eastern Army on 16 October 1943 he was still a substantive Colonel.
7. File 129, Auchinleck Papers.
8. File 130, Auchinleck Papers.
9. Auchinleck's letter confirming Quinan and Slim's departure for Iraq on 4 May 1941 is in British Library L/WS/1/535.
10. File 199, Auchinleck Papers.
11. Quoted in Duncan Anderson, 'Slim', in J. Keegan (ed.) *Churchill's Generals* (London, Weidenfeld and Nicholson, 1991), p. 306.
12. The story of Slim's appointment is in Appendix 1.

# Chapter 1 – Poisoned Chalice

1. Of the eighteen infantry battalions in Burma in 1941 sixteen were Burmese and two were British. The three regular battalions of the Burma Rifles ('Burifs') in 1939, together with a training battalion, were rapidly expanded to eight by 1941. This had the effect of immediately reducing

their operational effectiveness. The seven territorial Burma Military Police (BMP) battalions, lightly armed with rifles and Lewis guns, were scattered around Burma's periphery with a largely para-military and border-surveillance role. These BMP battalions were converted, in 1941, into units of the Burma Frontier Force (BFF). However, because of a number of fault lines within Burmese society a decision made in 1927 (later repealed in 1940) prevented Burmese from joining the Burma Army. By 1939 only 472 out of 3,669 soldiers in the Burma Army were actually Burmese. The remainder were the more politically safe Karens, Chins and Kachins.

2.    Michael Calvert, *Slim* (London: Pan, 1973), p. 50.
3.    J.D. Lunt, *'A Hell of a Licking': The Retreat from Burma 1941–2* (London, Collins, 1986), p. 106.
4.    I.L. Grant and K. Tamayama, *Burma 1942: The Japanese Invasion. Both sides tell the Story of a Savage Jungle War* (Chichester, The Zampi Press, 1999), pp. 26–27.
5.    Alexander, *'Despatch'*, *The London Gazette*, 5 March 1948, p. 1698.
6.    W.G.F. Jackson, *Alexander as Military Commander* (*London, Batsford, 1971*), p. 115.
7.    S. Woodburn Kirby, *The War Against Japan*, Volume II (London, HMSO, 1958), p. 86.
8.    Alexander's draft reply, which was terser still, was never sent. See File 229 PRO/WO/106/2681.
9.    Wavell, *'Despatch'*, *The London Gazette*, 5 March 1948, p. 1672.
10.   Lunt, op. cit., p. 98.
11.   File 2/13, Hutton Papers.
12.   Alexander, *'Despatch'*, *The London Gazette*, 11 March 1948, pp. 1711–1712.
13.   Jackson, op. cit., p. 139.
14.   Private communication to author December 2000.
15.   Lewin, op. cit., p. 87.
16.   Ibid.
17.   File 283A PRO/WO/106/2682.
18.   Lunt, op. cit., p. 206.
19.   File 276A PRO/WO/106/2682.
20.   File 293A PRO/WO/106/2682.
21.   File 293 PRO/WO/106/2682.
22.   File 310 PRO/WO/106/2682.
23.   File 300A PRO/WO/106/2682.
24.   Quoted in Woodburn Kirby, Vol II, op. cit., p. 161.
25.   Private communication to author December 2000.
26.   Lunt, op. cit., 189.
27.   File 283A PRO/WO/106/2682.
28.   Lunt, op. cit., p. 217.
29.   J.Hedley, *Jungle Fighter* (Brighton, Tom Donovan, 1996), p. 26.
30.   Grant and Tamayama, op. cit., p. 234.
31.   Calvert, op. cit., p. 32.

32. Grant and Tamayama, op. cit., p. 239.
33. Ibid.
34. Ibid., p. 244.

## Chapter 2 – Through the Shadows of Darkness

1. Grant and Tamayama, op. cit., p. 230.
2. Ibid., p. 249
3. Quoted in Lewin, op. cit., p. 93. Brian Montgomery was the younger brother of General Bernard Law Montgomery.
4. I am indebted to Major-General Ian Lyall Grant for this observation.
5. Lunt, op. cit., p. 203.
6. Major-General Sir John Kennedy, *The Business of War* (London, Hutchinson, 1957), p. 210.
7. Quoted in Grant, op. cit., p. 267.
8. Lunt, op. cit., p. 223.
9. Grant and Tamayama, op. cit., p. 281.
10. Jackson, op. cit., p. 136.
11. Woodburn Kirby, Vol. II, op. cit., p. 199.
12. Quoted in Lunt, op. cit., p. 242.
13. Lunt, op. cit., p. 223
14. Lewin, op. cit., p. 101.
15. PRO/WO/172/403 27 April 1942.
16. Lunt, op. cit., p. 228
17. Alexander, 'Despatch', *The London Gazette*, 5 March 1948, p. 1707.
18. File 3/9 Slim Papers.
19. Woodburn Kirby, Vol. II. op. cit., p. 210.
20. T.H. White (ed.), *The Stilwell Papers* (New York, Da Capo Press, 1991), p. 106.
21. Slim had urged Alexander as early as 21 April for direction as to the 'axis by which Corps HQ withdraws.' PRO/WO/172/403.
22. John Marsh (ed.), *Alexander, The Memoirs 1940–1945* (London, Cassells, 1962), p. 92.
23. Nigel Nicholson, *Alex: The Life of Field-Marshal Earl Alexander of Tunis* (London, Weidenfeld and Nicholson, 1973), p. 137.
24. File 2/13 Hutton Papers.
25. Marsh, op. cit., p. 83.
26. Lunt, op. cit., p. 160.
27. PRO/WO/106/2682.
28. See Nigel Hamilton, *Monty: Master of the Battlefield 1942–1944* (London, Hamish Hamilton, 1983), pp. 466–474; Nigel Nicholson, Field Marshal The Earl Alexander in Field Marshal Michael Carver, *The War Lords: Military Commanders of the Twentieth Century* (London, Weidenfeld and Nicholson, 1976), p. 332 and Jackson, op. cit., p. 138.

29. File 5/4, Slim Papers. Slim's admission was made to Lieutenant-General Sir Ian Jacob. Quoted in Nigel Hamilton *The Full Monty: Montgomery of Alamein 1887–1942* (London: Allen Lane, 2001), p. 490.
30. File 3/9, Slim Papers.
31. Jackson, op. cit., p. 139. See also Smyth, *Leadership in War 1939–1945: The Generals in Victory and Defeat* (London, David and Charles, 1974), pp. 180–83; Marsh, op.cit., p. 79.
32. Lunt, op. cit., p. xviii.
33. Grant and Tamayama, op. cit., p. 299.
34. Calvert, *Slim*, op. cit., p. 45.
35. Stilwell Papers.
36. Quoted in M. Hickey, *The Unforgettable Army: Slim's XIVth Army in Burma* (Tunbridge Wells, Spellmount Limited, 1992), p. 260.
37. Calvert, op. cit., p. 31.
38. Lunt, op. cit., pp. 197–98.
39. Quoted in Evans, op. cit., p. 67.
40. Ibid.
41. Duncan Anderson, '*Slim*' in John Keegan (ed.) *Churchill's Generals* (London, Weidenfeld and Nicholson, 1991), p. 308.
42. Grant and Tamayama, op. cit., p. 233.
43. Calvert, *Slim*, op. cit., p. 45.
44. Lewin, op. cit., p. 67.
45. See B. Fergusson, '*Slim*' in *The Army Quarterly* (Vol. 4, 1971), p. 272. On 24 November 1944 General Sir Oliver Leese, then Commander Allied Land Forces South East Asia (ALFSEA) in a letter to his wife claimed that Slim 'has the usual Indian Army complex. I am sure he neither understands nor appreciates British troops.' See Leese Papers Box 3. This judgement, however, accords with no other assessment of Slim. See also Norman Dixon, *On the Psychology of Military Incompetence* (London, Jonathan Cape, 1976), p. 341.
46. Quoted in Evans, *Slim as Military Commander*, op. cit., p. 87.
47. Grant and Tamayama, op. cit., p. 319.
48. White, op. cit., p. 98.

## Chapter 3 – In the Wilderness at Ranchi

1. Calvert, *Fighting Mad* (London, The Adventurers Club, 1964), p. 120.
2. Irwin's frantic request to GHQ India on 18 May 1942 for 'twenty thousand ground sheets, cooking pots for five thousand and tarpaulins to accommodate twenty thousand troops' is in PRO/WO/172/369.
3. R. Callahan, *Burma 1942–45* (London, Davis-Poynter, 1978), p. 43.
4. Quoted in J. Connell, *Wavell: Supreme Commander* (London, Collins, 1969), p. 236.
5. Slim comments that 'even with superior force, [it] would be slow and

costly and, knowing the Japanese tenacity in defence might be held up.'
Slim might well have been recalling too much in retrospect, as in 1942
no one had any knowledge of Japanese tenacity in defence.

6. Quoted in Lewin, op. cit., p. 105.
7. Anderson, op. cit., p. 305.
8. File 3/9 and File 5/4. Slim Papers.
9. File 5/4. Slim Papers.
10. He supported Lomax's 'clean sweep' of 26 Indian Division in April 1943,
    even to the extent of lending officers to Lomax from 15 Corps HQ.
11. Connell, op. cit., p. 239.
12. Ibid., p. 240. 'V' Force were locally enlisted 'irregular' troops officered
    from the British Army for reconnaissance and intelligence tasks behind
    Japanese lines.
13. Irwin to Wavell, 29 October 1942. Irwin Papers.
14. Ibid., 14 November 1942. Irwin Papers.
15. Ibid., 8 December 1942. Irwin Papers.
16. Wavell's Despatch, op. cit., p. 2512.
17. Wavell to Irwin, 26 March 1943. Irwin Papers.
18. Evans, *Desert and Jungle* (London, Kimber 1959), p. 140.
19. 'Jungle Jinks', Volume 1, HQ 12 Army, 1945 (MOD Whitehall Library).
20. Hedley, op.cit., p. 95.
21. Wavell to Irwin, 15 January 1943. Irwin Papers.
22. Wavell's Despatch, op.cit., p. 2512.
23. Irwin to Wavell, 23 February 1943. Irwin Papers.
24. Wavell's Despatch, op. cit., p. 2513.
25. Irwin to Wavell, 9 March 1943. Irwin Papers
26. Ibid., 9 March 1943. Irwin Papers.
27. Wavell to Irwin, 7 March 1943. Irwin Papers.
28. Irwin to Wavell, 20 March 1943. Irwin Papers.
29. Wavell to Irwin, 22 March 1943. Irwin Papers.
30. Wavell's Despatch, op. cit., p. 2514
31. Wavell to Irwin, 22 March 1943. Irwin Papers.
32. Ibid., 25 March 1943. Irwin Papers.
33. 'Report on Visit to Maungdaw Front from 4–9 May 1943'. Irwin Papers.
34. Quoted in Indian Official History, Vol. 2, p. 76.
35. Irwin to Wavell, 9 April 1943. Irwin Papers.

## Chapter 4 – Architect of Victory

1. Bisheshwar Prasad (ed.), *Official History of the Indian Army Forces in the
   Second World War: Campaigns in the Eastern Theatre, Arakan Operations
   1942–45*, p. 81.
2. Wavell to Irwin, 9 April 1943. Irwin Papers.
3. Irwin to Hartley, 20 April 1943. Irwin Papers.

4.  Irwin to Wavell, 9 April 1943. Irwin Papers.
5.  Slim to Irwin, 18 April 1943. Irwin Papers.
6.  Ibid.
7.  Slim to Irwin, 7 May 1943. Irwin Papers.
8.  Ibid., 18 April 1943. Irwin Papers.
9.  Irwin to Slim, 10 May 1943. Irwin Papers.
10. Irwin to Hartley, 8 May 1943. Irwin Papers.
11. Brooke to Churchill, 23 May 1943, Alanbrooke Correspondence. Giffard was at the time the senior general of the British Army. Irwin did not receive news of his sacking until 26 May.
12. The original signals no longer exist, but of the several accounts of this incident Lewin's is the most trustworthy. See Lewin, op. cit., p. 124. Calvert's account contains serious errors in date, personalities present and the contents of Irwin's second signal to Slim. See Calvert, op. cit., p. 52.
13. Lewin, op. cit., p. 122.
14. Churchill to Brooke, 21 May 1943, Alanbrooke Correspondence.
15. Callahan, op. cit., p. 62.
16. Ibid., pp. 59, 60. See also Lewin, op. cit., p. 116.
17. Wavell's Despatch, op. cit., p. 2514.
18. Ibid., p. 2514.
19. Calvert Fighting Mad, op. cit., p. 77.
20. Wavell's Despatch. For Irwin's support of Wingate's first expedition see Irwin to Kirby, 4 January 1956, Irwin Papers.
21. It would take a Chindit brigade, marching in single file, several hours to pass a given spot.
22. L. Allen, Burma, the Longest War (London, Dent, 1984), p. 118.
23. Sykes, Orde Wingate (London, Collins, 1959), p. 436.
24. A.J. Barker, The March on Delhi (London, Faber and Faber, 1963), p. 62.
25. Greenwood, Field Marshal Auchinleck (Durham, The Pentland Press, 1991), p. 240.
26. Ibid., p. 249.
27. W.S. Churchill, The Second World War, Volume V, Closing the Ring (London, Cassell, 1952), p. 494.
28. Brooke to Wavell, 20 February 1943. Alanbrooke Correspondence.
29. Evans, Slim as Military Commander, op. cit., p. 99.
30. File C324, Mountbatten Papers.
31. Lewin, op. cit., p. 124.
32. File K261, Mountbatten Papers.
33. Giffard, who had spent most of his military career in Africa, placed considerable and ultimately unwarranted store by these troops. He told Messervy when the latter was Director Armoured Fighting Vehicles in GHQ India that 'the real decisive factor is not going to be tanks. It is going to be the new West African Division.' See H.R. Maule, Spearhead General: The Epic Story of General Sir Frank Messervy and

*his Men at Eritrea, North Africa and Burma* (London, Odhams Press, 1961), p. 213.
34. Barker, op. cit., p. 75.
35. P.Christison, *Autobiography* (Imperial War Museum), p. 126. General Sir Oliver Leese criticized Briggs for being slow and dull but by all accounts this is a particularly unfair assessment.
36. Auchinleck's Despatch, pp. 2651 and 2666.
37. Auchinleck to Brooke, 18 September 1943, File 1037, Auchinleck Papers.
38. File C11, Mountbatten Papers.
39. File 1302, 5 December 1947, Auchinleck Papers.
40. File 3/2, Slim Papers.
41. Maule, op. cit., p. 219.
42. M.R. Roberts, *Golden Arrow: The Story of the 7th Indian Division in the Second World War 1939–1945* (Aldershot, Gale and Polden, 1952), p. 12.
43. Maule, op. cit., p. 225.
44. A. Brett-James, *Report my Signals* (London, Hennel Locke Limited, 1948), p. 181.
45. A. Brett-James, *Ball of Fire* (Aldershot, Gale and Polden, 1951), p. 252.
46. Ibid.
47. Slim was not alone in seeking the development of air transport to overcome the enormous logistical difficulties faced in eastern India and Burma. In May 1942 Irwin had asked New Delhi to investigate the possibility of air-dropping supplies on Imphal to support the recently arrived Burma Corps. See PRO/WO/172/369.

# Chapter 5 – Army Commander

1. The move took place two weeks later. Anderson infers that this move was partly intended to move Slim further way from Giffard in Delhi. Given that Slim decided to move as soon as he took up the appointment, this claim is unfounded. The act of moving out of Calcutta freed up the HQ in Barrackpore for Giffard's 11 Army Group HQ, which moved there from New Delhi in 1944.
2. G. Evans and A. Brett-James, *Imphal: A Flower on Lofty Heights* (London, Macmillan, 1962), p. 107.
3. File 3/9, Slim Papers. See also Mountbatten to Lewin, 6 May 1975, File K19B, Mountbatten Papers.
4. P. Ziegler (ed.), *Mountbatten's Diaries* (London, Collins, 1988), p. 19.
5. Mountbatten to Lewin, 6 May 1975, File K19B, Mountbatten Papers.
6. Ziegler, op. cit., p. 250.
7. File 3/9, Slim Papers.
8. File K261, Mountbatten Papers.

9.   Lewin to Mountbatten, 11 September 1975, File K19B, Mountbatten Papers.
10.  J. Masters, *The Road Past Mandalay* (London, Michael Joseph, 1961), p. 45.
11.  File 3/2, Slim Papers.
12.  Julian Thompson, *The Lifeblood of War: Logistics in Armed Conflict* (London, Brasseys, 1991), pp. 90–91.
13.  File 3/2, Slim Papers.
14.  Thompson, op. cit., p. 90.
15.  Christison, op. cit., p. 123.
16.  Thompson, op. cit., p. 87.
17.  Leese to Brooke, 15 December 1944. CAB106/106 Letter 1.
18.  Christison, op. cit., p, 123.
19.  File 3/2, Slim Papers.
20.  G. M. Fraser, *Quartered Safe Out Here* (London, Harper Collins, 1992), p. 35.
21.  M.R. Roberts, *Golden Arrow*, op. cit., p. 39.
22.  Ibid.
23.  File 5/3, Messervy Papers. 7 Indian Division Commander's Operational Notes No.8. 3 January 1944.
24.  File 5/3, Messervy Papers. 7 Indian Division Commander's Operational Notes No.2. 28 October 1943.
25.  File 5/5, Messervy Papers. 7 Indian Division Commander's Operational Notes No.5. 15 November 1943.
26.  Christison, op cit., p. 125.
27.  Quoted in Evans, *Slim as Military Commander*, op. cit., p. 163.
28.  Quoted in Maule, op. cit., p. 246.
29.  Christison, op. cit., p. 128.
30.  Roberts, op. cit., p. 76.
31.  Ibid., p. 59.
32.  Ibid., p. 87.
33.  Masters, op. cit., p. 243.
34.  A. Brett-James, *Ball of Fire*, op. cit., p. 294.
35.  Calvert, *Slim*, op. cit., p. 83.
36.  Maule, op. cit., p. 314.

# Chapter 6 – Operation U-Go

1.   Churchill, op. cit., pp. 576–77.
2.   Slim knew of this date because of his access to 'other sources of intelligence', a reference to the Far Eastern version of Ultra. See Lyall Grant, *Burma; The Turning Point* (Chichester, Zampi, 1993), p. 54.
3.   The INA consisted of Indian soldiers recruited by the Japanese from the large number of prisoners captured in Malaya and Singapore. It

was the military wing of Subhas Chandra Bose's nationalistic Indian
Independence League. Most INA soldiers joined to escape the prospect
of Japanese captivity.

4.   HQ 4 Corps arrived in Imphal in May 1943 and assumed responsibility
     for the defence of Manipur and thus the whole of Eastern India from
     Major-General Reginald Savory's 23 Indian Division, which remained as
     part of Scoones' corps.

5.   Commanded, from the end of 1943, by Brigadier R.A.L. Scoones, brother
     of the corps commander. The brigade contained the 7th Indian Light
     Cavalry with Stuart (Honey) tanks and the 3rd Carabiniers, with the
     Lee-Grant.

6.   File 3/2, Slim Papers.

7.   Mountbatten Papers. RUSI lecture, 9 October 1946.

8.   Harry Seaman, *The Battle at Sangshak* (London, Leo Cooper, 1989),
     p. 32.

9.   File 1/4, Gracey papers.

10.  Roberts Papers.

11.  This hard-won experience was gathered in operations such as 63 Brigade's
     attacks on Milestone 22 on the Tiddim Road in December 1943, and 32
     Brigade's attacks on Kyaukchaw in January 1944. Neither was successful
     at first, but a rapid alteration of tactics to overcome stubborn Japanese
     defensive positions eventually brought success. See Lyall Grant, op.
     cit., p. 46.

12.  File 3/2, Slim Papers. This comment could be read as criticism of
     Wingate.

13.  Box C247A, Mountbatten Papers.

14.  Evans & Brett-James, op. cit., p. 107.

15.  By February 1944 the seven squadrons of 221 Group RAF enjoyed
     air superiority over Japanese in the skies over north-east India and
     northern Burma. The infantry strength between 4 Corps and *15 Army*
     was roughly equal.

16.  Slim replaced Scoones with Messervy at the end of 1944.

17.  *Sato's 31 Division*, with 5,000 cattle on the hoof, carried the equivalent
     of fifty-nine days' supply.

18.  Churchill to Ismay, 24 July 1943. PRO PREM 3 143/8.

19.  This force was based on 70 British Division, which Wingate broke up
     in columns based on infantry companies. Wingate was also later given
     14 Brigade and 3 West African Brigade. The breaking up of 70 British
     Division was bitterly opposed by many, not least of all Auchinleck and
     Slim. 'I was convinced', wrote Slim, '– and nothing I saw subsequently
     caused me to change my mind' that 70 British Division would have had
     'more effect against the Japanese than a special force of twice its size . . .
     It was a mistake to break it up.'

20.  This dedicated air wing consisted of thirteen Dakotas (C47s), twelve
     Commando transports (C46s), twelve Mitchell medium bombers (B25s),

thirty Mustang fighter-bombers (P51s), 100 light planes (L5s), 225 gliders for transporting the men and six newly developed helicopters.

21.  Quoted in Allen, op. cit., p. 320.

22.  Slim commented in 1952 in a letter to a friend that: 'I doubt if Wingate was altogether a genius. He had flashes of genius but he had some pretty black spots too . . . The trouble is no one will write what they really think about him.' Letter to Lt. Col. H.R.K. Gibbs, 14 July 1952 (IWM).

23.  David Rooney, *Burma Victory: Imphal and Kohima March 1944 to May 1945* (London, Arms and Armour Press, 1992).

24.  Sykes, op. cit., p. 494.

25.  B. Bond (ed.), *Chief of Staff, The Diaries of Lieutenant General Sir Henry Pownall* (London, 1974), p. 111.

26.  Ibid., p. 126.

27.  Connell, op. cit., p. 762. See also Sykes op. cit., p. 472.

28.  Sykes, op. cit., p. 538.

29.  Woodburn Kirby (ed.), op. cit., Vol. 3, p. 220.

30.  According to Pownall's diary entry for 19 February 1944, knowledge of SEAC's strategic plan for 1944–45 'sent Wingate straight up into the air – he has been ruminating over continental operations right through to Bangkok-Saigon – along the south coast of China and so on. When he found we proposed no such thing but rather to give Burma a miss (as far as possible) and go south about by sea he went through the roof . . . Wingate replied with a long-winded diatribe of many pages accusing almost everyone of stupidity, ignorance, obstruction and much else besides.' Bond, op. cit., p. 141.

31.  Slim discussed LRP operations with Wingate twice in November, four times in December, and eight times in January 1944.

32.  Letter to Lt.-Col. H.R.K. Gibbs, 14 July 1952 (IWM).

33.  Quoted in Lewin, op. cit., p. 143.

34.  Bond, op. cit., p. 113.

35.  Ibid, p. 130.

36.  Skyes argues that this is to view Wingate superficially. But the evidence points clearly to Wingate's unbalanced, even fanatical, fixation with all things LRP to the extent that he saw LRP action as the panacea for all the strategic difficulties in SEAC. See Sykes, op.cit., p. 541.

37.  Bidwell, *The Chindit War: The Campaign in Burma, 1944* (London, Hodder and Stoughton, 1979), p. 150.

38.  Evans, *Slim as a Military Commander*, op. cit., p. 163.

39.  Lewin, op. cit., p. 144.

40.  Bond, op. cit., p. 141.

41.  It is axiomatic to some of Wingate's supporters that Slim deliberately and maliciously denigrated Wingate's achievements, before and after his death. There is, of course, not a shred of evidence to support these accusations and therefore no purpose in rebutting them in detail. See, for example, Sykes, op. cit., p. 457.

42. Ibid., 496.
43. Quoted in Lewin, op.cit., p. 146.
44. Wavell to CIGS, July 1944, Alanbrooke Papers.
45. File PRO/WO/172/4188.
46. Most histories follow the inaccurate account in the Official History, Lyall Grant being the honourable exception, following the clear evidence of the records in the PRO that Scoones had been informed as early as 8 March of Japanese activity in the Tiddim area, and of Cowan's concern to initiate preparations for a withdrawal of his division at the earliest opportunity.
47. Roberts Papers. Diary entry for 29 October 1945.
48. Numbering two battalions of 2,000 troops. The British Official History erroneously overestimates the numbers to be three battalions of 3,500. Indeed, when the Japanese were first contacted on 19 March in the Ukhrul area only one battalion had arrived from Kohima, the other arriving only after the Japanese attack had begun.
49. The full story is retold in Harry Seaman, *The Battle at Sangshak* (London, Leo Cooper, 1989).
50. 152 Bn lost 80 per cent of its strength and 153 Bn lost 35 per cent.
51. Seaman, op. cit., p. 56. Scoones was widely respected both for his capacity for hard work and for his acknowledged analytical prowess and intellectual strengths, for which Slim gave him warm praise in *Defeat into Victory*. But he did not possess the personality to dominate the battle and provide the dynamic leadership required at so desperate an hour. See also Brett-James, *Report my Signals*, op. cit., p. 187. Scoones' BGS, Brigadier Bayley, was new and did not possess the confidence of the divisional commanders in the early stages of the battle. See Gracey Papers. Evans and Brett-James accuse HQ 4 Corps of deliberately withholding information from commanders in the field.
52. See Roberts' unpublished memoirs (p. 294) and Lyall Grant, op. cit., p. 61.
53. File 1/23, Gracey Papers.
54. Ibid.

## Chapter 7 – The Bloody Plain

1. Slim Papers. 1946 lectures.
2. Seaman argues that Slim could not have received crucial intelligence in the form of a map showing Japanese intentions that 50 Brigade had captured at Sangshak on 23 March and conveyed at great risk by courier by foot across the thirty-six miles of mountains and jungle to 4 Corps at Imphal, because otherwise he would have gone all out to defend Kohima. Slim did not know that there were as many as three Japanese regiments bearing down on the weakly defended Kohima, and decided to defend Dimapur instead. Seaman op. cit., p. 83.

3.  Roberts, op. cit., p. 299. See also Evans and Brett-James, p. 157.

4.  Mountbatten had no direct control over the aircraft, which remained a US national asset under Stilwell's command. On 18 February Mountbatten asked Washington – in Stilwell's absence – for thirty-six DC3s from the Hump route for the emergency in Arakan. Twenty C47s were granted, but only because it was an emergency and Roosevelt told Mountbatten that he was not to ask for any more.

5.  In his diaries Pownall wrongly accuses both Slim and Giffard of lacking sufficient urgency in reinforcing Imphal. Bond, op. cit., p. 151. See also Box C247A, letter dated 1 February 1946, Mountbatten Papers.

6.  Box MB1/C82, Mountbatten Papers.

7.  Evans and Brett-James, op. cit., p. 204.

8.  161 Brigade (Brigadier Warren) was diverted by Slim to Dimapur for the defence of Kohima while 123 Brigade (Brigadier G.C. Evans) and 9 Brigade (Brigadier J.A. Salomons) were flown into Imphal as planned.

9.  Some accounts give this date as 30 March. *31 Division* cut the road on 29 March, with *15 Division* following suit north of Imphal on the 30th.

10. Evans, *Slim as Military Commander*, op. cit., p. 161.

11. Allen, op.cit., p. 235.

12. Brigadier A.D.R.G. Wilson, Unpublished Memoirs, Chap. 6., p. 4.

13. File 3/9, Slim Papers.

14. Brett-James, *Report My Signals*, op. cit., pp. 29–30.

15. Wingate's concept of strongholds with 'floater columns' to protect them was actually Scoones' idea for 4 Corps. Slim suggested that this might usefully be employed by Special Force. Wingate subsequently claimed that the idea had been his and this view is repeated by many. See for example Sykes, op. cit., p. 543. For Slim's view see *Defeat into Victory*, op. cit., p. 220.

16. Slim, *Defeat into Victory*, op. cit., p. 259. Accounts of the start of Operation Thursday at Lalaghat airfield have caused heated controversy. For a good assessment of this incident, and its subsequent reporting, see Bidwell, op. cit., p. 106. Some have contended that Slim's account in *Defeat into Victory* was untrustworthy because it was written so long after the event. Slim, however, submitted a full account of this incident to Mountbatten on 13 September 1944, and it was this account that was subsequently placed in *Defeat into Victory*. See Box C247A, Mountbatten Papers.

17. Quoted in Sykes, op cit., p. 502.

18. Slim never knew that Brodie's brigade had not supported Fergusson's attack on Indaw: even in *Defeat into Victory* he did not realize that Fergusson had attacked the town entirely unsupported.

19. There is considerable confusion on this point. Wingate, for instance, appeared to have decided not to use 14 Brigade in support of 16 Brigade's attack on Indaw, and despatched him to his guerrilla task along the Chindwin instead. He did not, however, tell Fergusson of this change

of plan. Nevertheless, it appears clear that Slim accepted this new role of one of Wingate's four deployed brigades, if only for a season.

20.  Bidwell, op. cit., p. 252.
21.  The Japanese actually showed themselves to be particularly adept at moving through 'difficult' country, as the *31 Division* advance on Kohima showed.
22.  Kirby, op.cit., Vol. III., Chap. XIV.
23.  Callahan, op. cit., p. 138.
24.  Sykes, op. cit., p. 536.
25.  Callahan, op. cit., p. 138.
26.  Wilson, op. cit., Chap. 6., p. 6.
27.  Arthur Swinson, *Four Samurai* (London, Hutchinson, 1968), p. 135.
28.  On the night of 15 April a Japanese suicide squad destroyed the suspension bridge on the track to Silchar thus removing the final land link between 4 Corps and the rest of India. In early April Slim sent 3 Special Service Brigade (No. 5 Army Commando and 44 Royal Marines Commando) to guard the western end of the Silchar track.
29.  1 Brigade went into Corps reserve while 49 Brigade guarded the Palel airfield.
30.  Allen, op. cit., p. 224.
31.  There was a daring small scale commando raid on Palel airfield in July, which did little apart from remind the Imphal garrison not to grow complacent.
32.  On 6 June Alanbrooke could still talk of a potential disaster at Imphal. Quoted in Lewin, op. cit., p. 188.
33.  Quoted in Bond, op. cit., p. xiv.
34.  Box C247A, Mountbatten Papers.
35.  As told to David Wilson. Wilson, op. cit., Chap. 6., p. 11.
36.  Mountbatten Papers.
37.  8,000 casualties in Arakan, 4,000 at Kohima and 12,000 at Imphal.
38.  Evans, *Slim as a Military Commander*, op. cit., p. 27.
39.  Quoted in Ibid., p. 212.
40.  Quoted in Ibid., op. cit., p. 134. Baldwin commanded the 3rd Tactical Air Force between 1943 and 1945. Strangely, Michael Calvert accused Slim of being 'slow to put his whole trust in air supply.' This criticism, however, is entirely without foundation. Calvert, *Slim*, op. cit., p. 159.

## Chapter 8 – The Masterstroke

1.  Churchill, *The Hinge of Fate*, The Second World War, Vol. IV (London, Cassell, 1951), p. 702.
2.  S. Woodburn Kirby, *The War Against Japan* (London, HMSO, 1969), Volume V, p. 419.
3.  Lewin, op. cit., p. 192.

4. Bernard Fergusson, *The Trumpet in the Hall* (London, Collins, 1970), p. 190.
5. Anderson, op. cit.
6. Lewin, op.cit., p. 194.
7. File 3/2 Slim Papers.
8. Quoted in Lewin, op. cit., p. 194.
9. Brett-James, *Report My Signals*, op. cit., pp. 29–30.
10. Box 3, Leese Papers.
11. John Masters, op. cit., p. 310.
12. Box 3, Leese Papers. Letters dated 10 February 1945 and 24 March 1945.
13. Box 3, Leese Papers. Letter dated 2 June 1945.
14. Mountbatten was sufficiently concerned about Slim's illness that he wrote: 'I do beg of you to take proper care of your health because to have a bad go of malaria on top of all you have been through is a serious matter and as much of our future operations depend on you retaining your health and strength, please look after yourself.' Box C247A, Mountbatten Papers.
15. W.J. Slim, *Campaign of the 14th Army 1944–45* (Melbourne, Australian Army Journal, 1950) p. 18.
16. W.J. Slim, *Higher Command in War* (US Army Military Review, May 1990), p. 13. See also Slim, *Unofficial History* (London, Cassells, 1959), p. 156.
17. Evans, *Slim as a Military Commander*, op.cit., p. 215.
18. File 13/2, Slim Papers.
19. Jack Masters' account of life in Pete Rees' division during Operations Capital and Extended Capital are described in John Masters, op. cit., pp. 292–322.
20. General Sir Oliver Leese, *Brief History of the Operations in Burma 1 November 1944–3 May 1945* (TAC HQ, ALFSEA, May 1945), p. 17.
21. Box C247A, Mountbatten Papers.
22. G.M. Fraser, *Quartered Safe Out Here* (London, Harper Collins, 1992), pp. 35–36.
23. File 3/9, Slim Papers.
24. Quoted in E. K. G. Sixsmith, *British Generalship in the Twentieth Century* (London, 1970), p. 290.
25. L. Allen, 'The Campaigns in Asia and the Pacific', in J. Gooch (ed.) *Decisive Campaigns of the Second World War* (London, Frank Cass, 1990) p. 168.
26. Evans, *Slim as a Military Commander*, op. cit., p. 202.
27. Lewin, op. cit., p. 210.
28. Browning to Alanbrooke dated 24 May 1945, Mountbatten Papers MBI/C50.
29. Christison's Unpublished Memoir, IWM.
30. PRO/CAB106/106 Leese to Alanbrooke, Letter 5, 5 May 1945.

31. Christison's Unpublished Memoir, IWM.
32. Letter from Mountbatten to Leese, 1 July 1945.
33. Quoted in Hickey, op. cit., p. 231.
34. Despite the erroneous claim of Michael Calvert that Slim appealed to the Army Council, Calvert op. cit., p. 155. This claim is repeated by Michael Craster in 'Cunningham, Ritchie and Leese', in J. Keegan (ed.), Churchill's Generals, op. cit., p. 220.
35. Quoted in Hickey, op. cit., p. 231.
36. Browning to Alanbrooke dated 24 May 1945, Mountbatten Papers MBI/C50.
37. A. Greenwood, Field Marshal Auchinleck (Durham, The Pentland Press, 1991), p. 256.
38. File 1091, Auchinleck Papers.
39. Box 3, Leese Papers. Letter dated 3 July 1945.
40. Anderson, 'Slim', op. cit., p. 319.
41. Mountbatten Papers: Obituary Speech, 15 December 1970.
42. Bernard Fergusson, Army Quarterly, 4/1971, pp. 268–272.

# Appendix 1 – Slim's appointment to Burma Corps: March 1942

1. Prasad (ed.), Official History of the Indian Armed Forces in the Second World War 1939–45 Campaigns in the Eastern Theatre: The Retreat From Burma (Calcutta, Orient Longmans, 1959), p. 234.
2. S. Woodburn, Vol. II, op.cit., p. 147.
3. See Evans, op. cit., p. 64; Lewin, op. cit., p. 82; Calvert, op. cit., p. 28; Anderson, op. cit., p. 306; Jackson, Alexander of Tunis as a Military Commander (London, Batsford, 1971), p. 124; and Michael Hickey, The Unforgettable Army, op. cit., p. 62.
4. John Marsh (ed.), Alexander, The Memoirs 1940–1945 (London, Cassells, 1962), p. 95.
5. File 3/1/1, Hutton Papers.
6. Wavell's Signal Reference was '3576/M20/2' and was sent on 15/16 February although a copy of the signal itself has not been traced.
7. Flie 2/13, Hutton Papers
8. Quoted in Arthur Bryant, The Turn of the Tide 1939–1943 (London, Collins, 1957), p. 256.
9. Evans, op. cit., p. 64.
10. File 3/1/3, Hutton Papers
11. When Slim, on his reconnaissance with Morris, met up with Alexander, Scott and Cowan, Slim commented that the latter two were surprised to see him. If they had played any part in persuading Alexander to bring him to Burma they would have been somewhat less surprised at his appearance. It is conceivable, however, that after meeting Slim at Maymyo, Cowan and

Scott, singly or jointly, urged Alexander to accept Slim's appointment of
Slim as Corps commander.

# Appendix 2 – Slim's appointment to Eastern Army: October 1943

1. Mountbatten to Alanbrooke, 23 October 1943, File MB1/C50, Mountbatten Papers.
2. Alanbrooke to Auchinleck, 30 October 1943, Alanbrooke Papers.
3. Mountbatten to Lewin, 6 May 1975, File K19B, Mountbatten Papers.
4. P. Ziegler (ed.), *Personal Diary of Admiral the Lord Louis Mountbatten 1943–1946* (London, Collins, 1988), p. 24.
5. With the exception of Geoffrey Evans, who got it right. See G. Evans, *Slim as Military Commander*, op. cit., pp. 105–106.
6. Age might have played a part in this friction. In October 1943 Giffard was fifty-eight, Slim was fifty-two and Mountbatten was forty-three.
7. PRO/WO/172/1698.

# MAPS

# Guide to Map Symbols

Note: Units and Formations have their number designation printed to the right of the symbol.

          Infantry Battalion

          Infantry Brigade

          Airlanded Infantry Brigade

          Infantry Regiment (Japanese, the equivalent of a British Brigade)

          Armoured Regiment (in the British Army this was the equivalent size of an Infantry Battalion)

          Infantry Division

          Artillery Regiment (in the British Army this was the equivalent size of an Infantry Battalion)

          Infantry Corps

          Army

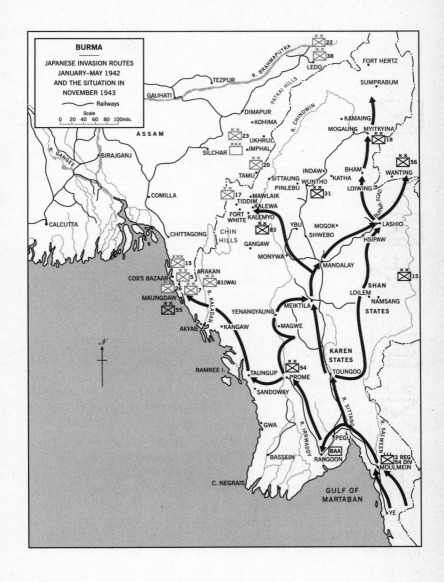

BURMA

JAPANESE INVASION ROUTES
JANUARY–MAY 1942
AND THE SITUATION IN
NOVEMBER 1943

⎯⎯⎯ Railways

Scale
0  20  40  60  80 100mls.

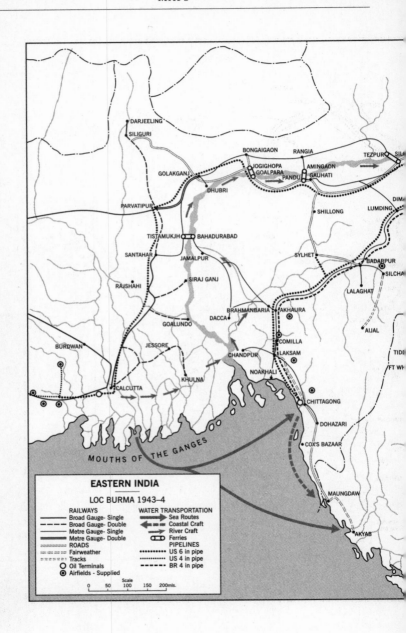

### EASTERN INDIA
#### LOC BURMA 1943–4

RAILWAYS
Broad Gauge- Single
Broad Gauge- Double
Metre Gauge- Single
Metre Gauge- Double
ROADS
Fairweather
Tracks
○ Oil Terminals
◉ Airfields - Supplied

WATER TRANSPORTATION
Sea Routes
Coastal Craft
River Craft
Ferries

PIPELINES
US 6 in pipe
US 4 in pipe
BR 4 in pipe

Scale
0 50 100 150 200mls.

MOUTHS OF THE GANGES

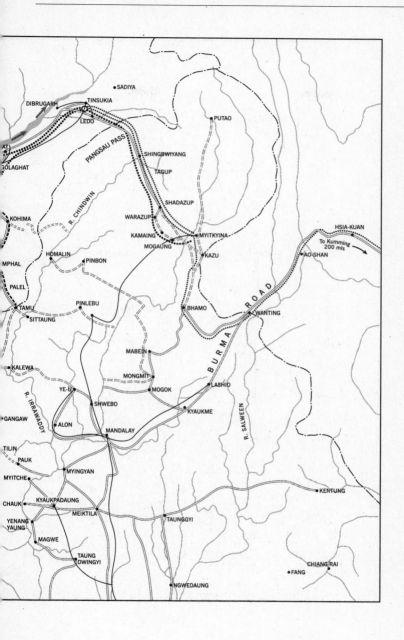

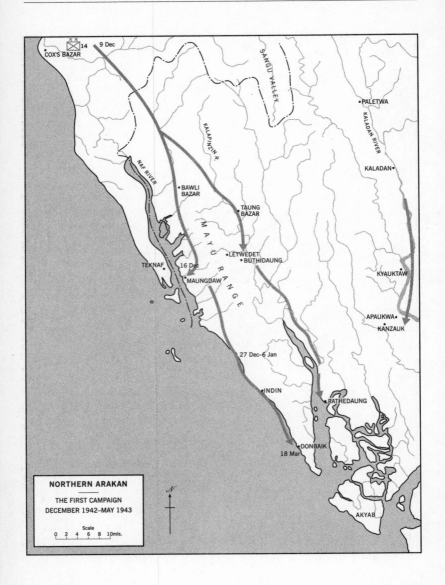

**NORTHERN ARAKAN**

THE FIRST CAMPAIGN
DECEMBER 1942–MAY 1943

Scale
0 2 4 6 8 10mls.

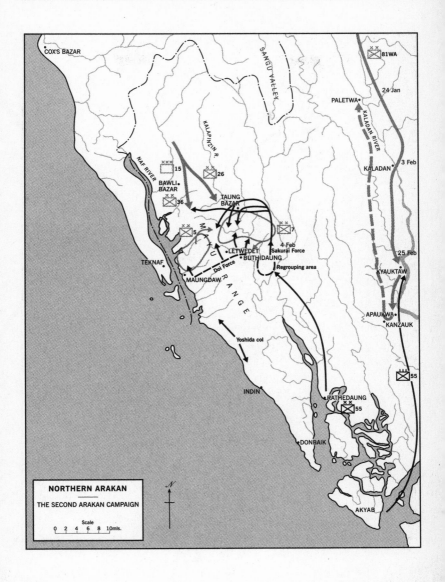

COX'S BAZAR

81WA

24 Jan

PALETWA

SANGU VALLEY

KALADAN RIVER

KALADAN 3 Feb

KALAPINZIN R.

15

26

BAWLI
BAZAR

36

NAF RIVER

TAUNG
BAZAR

5

7

MAYU RANGE

4 Feb
LETWEDET Sakurai Force
BUTHIDAUNG

TEKNAF

Doi Force

MAUNGDAW

Regrouping area

25 Feb

KYAUKTAW

APAUKWA

KANZAUK

Yoshida col

55

INDIN

RATHEDAUNG

55

DONBAIK

AKYAB

## NORTHERN ARAKAN

THE SECOND ARAKAN CAMPAIGN

Scale
0  2  4  6  8  10mls.

N

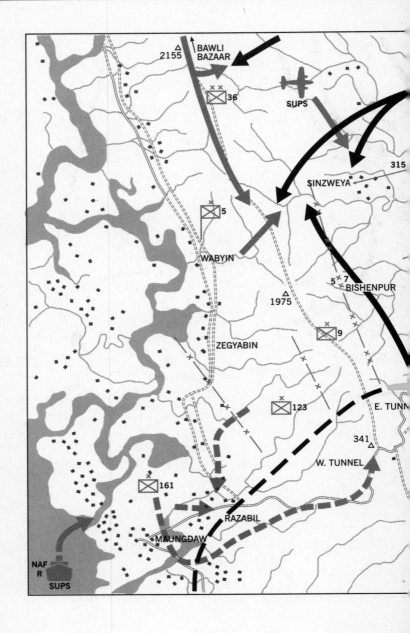

BAWLI BAZAAR
△ 2155
36
SUPS
315
SINZWEYA
5
WABYIN
5 7 BISHENPUR
△ 1975
ZEGYABIN
9
123
E. TUNN
△ 341
W. TUNNEL
161
RAZABIL
MAUNGDAW
NAF R
SUPS

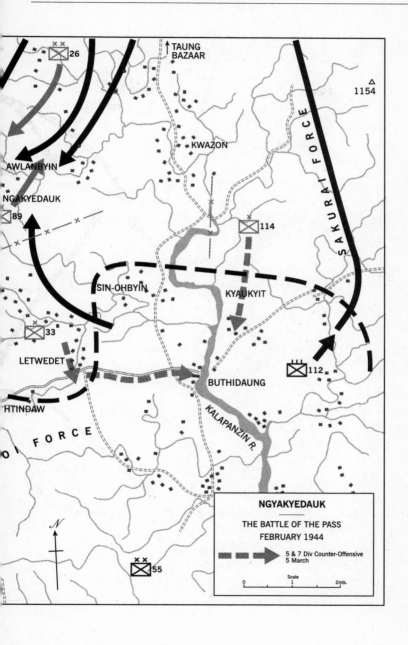

TAUNG
BAZAAR

1154

KWAZON

SAKURAI FORCE

AWLANBYIN

NGAKYEDAUK

89

114

SIN-OHBYIN

KYAUKYIT

33

LETWEDET

112

BUTHIDAUNG

HTINDAW

KALAPANZIN R.

FORCE

N

55

**NGYAKYEDAUK**

—

THE BATTLE OF THE PASS

FEBRUARY 1944

5 & 7 Div Counter-Offensive
5 March

Scale

0                    1                    2mls.

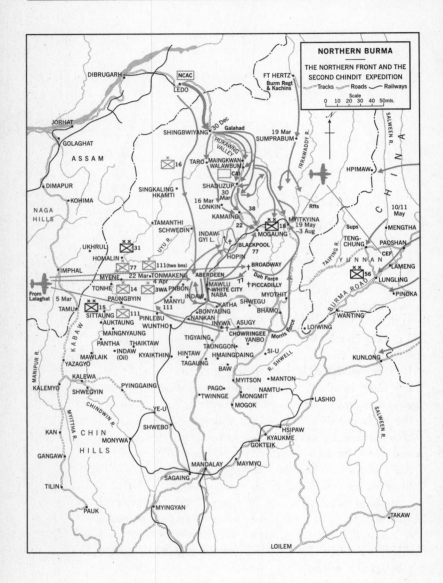

NORTHERN BURMA

THE NORTHERN FRONT AND THE
SECOND CHINDIT EXPEDITION

Tracks — Roads — Railways

Scale
0  10  20  30  40  50mls.

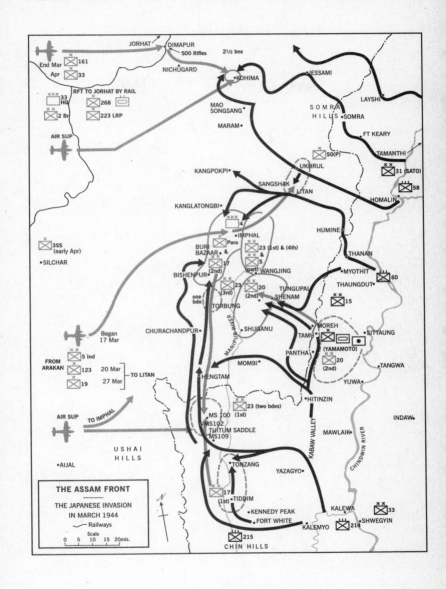

**THE ASSAM FRONT**

THE JAPANESE INVASION
IN MARCH 1944

—— Railways

Scale
0   5   10   15  20mls.

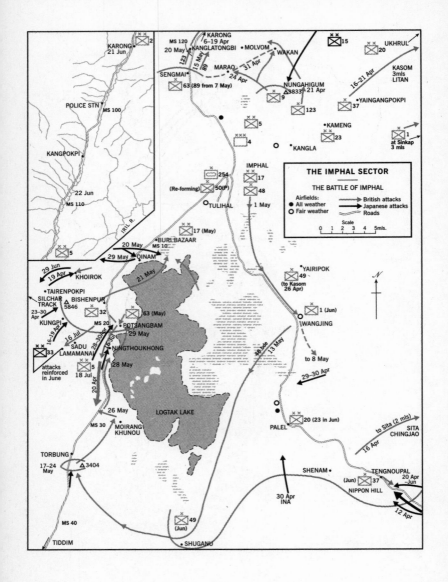

KARONG
21 Jun
×× 2

KARONG
6–19 Apr
MS 120
20 May
KANGLATONGBI
123
15 May
89
•MOLVOM
•WAKAN
×× 15
UKHRUL
×× 20

SENGMAI
MARAO
24 Apr
31 Apr
NUNGAHIGUM 21 Apr
△3833
16–21 Apr
KASOM
3mls
LITAN

63 (89 from 7 May)

9
123
37 •YAINGANGPOKPI

POLICE STN
MS 100

×× 5
•KAMENG
×× 23
×× 1
at Sinkap
3 mls

KANGPOKPI
×× 4
○ •KANGLA

22 Jun
MS 110

IRIL R.

254
50(P)
(Re-forming)
IMPHAL
17
48
×× 5

○TULIHAL
1 May

×× 5

20 May
17 (May)
•BURI BAZAAR
MS 10

29 May
QINAM
21 May
•YAIRIPOK
49
(to Kasom
26 Apr)

THE IMPHAL SECTOR
THE BATTLE OF IMPHAL
Airfields:
● All weather    British attacks
○ Fair weather   Japanese attacks
Roads
Scale
0 1 2 3 4 5mls.

29 Jun
19 Apr
KHOIROK

N

•TAIRENPOKPI
SILCHAR
TRACK
△5846
BISHENPUR
32
63 (May)
1 (Jun)
WANGJING

23–30
Apr
KUNGPI
MS 20
•POTSANGBAM
29 May

16 Jul
SADU
LAMAMANAI
NINGTHOUKHONG
to 8 May

×× 33
5
28 May
29–30 Apr

attacks
reinforced
in June
18 Jul

26 May
LOGTAK LAKE
20 (23 in Jun)
PALEL
to Sita (2 mls)
SITA
CHINGJAO

MS 30
•MOIRANG
KHUNOU
16 Apr

TORBUNG•
17–24
May
△3404
SHENAM •
(Jun) 37
TENGNOUPAL
20 Apr
–Jun
NIPPON HILL

30 Apr
INA
12 Apr

MS 40
49
(Jun)

TIDDIM
•SHUGANU

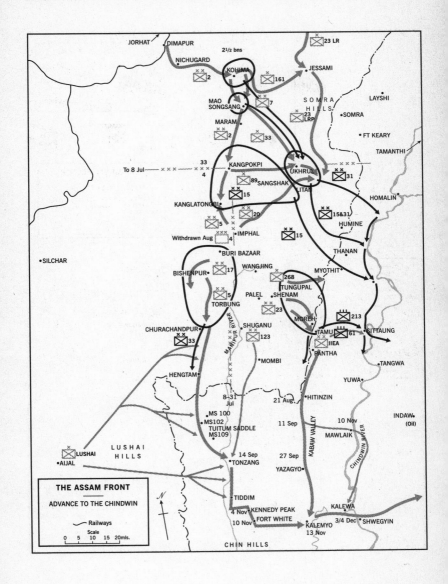

JORHAT    DIMAPUR
NICHUGARD
2½ bns
KOHIMA
2
161
JESSAMI
MAO
SONGSANG
7
S O M R A
H I L L S
SOMRA
LAYSHI
FT KEARY
MARAM
23
LRP
2
33
TAMANTHI
To 8 Jul
33
4
KANGPOKPI
SANGSHAK
89
UKHRUL
ITAM
31
HOMALIN
KANGLATONGBI
15
15&31
HUMINE
20
5
IMPHAL
15
THANAN
Withdrawn Aug
4
BURI BAZAAR
WANGJING
MYOTHIT
SILCHAR
BISHENPUR
17
268
TUNGUPAL
SHENAM
5
PALEL
MOREH
213
TORBUNG
23
TAMU
GITTAUNG
CHURACHANDPUR
SHUGANU
IIEA
161
33
123
PANTHA
TANGWA
HENGTAM
MOMBI
YUWA
8-31
Jul
21 Aug.
HITINZIN
INDAW
(Oil)
MS 100
MS102
TUITUM SADDLE
MS109
11 Sep
10 Nov
MAWLAIK
LUSHAI
HILLS
14 Sep
27 Sep
LUSHAI
AIJAL
TONZANG
YAZAGYO
TIDDIM
4 Nov
10 Nov
KENNEDY PEAK
FORT WHITE
KALEWA
KALEMYO
13 Nov
3/4 Dec
SHWEGYIN
CHIN HILLS

THE ASSAM FRONT
ADVANCE TO THE CHINDWIN

Railways

Scale
0  5  10  15  20mls.

MANIPUR RIVER
KABAW VALLEY
CHINDWIN RIVER
N

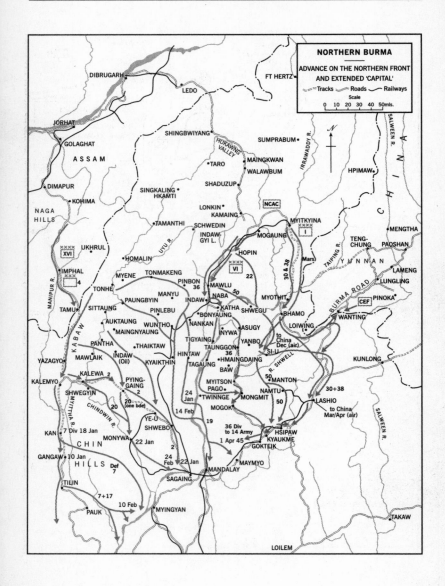

NORTHERN BURMA

ADVANCE ON THE NORTHERN FRONT
AND EXTENDED 'CAPITAL'

Tracks    Roads    Railways

Scale

0  10  20  30  40  50mls.

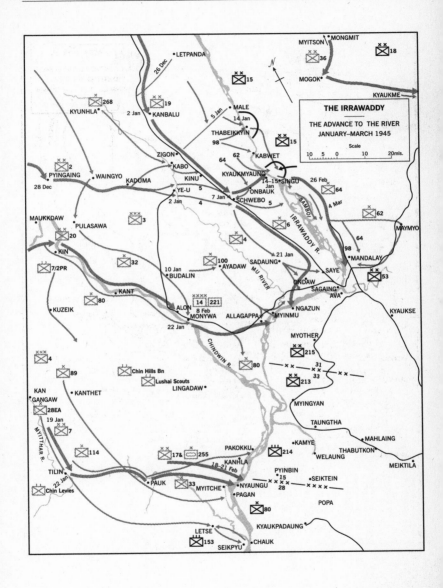

MYITSON • MONGMIT

⊠⊠ 36

MOGOK •

KYAUKME →

LETPANDA •

26 Dec

⊠⊠ 268

KYUNHLA •

2 Jan

⊠⊠ 19

KANBALU

5 Jan MALE •

14 Jan

THABEIKKYIN •

98

⊠⊠ 15

MALE

⊠⊠ 18

N

**THE IRRAWADDY**

THE ADVANCE TO THE RIVER
JANUARY–MARCH 1945

Scale
10  5  0        10        20mls.

⊠⊠ 15

⊠⊠ 2

PYINGAING •

28 Dec

WAINGYO •

KADUMA •

ZIGON •

KABO •

KINU •

YE-U •

2 Jan

5

62    KABWET

64    KYAUKMYAUNG •

14–15 • SINGU

Jan

ONBAUK

7 Jan    SCHWEBO •

4    5

⊠⊠ 15

26 Feb    ⊠ 64

4 Mar

⊠ 62

MAYMYO •

MAUKKDAW •

⊠⊠ 20

• KIN

⊠ 7/2PR

• KUZEIK

⊠ 80

⊠⊠⊠ 3

⊠ 32

KANT

10 Jan    • BUDALIN

ALON •

⊠⊠⊠⊠ 14  221

8 Feb    MONYWA •

22 Jan

⊠ 100

AYADAW •

MU RIVER

SADAUNG •

21 Jan

⊠ 4

6

ONDAW •

SAGAING • AVA •

NGAZUN •

ALLAGAPPA •    • MYINMU

98

64

MANDALAY •

SAYE •

⊠⊠ 53

KYAUKSE •

IRRAWADDY R.

SAMBON

⊠⊠⊠ 4

⊠ 89

KAN • GANGAW •

⊠ 28EA

19 Jan

⊠ 7

⊠ 114

TILIN •

22 Jan

⊠ Chin Levies

• KANTHET

⊠ Chin Hills Bn

⊠ Lushai Scouts

LINGADAW •

⊠ 80

x x    31

33

x x

⊠⊠ 215

MYOTHER •

⊠⊠ 213

MYINGYAN •

TAUNGTHA •

• MAHLAING

⊠ 17 & ⊞ 255

KANHLA

18–21 Feb

⊠ 33

PAUK •    • MYITCHE

• PAGAN

PAKOKKU •

⊠ 214

• KAMYE

WELAUNG •    THABUTKON •

MEIKTILA •

PYINBIN •

x x x  15

x x x x x    28

NYAUNGU •

• SEIKTEIN

⊠ 80

POPA

LETSE •

⊠ 153

SEIKPYU •    • CHAUK

KYAUKPADAUNG •

MYITTHAR R.

CHINDWIN R.

PULASAWA •

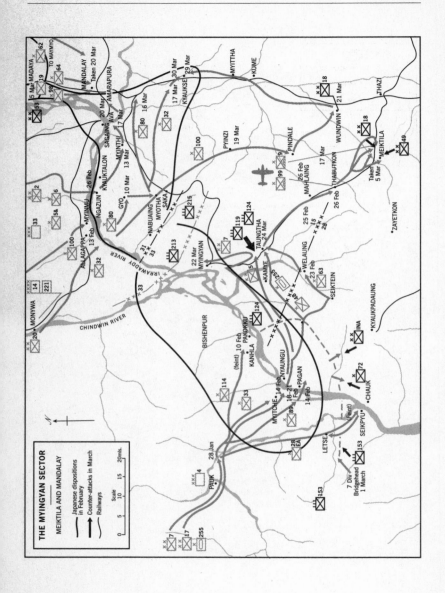

THE MYINGYAN SECTOR

MEIKTILA AND MANDALAY

Japanese dispositions in February
Counter-attacks in March
Railways

Scale
0 5 10 15 20 mls.

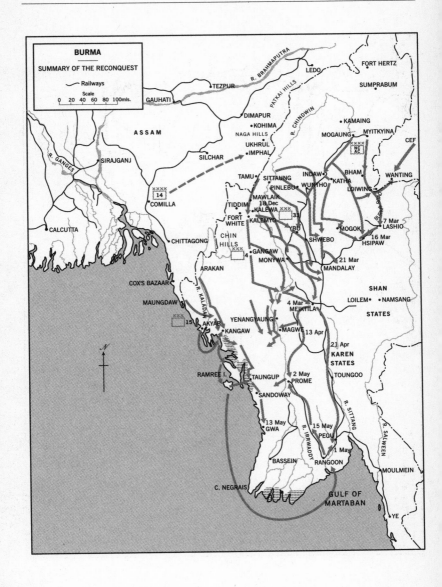

BURMA

SUMMARY OF THE RECONQUEST

⌐ Railways

Scale
0  20  40  60  80  100mls.

# Select Bibliography

*Except where otherwise recorded, all quotations from Slim come from W.J. Slim,*
Defeat into Victory (London, Cassell, 1956)

## Manuscript Sources

The Public Record Office (PRO), Kew
The British Library
Liddell Hart Centre, King's College, University of London: Papers of Field
  Marshal Lord Alanbrooke, General Sir Ouvry Roberts, Lieutenant-General
  Thomas Hutton, Lieutenant-General Sir F.W. Messervy.
John Ryland Library, University of Manchester: Papers of Field Marshal Claude
  Auchinleck.
Churchill Archives, Churchill College, Cambridge: Papers of Field Marshal
  Lord Slim.
Imperial War Museum: Papers of Lieutenant General N.M.S. Irwin, General
  Sir Alexander Frank Philip Christison, Lieutenant-General Sir Geoffrey
  Charles Evans.
Hartley Library, University of Southampton: Papers of Admiral Mountbatten
  (Broadlands Papers).
Unpublished memoirs of Brigadier A.R.D.G. Wilson.

## Official Publications

S. Woodburn Kirby, *The War Against Japan*, Volume II (London, HMSO, 1958); Volume III (1961); Volume IV (1965); Volume V (1969)

Bisheshwar Prasad, *Official History of the Indian Army Forces in the Second World War: Campaigns in the Eastern Theatre* (Calcutta, Orient Longmans, 1954–1958). Retreat from Burma 1941–42 [First Volume of Series]; Arakan Operations 1942–45 [Second Volume of Series]; Reconquest of Burma Volume 1 [Third Volume of Series]; Reconquest of Burma Volume 2 [Fourth Volume of Series].

Despatch by General Sir A.P. Wavell (*The London Gazette*, 11 March 1948) '*Operations in Burma from 15 December 1941 to 20 May 1942*'.

Vice Admiral The Earl Mountbatten of Burma, Report to the Combined Chiefs of Staff by the Supreme Allied Commander South East Asia 1943–1945 (HMSO,1951).

Despatch by Field Marshal Sir Claude Auchinleck, (*The London Gazette*, 27 April 1948), '*Operations in the Indo Burma Theatre based on India from 21 June 1943 to 15 November 1943*'.

Despatch by General Sir George Gifford (*The London Gazette*, 19 March 1951), '*Operations in Burma and North-East India from 16 November 1943 to 22 June 1944*'.

Despatch by General Sir George Giffard (*The London Gazette*, 19 March 1951), '*Operations in Assam and Burma, 23rd June 1944 to 12 November 1944*'.

Despatch by Lieutenant-General Sir Oliver Leese (HMSO, 1951), '*Operations in Burma from 12 November 1944 to 15 August 1945* (HMSO, 1951).

## Books and Articles

D. Anderson 'Slim' in J. Keegan (ed.), *Churchill's Generals* (London, Weidenfield and Nicholson, 1991)

L. Allen, *Burma, the Longest War* (London, Dent, 1984)

A.J. Barker, *The March on Delhi* (London, Faber and Faber, 1963)

S. Bidwell, *The Chindit War: The Campaign in Burma, 1944* (London, Hodder and Stoughton, 1979)

B. Bond (ed.), *Chief of Staff, The Diaries of Lieutenant General Sir Henry Pownall*, Vol II 1940–44 (London, Leo Cooper, 1974)

A. Brett-James, *Report my Signals* (London, Hennel and Locke, 1948)

A. Brett-James, *Ball of Fire: The Fifth Indian Division in the Second World War* (Aldershot, Gale and Polden, 1951)

R. Callahan, *Burma 1942–45* (London, Davis-Poynter, 1978)

M. Calvert, *Slim* (London, Pan/Ballantine, 1973)

T. Carew, *The Longest Retreat: The Burma Campaign 1942* (London, Hamish Hamilton, 1969)

W.S. Churchill, *The Second World War, Volume IV, The Hinge of Fate* (London, Cassell, 1951); *Volume V, Closing the Ring* (1952); *Volume VI, Triumph and Tragedy* (1954)

N. Dixon, *On the Psychology of Military Incompetence* (London, Jonathan Cape, 1976)

G. Evans, *Slim as Military Commander* (London, Batsford, 1969)

G. Evans and A. Brett-James, *Imphal, A Flower on Lofty Heights* (London, Macmillan, 1962)

G. M. Fraser, *Quartered Safe Out Here* (London, Harper Collins, 1992)

I. L. Grant, *Burma: The Turning Point* (Chichester, The Zampi Press, 1993)

I. L.Grant and K. Tamayama, *Burma 1942: The Japanese Invasion. Both sides tell the Story of a Savage Jungle War* (Chichester, The Zampi Press, 1999)

J. Hedley, *Jungle Fighter* (Brighton, Tom Donovan, 1996)

M. Hickey, *The Unforgettable Army: Slim's XIVth Army in Burma* (Tunbridge Wells, Spellmount Limited, 1992)

R. Lewin, *Slim: The Standard Bearer* (London, Leo Cooper, 1976)

R.M. Lyman, *The Art of Manoeuvre at the Operational Level of War: Lieutenant-General W.J. Slim and Fourteenth Army 1944–5*, in G. Sheffield and G. Till (eds.) The Challenges of High Command – The British Experience (Basingstoke, Palgrave MacMillan, 2002)

J.D. Lunt, '*A Hell of a Licking*': *The Retreat from Burma 1941–2* (London, Collins, 1986)

T. Mains, *The Retreat From Burma* (London, W. Foulsham, 1973)

J. Masters, *The Road Past Mandalay* (London, Michael Joseph, 1961)

H. Maule, *Spearhead General* (London, Odhams Press, 1961)

J. North (ed.), *The Alexander Memoirs 1940–45* (London, Cassell, 1962)

F. Owen, *The Campaign in Burma* (London, HMSO, 1946)

M.R. Roberts, *Golden Arrow: The Story of the 7th Indian Division in the Second World War 1939–1945* (Aldershot, Gale and Polden Ltd, 1952)

E.K.G. Sixsmith, *British Generalship in the Twentieth Century* (London, Arms and Armour Press, 1970)

W.J. Slim, *Campaign of the Fourteenth Army 1944–1945* (Melbourne, Australian Army Journal, August 1950)

W.J. Slim, *Higher Command in War* (US Army Military Review, May 1990)

W.J. Slim, *Unofficial History* (London, Cassell, 1959)

A. Swinson, *Four Samurai* (London, Hutchinson, 1968)

A. Swinson, *Kohima* (London, Cassell, 1966)

E.D.Smith, *Battle for Burma* (London, Batsford, 1979)

Sir John Smyth, *The Valiant* (London, Mowbray, 1970)

P. Ziegler (ed.), *Mountbatten's Diaries* (London, Collins, 1988)

P. Ziegler, *Mountbatten* (London, Guild Publishing, 1985)

# Index